Business in Asia Pacific

Business in Asia Pacific

Text and Cases

Sonia El Kahal

OXFORD
UNIVERSITY PRESS

OXFORD

UNIVERSITY PRESS

Great Clarendon Street, Oxford OX2 6DP

Oxford University Press is a department of the University of Oxford.
It furthers the University's objective of excellence in research, scholarship,
and education by publishing worldwide in

Oxford New York

Auckland Cape Town Dar es Salaam Hong Kong Karachi
Kuala Lumpur Madrid Melbourne Mexico City Nairobi
New Delhi Shanghai Taipei Toronto

With offices in
Argentina Austria Brazil Chile Czech Republic France Greece
Guatemala Hungary Italy Japan Poland Portugal Singapore
South Korea Switzerland Thailand Turkey Ukraine Vietnam

Oxford is a registered trade mark of Oxford University Press
in the UK and in certain other countries

Published in the United States
by Oxford University Press Inc., New York

First published 2001
Reprinted 2002, 2003, 2004, 2005 twice, 2007, 2010

British Library Cataloguing in Publication Data
Data available

Library of Congress Cataloging in Publication Data
Data available

ISBN 13: 978-0-19-878219-3

10 9

Printed in Great Britain
on acid-free paper by
CPI Antony Rowe,
Chippenham, Wiltshire

Thus we may know that there are five essentials for victory:
He will win who knows when to fight and when not to fight;
He will win who knows how to handle both superior and inferior forces
He will win whose army is animated by the same spirit throughout all its ranks
He will win who prepares himself, waits to take the enemy unprepared
He will win who has military capacity and is not interfered with by the sovereign.

Hence the saying: If you know the enemy and know yourself, you can fight a hundred battles without defeat. If you know yourself but not the enemy, for every victory gained you will also suffer a defeat. If you know neither the enemy nor yourself, you will succumb in every battle.

(The Art of War. 770–475 BC Concise Edition of the Chinese Philosophy)

For my dear husband John MacLean

Preface

Asia Pacific represents 25 per cent of the world economy and about 50 per cent of the world's population. It is for this reason that few international companies can afford to ignore Asia as a market of primary importance, despite the crisis which hit a large part of the region in 1997. Western firms without a presence in the region often fail to perceive the opportunities they miss in Asia to generate sales and profits. Asia Pacific is a vibrant region with numerous investment opportunities. Investing and carrying on business in Asia Pacific region is a matter which involves knowledge of a number of facets affecting each country. The failure to assess Asia's market potential and the competition it represents is largely due to the lack of adjustment in Western approaches to the region. Many managers of Western multinational firms are inculcated with the belief that Western management concepts, mostly American in origin, are universally acceptable and applicable. Only when Western firms confront the very different realities of doing business in the Asia Pacific region with Asian managers do they understand their limitations. Fundamental differences exist between their home territories and the Asia Pacific region. This book is intended to provide an overview of the region, its so-called miracle, and the subsequent crisis; the business environment in the light of the recent period of recovery; and strategic formulation and policy-making post-crisis.

Many multinational and global firms see the Asian economic meltdown as an opportunity to buy out their financially strapped local partners or to invest in new ventures on the cheap. On the Asian side, the recession is squeezing local companies' finances. Those already involved in joint ventures may feel increased pressure to sell out or at least to reduce their participation. It is a tempting time to buy out local partners in existing joint ventures or to increase stakes in partnership. The most important truth to remember about Asia Pacific is that most countries in the region are still developing and are not yet fully developed. But Asia Pacific is no longer suitable for short-cut instant profits. Companies traditionally focused almost exclusively on volume, growth, and relative market shares in Asia, rather than the quality of their earnings. Following the Asian crisis, they are now having to shift their focus into developing a deeper understanding of customers' needs and then pricing and/or building a differentiated value proposition for their product in the market-place. Real examples of what companies are already doing to position themselves for post-crisis growth are provided throughout the text. What should business managers reasonably expect from this region? How long should they be prepared to wait before succeeding? How can they develop effective strategies for dealing with the diversity of these markets? How should their company organize itself to compete for new business following the crisis? What specific lessons might be gleaned from the Asia Pacific experience? To what extent are they transferable to the West? This book teases out answers to these and other related questions. Rather than thinking of a model of Asian growth, this book suggests several different models that one might consider. The models suggested, however, do not warrant a claim to universality because each country differs in its initial conditions. This book will contribute to a better understanding of this part of the world. Asia Pacific represents both an opportunity and threat for business. The overall aim of the book therefore is to provide business managers and students with a methodology for developing their own regional and country strategies for Asia Pacific. Given the rapid pace of change in the region the approach adopted emphasizes potential as much as current strategies.

The term Asia Pacific has been widely used by economists, journalists, and business professionals, though it is often unclear which countries are referred to. For the purpose of this book, the Asia Pacific region comprises China, Hong Kong, Indonesia, Malaysia, Myanmar, the Philippines, Singapore, South Korea, Taiwan, Thailand, Vietnam, and Japan. Australia and New Zealand have been excluded: although economically these two countries have become intertwined with the region, they cannot claim to be Asian in culture or to show many of the characteristics of Asia Pacific. India and Pakistan are not included either because of their lack of close economic and political ties with the region. Most importantly the framework for this book has been based upon the historical developments understood generally as first the Asian miracle, secondly the Asian crisis, and at the present time the Asian recovery. And it is in relation to these events that I have chosen to focus on those countries more central to these developments. References throughout the book to the Republic of (South) Korea, will be shortened to Korea.

Distinctive Features of the Book

The title of this book expresses its basic objective which is to further our understanding of doing business in Asia Pacific. Since the end of the Second World War, the region has experienced dynamic changes and upheavals. In the early 1980s when the region became the home of the fastest growing economies in the world, much was written and said about the so-called 'Asian Miracle'. The competitiveness of Asian multinationals, Asian management principles and practices, whether Japanese, Korean, or Chinese have also fuelled the publication of several books prescribing various business models, management tools, and strategies for direct application in the West. From the mid-1990s, the Asian crisis which spread across Asia Pacific also captured the attention of politicians, economists, business people, and academics. The road to recovery is now becoming a further subject of considerable increase in research. A review of the literature on business in Asia Pacific published so far indicates a major omission of a single and comprehensive textbook dealing with economic, political, and business developments that have occurred in the region over the last two decades, from the miracle through the crisis to the recovery, under one cover. This book has been developed to fill that gap. The overall aim is to provide an insight into the region as far as international business is concerned and to guide strategic management and decision-making in the region, post-crisis. In summary then this book lays a foundation of facts about developments in Asia Pacific since its phenomenal growth, through the crisis and current recovery, and then proceeds to discuss the changes introduced since the crisis and their implications for international business.

This book will be the first of its kind providing an introductory but comprehensive understanding of the region's turbulent economic, political, and business environment. A second distinguishing feature of this textbook is in its overall framework where each issue raised is then followed consistently from the 'miracle' days, through the crisis, and into the recovery. A third distinguishing feature is the analysis provided of post-crisis survival and competitive strategies adopted by various businesses in the region. Detailed and practical examples of Western and Asian firms operating in the region are provided. These cases are useful in illustrating more concretely industry's response to the changing environment of Asia Pacific following the crisis. Since most issues raised in this textbook are covered at an introductory level, each chapter ends with a list of suggested further readings for those who wish to extend their knowledge more deeply. Review questions have been added to encourage and stimulate students' critical analysis and evaluation of facts and events. Practical exercises at the end of each unit should provide an opportunity for further concrete experiential learning within the classroom. Some exercises are mainly aimed at developing students' skills in conducting a debate, in choosing the main issues to be discussed, and in reaching an acceptable position between the different points of view involved. Others, such as the group projects, are specifically designed with the internet in mind. In the light of the rapidly and constantly changing events occurring on a daily basis in Asia Pacific, the purpose here is to familiarize students with the vast amount of information available, to develop their surfing skills in selecting relevant Asian websites, to update their normative knowledge and adjust their practical skills towards rapid decision-making, and to present their findings in the form of either a group presentation or a consultancy report. Finally, the case studies provided should further develop students' knowledge and critical examination of business policy and strategies of firms operating in the region. The book will be useful as an introductory, yet comprehensive text for courses on business in Asia Pacific in the undergraduate curriculum and for post-graduate post-experience diplomas in Business Management. It will also provide useful resources for MBA regional studies within MBA programmes. The book should also be valuable to first line managers and junior managers who want to acquire a general insight into the Asia Pacific region.

Structure of the Book

The content of the book is structured around four major parts:

Part I Towards a Better Understanding of the Asian Crisis

The Asian crisis has often been viewed essentially as a currency crisis, as falling exchange rates inflating foreign debt, and so on. Popular blame for the crisis has been spread among government policies, foreign speculators, and poorly run financial institutions. Prescriptions have mainly focused on government policies and financial systems. In order to fully appreciate the complete transformation of the region part I provides an insight into the region. This part itself is a mixture of relevant facts and first impressions surveying the debate over the reasons for the Asian crisis which have become one of the most important intellectual *causes célèbres* of the century. A special analysis of the Asian Miracle, the financial crisis as well as the contemporary recovery and business opportunities for doing business in the region, is thus provided.

Part II Asian Management: Theory and Practice

Asia Pacific by no means represents a group of homogenous economic and political systems—national and business cultures vary significantly, but despite all these variations, common characteristics can be found. The most important aspect of business in the Asian Pacific region is learning to deal with the people and their very different cultures. The countries of the region are economically, socially, and culturally diverse. In addition to the diverse Asian racial mix, various religious allegiances co-exist. Asian cultures are at a crossroad between the different streams of Confucianism, Buddhism, Taoisim, Islam, Shintoism, Hinduism, and Christianity. Additionally, most of these countries have followed a diversity of historical routes to the modern world. And, despite the obvious differences within the continent, a few common features are distinguishable. Despite the multiplicity of cultures in Asia, there are many characteristics that are more or less common across many Asian cultures. Examples are the importance of the family, group orientation, and the issue of saving face, all of which have an impact on consumers and business conduct. They do not deny the existence of cultural heterogeneity in the region, but imply that the differences within Asia Pacific are less significant than the differences from the world outside. The intention, however, is not to provide a catalogue of cultural behaviour practices in all Asia countries. Instead, Part II is intended to illustrate how Asian culture is different from Western culture and the implications of this for doing business in the region.

The overall aim of Part II is to provide an understanding of the fundamental difference between so-called Western and Asian management principles and practices. To begin with, it is difficult to identify just what is Western business culture. Equally, it is impossible to stereotype all Asian business into one homogeneous cultural identify. Like the nations of Europe, these countries have different histories, cultures, languages, and ways of doing business. Moreover, most of these countries have some common historical experiences, for example, colonization for all except China, Japan, and Thailand. These experiences have made them more comfortable with absorbing new ideas and practices, including those introduced by foreigners. Notwithstanding this, there are some verifiable, general, but fundamental characteristics which when explained help towards achieving a better understanding of business practices in the region. An introduction to Japanese, South Korean, and Chinese management principles and practices is thus provided. These three countries have been selected because they have been, on the one hand, the dominant forces in the region, and have contributed to their respective country's economic growth post-Second World War, and on the other hand because they are currently experiencing difficulties in the post-crisis context.

Part III Strategic Planning for Asia Pacific after the Crisis

The crisis has paradoxically opened several opportunities for doing business in Asia Pacific. Although a reservoir of business opportunities now exists, the region is also a source of threatening competition for Western firms. Part III aims at providing a deeper understanding of strategic analysis and business policy. Rather than simply thinking of where to make a splash in Asia, various strategies for entering the market and succeeding are offered in Part III. The relaxation of restrictions on foreign investment can now allow multinational and global firms to rethink their strategy for Asia Pacific completely. A close examination of firms' strategic operations in the region is thus covered.

Part IV Case Studies

The cases selected in Part IV have been primarily designed for teaching purposes. They are not intended to be used either as examples of 'best practices' or of ineffective management. They illustrate real-life examples of Western and Asian multinational corporations' (MNCs) experiences in the region. The aim is to provide students with an overall picture of doing business in Asia Pacific. Subjects covered range from dealing with the Asian crisis, restructuring, seeking new potential in Asia Pacific post-crisis, entering newly opened markets, handling crises and ethical problems, to adopting appropriate strategies for global competition.

Contents

Part II **Asian Management: Theory and Practice**

Part III **Strategic Planning for Asia Pacific after the Crisis**

Part IV Case Studies

List of Figures

List of Tables

Part I

Towards a Better Understanding of the Asian Crisis

Introduction

Crises can be useful only if we learn from them and can make a fresh start.

(Jomo, 1998)

The Chinese written expression for 'crisis' is a combination of the character signifying danger, and the one signifying opportunity. The Asian crisis has both these elements. The implications of the present crisis as danger are all too clear, with a devastated financial sector and a deeply troubled corporate sector, but the crisis, as an opportunity may be more difficult to recognize (Abonyi, 1999).

Since 1997, the Asian crisis has captured the attention of politicians, business people, and academics. Analysis of the origins and causes of the crisis has become the subject of considerable interest in publications and academic research. The same Asian countries that were held up as models for other developing countries are now being heavily criticized. Critics are condemning them for their unworkable economic systems, after praising them from their outstanding economic performance over several decades. Prior to 1997, these Asian 'tigers' or 'dragons', it was claimed, were threatening to dominate the world. 'Caging the tigers' became a preoccupation of policy-makers and Western business people. Today, as Stanley Fisher, first Deputy Managing Director of the International Monetary Fund, put it: 'It is in the global interest, and indeed the US interest lies in an economically strong Asia . . . we are ready to do our duty, which is to provide assistance to help mobilize the economy' (Fisher, 1998*b*).

The Asian crisis erupted in Thailand in the summer of 1997 with the so-called 'contagion' that spread to other economies in the region. The causes and circumstances surrounding the crisis will be examined in order to assess the extent to which they provide us with a satisfactory explanation. The crisis has been constructed as a pathological condition. The dominant assumption here is that these economies have internal problems in need of correction. To stop this 'contagion' from spreading, the assistance of the International Monetary Fund was seen as essential. A re-examination of the factors behind the Asian 'Miracle' is essential to establish the economic and strategic importance of the region to the global economy and its implications for international business in general. Chapter 1 provides a review of the Asian 'Miracle', while Chapter 2 covers the causes and circumstances surrounding the crisis. Chapter 3 examines the crisis within a global context and evaluates the role of the IMF in dealing with the crisis. Chapter 4 concludes with an overview of recent trends towards recovery including reforms recently introduced to ride the crisis and business opportunities available in the region post-crisis.

Chapter 1

The Roaring Tigers and the Asian Miracle

Until a few years ago one could not open the pages of a public affairs magazine without running into a commentary claiming for example that 'Asian countries have developed a new and superior form of capitalism that is beating the pants off Western, free market economies' (Altfest, 1998). Between 1965 and 1990 the economy of East Asia grew faster than all other regions of the world, roughly three times as fast as other developing regions and twenty-five times faster than Sub-Saharan Africa. The export performance of these East Asia economies has been particularly dramatic, with their share of world exports of manufactures leaping from 9 per cent in 1965 to 21 per cent in 1990, thus significantly outperforming the industrial economies and the oil-rich Middle East–North Africa region (World Bank, 1993). Most of this achievement was attributable to six economies: Japan, Hong Kong, the Republic of Korea, Singapore, Taiwan, and China; and the three newly industrializing economies of South East Asia, Indonesia, Malaysia, and Thailand.

Real income per capita also increased more than four times in Japan and the Four Tigers (Hong Kong, Korea, Singapore, and Taiwan), and more than doubled in the South East Asian newly industrialized economies. Annual GDP growth in the ASEAN Five (Indonesia, Malaysia, the Philippines, Singapore, and Thailand) averaged close to 8 per cent over the last decade. Indeed, during the thirty years preceding the crisis per capita income levels had increased tenfold in Korea, fivefold in Thailand, and fourfold in Malaysia (Yellen, 1998). Human welfare also improved dramatically. In South Korea and Singapore, for example, real per capita income grew more than 700 per cent between 1965 and 1995. Over the same period Taiwan and Hong Kong logged increases of more than 400 per cent, while Malaysia, Thailand, and Indonesia each experienced real per capita income growth of over 300 per cent. South Korea specifically experienced an unprecedented growth in per capita GNP from 6.9 per cent over the period 1960–81 and 8.5 per cent over the period 1980–94 with increased incomes from US$1,700 in 1981 to US$8,260 in 1994. Equally impressively, Indonesia's GNP rose from US$90 in 1972 to US$880 in 1994, Thailand's rose from US$220 to US$2,410 and Malaysia's from US$450 to US$3,480 during the same period (Sharma, 1998).

Not only did these nine economies grow rapidly, they were also successful in sharing the fruits of growth, with low and declining inequality of income. For example in Malaysia, the percentage of the population living in absolute poverty has dropped from 37 per cent in 1960 to less than 5 per cent in 1990 (Yellen, 1998). Thailand poverty (measured on purchasing power parity) had been reduced from over 57 per cent in the late 1960s to about 13 per cent in 1996, with Thais enjoying dramatic improvements in social welfare such as food security, education, infant mortality, and life expectancy. Similarly, in Indonesia, despite remaining disparities, the benefits of growth had extended to all of the twenty-seven culturally diverse provinces. Between 1970 and 1996 the proportion of population living below the official poverty line declined from 64 per cent to an esti-mated 11 per cent. The quality of life for the average Indonesian had improved greatly: infant mortality declined from 145 per 1,000 live births in 1970 to 53 per 1,000 in 1995. Life expectancy rose from 46 to 63 during the same period, and the country achieved universal primary education in 1995 (Sharma, 1998). Life expectancy increased from 56 years in 1960 to 71 years in 1990. The proportion of people living in absolute poverty, lacking such basic necessities as clean water, food, and shelter, dropped from 58 per cent in 1960 to 17 per cent in 1990 in Indonesia, and from 37 per cent to less than 5 per cent in Malaysia during the same period (World Bank, 1993: 5). Additionally, until the current crisis Asia attracted almost half of total capital inflows to developing countries—nearly $100 billion in 1996. In the last decade, the share of developing and emerging market economies of Asia in world exports has nearly doubled to almost one-fifth of the total. Prior to the crisis, East Asian countries also had one of the highest savings rates in the world—above 30 per cent on average over the 1975–95 period and their investment rates were 30–40 per cent of GDP (Yellen, 1998).

Although there is no single explanation for such impressive growth rates in South East Asia, a considerable amount of research and publication by policy analysts, investors, and academics has been developed with often repeated praises for the virtues of East Asian-style state-guided capitalism. What follows is a brief synthesis of the literature developed to explain the factors which only a few years ago were in fact praised for contributing to the outstanding growth between 1960 and 1990, the so-called 'Asian Miracle' period.

Causes and Circumstances surrounding the 'Asian Miracle'

There have been several explanations offered for the extraordinary Asian economic growth. Although several factors have been identified as significant to the so-called 'miracle', most of the studies reviewed seem to attribute the successful East Asian growth to the following main factors: stable macroeconomic and stable financial systems, state-guided capitalism, administrative competence of the government, political and economic stability, and social cohesion.

Stable Macroeconomic and Stable Financial Systems

According to World Bank reports, most East Asian economies generally limited fiscal deficits to levels that could be prudently financed without increasing inflationary pressures and responded quickly when fiscal pressures were perceived to be building up. Between 1960 and 1990, annual inflation averaged approximately 9 per cent in these economies compared with 18 per cent in other low and middle-income economies. When macroeconomics control lapsed, it was swiftly re-established. For example when Korea's inflation rate rose to 20 per cent in the late 1970s as a result of the expensive drive to develop the heavy and chemical industries, the government acted decisively to cut fiscal spending. Indonesia's public sector deficit exceeded 4 per cent of GDP in 1986 as oil prices declined, but the government made sharp budget cuts and reduced the deficit to a manageable 1.3 per cent by 1989. In some countries, prudent fiscal behaviour was aided by legislation that limited the size of public deficits (e.g. Indonesia, Taiwan, Thailand), while in others the anti-inflation stance of the political leadership (e.g. Korea, Malaysia, and Singapore) served to keep macroeconomic control high on the policy agenda (Leipziger and Vinod, 1994: 6). Because inflation was both moderate and predictable, real interest rates were far more stable than in other low and middle-income economies. This macroeconomic stability encouraged long-term planning and private investment, and through its impact on real interest rates and the real value of financial assets helped to increase financial savings (World Bank, 1993).

Flexible and Prudential Regulations, Good Supervision and Secure Financial Systems

The East Asia economies increased savings by using generally positive real interest rates on deposits and creating secure bank-based financial systems through strong prudential regulation, good supervision, and institutional reforms. In addition Japan and Taiwan established postal savings systems to attract small savers. These systems offered small savers greater security and lower transaction costs than the private sector, and made substantial resources available to government. Some governments also used a variety of more interventionist mechanisms to increase savings. Malaysia and Singapore, for example, guaranteed high minimum, private savings rates through mandatory provident fund contributions. Japan, Korea, and Taiwan all imposed stringent controls and high interest rates on loans for consumer items as well as taxes on luxury consumption.

As far as investment control is concerned, the East Asia economies encouraged investment by several means. They created an investment-friendly environment through a combination of tax policies and measures that kept the relative prices of capital goods low, largely by maintaining low tariffs on imported capital goods. Most countries kept deposit and lending rates below market-clearing levels (Page, 1994). Furthermore, East Asian economies' governments gradually but continuously liberalized the trade regime and supplemented it by institutional support for exporters, to achieve an export push. Exchange rate policies in all economies were liberalized and currencies frequently revalued to support export growth (Page, 1994).

Pegging Currency to the US Dollar

Rapidly growing economies often peg their exchange rates to encourage trade and investment, to maintain a nominal anchor for domestic prices and restrain inflation, and to signal their commitment to prudent monetary policies. The formal pegging of the Thai baht, Malaysian ringgit, the Philippine peso, and other regional currencies to the US dollar provided a strong impetus to export-led growth. The mid-1980s export boom for Thailand, for example, was driven largely by the depreciation of the US dollar in relation to other countries and by the fact that the baht was pegged to it. This made Thailand's labour-intensive exports such as apparel, footwear, and toys more price competitive internationally. It also promoted a massive influx of Japanese, Taiwanese, and Hong Kong investment into the country because the former wished to avoid rising labour costs in their own countries. As a result the terms of trade improved, and the economy recorded a GDP growth rate of 12 per cent a year between 1987 and 1990, and 8.6 per cent growth between 1991 and 1996. Thailand's exports from the manufacturing sector rose from 35 to 80 per cent of total merchandise exports, the largest percentage of any ASEAN country. Between 1994–96 ASEAN and East Asia countries that pegged their currency to the US dollar recorded the highest rates of increase in merchandise trade. The region's imports were up 15.6 per cent and reached US$1.01 trillion. Exports rose by 15.2 per cent to US$1.1 trillion, and Asia, which only controlled 17 per cent of the world's GDP in 1950, saw its share jump to 40 per cent by 1997. In Taiwan, Hong Kong, South Korea, Malaysia, Thailand, and Singapore, exports were up by 18.1 per cent to US$418 billion, a 9 per cent increase over 1993–94 (World Trade Orgranization, 1997).

State-Guided Capitalism and Administrative Competence of the Government

Most explanations of the extraordinary growth of several Asian Pacific economies since the early 1960s in one way or another acknowledge the significant contributions of the government in setting out and creating an environment favourable to growth and economic development. Governments' interventions despite the variations ranging from heavy intervention in South Korea, Indonesia, and Malaysia to a more flexible form in Hong Kong and to some extent in Thailand, were seen as the major reason for East Asia success.

Government Selective Intervention

Almost all of the East Asian governments engaged in some form of intervention. Subsidized lending and tax incentives to selected industries and export promotion were widespread. All the East Asian countries, with the exception of Hong Kong and Singapore, relied on import barriers to protect their domestic industries in their early stages of development. Even by the early 1980s most of South Korea's industries were still protected by some combination of tariffs and non-tariff barriers. In Taiwan as late as 1980 more than 140 per cent of imports faced rates of protection of more than 31 per cent. Indonesia, Malaysia, and Thailand all had import-substitution regimes that favoured manufactured goods in their early years of development. In the South-east Asia newly industrializing economies, government intervention played a much less prominent and frequently less constructive role in economic success, while adherence to policy fundamentals remained important.

A 390-page study, *The East Asian Miracle*, was conducted by the World Bank to identify the main policies that characterized East Asia's unique success between 1960 and 1990 (World Bank, 1993). According to the report, East Asia's success during those twenty years was largely attributable to a combination of policies ranging from market-oriented (fundamental policies) to state policies (selective interventions). These were introduced to achieve macroeconomic stability and rapid export growth. Fundamental policies included high investments in physical and human capital, stable and secure financial systems, limited price distortions, and openness to foreign technology. Selective interventions included mild financial repression (keeping interest rates positive but low), directed credit, selective industrial promotion, and trade policies that pushed non-traditional exports.

Government intervention took many forms: targeting and subsidizing credit to selected industries, keeping deposit rates low, and maintaining ceilings on borrowing rates to increase profits and retained earnings, protecting domestic import substitutes, subsidizing declining industries, establishing and financially supporting government banks, making public investments in applied research, establishing firm- and industry-specific export targets, developing export-marketing institutions, and sharing information widely between public and private sectors. Given the 'unusually' rapid growth in the region, these selective interventions could not have significantly inhibited growth.

... Our judgment is that in a few economies mainly in North East Asia, in some instances, government interventions resulted in higher and more equal growth than otherwise would have occurred ... First governments in North East Asia developed institutional mechanisms, which allowed them to establish clear performance criteria for selective interventions and to monitor performance. Intervention has taken place in an unusually disciplined and performance-based manner. Second the costs of interventions, both explicit and implicit, did not become excessive. When fiscal costs threatened the macro-economic stability of Korea and Malaysia during the heavy and chemical industries drives, governments pulled back. In Japan the Ministry of Finance acted as a check on the ability of the Ministry of International Trade and Industry to carry out subsidy policies and in Indonesia and Thailand balanced budget laws and legislative procedures constrained the scope for subsidies. Indeed when selective interventions have threatened macro-economic stability, governments have consistently come down on the side of prudent macro-economic management. Price distortion arising from selective interventions were also less extreme than in many developing economies. (World Bank, 1993: 9)

The World Bank report acknowledges further that although the East Asian experience does not make a clear case for a *laissez-faire* approach to economic policy-making or for a heavy hand on the tiller, the studies do show, however, that the way governments supported markets and fashioned an institutional framework for effective policy implementation was critical (Leipziger and Vinod, 1994: 6).

Export Promotion and Direct Credit

Export promotion and direct credit were the most successful forms of intervention. Governments in South East Asia used a variety of approaches to promoting exports. All except

Hong Kong began with a period of import substitution, and a strong bias against exports. But each moved to establish a pro-export regime more quickly than other developing economies. First Japan, in the 1950s and early 1960s, and then the Four Tigers, in the late 1960s, shifted trade policies to encourage manufactured exports. In Japan, Korea, Taiwan, and China, governments established a pro-export incentive structure that coexisted with moderate but highly variable protection of the domestic market. A wide variety of instruments was used, including export credit, duty-free imports for exporters and their suppliers, export targets, and tax incentives. In the South East Asia newly industrialized countries, the export push came later in the early 1980s and the instruments were different. Reductions in import protection were more generalized and were accompanied by export credit and supporting institutions.

Each of the Asian economies also made some attempts to direct credit to priority activities: all except Hong Kong gave automatic access to credit for exporters. Housing was a priority in Hong Kong and Singapore, while agriculture and small and medium-sized enterprises were targeted sectors in Indonesia, Malaysia, and Thailand. Taiwan has targeted technological development, while Japan and Korea have at various times used credit as a tool of industrial policy to promote the shipbuilding, chemical, and automobile industries (Page, 1994).

Rigorous Performance-Based Directed Credit Mechanisms

Directed credit programmes included strict performance criteria. In Japan, public bank managers employed rigorous economic and financial evaluations to select among applicants from sectors that were being targeted by the government. In Korea, the government individually monitored the large conglomerates using market-oriented criteria, such as exports and profitability (Page, 1994). In addition, to minimize the costs of intervention, governments set up institutional mechanisms for rigorous screening and monitoring of the selected industries according to their performance. In Japan and South Korea, for example, governments created 'contests' between firms, with exports as the yardstick of success, and subsidized credit, foreign exchange, or investment licences the reward. Assessments of the directed-credit programmes in Japan and Korea provide micro-economic evidence that such programmes increased investment in these economies, promoted new activities and borrowers, and were directed at firms with high potential for technological spillovers. Thus the performance-based directed-credit mechanisms appear to have improved credit allocation, especially during the early stages of rapid growth (Page, 1994). According to the World Bank report, the success of these 'contests' to allocate resources depended crucially on a unique institutional factor: the competence and relative lack of corruptibility of civil servants. Hong Kong, Japan, South Korea, Singapore, and Taiwan have, by Asia standards, been successful in building professional and honest bureaucracies, thanks partly to generous pay and perks that are competitive with the private sector (World Bank, 1993).

Administrative Competence of the Government

Economic developments in Asia Pacific during the 'Miracle' were also attributed to the competent guidance and policies implemented by their respective governments.

Public Spending on Human Capital

Much of East Asia's dramatic growth between the 1960s and 1990s was due to superior accumulation of physical and human capital. Education policies focused on primary and secondary education vital for a skilled workforce, rather than on universities. This generated rapid increases in labour-force skills. For example, in the mid-1980s, Indonesia, South Korea, and Thailand all devoted more than 80 per cent of their education budget to basic education, compared with less than 50 per cent in Argentina and Venezuela (World Bank, 1993). The limited public funding for post-secondary education was used primarily for science and technological education (including engineering), while university education in the humanities and social sciences was handled through the private system. Some East Asian economies also imported education services on a large scale, particularly for disciplines requiring specialized skills (Page, 1994). The result of these has been a broad, technically inclined human capital base well suited to rapid economic development.

Productivity Growth

Productivity growth in the Asian economies has often been linked to the quality of the labour force, specially its education and training. This was clearly an East Asian strength. The high quality labour, as seen in South Korea and Singapore, for example, aided industrial flexibility, increased economic efficiency, and promoted greater equity (Leipziger and Vinod, 1994: 6).

Flexible Policy-Making

Another common feature attributed to the productivity growth is the flexibility of government policy-making. Governments did not merely provide protection for a local industry but supported many kinds of industries to help them achieve export competitiveness. It is important to note that governments guided, but did not override, the decision of firms. International price signals were used to gauge efficiency and success and firms were offered support in exchange for specific performance requirements. Policies were constantly subject to review and scrutiny. When policies appeared ineffective, or when sectoral polices conflicted with macroeconomic equilibrium, they were abandoned. Policy-makers were aware that they were accountable for performance and the standards of performance were known. There are several examples to illustrate this, such as South Korea's sharp policy reversal with respect to its long support of heavy industry by reversing its credit allocation policies and introducing drastic stabilization measures following the second oil shock and overheating of the domestic economy. Trade liberalization replaced protection, commercial banks were privatized, and the attempts to pick winners abandoned (Leipziger and Vinod, 1994). Indonesia and Malaysia scrapped their import-substitution policies in the 1980s. Indonesia began to open up its economy. In Malaysia, the government shifted from promoting heavy industries relying on public sector investments to a reform programme centred on privatization.

Effective Bureaucracy

An effective bureaucracy further aided effective policy-making. In most East Asia countries, because government service conferred status, governments were able to select the most highly qualified individuals. In South Korea, Singapore, Taiwan, Indonesia, and Malaysia, bureaucracies tended to work well and they enjoyed strong political support.

Political and Economic Stability and Social Cohesion

Between the 1960s and the 1990s Asia Pacific countries displayed a record of maintaining political and economic stability and of pursuing long-term economic goals. Most of the East Asia economies were able to develop a national consensus concerning the direction of economic policy, beginning with land redistribution in South Korea and Taiwan and large-scale public housing investment in Hong Kong and Singapore. This political and economic consensus was seen formally in Singapore, for example, where a tripartite apparatus was established combining government, business, and labour. In Malaysia, it took the form of a pro-Malay development strategy that became the central driving force. In South Korea a symbiotic relationship between business and government was formed which helped produce the business conglomerates known as the Korean Chaebols (Leipziger and Vinod, 1994). It was the Chaebols that initiated the industrialization of South Korea. In 1990 it was reported that the total earnings of Korea's top thirty Chaebols contributed about 95 per cent of the gross national product (GNP) (Bank of Korea, 1990, quoted in Leggett and Bambeer 1996).

The Principle of Wealth Sharing

To establish their legitimacy and win the support of the society at large, East Asian leaders established the principle of shared growth, promising that if the economy expanded all groups would benefit. South Korea and Taiwan carried out comprehensive land reform programmes; Indonesia used rice and fertilizer price policies to raise rural incomes; Malaysia introduced explicit wealth-sharing programmes to improve the lot of ethnic Malays *vis-à-vis* the better-off ethnic Chinese; Hong Kong and Singapore undertook massive public housing programmes. In several economies, governments assisted workers' cooperatives and established programmes to encourage small and medium-sized enterprises (Page, 1994).

Cooperation between the Public and Private Sectors

To reassure each competing group that each would benefit from growth, governments realized the importance of building a business-friendly environment. They recruited a competent and relatively honest technocratic cadre and insulated it from day-to-day political interference. The power of these technocracies has varied greatly. In Japan, South Korea, Singapore, Taiwan, and China, strong, well-organized bureaucracies wielded substantial power while others had small, general-purpose planning agencies. But in each economy, these economic technocrats' mission was to help leaders in devising a credible economic strategy, a legal and regulatory structure that was generally hospitable to private investment, and enhanced communication between business and government. In contrast to lobbying, where rules are unclear and groups often seek secret advantage over one another, Japan, South Korea, Malaysia, and Singapore established 'deliberation councils'. These were forums in which private sector groups were invited to help shape and implement the government policies relevant to their interests. In Japan and South

Korea, technocrats used these deliberation councils to establish contests among firms. Because the private sector participated in drafting the rules, and because the process was transparent to all participants, private sector groups became more willing participants in the leadership's development efforts. Deliberation councils also facilitated information exchanges between the private sector and government, among firms, and between management and labour.

Neo-Confucian Ethics and Values

Finally, neo-Confucian ethics and values are believed to have contributed to the high economic growth in East Asia, in particular its collectivist orientation whether inherent, as in South Korea, or deliberately propagated by government as in Singapore (Leggett and Bambeer *et al.*, 1996) and the Confucian values of education, hard work, thrift, and social order (Schültz and Pecotich, 1997). Cultures that eschew adversity and give and take in favour of an ethic of group relationships rather than individual responsibility, it was also argued, help explain East Asia's remarkable economic success (*The Economist*, 1998). Another important factor to consider is the important role of business families in Asia Pacific ranging from the Japanese Zaibatsus and the Korean Chaebols to the Overseas Chinese family networks extending from Taiwan and Hong Kong, through South-East Asia to Australasia and the Pacific.

The Myth of the Asian Miracle

Any overview of the Asian Miracle would be incomplete without a reference to Krugman's provocative article 'The Myth of the Asian Miracle' (Krugman, 1998). In this article Professor Krugman argued that there had been no economic miracle in East Asia. The region's growth, he said, had largely been achieved through heavy investment and a big shift of labour from farms into factories, rather than from productivity gains based on technological advance or organizational change. He linked the Asian economies to the Soviet Union: once inputs are exhausted and capital output ratios rise towards rich country levels, diminishing returns will set in and growth will slow sharply. However, a study by a Swiss bank using the same up-to-date figures for 1970 and 1990 came to a very different conclusion. In this study, five East Asian countries, Hong Kong, Thailand, Singapore, South Korea, and Taiwan ranked in the top twelve countries (out of 104) for average total factor production (TFP) growth. In all five, productivity was roughly as important as investment in explaining growth. In another study of ASEAN countries, Michael Sarel of the IMF also found higher productivity growth. He estimated that Singapore, Malaysia, and Thailand all had a TFP growth of 2 to 2.5 per cent between 1978 and 1996 compared with only 0.3 per cent in the USA. Moreover, TFP growth increased in most ASEAN countries between the 1980s and the 1990s (Sarel, 1996). Another study by the Brookings Institute found that productivity growth in the East Asian Tigers had increased over time: Taiwan's rate of TFP growth quickened from an annual average of 1.6 per cent in 1960–84 to 8 per cent in 1984–94, and Thailand's from 1.3 per cent to 3.3 per cent in the ten years to 1994 (Collins and Bosworth, 1996).

Whatever the precise estimate of East Asian productivity growth, it remains true that low-income countries can grow faster than those further up the development ladder. Obviously Asian growth will slow down but this cannot be simply regarded as a consequence of 'diminishing returns to the inputs' (Crosby, 1997), or as a result of 'perspiration, not inspiration' (Krugman, 1998) . For the moment the East Asian economies are still much less capital-intensive than the rich economies. The average South Koran has only two-fifths as much capital to work with as his American counterpart, the average Thai only one-eighth as much, so there is plenty of room for catching up. The same is true for education, which also boosts productivity. The average East Asian worker aged over 25 has had only seven years of education, compared with at least ten in the developed economies. So even if Krugman is right and most of East Asia's growth has come from pumping capital and labour, those two sources are far from exhausted (Mitsuru, 1995).

Review Questions

1 Why were the Asian economies often referred to as 'Tigers' and 'Dragons' during the 'Miracle' period and did they pose a real threat to free-market economies in the world?

2 To what extent can the Asian 'Miracle' be attributed to Asian governments' intervention in their respective economies?

3 Identify and evaluate the main factors attributed to the Asian Miracle.

Group Project

During the 'Asian Miracle', Western firms actively pursued the tremendous potential of Asia Pacific's massive and unmet infrastructure and upscale consumption requirements. Business opportunities were there in unprecedented abundance. Choose either a Western or Asian multinational firm operating in Asia Pacific and investigate the extent of its success in the region during that period. In your report identify and evaluate the main internal and external factors that have contributed to such success.

Further Reading

Krugman, M., 'The Myth of the Asian Miracle', *Foreign Affairs*, 73(6), 1998.

Sharma, S. D., 'The IMF and Asia's Financial Crisis: Bitter Medicine for Sick Tigers', http://www.usfca.edu/pac-rim/pages/publications/report8.html, 1998.

World Bank, *The East Asian Miracle: Economic Growth and Public Policy*, New York: Oxford University Press, 1993.

Yellen, Janet, 'Lessons from the Asian Crisis', Chair Council of Economic Advisers, *Council on Foreign Relations*, New York, 15 Apr. 1998.

Chapter 2

The Ailing Tigers: From 'Miracle' to Crisis

The Asian crisis erupted publicly in Thailand on 2 July 1997, when Thailand's newly appointed finance minister allowed the Thai baht to float freely against the world's currencies. However the *Financial Times* places the beginning of the crisis back in early February 1997, when the first Thai financial institution missed payments on foreign debt (Connelly, 1998). Starting in 1996 domestic and external shocks revealed weaknesses in the Thai economy that until then had been masked by the rapid pace of economic growth and the weakness of the US dollar to which the Thai currency was pegged. Thailand's difficulties, it was claimed, resulted from its earlier economic success. Strong growth, averaging almost 10 per cent per year from 1987 to 1995 and generally prudent macroeconomic management, as seen in continuous public sector fiscal surpluses over the same period, had attracted large capital inflows, much of them short term—and many of them attracted by the establishment of the Bangkok International Banking Facility in 1993. But while these inflows had permitted faster growth, they had also allowed domestic banks to expand lending rapidly, fuelling imprudent investments and unrealistic increases in asset prices. Thailand was running an exceptionally large current account deficit at 8 per cent of GDP (Fisher, 1998a). A domino effect followed in early July, first with the collapse of the Thai baht and, in quick order, the Malaysian ringgit, the Philippines peso, and the Indonesian rupiah. South Korea on Christmas Eve 1997 agreed on the rollover of their debt. At the start of 1998, the Thai baht was worth about 40 per cent less and the South Korean won 36 per cent less in terms of dollars than in June 1997, a year before. The currencies of Malaysia and the Philippines had also gone down by about 35 per cent in one year. The South Korean and Thai stock markets had fallen by large amounts since mid-1997, 47 per cent and 50 per cent respectively. Economic activity dropped, with a noticeable 5 per cent decline in output in 1998 for both Thailand and Korea. Indonesia's output fell by more than 10 per cent, and a similar decline was also noticed in Malaysia. The worst-hit crisis country has been Indonesia, whose currency has lost an astonishing 83 per cent of its value since the middle of 1997, and 67 per cent of its value since the beginning of 1998 (Fisher, 1998a).

Although the crisis began in Thailand, it rapidly affected other countries in the region. Funds began to flow out of the region, starting a highly damaging chain reaction. The exchange rates depreciated and domestic borrowers with unheeded foreign exchange positions rushed to buy dollars. While this was occurring, foreign lenders became worried that their customers would not be able to repay their debts, which led them to call in their loans. This prompted further falls in the currencies. The withdrawal of funds also started a liquidity crunch. Many firms have found it difficult to obtain working capital or export credit. As a result, even profitable firms have become insolvent, which has added further to pressures on the banking system and depositors' confidence. The Institute of International Finance estimated that net private capital flows to Indonesia, South Korea, Malaysia, the Philippines and Thailand, which had increased from US$38 billion in 1994 to US$97 billion in 1996 collapsed to an estimated minus US$12 billion in 1997—a reversal of $109 billion or more than 10 per cent of the combined pre-shock GDP of these five countries. Commercial bank credits which had risen from $32 billion in 1994 to $56 billion in 1996 turned to a deficit of $27 billion in 1997—a reversal of $83 billion or the equivalent of over 8 per cent of the aggregate GDP of these countries (Fisher, 1998*b*).

Background to the Current Crisis

Most Asian countries have experienced a serious decline in their manufactured exports since the middle of 1995. Two factors have been most commonly cited: the saturation of developed country markets, particularly for machinery and transport equipment, semiconductors, and office automation equipment, which accounted for a significant share and constituted the most dynamic segment of the total exports of many of these countries; and increased protectionism despite the General Agreement on Tariffs and Trade (GATT), and the World Trade agreements, by industrial countries in the area of textiles and clothing imports, which remain the mainstay of the newly industrialized countries. Such export patterns were not accompanied by equivalent reductions in imports, thus leading to widening trade and current account deficits throughout most of South East Asia. The decline in export growth not only hit the profitability of domestic exporters and employment in export-oriented industries, but also adversely affected investor expectations, which had become dependent upon very high growth rates; this proved to be a catalytic factor in the subsequent financial debacle (Montes, 1998: 66) . According to another school of thought, these current account imbalances led to precipitous declines in foreign investor confidence and consequently to the current crisis.

According to the Institute of International Finance, a think-tank funded by global financial institutions, net private capital flows to the five East Asian economies most afflicted by the crisis (Indonesia, Malaysia, Philippines, South Korea, and Thailand) fell sharply in 1997. Whereas in 1996, these economies attracted net capital flows to the tune of US$93 billion, they suffered an outflow of US$12 billion in 1997, or a loss of US$105 billion in terms of net inflows. (These figures are reported in 'Emerging Market Indicators', *The Economist* 7–13 Feb. 1998. The Institute of International Finance's report was released at the end of January 1998. Montes, 1998: 66). This amount equals two-thirds of the capital funnelled into all of Asia the previous year. According to this report, South Korea alone received US$50 billion less than it did the year before. Much of this outflow occurred, it appears, because of the refusal of international banks to roll over the large sums of short-term credit they had provided these countries with in the recent past.

Genesis of the Crisis

Chronology of the financial crisis

1997

May/June/July

14–15 May	Bank of Thailand intervenes to defend baht from attack by speculators.
27 June	Bank of Thailand suspends operation of sixteen finance companies which have high level of bad debt and orders them to merge with healthier ones.
2 July	Bank of Thailand abandons the fixed exchange rate for the baht against the US dollar. The baht depreciates by 20 per cent.
11 July	Philippines central bank gives up defence of the peso. The peso depreciates by more than 10 per cent against the US dollar.
13 July	Kia group, Korea's eighth largest Chaebol is put under the control of a government alliance of banks to avoid bankruptcy.
14 July	Malaysia's Bank Negara gives up defence of the ringgit.
24 July	Indonesia and Malaysia regional stock market plunge.
28 July	Thailand seeks for help from the IMF.

August

11 Aug.	IMF approves Thailand bail-out package of $17 billion in loans to Thailand.
14 Aug.	Indonesia abandons its fixed exchange rate for the rupiah against the US dollar.

September

4 Sept.	Bank of Korea agrees to lend 1 billion won to troubled Korea First Bank. Korean government also announces measures including soft loans to banks to try to prevent bad debts overwhelming the banking system.
22 Sept.	Regional stock markets plunge again.
28 Sept.	Stock exchange of Thailand suspends forty-eight listed companies including twenty-six finance companies.
29 Sept.	Kia Motors receives South Korea court order, freezing debt obligations and assets but avoiding immediate bankruptcy.

October

1 Oct.	Regional currency plunge to new lows creating panic in the region.
8 Oct.	Indonesia government asks for help from IMF to help stabilize its financial sectors in the face of recent sharp depreciation of the rupiah.
14 Oct.	Thailand unveils its plan for financial restructuring.

17 Oct.	Malaysia unveils 1998 budget cutting state infrastructure spending, increasing import duties.
18 Oct.	Taiwan dollar falls to its weakest level in a decade.
22 Oct.	Korea government announces court receivership of the Kia group, effectively nationalizing it.
23 Oct.	Hong Kong stock market crashes 40 percent during the month, but Hong Kong monetary authority is able to counter heavy selling of the Hong Kong dollar and maintain exchange rate with the US dollar.
31 Oct.	IMF assistance package for Indonesia is announced at $23 billion.

November

4 Nov.	Thai prime minister announces that he would resign by the end of the week.
17 Nov.	New Taiwan dollar weakened.
21 Nov.	Korea seeks help from the IMF in the form of standby credit of $20 billion.

December

1 Dec.	Taiwan and Malaysia stocks plunge.
3 Dec.	Korea and the IMF reach agreement on bail-out package totalling $57 billion.
5 Dec.	Malaysia government announces cutting its spending to match slower revenue.
31 Dec.	Indonesia announces planned merger of former state banks and will open them to foreign investors.

1998

5 Jan.	Political instability in Indonesia. Attack targeted against ethnic Chinese minority.
8 Jan.	Indonesia market plunge.
12 Jan.	Meeting between the IMF and US government officials and President Suharto of Indonesia. Peregrine Investment, Hong Kong's Investment Bank, files for liquidation procedures.
15 Jan.	Indonesian President Suharto and the IMF reach agreement.
22 Jan.	Collapse of Indonesian rupiah continues.

Sources: Gough, Leo, *Asia Meltdown: The End of the Miracle*, Oxford: Capstone Publishing, 1998.
Montes, Manuel, F., *The Currency Crisis in Southeast Asia*, Singapore: Singapore Institute of Southeast Asian Studies, 1998.

When discussing the causes and consequences of the crisis, there is a tendency among the commentators to lump together all countries in Asia. It is important to note that not all countries in Asia Pacific have been affected by the crisis in the same way. During the crisis, Hong Kong and Singapore, for example, were more resistant to foreign economic contagion than others. They were able to avoid such serious damage to their currencies and economies as suffered by other Asian countries by avoiding excessive debt and asset bubbles. They also had adequate financial disclosure, well-developed procedures allowing unsuccessful businesses to fail, and had husbanded enough foreign exchange reserves to finance their international trade. Further they avoided the worst problems by limiting cross-border financial flows and placing restrictions on such flows (Aggarwal, 1999*a*).

Singapore's sound economic base was not shaken too much by the crisis. Damage caused by the crisis was far smaller than for neighbouring countries. The reasons for this are that the government of Singapore had adopted several precautionary measures against financial instability before the crisis. For instance, it had upgraded to high-tech and high value-added industries in the late 1980s and early 1990s, successfully avoided the competition in exports from China and India, as well as the North American Free Trade areas; it had also strictly restricted the domain of the business-type financial sector and monitored financial operations closely. In 1996 measures were taken to cool down the real estate market. The government also kept a positive balance on the current account and a positive government budget surplus in the long term, in addition to maintaining an efficient and clean government and transparency policy (Yunhua, 2000).

The Asian crisis had a light impact on Taiwan as well, where investments, both in the public and private sectors, were essentially funded from domestic savings, rather than by incurring foreign debt. Taiwan had run a current account surplus for many years prior to the crisis (US$7.7 billion in 1997), as opposed to the enormous current account deficits sustained by other countries affected by the crisis (Siew, 1998). Public external debt was also very limited (less than US$100 million at the end of 1997) (Rong, 1998). As far as the financial sector is concerned, banks in Taiwan were prudent in lending, ensuring any extension of loans was secured by stocks. For lending purposes, the valuation of stocks was set at 60 per cent of the market price. For all domestic banks, the rate of non-performing loans was 3.8 per cent on average in 1997 (Siew, 1998). Furthermore, at the time of the currency fallout, Taiwan had huge foreign reserves (US$83.5 billion at the end of 1997). These huge foreign reserves allowed the Central Bank to defend unexpected speculative attacks (Yi-Chi, 1998). Additionally, foreign capital flowing into Taiwan was mostly of the nature of direct investment in production activities, and less in stock market and real estate. Therefore a 'bubble phenomenon did not exist' (Wu, 1998). Finally, Taiwan had a floating exchange rate unlike the dollar-peg schemes of crisis-ridden countries.

China weathered the economic and financial turbulence in East Asia in 1997 because of its sound external balances and rising foreign currency reserves, and having only partially liberalized the capital account. The financial crisis as a result did not spread into China as quickly as other Asian economies. The renminbi even appreciated marginally against the US dollar in 1997. The following factors explain the strength of the renminbi compared to other currencies in Asia Pacific. First, China's capital account was not convertible. Secondly, the bulk of foreign capital inflows during the first half of the 1990s went into production sectors as direct investment as opposed to portfolio investment. Thirdly, China has adopted prudent policies with regard to external borrowing, with about 82 per cent of its external debt being medium and long term, and its debt to GDP and debt-service ratios being significantly below the thresholds at which the International Monetary Fund expresses concern. Finally, because of massive foreign capital inflows and strong export performance, China maintained a robust external position, with foreign currency reserves exceeding total foreign debt. By the end of 1998, China had about $149 billion in total reserves less gold (including about $145 billion in foreign exchange). The growth in foreign reserves has slowed since 1997. However, reserves began increasing again at the end of 1998 (Henderson, 1998). China also reported external debt of $130 billion in mid-1998. This debt remains moderate compared to other Asian economies (Henderson, 1998: 258–9).

Thailand, Malaysia, Indonesia, and South Korea, on the other hand, were the countries worst hit by the crisis. A brief summary of these economies follows in the chronological order that they experienced the crisis.

Thailand and the Crisis

Basically, the financial crisis in Thailand was due to excessive investments, many of which turned out to be too optimistic and too unproductive. Many investments were based on money borrowed abroad. Due to high interest rates in Thailand and a fixed exchange rate policy linking the baht to the US dollar, foreign investors were eager to place their money in Thailand, preferring to lend on a short-term basis for which they could obtain 10 to 11 per cent interest rates. Domestic borrowers were also eager to borrow offshore because such money was cheaper (low interest rates) and the virtually pegged exchange rate encouraged borrowers to think that there was no currency risk. Corporate borrowers discovered they could thus borrow at an interest rate of 5 to 8 per cent instead of paying more than 13 per cent when borrowing domestically. They could even earn money simply by borrowing from abroad and depositing baht in Thailand (Lauridsen, 1998: 136–61).

In 1992, as part of a broader financial liberalization package, the Thai government deregulated the foreign exchange. The Bangkok International Banking Facility (BIBF) was established in 1993 to attract more foreign funds to cover the increasing current account deficits, to turn Thailand into a regional financial centre, and to ensure a greater degree of competition in the banking sector. The BIBF made it possible for local and foreign commercial banks to take deposits or to borrow in foreign currencies from abroad and to lend the money both in Thailand and abroad (Chaiyasoot, 1995: 172). As a consequence, Thailand undertook too much offshore borrowing. The external debt increased from almost US$40 billion in 1992 to US$80 billion in March 1997. Therefore, total outstanding debt as a share of GDP increased from 34 per cent in 1990 to 51 per cent in 1996, an increase generated almost exclusively by the private sector. Of the total debt stock, 80 per cent was private debt and almost 36 per cent was short term, maturing in 12 months or less. In August 1997, the Bank of Thailand realized that the foreign debt was about US$90 billion, of which US$73 billion was by private companies, with US$20 billion falling due by the end of 1997. In January 1998, the Thailand Development Research Institute showed that the ratio of short-term debt to foreign reserves increased from 0.6 in 1990 to 1.0 in 1995 (and 1996), implying that the ability of the country to service short-term debt had deteriorated during the first half of the 1990s. Misallocation of loan funds was one problem. A second problem was vulnerability. Most of the loans, even those going to the industrial sector, were not hedged against currency fluctuations. Secondly, a currency mismatch arose as much of the foreign money went into non-tradable sectors of the economy, that is, with no foreign exchange receipts. Thirdly, there was a term mismatch as short-term borrowing was utilized to finance long-term projects with longer-term returns. Finally, financing of equity purchases by loans without taking the foreign exchange risk into account was not unusual (Lauridsen, 1998: 136–61). A third problem was related closely to Thailand's property boom. In Thailand, people who wanted loans for property, cars, and other consumer durables went to the country's finance companies. These finance companies had found that it was easy to raise money by borrowing from abroad or by selling stocks and bonds to institutional investors—such as South Korean banks. In the early 1990s, foreign lenders were too eager to lend to Thai institutions and were not looking too closely at the financial fundamentals of the borrowers. Furthermore, many banks in Asia were so anxious to develop good relations with Thai banks that they were willing to lend simply to cement their relationships rather than to make profits (Gough, 1998: 110). As a result, finance companies in Thailand were able to borrow US dollars cheaply and then lend baht to local consumers at high rates of 14 to 20 per cent not only for short-term consumer loans but also for property purchases. However, property loans could only be sustained at such high rates if there was a property boom. But this did not seem to be an obstacle. Thai finance companies and banks had plenty of cash and were simply looking for quick gains. Property in the early 1990s was the quickest way to make money in Thailand. Not only did the finance companies lend to property developers, but they themselves, like the high-flying Finance One, became involved in property speculation. Everyone was doing it—even the manufacturers began to channel their profits into property instead of ploughing it back into their businesses (Gough, 1998).

By the beginning of 1997, there was an estimated $4 billion worth of non-performing loans. The Thai finance companies and banks did not declare their real estate borrowers insolvent. Instead, they covered up the problem to protect their own financial standing. This worked for a while, but when Thailand's largest finance company, Finance One, and a big property company, Somprasong Land, failed to pay due debts to foreign leaders early in 1997, it became apparent to overseas observers that Thailand was in trouble (Gough, 1998). By June 1997, when foreign investors started pulling their money out, the currency speculators pounced, sparking the crisis.

Indonesia and the Crisis

In July 1997, shortly after the Thai baht was unpegged from the US dollar, Indonesia saw its stock market drop by 50 per cent. Its currency plunged more than 70 per cent. The weaknesses in the Indonesian economy which made it vulnerable to currency attacks were similar to Thailand's, that is, rising external liabilities, private sector debt problems and poor loan quality, lack of confidence in the government's ability to resolve the problems, excessive amounts of foreign investment inflating an expanding asset bubble, and an overvalued currency pegged to the strengthening US dollar. Although most of the macroeconomic indicators were deemed sound, the financial sector was deeply suspect and proved to be the weakest link in the chain (Congressional Report, 1997).

Early in the crisis, the Indonesian government attempted to calm the situation by defending the currency, using central bank reserves, and loosening its control on the exchange rate. However, by 13 August 1997, just as Thailand was signing a deal with the IMF, the rupiah hit a then historic low of 2.682 to the dollar, from a pre-July level of 2,400. On 14 August 1997 the government abolished the managed exchange rate and the rupiah slid immediately to 2,755. Even though the central bank attempted to defend the currency by raising interest rates and the government announced that projects worth

39 trillion rupiah would be postponed to meet the budget shortfall, the situation continued to deteriorate and by 6 October the rupiah was at a new low of 3,845 to the dollar. Two days later, faced with declining reserves, collapsing financial institutions, and capital haemorrhaging from the country, the government announced its intention to seek IMF assistance. By 31 October, Indonesia had agreed to a US$43 billion loan agreement. Of this, US$23 billion was first-line financing made up of US$10 billion from the IMF, US$4.5 billion from the World Bank, US$3.5 billion from the Asian Development Bank and US$5 billion from Indonesia's own international reserves. Second-line supplementary financing, totalling about US$20 billion, included US$6 billion from the USA, US$5 billion each from Japan and Singapore, and US$1 billion each from Australia and Malaysia. The agreement represented about 490 per cent of Indonesia's special drawing rights, just below the 500 per cent threshold requiring special approval. The objectives of the package were to stabilize exchange market conditions, ensure an orderly adjustment of the external current account in response to lower capital inflows, and lay the groundwork for a resumption of sustained rapid growth (IMF, 1997).

Malaysia and the Crisis

The first signs of the crisis for Malaysia emerged in mid-May 1997 when the ringgit came under pressure, triggered by speculative attacks on the Thai baht. Bank Negara's (Malaysia's central bank) immediate response was to intervene in the foreign exchange market to uphold the value of the ringgit. It tried to uphold its value for about a week before it was finally forced to float the ringgit on 14 July. By that time, the bank had already lost close to US$1.5 billion in the effort to prop up the ringgit. By the second half of 1997, the strengthening of the US dollar and the pound sterling and the escalation of the regional financial crisis set the stage for the depreciation of the ringgit to unprecedented levels. The depreciation was concentrated in the last four months of 1997 when the ringgit depreciated against the dollar by almost 50 per cent, hitting a high of US$1 = RM 4.88 on 7 January1998 (Ariff and Abubakar, 1999: 418).

Malaysia also experienced the biggest stock market plunge in the region. Between July and December 1997, the composite index of the Kuala Lumpur Stock Exchange fell by 44.9 per cent. On the whole, between 1 July 1997 and September 1998 market capitalization in the Kuala Lumpur Stock Exchange fell by about 76 per cent to RM 181.5 billion. The crash was then followed by massive capital outflows as confidence in the Malaysian economy became increasingly shaky. As a result, the banking system began to experience increasing non-performing loans which, according to Bank Negara data, rose from a modest 2.18 per cent in June 1997 to 4.08 per cent in December 1997, and then to a high of 11.45 per cent in July 1998 (EPU White Paper, 1999: 419). Many companies began to roll over debt as part of their survival strategy. This was followed by a general contraction in domestic demand. Consequently, domestic-oriented industries such as the construction and service sectors were severely hit. FDI too displayed a declining trend. The government, effective from 2 September 1998, fixed its value at US$1 = RM3.8. At the same time, trading in Malaysian shares and currency outside of Malaysia was halted and selective capital controls were put in place.

The impact of the financial crisis in the region began to have an effect on the level of domestic economic activity in 1998. While employment growth had been growing stead-ily at 4.9 and 4.6 per cent in 1996 and 1997 respectively, it contracted by 3 per cent in 1998. For the whole of 1998, the number of workers retrenched was 83,865, a sharp increase from the 19,000 retrenched in 1997. Inflation levels rose as well, reaching a high of 6.2 per cent in June 1998. The inflation rate was 5.3 per cent in 1998 (Ariff, and Abubakar, 1999: 420). Consequently, with such a high rise of unemployment and infla-tion, the erosion of household income and welfare became unavoidable. In addition to the existing poor, a new group of poor has emerged for whom there are no social safety nets available to cushion the effects of sudden loss of income. Urban families experienced the worst of the impact due to an increased cost of living, including the cost of food, household necessities, health care, tertiary education, and transportation. Finally, it is important to note that, unlike Thailand, Indonesia, and South Korea, recovery efforts in Malaysia did not rely on IMF assistance. Malaysia, in fact, flatly rejected the financial package offered by the IMF, although the reforms introduced by the Malaysian govern-ment advocated similar austerity measures (further details on these reforms are provided in Ch. 5).

Korea and the Crisis

It is argued that Korea, even while sharing some of the basic underlying economic prob-lems plaguing Thailand and Indonesia, is in many respects structurally different in the sense that the problem is one of liquidity rather than insolvency, or that it is only tem-porarily unable to pay current foreign obligations, not permanently unable to earn for-eign currency to repay debts (Sharma, 1998). On the eve of the crisis the Korean economy was performing well as real GDP grew at 8 per cent per year through the 1980s and 1990s and the current account deficit was only over 3 per cent of GDP compared to 8 per cent in Thailand. Also the bulk of foreign loans was used to finance investments in the export sector rather than real estate developments or imports of consumer goods, as was the case elsewhere in South East Asia. Finally, the gross public debt amounted to only 3 per cent of GDP, there was little inflationary pressure in the economy, and in June 1995 the coun-try's seasonally adjusted unemployment rate stood at 2.1 per cent, the lowest in the country's history (*Far Eastern Economic Review*, 1996).

In the early 1990s, three factors were central to the crisis in Korea. The first was distrac-tion from the previous focus on building up industrial and technological capabilities by real estate and other such unproductive investments. The second was the massive trade blitz unleashed on Korea by the USA. The third was membership of the OECD, which forced Korea to adopt a more liberal stance towards foreign capital and finance. Instead of focusing investments on turning out high value-added commodities and developing more sophisticated production technologies, Korea's conglomerates went for quick and easy profits, buying up real estate or pouring money into stock market speculation. For example in the 1980s, over US$16.5 billion in Chaebol funds went into buying land for speculation and setting up luxury hotels and golf courses. Additionally, Korea's inability to advance from labour-intensive assembly with Japanese inputs using Japanese tech-nology resulted in a massive trade deficit with Japan which came to over US$15 billion in 1996 (*Far Eastern Economic Review*, 1996).

The Hanbo Scandal in Korea

In Korea the first big sign of trouble was in January 1997 when Hanbo Steel, a company in the Hanbo group, defaulted on its loans. The scandal erupted when it was discovered that Hanbo, the country's fourteenth largest Chaebol which had grown immensely during the 1990s, had massive debts of around US$6 billion or sixteen times its own capital. The Hanbo group's chairman and his son were convicted of taking some US$400 million from the group to bribe government officials and bankers in a futile attempt to keep the group afloat (Gough, 1998). After the Hanbo problem was exposed, banks began taking a closer look at their loans and started calling in loans to the most indebted firms. This created a domino effect as more companies failed. The biggest blow was when Kia Motors, the country's eighth largest Chaebol collapsed (Gough, 1998).

By October 1997, it was estimated that non-performing loans by Korean enterprises had escalated to over US$50 billion. As this surfaced, foreign banks, which already had about US$200 billion worth of investments and loans in Korea, became reluctant to release new funds to Seoul. By late November 1997, saddled with having to repay some US$66 billion out of a total foreign debt of US$210 billion within one year, Korea joined Thailand and Indonesia in the queue for an IMF bail-out.

Causes and Circumstances surrounding the 'Crisis'

The Asian crisis engendered interesting economic and political debates. A review of the literature, however, indicates a particular problem in establishing an overarching causal explanation of the financial turmoil. While different interpretations have so far been developed, a comparative analysis of the factors attributed to the 'Miracle' discussed earlier reveals how the same factors that were praised for contributing to the outstanding growth between 1960 and 1990, only a few years later have come to be identified as also contributing to the crisis. What follows is a brief synthesis of the literature developed to explain the factors which have contributed to the crisis in Asia Pacific. For comparative purposes, the framework adopted is similar to the one used in explaining the 'Miracle'.

Financial Turbulence, Economic Instability, and Weak Financial Systems

During the 'Miracle' period, the relatively stable macroeconomic environment was mainly attributed to the stability of interest rates and to the flexible and prudential fiscal policies. The crisis that followed was then attributed to the fixed rate regimes, pegged currency against the US dollars, and the inflexibility of the financial system.

Currency Crisis and Fixed Rate Regimes

The crisis in Asia Pacific is often claimed to be simply or mainly a currency crisis. By 1997 most of the regional currencies were overvalued and fixed rate regimes and excessive short-term capital inflows led to significant real appreciation. The problem, it is argued, began building more than a decade ago, when American manufacturers started flocking to Singapore, Indonesia, Malaysia, and the Philippines to take advantage of cheap labour and low-price land. They were followed by US-based mutual funds and investment banks, all anxious to cash in on the Asian boom. Wages inevitably rose throughout Asia, and real estate costs went through the roof all along the Asia Pacific. Meanwhile one Asian government after another began printing more local currency, to meet investment demand. Then one by one they were forced to devalue their currencies as markets flooded with new money (Welsh, 1998).

Inflexibility of Domestic Policies and Lax Prudential Rules

Many argue that the fundamental cause of the recent crisis is to be found in the financial systems. Thailand, Indonesia, and South Korea had weak financial institutions. Domestic institutions were not strong enough and domestic policies were not flexible enough to meet the increasing demands of economic success. These institutional and policy short-comings manifested themselves in various ways, including: the failure to address the overheating pressures seen in the countries' excessive credit expansion, inflated real estate prices, and widening current account deficits; in the lack of sufficient exchange rate flexibility, which undermined competitiveness and which together with implicit guarantees of support to banks and corporations, led to excessive external borrowing and foreign exchange exposure, often at short maturities; in lax prudential rules, inadequate supervision, and lending based on personal connections and government directive, which led to inefficient investment and a deterioration in the quality of bank balance sheets; and in the lack of data and transparency (Camdessus, 1998*c*). In summary, a combination of inadequate financial sector supervision, poor assessment and management of financial risk, and the maintenance of relatively fixed exchange rates led banks and corporations to borrow large amounts of international capital, much of it short term, denominated in foreign currency, and unhedged (IMF home page, 1998).

Pegged Currency Leading to Debt Crisis

Debt is one of the major factors identified as the cause of the crisis. Companies, in the worst-hit countries, South Korea, Indonesia, and Thailand, borrowed vast sums of money as their economies boomed. They borrowed mostly in US dollars because interest rates were much lower than on their own currencies. The exchange rates of local currencies were pegged against the dollar, so they had no fears about having to earn money in local currency to pay back loans in US dollars. This was fine while the economy was booming until 1995 when the US dollar started to appreciate sharply against the yen and the European currencies (Flight, 1997). From the middle of 1995 while the US dollar was rising against most of the world's other currencies, Asian currencies pegged against the dollar rose with it. Asia's exports, as a result, became more expensive and less competitive on world markets. From May 1997, international banks and money traders came to the view that Asian currencies would have to abandon the dollar peg and devalue in order to revive exports. Asian governments tried to resist, knowing that devaluation would cripple firms which had borrowed huge sums in dollars and would now have to earn much more in local currency to pay back the loans.

Government Involvement in the Private Sector: Capital Cronyism and Corruption

Government interventions in Asia Pacific during the 'Miracle' were acknowledged by the World Bank as success factors. During the crisis, however, analysts argued that the problems of Asian economies were deeply embedded in those nations' institutions, for example, the cosy relationships between politicians and key bankers and industrialists.

Capital Cronyism and Corruption

Although private sector expenditure and financing decisions led to the crisis, this, it was claimed, was exacerbated by issues of governance, notably government involvement in the private sector and lack of transparency in corporate and fiscal accounting and the provision of financial and economic data. It is thus argued that public policy failures had to do mainly with the governments' inaction and their underestimation of the importance of strong financial institutions and sound corporate governance and disclosure rules. Government policies—or the lack thereof—it is claimed fostered the incentives that led to the excessive short-term, foreign currency borrowing and to the misallocation of those funds to unproductive investments. Exchange rate policy, combined with underdeveloped domestic financial systems, provided strong incentives to borrow abroad. Weak supervision of the financial sector, inadequate corporate governance, and the general lack of transparency allowed the problems to grow and fester for much longer than was prudent.

It is further argued that easy money was partly to blame for over investment and hence excess capacity in several areas, including semiconductors, consumer electronics, and petrochemicals. In many countries the problem has been compounded by governments' attempts to pick winners by directing cheap credit to favour industries, while small firms were starved of cash (Franklin, 1998). It is, however, important to note that the so-called 'tigers' do not all share the same policies and problems. There are huge differences between them. For example, the role of the state ranges from hands-off in Hong Kong to a heavy interventionism in South Korea, Indonesia, and Malaysia. The quality of government is corrupt in Indonesia, squeaky clean in Singapore, and in-between elsewhere. Bank supervision is shaky in Thailand and Indonesia but rock solid in Hong Kong and Singapore. South Korea and Taiwan still restrict some kinds of international capital flows; others, particularly Thailand, have flung their doors open (Woodall, 1998). This concrete manifestation of financial weakness filtered from country to country. In South Thailand, for example, essentially unregulated operations of (non-bank) finance companies constituted a major problem. In Korea, government-directed bank lending and lack of transparency resulted in non performing debt (Nunnenkamp, 1998).

Relationship Lending

It is also claimed that the countries in crisis often favoured centralized and behind-the-scenes mechanisms for the allocation of capital. A large part of capital allocations were not made by a decentralized open capital market via arm's-length transactions. Instead decisions were made out of the public eye and were often based on personal and business relationships or governmental influence more than on reliable accounting or other information about the borrowers or their investment projects. It is useful to recall here that this 'relationship lending' system or the reliance on personal, business, or governmental ties in the allocation of capital did work remarkably well during the early stages of development simply because borrowers were able to reap large economic rewards from pursuing the high-return projects (Yellen, 1998).

Political Instability and Regional Insecurity

Between the 1960s and the 1980s, Asia Pacific region was generally praised for maintaining political stability and social cohesion through the introduction of policies such as wealth sharing, cooperation between the private and public sectors, and neo-Confucian values. This, however, did not seem to be the case any longer during the crisis. Significant political uncertainty, it was claimed, led to serious policy uncertainty. The government weakness, cabinet reshuffling and eventual government collapse in Thailand; the inflammatory statements by the Malaysian prime minister against rogue speculators; the elections in Indonesia, political tensions, and continued news about the health of the Indonesian president Suharto who had no apparent successor, presidential elections and contradictory policy signals sent by then candidate Kim Dae Jun, in Korea, and threat of labour unrest in the region were all factors that added to the seriousness of the crisis (Roubini, 1998).

Manuel Montes's Explanation of the Crisis in Asia Pacific

In late 1997, Manuel Montes published an interesting book, *The Currency Crisis in Southeast Asia* (1998), in an attempt to understand the crisis in South East Asia. In his analysis, he begins by considering the most often cited popular explanations, suggesting that the crisis stemmed from the banking sector due to imprudent expansion and diversification of domestic financial markets, fuelled by short-term private borrowings. He then explains how the South East Asian currency crisis can be attributed to the twin liberalization of domestic financial systems and opening of the capital account. Montes argues that financial liberalization induced some new behaviour in the financial system notably:

- domestic financial institutions had greater flexibility in offering interest rates to secure funds domestically and in bidding for foreign funds;

- they became less reliant on lending to the government;
- regulations, such as credit allocation rules and ceilings, were reduced;
- greater domestic competition has meant that ascendance depends on expanding lending portfolios, often at the expense of prudence.

Meanwhile liberalizing the capital account has essentially guaranteed non-residents' ease of exit as well as fewer limitations on nationals holding foreign assets, thus inadvertently facilitating capital flights.

Overall Summary of Analysis of the Crisis in Asia Pacific

First, several Asian currencies had appreciated in real terms in the 1990s and large and growing current account balances had emerged in the countries that faced a speculative attack in 1997. The overvaluation was due in part to the widespread choice of fixed exchange rate regimes in the region and the related large capital inflows in the 1990s. By 1997, it was clear that several regional currencies were seriously overvalued and that such overvaluation was a factor in the worsening of the current account of many countries in the region. Secondly, the current account imbalances and an investment boom (as well as a consumption boom) also drove a related growth of foreign debt. Such investment boom was excessive and often in the wrong sectors: real estate, speculative assets build-up, and so on. Thirdly, interest rates at which domestic banks could borrow abroad and lend at home were too low so that domestic firms were able to invest in many projects, which were marginal if not outright unprofitable. Once these investment projects turned out not to be profitable, the firms and the banks that lent them large sums found themselves with a huge amount of foreign debt, mostly in foreign currencies that could not be repaid. The exchange rate crisis that ensued exacerbated the problem as the currency depreciation dramatically increased the real burden in domestic currencies of the debt that was denominated in foreign currencies. Fourthly, a significant fraction of the borrowing and lending was not going to finance new investment projects. Instead the loans were financing speculative demand of existing assets in fixed supply (land, real estate, and so on). While it is true that weak financial systems, excessive unhedged foreign borrowing by the domestic private sector, lack of transparency about the ties between government, business, and banks may have led to the crisis, it is interesting to note that the same reasons now attributed to the crisis were praised only a few years ago for their contribution to the so-called 'Asian Miracle' as illustrated in Table 2.1.

Table 2.1 Summary of the causes and circumstances surrounding the Asian Miracle and the subsequent crisis

Asian Miracle		Asian Crisis	
1.	Stable macroeconomics and financial systems	1.	Financial turbulence and weak economic and financial systems
	(a) Stability of interest rates		(a) Currency overvaluation
	(b) Flexible and prudential fiscal policies and institutions reforms and good supervision		(b) Inflexibility of domestic policies and lax prudential rules
	(c) Pegging currency to the US dollar providing strong impetus to export-led growth		(c) Pegging of currency leading to debt crisis
2.	State-guided capitalism	2.	Government involvement in the private sector
	(a) Government selective interventions; directed credit, selective promotions		(a) Capital cronyism and corruption
	(b) Performance-based directed mechanisms		(b) Relationship lending
	(c) Administrative competence of the government		(c) Inefficient control
3.	Political and economic stability and social cohesion	3.	Political instability and regional insecurity
	(a) Wealth sharing		(a) Cabinet reshuffling
	(b) Cooperation between public and private sectors		(b) Policy uncertainty, cabinet reshuffling, and government collapse
	(c) Neo-Confucian ethics and values		(c) Political and labour unrest

Review Questions

1   Explain why and how some Asian countries were able to resist or at least minimize the impact of the Asian crisis.

2   Is the spread of the so-called 'Asian flu' a matter of contagion or of separate political economies at similar stages of development?

3   With the Mexican crisis and the crisis in Central and Eastern Europe in mind, what is 'Asian' about the Asian crisis? Discuss.

Class Debate: Was the Asian 'Miracle' a 'Myth or Reality'?

Aim This exercise is designed to illustrate the complexity of the ongoing debates related to the Asian Miracle. It also aims at improving students' skills in conducting a debate, in choosing the main issues to be discussed, and in reaching an acceptable position between the different points of view involved.

Assignment The class is divided into two groups. Each group has a specific assignment. Group 1 should introduce, analyse, and evaluate the factors that have contributed to the 'Miracle' in Asia Pacific. Group 2 should introduce the arguments so far developed against the existence of a so-called 'Miracle'.

Relevant Case Study

- Peregrine: Bad Luck or Bad Management (Part IV)

Further Reading

Gough, Leo, *Asia Meltdown: The End of the Miracle*, Oxford: Capstone Publishing, 1998.

Montes, Manuel F., *The Currency Crisis in Southeast Asia*, Singapore: Singapore Institute of Southeast Asian Studies, 1998.

Roubini, Nouriel, 'An Introduction to Open Economy Macroeconomics: Currency Crises and the Asian Crisis', http/www.stern.nyu.edu/~nroubini/NOTES/macro5.htm#9.

Chapter 3

Disciplining the Tigers: Globalization and the Crisis in Asia Pacific

In the previous chapter we have shown how the same factors that were praised for contributing to the Asian Miracle, were also identified as contributing to the crisis. A wider examination of the causes and circumstances surrounding the crisis, and the role of the IMF within it, reveals that the causes of the 'Miracle', the crisis, and the recovery are not limited to specific factors in the region itself. Global factors in the world economy have also played a major role in the crisis and the subsequent recovery.

The USA, the International Monetary Fund (IMF), and the Asian Crisis

The USA and particularly the IMF immediately responded to Asian governments' calls for assistance by dispatching teams of economists to negotiate bail-out agreements and to restore economic health and stability in the region. The main reason for the USA's active involvement in the Asian crisis, is that so many of its own national interests, economic and strategic, were bound up in East Asia's future. A US Treasury press statement was released on 21 January 1998 clearly stating that 'the United States has enormously important economic and national security interests at stake in promoting restoration of financial stability in Asia. When we act to resolve the Asian crisis, we act to protect and benefit the American people' (Rick, 1998).

The Asian continent, from India to Japan, from below the old Soviet Union down to Indonesia, accounts for more than half of the world's population. The market is roughly the size of the USA and Europe combined, with 3 billion people. Until the Asian crisis, more than 40 per cent of US trade was conducted with Asia Pacific. From early 1993, US firms began actively to pursue the tremendous potential of East Asia's massive unmet infrastructure and upscale consumption requirements (Erland, 1994). Business opportunities were there in unprecedented abundance, and they favoured US interests. Furthermore, Asian economies have actively sought foreign technology in the form of licences, capital goods imports, and foreign training. Openness to foreign direct investment speeded technology acquisition in Hong Kong. Malaysia, Singapore, and more recently Indonesia and Thailand. Japan, South Korea, and to a lesser extent Taiwan restricted foreign direct investment but offset this disadvantage by aggressively acquiring foreign knowledge through licences, overseas education, and capital goods imports. According to World Bank estimates, developing East Asia in the early 1990s needed an average of at least $150 billion of new infrastructure spending in each of the next five years. China alone had identified over $1 trillion of infrastructure projects needed by 2000. China greatly increased the accessibility of these opportunities by opening a broad range of public utility projects, previously the exclusive domain of national or provincial governments, to foreign investors to build, operate, and even own. This included such utilities as local telephone systems, power generation, toll-roads, and railways. US construction, power generation, telecommunications, information, and transportation equipment companies and utilities pursued these massive opportunities with considerable success (Erland, 1994). During that period there was also an outburst of upscale consumer spending as cellular telephones, colour televisions, refrigerators, and even foreign luxury cars became the status symbols of the times. Asian economies have not only been major importers of US goods but also a source of attractive investment returns. Asian countries also provided high quality production bases for US firms. The USA's critical role in promoting growth, development, and integration in the Asia Pacific region can thus be summarized in terms of the following: providing markets for products made in Asia, providing capital to Asia, providing technology to Asia, providing training for Asian students, promoting the multilateral open trading system, providing aid, and providing a security umbrella, as well as massive infusions of war-related demand during the South Korea and Vietnam conflicts (Gough, 1998).

A prolonged period of economic slowdown or a recession in Asia Pacific would consequently have a serious impact on the US economy. A sharp drop in the demand for US exports could slow economic growth (Saving *et al.*, 1998). Major sectors like energy, infrastructure, tourism, the aircraft industry, and the defence industry could be seriously affected. It was also feared that the currency depreciation and asset deflation in the region might knock the profits of US multinationals which might be forced to respond with layoffs and cutbacks in spending (Gwynne, 1998). This may in due course contribute to a sustained setback in the US equity market (Flight, 1997). Another danger was that Japan and Korea might slash prices of exports to the USA to restart their economic engines and thereby ignite a trade war (Naisbitt, 1996). The financial crisis will not only reduce US export growth but might raise import growth from South East Asia, thus leading to a much larger US trade deficit adding to this higher unemployment, greater loan delinquencies, and bankruptcies (Rick, 1998).

Another serious risk is that deep recession could lead to widespread ethnic violence and a breakdown of social and political order. It could also provoke a backlash against free trade globalization and a general resentment of Westerners (Woodall, 1998). Trade liberalization may be jeopardized. Asian governments might become more preoccupied with addressing social problems than expediting trade liberalization. They might delay trade liberalization to provide more protection somewhere (Saving *et al.*, 1998). This fear has in fact been confirmed to some extent by the action taken by certain governments in Asia following the crisis. While Asia has generally held a positive attitude towards trade liberalization during the crisis, there has been some regressive action taken on both sides of the Pacific. Malaysia took bold steps in October 1997 when it raised import duties on construction machinery and materials, as well as durable consumer goods, in an effort to curb imports and improve the trade deficit. It raised the walls of protectionism even higher when it required foreigners investing in Malaysian stocks to hold onto those investments for at least one year. Likewise, Thailand has hiked import duties on intermediate goods to protect domestic manufacturers in certain industries like iron and steel, to offset the effects of the crisis. The Philippines has raised import tariffs 3 per cent to 5 per cent on, among other things, fabric, thread, yarn, and garments (which will make products made in the Philippines using these materials more expensive (Sowinski, 1999). The Asian crisis might thus bring in a rising tide of global protectionism, including controls not only on trade but also on flows of capital. Thus, the US presence in the region seemed crucial. However, instead of depending as they once did, on economic weight in bilateral relationships and a strong forward military presence in the Pacific (Gibney, 1993), this time they had to rely on the intervention of an international organization such as the IMF to monitor and regulate further developments in the region.

The Role and Function of the IMF

The goal of the representatives of the forty-four countries who met at the United Nations Monetary and Financial Conference in Bretton Woods, New Hampshire in 1944 was to rebuild the international economic system, whose collapse was seen as contributing to the Great Depression and the outbreak of war. To this end they proposed setting up the International Monetary Fund and the World Bank, later to be supported by the GATT in 1948.

The primary purposes of the IMF, set out in Article I of its Articles of Agreement, have remained essentially unchanged over the past fifty years:

- to promote international monetary cooperation through a permanent institution which provides the machinery for consultation and collaboration on international monetary problems;

- to facilitate the expansion and balanced growth of international trade, and to contribute thereby to the promotion and maintenance of high levels of employment and real income;

- to promote exchange stability, to maintain orderly exchange arrangements among members, and to avoid competitive exchange depreciation;

- to assist in the establishment of a multilateral system of payments in respect of current transactions and in the elimination of foreign exchange restrictions which hamper the growth of world trade;

- to give confidence to members by making the general resources of the Fund temporarily available to them under adequate safeguards, thus providing them with the opportunity to correct maladjustments in their balance of payments without resorting to measures destructive of national or international prosperity;

- in accordance with the above, to shorten the duration and lessen the degree of disequilibrium in the international balances of payments of members (quoted in Fisher, 1998c: 3).

The IMF promotes international trade directly by encouraging trade liberalization, through both surveillance and its lending programmes with member countries and indirectly by encouraging countries to liberalize foreign exchange controls on trade in goods and services.

Evolution of the IMF

While the purpose of the IMF has not changed, it has over the years been called upon to advise and assist an ever-wider array of countries facing an ever-greater diversity of problems and circumstances—not only industrial economies with temporary balance of payments difficulties, but also low-income developing countries with protracted balance of payments problems, transition countries struggling to establish the institutional infrastructures of full-fledged market economies, and emerging market countries seeking to secure the private capital inflows intended to maintain high rates of economical human development. Indeed, it might be argued that since the so-called 'Nixon Shock' of August 1971, the IMF became of much less importance directly to the advanced political economies, with the development of the Group of Seven (G7—now G8) and the shift of their activity with the OECD. Apart from a small number of exceptional cases, such as the UK Labour government's huge loan of $8.5 billion in 1976, the IMF came to focus its policy formulation much more upon the developing economies, and shifted its policy basis of loans from conditionality to structural adjustment (Biersteker, 1990).

The IMF, it is claimed, has maintained its primary focus on sound money, prudent fiscal policies, and open markets as preconditions for macroeconomic stability and growth. But increasingly, the scope of its policy concerns has broadened to include other elements that also contribute to economic stability and growth. Thus, to different degrees in different countries, the IMF is also pressing, generally together with the World Bank, for sound domestic financial systems; for improvements in the quality of public expenditure, so that spending on primary health care and education is not squeezed out by costly military build-ups and large infrastructure projects that benefit the few at the expense of many; for increased transparency and accountability in government and corporate affairs to avoid costly policy mistakes and the waste of national resources; for adequate and affordable social safety nets to cushion the impact of economic adjustment and reform on the most vulnerable members of society; and in some countries, for deregulation and demonopolization to create a more level playing-field for private sector activity (Fisher, 1998).

Containing the Crisis: IMF Intervention

Through history and all around the world, IMF structural adjustment and economic reform programmes have had a common impact on the countries hosting the IMF programmes. Consequences include the following: forced devaluation, forced privatization, a free fall in the value of the domestic currency, lower purchasing power, a fall in the standard of living, unemployment and retrenchment of workers, inflation and the phenomenon of rising prices, food riots and social unrest, challenges to trade unions and labour, substantial challenges to human rights organization, increased mortality with the mandatory removal of subsidies on health, declines in school attendance along gender lines, challenges to democratic governance, the rise and or consolidation of military dictatorship, de-industrialization as the economies are inundated with cheap foreign products, reduction in the number of nationals owning industries due to privatization and an invasion of foreign capital, intensified unequal development among ethnic groups, ethnic tension, transfer of as much as 40 per cent of the domestic budget in debt repayment to the creditors/bankers of Euro-America, *de facto* loss of sovereignty and the feminization of poverty. These effects have been documented extensively in Nigeria, Zimbabwe, Zambia, Kenya, Sierra Leone, Somalia, Rwanda, and other African countries. In the case of the Caribbean, Jamaica and Trinidad are outstanding cases (Nunnenkamp, 1998). Despite these devastating effects on local economic life, IMF assistance is still sought by governments in crisis.

IMF Intervention in Asia Pacific

Among Asia's crisis countries, Thailand, Korea, and Indonesia all went to seek for IMF support. Malaysia proceeded to ride the crisis on its own, while the Philippines had already been on precautionary arrangements with the IMF for some time.

On 28 July 1997 the Thai government asked the IMF for technical assistance in order to forestall a balance of payment crisis. The IMF immediately responded by providing a $17.2 billion emergency international financial 'bail-out' package. This was, however, attached to a stand-by adjustment programme which the Thai authorities agreed to in early August 1997 (Sharma,1998). This austerity plan (or the 1997–2000 programme) immediately suspended 48 finance firms out of a total of 91 (Saving *et al.*, 1998) and provided a blueprint for the complete restructuring of the financial sector. At the core of the 1997–2000 programme is the so-called 'second generation' reforms designed to re-establish domestic and external confidence in Thailand's financial system by requiring that 'surviving' banks meet tough new reserve and prudential supervision requirements. These include a tight monetary policy to stop authorities from printing money in order to rescue failed or failing financial and property companies. That was to be complemented by an array of the usual IMF fiscal belt-tightening measures such as expenditure cuts, shifts in domestic savings–investment balances to reduce the external current account deficit to a more sustainable 5 per cent in 1997 and 3 per cent of GDP in 1998, and the maintenance of GDP growth at 3 to 4 percent and the capping of year-end inflation at 9.5 per cent in 1997 and 5 per cent in 1998. Also, state enterprises were required to maintain their overall financial balance by phasing out low-priority investments and seeking private sector participation in infrastructure programmes, and the government was virtually ordered to reduce its budget deficit by 1998 through an increase in the rate of value-added tax (VAT) from 7 to 10 per cent, as well as cuts in fiscal spending by 100 million baht (Sharma, 1998).

In the case of Korea, the IMF provided a record-breaking $58.4 billion rescue package. In return, the Korean government had to sign a three-year stand-by arrangement under which it agreed to a fundamental overhaul of its economy and a contractionary macro-economic policy of higher taxes, reduced spending and higher interest rates. More specifically it agreed:

- to immediately suspend some 15 of the country's 30 ailing merchant banks with huge non-performing loans to submit rehabilitation plans regarding capitalization, liquidity, and management;

- to provide more transparent financial data by requiring independent external auditors;

- to oversee the bookkeeping practices of the financial ministry and the major con-glomerates, including banning Chaebols from making debt guarantees for affiliates, as well as forcing the government to disclose all data relating to foreign-exchange reserves, ban capitalization and Chaebol ownership in consolidated financial statements;

- to open its financial markets by liberalizing capital account transactions and increasing foreign access to domestic money market instruments, corporate bond markets, and direct investment;

- to increase the ceiling for foreign ownership of listed shares from 26 to 50 per cent by the end of 1997 and to 55 per cent by the end of 1998;

- to end restrictive trade practices, including providing trade-related subsidies to pro-mote exports and the elimination of import licensing; and finally

- to raise taxes and tighten monetary policy, including facilitating labour market restructuring by easing lay-off and dismissal restrictions under mergers, acquisitions, and corporate downsizing (IMF Press Release, 1997).

The IMF has thus imposed severe conditionality, rather than aiming for domestic 'owner-ship' of adjustment programmes. Some of the measures forced on Korea are beside the IMF's principal business of restoring stability and stopping the drain on foreign reserves, for instance, forcing the Korean government to agree to liberalize the import regime for cars. In the longer run, this step may well be in Korea's own interest; but it is hard to see how it helps to overcome acute balance of payments troubles. It is suspected that the IMF raised the issue of Korean car imports because it figured high on the US administration's bilateral agenda (Nunnenkamp, 1998).

The IMF $42.3 billion rescue package for Indonesia consisted of a similar agenda of sweeping structural reforms. Negotiations between the IMF and the government of Indonesia continued without success in the first half of 1998. On 15 January 1998, the government of Indonesia finally agreed:

- to contain inflation to 20 per cent in 1998, with the aim of bringing it back to the single-digit level by 1999, despite the sharp depreciation of the rupiah; and to move the external current account balance from a deficit into a sizeable surplus in order to generate additional foreign exchange to help the country to repay its external debt;

- to revise the 1998/99 budget to record a small deficit, of about 1 per cent of GDP;

- to phase out energy subsidies gradually by raising both fuel and electricity prices. These, according to the IMF have grown to unsustainable proportions as the rupiah's depreciation has pushed domestic prices far below world levels;

- to ensure that the public is kept fully informed of all government activities by bringing the accounts of the Reforestation and Investment Funds onto the budget in 1998/99;

- to limit public spending only to those items that are of vital importance to the country and to curtail development spending, including the immediate cancellation of 12 infrastructure projects, and the elimination of budgetary and extra budgetary support and credit privileges granted to IPTN's aeroplane projects. In addition, the Indonesian government agreed to revoke immediately all special tax, customs, and credit privileges for the National Car project;

- to restructure the banking system and restore it to financial health;

- to implement a series of structural reforms by removing all the restrictions that have been put in place previously such as:

    (a) to limit BULOG's monopoly solely to rice and to eliminate its existing monopoly over the import and distribution of sugar, as well as its monopoly over the distribution of wheat flour;

    (b) to fully deregulate domestic trade in all agricultural products and to eliminate the Clove Marketing Board by June 1998;

    (c) to abolish all restrictive marketing arrangements and to specifically dissolve all cartels related to cement, paper, and plywood;

    (d) to remove all formal and informal barriers to investment in palm oil plantation, as well as lifting all restrictions on investment in wholesale and retail trade;

    (e) to cut tariffs on all food items and non-food agricultural products by a maximum rate of 5 per cent (Camdessus, 1998a).

The IMF has thus imposed severe conditionality in Indonesia too. But as Michel Camdessus, managing director of the IMF acknowledged: 'my thoughts go to those who may experience hardships—hopefully for only a short period of time—because of the very strength and rapidity of the adjustment process. The program provides for strengthened measures targeted to alleviating the plight of the most vulnerable people in the country' (Camdessus, 1998a). Martin Feldstein, Professor of Economics at Harvard University and President of the National Bureau of Economic Research, however, questioned the need for such a comprehensive restructuring of the Indonesian economy to restore access to international capital markets.

. . . In Indonesia, the IMF insisted on a long list of reforms, specifying in minute detail such things as the price of gasoline and the manner of selling plywood. The government has also been told to end the country's widespread corruption and curtail the special business privileges used to enrich President Suharto's family and the political allies that maintain his regime. Although such changes may be desirable in many ways, past experience suggests that they are not needed to maintain a flow of foreign funds . . . Is this reform really needed to restore the country's access to international capital markets? Is this a technical matter that does not interfere unnecessarily with the proper jurisdiction of a sovereign government? If the policies to be changed are also practiced in the major industrial economies of Europe, would the IMF think it appropriate to force similar changes in those countries if they were subject to a fund program? (Feldstein, 1998)

Malaysia, on the other hand resisted turning to the IMF for a financial bail-out. On 1 September 1998 Malaysian prime minister Mahatir Mohammed ignored advice from the IMF setting a year-long block on the removal of foreign capital from Malaysia and suspending offshore trading of the Malaysia ringgit. The Malaysian government introduced capital controls and pegged the exchange rate of the ringgit to the dollar, in order to insulate domestic interest rates from continuing pressures and volatility in the foreign exchange market. These measures were followed by interest rate reductions as well as more direct measures aimed at stimulating credit growth, an expansionary government budget, and accelerated implementation of the financial and corporate sector and restructuring programme. In February 1999 the capital controls were modified with the replacement of the one-year holding restriction on portfolio capital flows with a system of exit levies (IMF, Public Information Notice, 1999).

Thus, the IMF prescribed standard contractionary macroeconomic adjustment policies—monetary and fiscal policy in Thailand, Korea, and Indonesia—despite the fact that the major underlying causes for the current account deficits did not lie in the government sector (Saving *et al.*, 1998). The government sector was not the source of the problem. Just as had been done in the 1930s, whenever faced with currency crises that endangered financial systems and whole economies, so too the IMF responded to the Asian crisis by giving priority to finance, assuring the world that restoring the confidence of lenders and investors worldwide in the soundness of governments' financial policies is essential for prosperity and growth, a view which prime ministers and presidents had to go along with. The interesting point here is that prior to 1997 the Asian tigers appeared to be model economies by IMF criteria. They were generally running budget surpluses, and money growth was moderate. Inflation rates were low, and saving rates high (Tobin, and Ranis, 1998).

As recently as the early 1990s economists were debating vigorously whether the Asian model of capital markets was superior to the Anglo-Saxon model. The widespread admiration of both financial and non-financial aspects of East Asian economies was obvious: these countries must have been doing something very right, because over the course of the last thirty years or so they had achieved the single greatest spurt of economic growth in the history of mankind (Yellen, 1998). The question, then, is why did the system suddenly fail after working so well for many years. On the eve of the crisis all of the governments were more or less in fiscal balance; nor were they engaged in irresponsible credit creation or runaway monetary expansion. Their inflation rates, in particular, were quite low. Although there had been some slowdown in growth in 1996, the Asian victims did not have substantial unemployment when the crisis began. There did not, in other words, seem to be the kind of incentive to abandon the fixed exchange rate to pursue a more expansionary monetary policy that is generally held to be the cause of the ERM crises in Europe. The IMF in its 1997 *Annual Report* reported: 'directors welcomed Korea's continued impressive macroeconomics performance and praised the authorities for their enviable fiscal record' (Yellen, 1988). Three months before there was not a hint of alarm, only a call for further financial sector reform, incidentally without mentioning the Chaebol or the issue of foreign ownership of banks, or banking supervision, all of which now figure so prominently in the IMF's Korea programme. In the same report, the IMF had this to say about Thailand which was then on the edge of the financial abyss: 'Directors strongly praised Thailand's remarkable economic performance and the authorities' consistent record of sound macroeconomic policies' (Yellen, 1998).

As these economies matured, their growth rates naturally had to slow down. Indeed, these 'tigers' are, to a large extent, victims of their own success. Years of breathtaking growth attracted vast inflows of foreign capital in the 1990s. At their peak, net private capital inflows accounted for as much as 17 per cent of Malaysia's GDP in 1993 and 13 per cent of Thailand's in 1995, causing overborrowing and overinvestment which could not continue indefinitely (*The Economist*, 1996). Rapid growth also concealed structural weaknesses such as inadequate bank regulation, a lack of transparency in business, and endemic cronyism, which made a dangerous mixture with the excessive borrowing (Woodall, 1998). As explained earlier, the 'tiger's' current 'illness' is caused in part by weaker demand in the rich world, sluggish demand in Europe, a cut in demand for electronic goods, the rise in the US dollar, to which many Asian currencies are in effect pegged and which has eroded the tigers' competitiveness. The question then arises, how do we explain this hegemonic intervention of the IMF?

The IMF Remedy to the Crisis: Expressing Universal Norms and Promoting Free Market Ideology

The IMF, it is claimed, is charged with safeguarding the stability of the international monetary system. In the case of the Asian crisis, its main priority is to restore confidence to the economies affected by the crisis (IMF home page).

We are ready to do our duty, which is to provide assistance to help stabilize economies that may need financial help, provided they are willing to undertake appropriately ambitious economic reform and adjustment measures. As we have shown in the last 12 months we are able to move rapidly and on a very significant scale to provide assistance to countries willing to undertake the necessary policy measures. . . . the global interest, and indeed the US interest lies in an economically strong Asia that imports as well as exports and thereby supports global growth. (Fisher, 1998*b*).

In relation to the IMF promotion of free market ideology and general rules of behaviour for states, the institution's approach in Asia, according to Michel Camdessus Managing Director of the IMF 'is to strengthen financial systems, improving governance and transparency, and enhancing domestic competition. This involves closing insolvent financial institutions and writing down shareholders' capital, recapitalizing undercapitalized financial institutions; putting weak ones under close supervision; and increasing foreign participation in domestic financial systems' (Camdessus, 1998*c*). Other efforts of the IMF in containing the crisis include the introduction of flexibility to exchange rates, the temporary tightening of monetary policy to stem pressures on the balance of payments, immediate action to correct the obvious weaknesses in the financial system, structural reforms to remove features of the economy that had become impediments to growth such as monopolies, trade barriers, and non-transparent corporate practices and to improve the efficiency of financial intermediation and the future soundness of financial systems, efforts to assist in reopening or maintaining lines of external financing and the maintenance of a sound fiscal policy. Finally, to address the governance issues that also contributed to the crisis, the reform of the financial systems is being buttressed by measures designed to improve the efficiency of markets, break the close links between business and governments, and prudently liberalize capital markets (IMF home page).

As far as the IMF second generation reforms are concerned, these include:

- reductions in unproductive government spending;
- higher spending on primary health care and education; and adequate social protection for the poor, the unemployed, and other vulnerable groups;
- the creation of a more level playing-field for private sector activity, by increasing openness, stepping up privatization, dismantling monopolies, and setting up simpler, more transparent regulatory systems;
- stronger banking systems that protect depositors, especially small savers, and reduce risks for shareholders and creditors by enforcing strict prudential standards and information disclosure requirements;
- tax systems that are effective, efficient, equitable, and as simple as possible; and
- greater transparency and accountability in government and corporate affairs. (Camdessus, 1998*d*).

It is important to note here that the IMF, by insisting that the Asian governments open their doors wider to international financial transactions and by encouraging inflows when exchange rates and local asset values are so depressed, created the image and the reality of arranging bargain-basement deals for foreigners, thus undermining the faith of many residents of these nations in the intentions of the international lenders, private and public (Tobin and Ranis, 1998). Another delicate issue concerns the deregulation of foreign banking in Asian financial markets. Again controversy is mainly about the timing of reforms. Foreign participation in banking may support financial restructuring and help achieve internationally accepted best practices. However, under conditions of financial turmoil, foreign banks, if allowed in immediately, may acquire local assets at seriously depressed prices. This may add to public resentment against foreign investors taking over domestic industries.

Furthermore, it is generally claimed that the IMF reform programmes in the affected countries were designed to bring about structural reforms that would strengthen financial systems, increase transparency in both the public and private sectors, and open markets, thereby restoring investors' confidence. To this end, non-viable financial institutions, including banks, have been closed down. Other weak, but viable, institutions were required to produce restructuring plans, including mergers and consolidations, and to comply, within a reasonable time, with internationally accepted best practices in terms of capital-adequacy requirements for banks and accounting practices and disclosure rules for companies. Other proposed structural changes included strengthening financial sector regulation and supervision. Together, these policies were intended to create a more level playing-field for the private sector and to intensify competition. According to the IMF, the Asian crisis was not an outcome of macroeconomic imbalances, but was caused principally by structural weaknesses in the financial and corporate sectors. The IMF programmes also recommended steep increases in interest rates and appropriate monetary policies to stem the outflow of capital, in the belief that higher interest rates would encourage companies to restructure their finances and move from debt towards equity. At the same time, since high interest rates have serious adverse effects on banks and corporate entities and slow down the economy, a final balance must be struck between these conflicting policy objectives. The timing and nature of monetary policy adjustment—particularly interest rate adjustment—should reflect the circumstances prevailing in individual economies. Some claim IMF actions caused banks to run. Rather than restoring confidence, the IMF directive, for instance, to close down sixteen insolvent banks in Indonesia caused panic and contributed to the further weakening of the financial sector and the erosion of faith in the economy. Furthermore, neither the IMF nor the investors had confidence in the determination of the Indonesian government to stick to the loan conditions.

The IMF Bowing towards Malaysia

Malaysia incurred the wrath of the international community when it brought in capital controls in 1998. These controls had been implemented against a backdrop of anti-IMF rhetoric (Reuters, 2000). Western experts strongly criticized the moves, proclaiming them to be merely a short-term fix, if not actually detrimental to Malaysia, and that only IMF-style austerity reforms could fix the economy. They argued further that capital trapped in Malaysia would fly out at the slightest relaxation of controls (Global Intelligence Update, 1999). However, one year later, when Mahatir removed many of the controls, a mere $328 million left the country—significantly lower than outside estimation of up to $2.6 billion. After contracting 6.7 per cent in 1998, Malaysia's gross domestic product in fact rose 4.1 per cent in the second quarter of 1999, with investors investing nearly $1 billion and applying for $1.85 billion from February to September 1999 compared to a total of $3.32 billion for all of 1998 (Global Intelligence Update, 1999).

IMF Director Michel Camdessus admitted that Malaysia's control had brought better than expected results and had been applied in a flexible and pragmatic way (Reuters, 2000). Accordingly and as reported in a Stratford Special Report (1999)

... the IMF after fumbling in the Asian crises, has signaled a departure from the one prescription for every illness cures of strict austerity measures, deep financial reforms, free markets and free-floating currencies, regardless of the social cost. The fund announced potential internal reforms which could result in more flexibility in its current system, including the possibility of considering alternate financial strategies other than the present systems for individual developing countries. Furthermore, The IMF's Executive Board acknowledged that Mahatir's actions gave Malaysia the breathing space it needed to rework its financial structure. This is extremely significant considering that Mahatir has been a strident critic of Western economics with his policy flying in the face of the IMF. (Quoted in Global Intelligence Update, 1999).

Globalization and the Asian Crisis

Analysis of the crisis in Asia cannot be limited only to reference to specific factors in the region itself. Global factors in the world economy have also contributed to the crisis, for example the economic problems in Japan, the slowdown of international trade, and the globalization of private sector lending. This shows that the causes of the 'Miracle', of the crisis, and of the recovery are not located only within the Asia Pacific region or reducible fully to the internal conditions of particular countries within the region. Consequently, in respect of doing business in the Asia Pacific region, it is important for managers to situate their analysis of opportunities arising from the recovery there within a global strategic framework, which draws explicit attention to trends and developments in the global political economy as a whole, including of course the relationship at any given time between the core triad markets (USA, EU, Japan, and Asia Pacific).

Japan's Economic Problem

Prior to the post-1985 yen appreciation, Japan's role in integrating the Asia Pacific region was primarily in terms of purchasing raw materials, investing in import substitution industries, and providing foreign aid. Since 1985, Japan's direct investment in the Asia Pacific region, its imports of manufactured products, and its foreign aid disbursements have been expanding rapidly. For example, the investment flow increased from US$1.4 billion in 1985 to a peak of US$7.8 billion in 1989 and continued to grow by another US$6.6 billion in 1990 (Simon, 1995). This led to the transfer of technology and management practices, and has created jobs throughout the region. Japan's massive foreign aid and portfolio investments were financing a large portion of Asia's capital requirements, and Japanese direct investments are integrating the Asian economies into Japan's production systems. Consequently, it is often claimed that the recession in Japan is one reason why the region is not experiencing growth anymore and that the economic problems in Japan, the leading regional economic power, exacerbated the crisis.

Japan's economy has several problems: short term, medium term, and long term. The short-term problems are the big gap between supply and demand with supply capacity exceeding 20 trillion yen to 30 trillion yen over demand. Non-performing loans by the banking sector is another short-term problem. Japan banks have 73 trillion yen non-performance loans, which account for approximately 15 per cent of the active Japanese GDP. Medium-term problems consist mainly of the budget deficit and low interest rate. In 1989 Japan budget deficit ratio to GNP was only 0.5 per cent. But in 1998, it was almost 15 per cent which was the largest among G7 countries. As far as the low interest rate is concerned, the Bank of Japan (BoJ) started reducing its discount rate in August 1990. Since then, the BOJ continuously lowered its rate. Up until 1999, the discount rate has been 0.5 per cent. The extremely low interest rate did help ailing banks suffering from bad loans and other corporations, especially those in the business of real estate. But individual depositors were sacrificed and this might be one reason why private consumption has been very weak. Finally, a high cost structure, risk-avoiding behaviour prevailing among both employers and employees, and an ageing society with declining birth rate are among the long-term problems (Hatakeyama, 1999). Despite these problems, Japan remains the world's leading bilateral aid donor in Asia Pacific. The total amount of Japanese commitment during the crisis was more than $44 billion as compared to $12 billion by the USA and $7 billion by the entire European Union (Embassy of Japan, 1998).

In addition to this $44 billion, Japan offered $30 billion which is called the Miyazawa Plan of 1999. Approximately $6 billion has been committed to Thailand, Malaysia, and the Philippines under this plan. The new Miyazama Initiative is to provide further support aimed at ensuring the recovery of Asian economies. This initiative is intended to help Asian countries overcome the financial crisis by providing the capital they need for (1) restructuring private companies and stabilizing the financial system, (2) strengthening the social safety net, (3) stimulating the economy, (4) addressing the credit crunch, and so on (Embassy of Japan, 1998a).

The main reasons for Japanese aid concentration in Asia are clearly historical and geographical, as well as economic. Aid, in the form of grants and low-interests loans, is mainly aimed at promoting the economic 'take-off' in recipient countries and to promote economic stability in developing regions. While Japan has invested to a significant extent in hospitals, sewage facilities, and rural water supplies, its overall investment in basic

Thailand
Total $17.2 billion

(IMF $4 billion)	*Japan*	*$4 billion*
(WB up to $1.5 billion)	Australia	$1 billion
(ADB up to $1.2 billion)	Malaysia	$1 billion
	Singapore	$1 billion
	PRC	$1 billion
	Hong Kong	$1 billion

Republic of Korea
Total $58 billion

(IMF $21 billion)	*Japan*	*$10 billion*
(WB up to $10 billion)	USA	$5 billion
(ADB up to $4 billion)	Canada	$1 billion
	Australia	$1 billion

Indonesia
Total above $40 billion

(IMF $10 billion)	*Japan*	*$5 billion*
(WB up to $4.5 billion)	Singapore	$5 billion
(ADB up to $3.5 billion)	USA	$3 billion

Fig. 3.1 Japan's assistance to Asian countries in financial turmoil

Notes: Japan is also providing bilateral assistance of approximately $24.5 billion by utilizing yen loans, non-project grant aid, emergency grant aid, and the finance capability of the Export-Import Bank of Japan.
WB = World Bank; ADB = Asian Development Bank; PRC = People's Republic of China.
Source: The Embassy of Japan, 'Japanese Economic Measures', 16 Nov. 1998.

human needs, such as rudimentary education and health, has been poor. Most of the aid has been aimed at building the economic infrastructure of the region and improving industrial production and services. The Asian continent has traditionally been attractive to investors for its cheaper production sites, but its attractiveness as a market has been increasing too. Japan is now the largest single investor in terms of stock in Thailand, Indonesia, and Malaysia and the second largest in the Philippines after the USA (Chi and Miyake, 1999). About 20 per cent of Japan's exports are to these countries. Additionally, between 15 to 25 per cent of these countries' trade is with Japan (Anon., 17 June 1998).

Slow Growth in International Trade

Companies in Korea and many other Asian countries have become formidable world-class producers in a number of manufacturing sectors using advanced technologies, but in a number of cases they permitted leverage to rise to levels that could only be sustained with continued very rapid growth. Asian economies, to varying degrees over the last half century, have tried to combine rapid growth with a much higher mix of government-directed production than has been evident in the essentially market-driven economies of the West. Through government inducements, a number of select, more sophisticated manufacturing technologies borrowed from the advanced market economies were applied to these generally low-productivity and hence, low-wage economies. Thus, for selected products, exports became competitive with those of the market economies, engendering rapid overall economic growth. There was, however, an inevitable limit to how far this specialized Asia economic regime could develop. As the process broadened beyond a few selected applications of advanced technologies, overall productivity continued to increase and the associated rise in the average real wage in these economies blunted somewhat the competitive advantage enjoyed initially. As a consequence of the slackening of export expansion caused in part by losses in competitiveness because of exchange rates that were pegged to the US dollar, which was appreciating against the yen, aggregate economic growth slowed somewhat even before the current crisis (Greenspan, 1998). In addition, the semiconductor market has experienced a serious slump since 1996. Memory-chip prices fell by more than 80 per cent in 1996. This hit South Korea and Singapore especially because electronics account for a big chunk of their exports (*The Economist*, 1996). The main problem here has been identified as nothing more than 'glut'. There is excess global capacity in virtually every industry, particularly in those that have experienced rapid growth in South East Asia. A slowdown in export growth has led to a fall in economic and corporate profitability growth, which in turn has meant that overall growth has been insufficient to sustain real estate development (Flight, 1997).

Globalization of Private Sector Financial Lending

It is also often argued that in their haste to blame the governments in the region for the crisis, many critics have forgotten the fact that every loan requires not just a borrower, but also a lender. The borrowers who misallocated their investments share responsibility for the problems with the lenders, many of them international commercial banks which provided them with the money in the first place (Stiglitz, 1998). The key trigger for the crisis was the build-up of excessive external liabilities largely in the form of short-term commercial bank credits to private borrowers in an increasingly integrated global financial system. In this context, not only domestic policies and institutions fell considerably short of the mark, but also the providers of external capital and their regulatory authorities failed to take due cognizance of the weaknesses of the borrowers in the East Asia countries and overlooked the danger signals. The problem emerged in the private sector, explains Jeffrey Sachs. International money market managers and investment banks went on a lending binge from 1993 to 1996. Short-term borrowing from abroad was used in most of those countries unwisely, to support long-term investments in real estate and other non-exporting sectors. However, a combination of rising wage costs, competition from China, and lower demand for Asia's exports (especially electronics) caused exports to stagnate in 1996 and the first part of 1997. It became clear that if the Asians were going to compete, their currencies would need to fall against the dollar so their costs of production would be lower. It also became clear that with foreign lending diverted into real estate ventures, there was some risk that the borrowers, especially banks and finance companies, would be unable to service the debts if the exchange rates weakened.

The international investment community needs to tell the truth: the currency crisis is not the result of Asian government profligacy. . . . This is a crisis made mainly in the private, financial markets. East Asian countries have a strong track record of prudent fiscal management. The countries of Thailand, Indonesia and Korea, and those markedly affected by the contagion, Malaysia and the Philippines, had been running surpluses or very small fiscal deficits in the immediate years preceding the crisis. Inflation had also been moderated and was declining. At the same time, however, the balance of payments current account deficits in several countries were rapidly rising in relation to their GDP and export growth and external private borrowing was growing sharply. This borrowing by financial and non-financial entities was largely unhedged and short-term leaving them highly vulnerable to exchange rate and maturity mismatch risks. (Fisher, 1998*b*).

As Fisher explained, the high level of unhedged private external indebtedness had three major causes. First, the international environment provided an abundant supply of funds at perceived low costs. Secondly, broad financial deregulation and the opening of the capital accounts of East Asia economies made it much easier for banks and domestic corporations to tap into foreign markets for financing their investments. At the same time, lax supervision and prudential regulation allowed banks and corporations to take on significant exchange rate and maturity risks. Thirdly, exchange rate policies that in effect pegged currencies to the US dollar reduced perceived risks for investors. Thus, the liberalization of capital account which took place before the liberalization of the domestic financial systems and its strengthening, was a major factor. Interest rate ceilings, government-directed lending, and insider relationships between banks and borrowers, and other weaknesses produced misallocation of resources. Foreign money exacerbated the misallocation. In essence, too much money was chasing too few investments with the requisite rates of return (Fisher, 1998*b*).

The banks offers two more reasons why these policies may not be repeatable today. When ceilings on interest rates helped to boost investment in Japan, South Korea, and Taiwan, financial markets were fenced by capital controls. In today's' increasingly integrated global capital market, governments wishing to attract foreign investment cannot close their financial markets to the outside world, so it is much harder to hold down interest rates. The global financial system has been evolving rapidly in recent years. New technology has radically reduced the costs of borrowing and lending across traditional national borders, facilitating the development of new instruments and drawing in new players. One result has been a massive increase in capital flows. Information is transmitted almost instantaneously around the word, and huge shifts in the supply and demand for funds naturally follow (Nunnenkamp, 1998).

The financial turmoil in South East Asia has revived the debate about whether capital liberalization is beneficial or harmful to developing countries. Unrestricted cross-border flows of capital in an increasingly globalized economy has become an article of faith for free market economists. They argue that the benefits of capital liberalization in terms of growth and investment are obvious. The unfettered mobility of capital can improve economic efficiency by injecting savings into viable and productive projects—irrespective of their location. Greater competition, they say, creates more efficient financial systems while restrictions on capital flows can prevent the entry of multinational firms and banks, allowing weak and inefficient companies to survive with consequent costs to the economy (Diddiqi, 1998). The overall pattern of the past decade, in which much capital has been invested in the developing world, has provided hefty returns for savers in the developed world. Capital flows to emerging markets are highly selective, however, and target only a few countries. Some argue that despite its undeniable advantages, international capital mobility can also bring economic and political penalties. Substantial inflows can become large outflows overnight and lead to catastrophic runs on a country's currency. The five Asian tigers suffered an outflow of $12 billion in 1997 compared with capital inflows of $93 billion in 1996 (Diddiqi, 1998). Capital liberalization requires competent regulation and supervision of markets and transparency. The Asian crisis has shown the danger of free capital flows when vital information is imperfect, domestic financial systems are weak, and governments pursue unsound economic policies. Almost all observers now concede that premature liberalization of capital markets (often pushed by the IMF itself) was one cause of the current crisis. It was financial-market 'reform' that allowed Thai and South Korean banks to tap into short-term international loans in the early 1990s. As Sachs explains '. . . developing countries are not trying to overturn Washington's vision of global capitalism, but rather to become productive players in it . . . they know that they cannot get by without the outside world. They know that technology and capital can come only from outside and they know that only markets can deliver the chance of sustained growth' (Sachs, J., quoted in Roubini, 1998). Thus by locating the concept of crisis within the global political economy, we have shown how the Asian crisis is not simply located within the region as it is generally claimed to be. Forces of globalization which have allowed many countries in Asia to accelerate investment and growth, create more jobs, and reduce poverty have also contributed to its collapse.

Global Implications of the Crisis

There has been a certain degree of ambivalence regarding the global impact of the crisis. While on the one hand it is increasingly argued that we are now all living in a global village as a result of significantly increased integration of markets and interdependence of economies, at the same time it is also maintained that the impact of the East Asian crisis on the global economy can be expected to be negligible since their share in global trade and production is small. While it is true that neither the USA nor Europe depends on Asia for a substantial proportion of their exports (the US exports less than 20 per cent and Europe little over 5 per cent), it is an integral part of the process of globalization; while the USA may not export much to Asia, US companies do import to and export from their production facilities in Asia, so that the overall impact on US income will be much higher. The developing countries in Asia Pacific have also come to play a crucial role in generating global demand and global growth. In the 1990s they accounted for roughly half of global expansion. The collapse of growth in the region would thus produce a global deflation. This would then make it more difficult for developed economies, particularly Europe and Japan, to expand at rates necessary to generate sufficient investment to produce reductions in unemployment. Recovery in the developed world outside the USA and the UK is thus at risk as a result of declining Asian growth. Indeed, if the USA cannot continue its current expansion, there is a clear risk of a global depression similar to that of the 1930s (Montes, 1998).

Thus, in many ways the Asian crisis was not simply an Asian crisis. It was a global crisis which has shown the impact of rapid financial liberalization and the inadequacies of markets, governments, and international institutions in coping with it. The crisis has also proved to be a human crisis with millions of people thrown out of work, and poverty and hunger on the increase. The crisis thus should be used as an opportunity to reassess the economic and political directions taken in the global political economy in the last decade, and to consider what factors need to be taken into account by anyone considering doing business in the Asia Pacific region.

Review Questions

1 Why did the Asia crisis raise such a global concern?

2 What can be learned from the Asian countries' experience with the crisis which might be useful for students and managers in International Business?

3 Does consideration of the 'globalization' of finance, markets, and production help us to better understand the crisis in Asia Pacific?

Group Project: The Impact of the Asian Crisis on Global Business

The class should be divided into four groups. Each group should investigate and evaluate the implications of a deepening recession in Asia Pacific on one of the following regions: USA, EU, Japan, and Asia.

Further Reading

Biersteker, T. J., Reducing the Role of the State in the Economy: A Conceptual Exploration of IMF and World Bank Prescriptions', *International Studies Quarterly*, 34, Sep. 1990: 477–92.

Fisher, Stanley, *The Asian Crisis: A View from the IMF*, Address by Stanley Fisher, First Deputy Managing Director of the International Monetary Fund at the Midwinter Conference of the Bankers' Association for Foreign Trade, Washington, 22 Jan. 1998.

—— The Asian Crisis and the Changing Role of the IMF, *Finance and Development*, June 1998.

IMF Home page, 'The IMF's Response to the Asian Crisis', Apr. 1998.

Sharma. S. D., 'The IMF and Asia's Financial Crisis: Bitter Medicine for Sick Tigers', http://www.usfca.edu/pac-rim/pages/publications/report8.html, 1998.

Chapter 4

The Business Environment in Asia Pacific, Post-crisis

Despite the crisis, economic growth in East Asia is far from over. According to a 1998 Survey of East Asian economies in the first decade of the twenty-first century, Thailand, Malaysia, and even Indonesia (if it embraces reform) could see annual growth of 6 per cent down from the 8 to 9 per cent growth of the 1990s but still much higher than the developed economies 2 to 3 per cent. The Philippines may enjoy a similar rate, up from only 3 per cent; over the past decade. The four richer tigers, Hong Kong, South Korea, Singapore, and Taiwan, are likely to slow to 4 to 6 per cent (from 7 to 8 in the past decade) (Woodall, 1998). Jeffrey Sachs, the Harvard economist, argues that while the weaknesses in the Asian economies were significant, they were 'far from fatal'. That is, the economies deeper strengths, including high rates of savings, budget surpluses, flexible labour markets, and low taxation remain in place and auger well for long-term recovery (Sachs, 1997). Most tigers' economies, in fact, could continue to grow at least twice as fast as the developed world for many years to come provided structural reforms are introduced (*The Economist*, 1997a). Some of the most important features of East Asia's development as discussed earlier were sound macroeconomic fundamentals: high savings, a commitment to education, technologically advanced factories, a relatively egalitarian distribution of income, and an aggressive pursuit of foreign exports. Since all of these elements are still present, East Asia's economic prospects could continue to be good (Stiglitz, 1998).

The prospects of a rejuvenated region are also equally good. Even though capital flight is occurring from the region, FDI is still pouring in. There is a unique window of opportunity to seize the advantages produced by the crisis. US companies have spent $8 billion in acquisitions in Asia in the first half of 1998. In an address at the National Press Club, Washington on 2 April 1998, Michel Camdessus, Managing Director of the International Monetary Fund, confirmed that 'There are a number of encouraging signs that some countries in the region are beginning to turn the corner' (Camdessus, 1998b). Regarding Thailand and South Korea, he went on to say that market confidence in both economies seems to be returning. The Thai baht has strengthened by over 40 per cent from its low point since January, and the South Korean won by over 30 per cent since its low point in mid-December. The Thai and South Korean stock markets are up 25 per cent and 30 per cent respectively since the beginning of the year. And in both countries, new foreign direct investment and portfolio investment are beginning to flow back in again.

Furthermore market participants are beginning to differentiate among countries—and cautiously returning to the countries where economic problems are being forcefully addressed. This is also a good sign (Camdessus, 1998b). The regional business environment remains competitive, with strong fundamentals, an abundance of raw materials, low-cost labour, hard-working populations and the desire for prosperity (Franklin, 1998), in addition to an excellent work ethics, high educational levels, strong private sectors, and high rates of saving and of growth-generating capital investment, and a strong desire for prosperity. Furthermore, many Asian countries now present unusually good bargains. For example, sourcing opportunities are especially good with the significant drops in currency values. Also, as asset prices have sunk to very low levels in local currency terms and even lower in dollar terms, these countries represent excellent opportunities for acquisitions. In fact, many large companies such as General Electric and General Motors are already making new direct investments in Asia and taking advantage of the new sourcing opportunities there. Such sourcing and direct investment activities by Western firms are also helping accelerate the economic recovery of these Asian countries (Aggarwal, 1999b).

A look at South East Asia's demography also suggests that the region's long-term future is still promising. The region, depending on which countries are included, contains as much as 50 per cent of the world's population while occupying only about 20 per cent; of the total land mass. This statistic includes China, the world's most populous nation, and five other nations with populations of more than 40 million (Indonesia 199.7 million; Myanmar 45.4 million; the Philippines 68.7 million; Thailand 59.4 million, and Vietnam 74 million. Some of the fastest growing populations are also found in South East Asia: Cambodia (9.9 million) and Laos (4.7 million) are both growing at annual rates of 2.9 per cent. The South East Asia population is younger than other parts of the world (more than half of the people are under 25 years of age, compared with the USA, in which the proportion is about a third, and Europe where it is about a quarter), so the demographic base for further economic growth also exists (Schultz and Pecotich, 1997). By 2010, according to figures compiled by Andrew Mason and Minja Kim Choe of the East-West Center in Hawaii, the workforce of China and South Korea will be around a quarter bigger than they were in 1990 (Maddison, 1991). One might argue that people in Asia also work longer hours. In the 1980s the South Korean working week was some ten hours longer than Japan's and more than fifteen hours longer than West Germany's.

The Road to Recovery: Is there a Light at the End of the Tunnel?

Generally speaking, a modest recovery is noticeable in Asia Pacific, but recovery to pre-crisis GDP growth rates and per capital income levels might take a number of years.

However, the region is still fundamentally strong. The capacity for resource mobilization (past savings rates exceeded 30%), the reasonably good infrastructure, the favourable

Table 4.1 Economic growth rates of Asia Pacific countries

	1992	1993	1994	1995	1996	1997	1998	1999	2000
Hong Kong	6.3	6.1	5.5	3.9	4.5	5.3	−5.1	−1.3	3.1
Indonesia	7.0	7.3	7.5	8.2	8.0	4.6	−13.7	−4.0	2.5
Korea	5.1	5.8	8.6	8.9	7.1	5.5	−5.5	2.0	4.6
Malaysia	7.8	8.3	9.3	9.4	8.6	7.7	−6.8	0.9	2.0
Philippines	0.3	2.1	4.4	4.7	5.8	5.2	−0.5	2.0	3.0
Singapore	6.2	10.4	10.5	8.9	7.5	8.0	1.5	0.5	4.2
Taiwan	6.8	6.3	6.5	6.0	5.7	6.8	4.9	3.9	4.8
Thailand	8.2	8.5	8.6	8.8	5.5	−0.4	−0.8	1.0	3.0

Notes: Figures for 1999 and 2000 are predicted rates of growth.
Source: International Monetary Fund, *World Economic Outlook*, up to May 1999.

demographics, the open trading system, and the general commitment to macroeconomic prudence should stimulate growth, which should resume once appropriate adjustment policies are implemented and take effect. The same people and resources that created the additional wealth over all these years are still in place. Governments and businessmen will have learned from their mistakes. More transparency, greater competence, fewer market distortions can be expected in future, probably leading to a higher degree of international competitiveness. The fundamental strength of the region also still prevails, characterized by high saving rates, entrepreneurship, young population, low taxes, high work ethic, and flexible labour markets.

Although the Asian crisis hit Thailand in July 1997 and quickly spread across Asia Pacific, by the middle of 1999 it was clearly evident everywhere in the region that these economies are slowly recovering. All governments in the region have been actively engaged in structural reforms and industrial restructuring. The Asian currencies have also stabilized with the exchange rates of the baht, ringgit, won, and peso converging to a level 30 to 35 per cent below their pre-crisis value, and the Taiwan and Singapore dollars to a 10 to 15 per cent lower value (Yamazawa, 1999). Consumers are beginning to spend, producers are rebuilding inventories, imports are rising, and even some banks are lending again. Positive economic growth is being witnessed in most countries in the region except in Indonesia where political uncertainty is handicapping recovery (Bhaskaran, 1999).

A number of key developments point to this somewhat rapid recovery. First, as previously acknowledged by the World Bank, Asian countries had the basics right—high savings rates, relatively low taxation, the creation of strong education systems, high productivity rates in both industry and agriculture, the maintenance of relatively low price pressures to ensure high savings rates, the acquisition of foreign know-how and technology, the creation of an investment-friendly atmosphere, and strategic government intervention in the economy (Henderson, 1998). Despite the crisis, these long-term fundamentals in Asia remained relatively unchanged. Also, despite the economic and financial problems that the region is currently experiencing, imports of raw materials and intermediate goods are beginning to recover. Recent trade data show a steady pick-up in Malaysia, Thailand, and South Korea, as well as a reduced rate of contraction in Singapore and the Philippines (Bhaskaran, 1999). Bank lending behaviour is also beginning to change positively. Corporate failures and financial distress are beginning to decelerate and as banks are being recapitalized, the stronger ones seem more prepared to lend to companies with letters of credit, at least for working-capital financing. This is now showing up in data for new loan approvals in Korea and Malaysia. Surveys in Singapore, Korea, and Malaysia also indicate an improvement from business expectations. Asian businesses are adjusting to a new equilibrium seeking out export markets and restructuring their balance sheets (Bhaskaran, 90). Exports of raw materials to the region are also on the rise. Hong Kong and Singapore are seeing slow and steady increases in exports from the USA. Export growth to Thailand, Indonesia, and Malaysia, which were hammered the hardest by the Asian flu, are improving more slowly. Reports from the Central Bank of Thailand suggest that the recession there has bottomed out, while the Malaysian Central Bank recently lowered its three-month intervention rate (Diederman, 1999).

Furthermore, although bank lending from the USA, Japan, and other countries decreased significantly during the crisis, foreign direct investment has been increasing in some countries, mainly in Korea and in Thailand, where the respective governments are increasingly making progress on economic structural reforms (Annual Report on the Asian Economies, 1999). Private consumption is also improving. The crisis triggered an unprecedented rise in precautionary savings across the region, flooding the banks with liquidity. This led to a collapse in real deposit rates, which in turn has encouraged people to spend again. What we are now seeing is a return to more normalized consumption patterns (Lall, 1999). Finally, governments of Asian countries are trying hard to build stronger financial systems. Although the stance and speed of financial reforms are divergent across the region, basic schemes of financial restructuring have been put in place in most countries (Annual Report on the Asian Economies, 1999). Having said this, it must be noted that much of the region's growth in the future would need to be supported by ongoing economic reforms, sustained capital inflows, low labour and resource costs. The role of Asian governments will be crucial for speeding and maintaining such a healthy recovery. Just as economic developments in Asia Pacific countries during the 'Miracle' were guided to a large extent by their governments, the road to recovery from the current 'crisis' also depends heavily on the role of these governments.

The Changing Role of the Government in Asia Pacific, Post-crisis

Although most countries in the region in the past have adopted an economic development strategy based on export-oriented industrialization, significant differences in other aspects of their economic policies exist, including the role of the state, industrial policy, the degree and nature of trade and financial liberalization, and the openness of their markets. The role of government in Asia economic development has been one of the most contentious issues. Until recently there has not been consensus among economists on whether government intervention in the market process played any positive role in the phenomenal economic growth in that region over past decades or whether it can now help those economies towards their recovery from the crisis. During the 'Miracle', governments in Asia Pacific were complimented for the successful institutional base they built for rapid growth. The Asian Development Bank (1997: 16–17), summarizes some of these policies as follows:

1. **Export promotion** Most Asian governments put relatively open trade, especially export promotion, at the top of their agenda. They have maintained a policy environment that supports exporters and insulates them from the negative effects of tariffs through specific institutions such as export-processing zones and duty-free rebate schemes, thus allowing these economies to export manufacturing goods successfully, even though they began from a low base of technology and industrialization. In turn, the rapid growth of manufactured exports allowed these countries to import productivity-enhancing capital goods and technology from abroad. Exports have also provided an objective criterion for measuring the effectiveness of state support for industry. Successful growth strategies during that period were also built upon private ownership and market-based economic organization.

2. **Agricultural transformation** Most East Asian governments did not repress their agricultural sectors. With the exception of the two city-states of Hong Kong and Singapore, most governments invested amply in agricultural research, local extension services, and rural infrastructure such as irrigation and electrification. This allowed rapid spread of the fruits of the Green Revolution. Food balances improved, as did standards of nutrition, and rising productivity in rural areas freed up labour for manufacturing exports, thereby allowing a rapid structural transformation of the economy.

3. **High saving rates** Public institutions supported high rates of national saving. The basic budgetary framework meant that East Asian governments were themselves large savers. They took in more revenues than they spent on current items, leaving plenty of money for public investment in basic infrastructure, such as roads and ports. They also kept social spending low, in turn allowing tax rates to stay low.

4. **Skill accumulation** East Asia's policies and supporting institutions led to rapid skill increases. This was not merely a matter of providing public education, although most East Asian governments did do that well. The broader upgrading of their skill base depended on more complex interactions; for example, exports accelerated the introduction and transfer of technology, creating a strong demand for skilled labour. This persuaded parents to invest in educating their children. Textiles, electronics, and other labour-intensive exports created a specific demand for female workers. As more young women began working, they married later and had fewer children. With fewer children, parents' investment in the health and education of each child rose.

5. **Economic flexibility** East Asia set up market-based institutions that allowed the economy to become more complex rapidly. Basic property rights existed and contracts were enforced and legal institutions were set up to settle disputes. This legal stability fostered the rise of a vigorous private sector and gave long-term confidence to foreign

investors. Governments furthermore relied mainly on private investors, both domestic and foreign, rather than on state enterprises, to organize manufacturing investments and production. Private firms generally built sophisticated production networks and linkages more successfully than state enterprises could. East Asian governments kept their labour markets flexible so that workers could readily shift between sectors as the economic structure changed. Many governments also began far-sighted programmes of scientific and engineering upgrading that are now contributing to rapid technological development. Korea, Taiwan, and China, for instance, are now benefiting from their governments' earlier technological foresight (Asian Development Bank, 1997: 16–17).

Thus during the 'Asian Miracle', most Asian governments played a direct role in the economy through owning or controlling enterprises and through targeting public procurement. The economies of China and Vietnam, for example, were dominated by state-owned enterprises. Indonesia nationalized most foreign firms in the 1960s. The Thai government controlled sectors such as fertilizers, commodities, distribution, air transport, and steel. Malaysia set up state companies to carry out its ambitions of becoming an industrialized country by the year 2020. Singapore controlled many firms through state holdings, while Korea and Japan relied on targeted procurement rather than state ownership. In Japan, business–government cooperation was formally institutionalized in 'deliberation councils', where government officials and representatives from the private sectors discussed policy projects and exchanged information (World Bank, 1993: 181–2). Government activity in Korea also took the form of 'administrative guidance'—a combination of notification, informal hints, invitations, and directed pressures that originated from ministries. The results up to the crisis had been rapidly rising prosperity and a profound change in Asia's quality of life. Asian governments thus, while intervening in their economic development, have tried to create a 'business-friendly', 'market-led environment', to use the World Bank's terminology.

During the Asian crisis, Asian governments' responses, including that of Japan, have been diverse and multifaceted. For example, Thailand, which triggered the crisis when it floated the baht in July 1997, has faithfully followed the IMF prescription. It has maintained the free movement of foreign capital both in and out of the country despite the fact that the Thai economy has suffered the consequences of this free movement (Krongkaew, 1999). The Korean government too requested assistance from the IMF during the crisis and has followed its severe prescription of contractionary policies despite the strong complaints of its citizens. However, when these policies started to threaten to break down the fundamentals of the real economy, the Korean government, in consultation with the IMF, changed to an expansionary policy to stimulate an early recovery. The government has also taken strong initiatives to strengthen the financial system and restructure its business groups. It is now pursuing its 'four plus one' reforms covering the financial sector, corporate structure, the public sector, industrial relations, and the liberalization of trade and investment. The Korean government is also now shifting its emphasis from Korea-owned industry to Korea-based industry (Dohyung, 1999).

The Malaysian government, on the other hand, responded to the crisis quite differently from Thailand and Korea. Malaysia did not resort to a rescue by the IMF but implemented a 'home-made' policy. It initially initiated contractionary macroeconomic policies, almost the same as the IMF's prescription, but quickly changed to expansionary measures to mitigate the depression. It then introduced a decisive financial policy in September 1998, returning to the dollar peg and restricting foreign capital outflow. The government is now taking the initiative in such domestic reforms as strengthening the financial system and industrial restructuring (Ariff and Abubakar, 1999). Japan, on the other hand has introduced its programme of Six Big Reforms and recently enacted the Industry Revitalization Act and implemented measures to nurture venture business (Kunimune, 1999) (details of the reforms introduced by the respective governments to ride the Asian crisis are provided in Chapter 5).

Overall, such efforts have been positive and by the first quarter of 1999 growth performance improved, with three countries showing positive growth rates: Korea 4.6 per cent, the Philippines 1.2 per cent, and Thailand 1.0 per cent. Industrial production has also started to resume and imports of industrial materials have been increasing (Yamazawa, 1999). Furthermore, foreign investments, both direct and portfolio, are now accelerating their return to the region to take advantage of depreciated currencies and deregulation (these are discussed in detail in Part III).

APEC, ASEAN, and the Asian Crisis

It is often argued that regional trade groupings could provide a strong integrative dimension to the highly diverse Asia Pacific region. The road to recovery in Asia Pacific would be incomplete without examining briefly the role of economic integration in the region during the crisis, and its impact upon the recovery in the region. In addition, such groupings could play an increasingly large role in stimulating economic growth and easing the participation of MNCs in individual countries and in the region as a whole. Unlike Europe or North America, and more like South America, Asia Pacific does not have one encompassing trade bloc but a wide variety of independent, overlapping arrangements. The most important ones are Asia Pacific Economic Cooperation (APEC) and the Association of South East Asian Nations (ASEAN).

Asia Pacific Economic Cooperation (APEC)[1]

APEC was an Australian initiative formed in 1989 in response to the growing interdependence among Asia Pacific economies. Begun as an informal dialogue group, APEC has become the primary regional vehicle for promoting open trade and practical economic cooperation. Its goal is to advance Asia Pacific economic dynamism and sense of community (APEC home page). APEC has gradually increased in size and prominence over the years to an organization of twenty-one members, whose economies comprise 55 per cent of world GDP. Members include: the USA, Canada, Mexico, Peru, Chile, Papua

---

[1] Information in this section is mainly derived from APEC's home page visited Dec. 1999.

New Guinea, Australia, New Zealand, China, Taiwan, Hong Kong, Japan, Korea, Russia, Singapore, Malaysia, Thailand, Brunei, Indonesia, Vietnam, and the Philippines. APEC has the ambitious aim of free and open trade and investment in the region by 2010 (and 2020 for developing countries). This aim was stated at the 1994 Bogo Leaders Summit.

APEC operates on a voluntary non-binding basis, through cooperation and peer pressure, and is built on two pillars: trade and investment liberalization and facilitation and economic and technical cooperation. The economies of members of APEC are due to meet their targets through action plans both collective and individual whereby they are able to reach their targets at their own pace. The Individual Action Plans (IAP) set down exactly what the economy aims to achieve, whereas the Collective Action Plans (CAP) cover activities on particular areas which involve all members of APEC. The CAP covers areas such as customs procedures, standards, and mobility of business people and so on. Each area has its own committee which reports to the Committee on Trade and Investment which in turn publishes a yearly progress report. APEC economic Trade Ministers meet on a yearly basis and also meet during the Joint Ministerial Meeting (with Foreign Ministers) which precedes the Leaders Summit. Dialogue with the business community is via the APEC Business Advisory Council, made up of representatives from every member economy, which meets regularly, reporting directly to the Leaders Summit.

The Asian economic crisis has been a major schock to APEC and has revealed the limitations of the cooperative efforts of APEC in overcoming the crisis (Akira, 1999). Unlike the European Union, which is comprised of relatively homogeneous members, APEC's member nations are in vastly differing stages of economic development and they cannot all be approached in the same manner. During the Asia crisis, there were large differences in the measures taken by APEC members. APEC is poorly suited institutionally, as it has no central institution-wide point of technical expertise such as the IMF has. Neither does it have a funding mechanism or resources of a scale to deal with such a crisis. One of the issues faced was how to incorporate discussions of financial and monetary matters into discussions of trade and investment, which has so far been outside the competence of the association (Adlan, 1998).

Association of South East Asian Nations (ASEAN)

The Association of South East Asian Nations (ASEAN) was established on 8 August 1967 in Bangkok. The formation of ASEAN was officially opened at the signing of the Bangkok Declaration on 8 August 1967 by five countries: Indonesia, Malaysia, the Philippines, Singapore, and Thailand. Brunei later joined the grouping in 1984. ASEAN currently consists of Singapore, Malaysia, Indonesia, Thailand, Philippines, Brunei, Vietnam, Myanmar, Laos, and Cambodia. Cambodia was the latest country to accede to ASEAN on 30 April 1999. Political and economic considerations have influenced these countries to form a regional cooperation. All the signatory countries saw the need to foster their economic development and promote regional security in the face of a growing communist threat in South East Asia, precipitated by the fall of Indo-China to communism and the declared intention of the West to withdraw their military forces from the region. Their common objectives, it was agreed, could be best achieved through mutual cooperation in the economic, social, and cultural areas (Tongzon, 1998).

During the initial stages of development, members of ASEAN faced several difficulties due to their diverse colonial traditions and influences, different economic priorities arising from their different stages of economic development, and differences in factor endowment. However, despite these differences, there were common grounds for regional cooperation. First, there was a realization that regional cooperation would confer economic benefits on member countries. Secondly, they realized that a common bargaining position and unified stance in their negotiations with outside countries would make them a significant force in the international sphere and thus enable them to influence the outcome of multilateral negotiations. Thirdly, the threat of growing protectionism and regionalization, as manifested in the formation of regional economic trade blocs and diminishing flows of capital to the developing countries, had made them more committed to regional cooperation. Fourthly, from the political perspective, the growing threat of communism, vulnerability to external powers, and the need for physical security have bound the ASEAN countries into one group. Fifthly, their geographical proximity and the importance of maritime trade, and finally the existence of quasi-authoritarian regimes and similarities in approach to development have facilitated cooperation and coordination (Tongzon, 1998). From a trade policy point of view, ASEAN is noted for two main things: their formation as a powerful bloc in the World Trade Organization (WTO) and their economic cooperation commitments which include the creation of the ASEAN Free Trade Area (AFTA) and the ASEAN investment area. In 1992, ASEAN agreed on the creation of the AFTA, which aimed to reduce tariffs on intra-ASEAN trade to between 0 and 5 per cent except for certain sensitive products, via a mechanism called the Common Effective Preferential Tariff scheme. Tariffs for external trade are unaffected and are controlled by individual countries. ASEAN's target for AFTA was 2003. However, the later members were given extended targets to meet the tariff reduction criteria; Vietnam until 2006 and Myanmar and Laos until 2008. ASEAN also applies a local content rule (which stands at 40% for the minimum requirement) and an industrial cooperation scheme which enables companies sourcing from within ASEAN to take advantage of accelerated tariff reductions. Also in association with AFTA, member countries are undertaking a number of trade facilitation measures including the harmonization of customs procedures and products standards.

When the financial crisis erupted in Asia in 1997, the leaders of ASEAN issued a statement on 'bold measures' which was designed to boost recovery in the region. The most important of the new measures was the acceleration of AFTA, whereby the AFTA target of 2003 would be implemented a year earlier (2002); by 2000 a minimum of 90 per cent of tariff lines would be between 0 and 5 per cent. The newer members also agreed to accelerate their tariff reductions. In order to encourage investments from both within and especially outside the region, ASEAN also adopted a framework agreement on the ASEAN Investment Area which has three programmes of action: cooperation and facilitation; promotion and awareness, and liberalization. As part of the above-mentioned 'bold measures', each ASEAN member agreed to extend a number of special privileges to investors in the manufacturing sector until December 2000. In addition, they have all agreed to extend national treatment to investors in this sector and accelerate the removal of exclusions by 2003 instead of 2010 (Tongzon, 1998).

Post-crisis Business Opportunities in Asia Pacific

Although shaken by the financial crisis that began in 1997, the Asia Pacific region as mentioned earlier is now slowly recovering and should provide most profitable prospects for business activity over the next several decades. According to the 1999 Annual Report on the Asian Economies, the Asian economies as a whole are expected to recover gradually and to grow by 4.4 per cent in 1999 (Annual Report on the Asian Economies, 1999). Following the currency devaluation in the region as a whole, the cost of assets has fallen in some cases by half or more, making them true bargains for foreign direct investors. Companies with export-oriented operations in Asia are finding that cheaper local currencies make their products less costly to manufacture in dollar terms and more competitive in global markets (Martin, 1998). Multinational firms are now regarding these countries as important investment destinations from a longer-term viewpoint (see case studies in Part IV). Furthermore, the region's poor environmental prospects create enormous opportunities for vendors of capital equipment and related services, including pollution control devices, waste disposal systems, water treatment plants, and environmentally sound technologies. The region's huge infrastructure rebuilding and development investment boom will generate strong demand for all types of goods and services (Strizzi and Kindra, 1998).

Country Reviews

The countries in Asia Pacific, however, do not represent a group of homogeneous economic and political systems. The speed of their economic revival is not uniform across the region. Post-crisis business opportunities also differ greatly from one country to another. To assist managers in MNCs, whether from North America, Western Europe, Asia, or other parts of the world, in formulating their strategies for doing business in Asia Pacific, country-specific business knowledge is essential.

Given the diversity of the countries in the region, it is not possible to provide a detailed individual study. This would be a mammoth task far beyond the scope of a single chapter. Chapter 5 gives a general overview of the business environment and business opportunities after the crisis in selected countries in the region. Some countries have been omitted either because their economies are too small or because their experience with foreign firms is too limited, or simply because of their lack of close economic and political ties with the region. The dynamic changes currently occurring in the region make it almost impossible to provide an up-to-date country profile. This information can be retrieved from the internet. The overall aim of the next section is simply to provide a brief overall view of the business environment, reforms introduced since the crisis to attract FDI and help the economy towards recovery, and to identify business opportunities post-crisis. The selected countries are presented in alphabetical order.

Review Questions

1 'With the economy turning the corner and key indicators showing signs of recovery, the time is perhaps ripe to look beyond the crisis at the new drivers of economic growth' (M. Arief, *et al.*, 1999: 436). Explain and evaluate this advice.

2 With the bitter and painful experience of the economic crisis behind them, what would be an appropriate role for Asia Pacific governments to adopt in relation to business?

3 Analyse and evaluate the impact of the IMF bail-out packages on those countries in Asia Pacific that were given little choice about accepting them? To what extent have they been successful?

Group Project

Aim This exercise aims at improving students' research skills. It should familiarize them with surfing appropriate Asian websites, selecting relevant information, establishing what is relevant, analysing data collected, writing a report and presenting a summary of their findings to the class.

Assignment Countries in Asia Pacific responded differently to the Asian crisis. Students are asked to review and assess various reform programmes that have been introduced so far by countries that were worst hit by the crisis in Asia Pacific. How successful have these reforms been in assisting their respective countries towards recovery?

Each group in the class should be assigned one particular country in Asia Pacific. At the end of all the presentations, students should be able to reach a common decision as to which country(ies) researched and discussed would be most attractive for business post-crisis.

Relevant Case Study (Part IV)

- Telecommunications in Thailand: The Mobile Phone Sector

Students could also be asked to use the above case study as an example of an industry analysis, and to conduct similar research on any other sector of interest to them, in their chosen country, such as, for example, e-commere in China, retail in Korea, and so on.

Further Reading

Aggarwal, Raj, 'Lessons for America', *Multinational Business Review*, 7(2), Fall, 1999: 22–31.

—— 'Restoring Growth in Asia after the late 1990s Economic Crisis: Need for Domestic and International Economic Reforms', *Multinational Business Review*, 7(2), Fall 1999: 22–31, Detroit.

Asian Development Bank, *Asian Development Outlook, 1998: Population and Human Resources*, New York: Oxford University Press, 1999.

Henderson, Callum, *Asia Falling: Making sense of the Asian Crisis and its Aftermath*, Business Week Books, New York: McGraw-Hill, 1998.

Chapter 5

Country Reviews

The People's Republic of China

Brief Overview

The Communist Party founded the People's Republic of China in 1949. The PRC pursued a closed-door and self-reliant development strategy in the first few decades. However in 1978 the PRC adopted an open-door policy and started to reintegrate with the global economy. Moreover, President Jiang Zemin's announcement in July 1997 at the People's Party Congress that most state-owned enterprises would shift to public ownership created huge opportunities for foreign investment. A new market for inward FDI has also developed recently, with the retail market gradually opening up to foreigners. Many consumer areas, from fast foods to laundry soap to shampoo, are now wide open. The personal computer (PC) market is also growing fast at a 40 per cent annual growth rate and was expected to reach 12 million units by 2000. Although the feverish pace of investment by multinational companies in China has slowed slightly since the crisis, reflecting the general caution about Asia, and the number of announced ventures has fallen, the size of individual projects has increased. In addition, more companies are opting for wholly owned projects rather than for joint ventures, and in some cases they have bought Chinese partners out of existing projects. China's continuous massive investment in infrastructure such as telecommunications and transport is moving this enormous nation forward slowly but steadily.

The Country and its People

China covers an area of 9,561,000 square kilometres, slightly larger than that of the USA. After the disintegration of the Soviet Union, China now shares borders with North Korea, Mongolia, Russia, Kazakhstan, Kirgizstan, Afghanistan, Pakistan, India, Nepal, Bhutan, Myanmar, Laos, and Vietnam.

China is the world's ninth largest economy, but if GDP per head is calculated on the basis of purchasing-power parity (PPP), then it would be battling with Japan for the number two position behind the US. China is also the world's most populous country (1.3 billion people) and thus has potentially a huge home market. It is the world's second largest country after Canada and the world's third richest in natural resources. Its large agricultural sector continues to make a significant contribution to GDP and provides employment to many of the country's 800 million rural dwellers. China's greatest resource and greatest problem remains its huge population. Indeed, the 1.2 billionth baby was born in February 1995 and the 1.3 billionth by 2000. Despite a tough family planning programme (one child per family) since 1971, the population has still been growing at a rate of 17 million people per year. By the year 2010, it is estimated that the total population of China will be about five times that of the USA. However it must be noted that China's per capita GNP would still only be-one fifth of the USA's. China therefore cannot be regarded as a superpower, unless the matter is looked at from a geo-political perspective. China still needs to absorb large amounts of foreign capital for its economic take-off.

The Business Environment

China is controlled by a communist government that has managed to maintain tight control of the economic and political arenas, making China the last large and stable communist fortress. Since 1979 China has made tremendous progress in its economic reform which has two major aspects: the internal restructuring of the economy, and the opening up of the economy to external trade and foreign investment.

China's Open-Door Policy

At the Third Plenary Session of the Eleventh Central Committee of the Communist Party in December 1978, the new leadership, headed by Deng Xiao Ping, restated that the primary national objective of China was to achieve the following four 'modernization' reforms.

First, control over production in agriculture was shifted from the centre to more local levels, with participants given incentives in the form of retained profit. This idea was translated into practice in a variety of ways with families, or family groups, or brigades or communes taking the responsibility and ordering their affairs. At the same time the area of private plots was increased. Overall, there was a rapid move to a decentralized system which combined broad planning at national and regional level and extensive scope for local-level or private initiative on land with long leases.

Secondly, in industry the Chinese Communist Party (CCP) began to relax central planning in the urban industrial sphere. A measure of freedom of labour was allowed in place of assignment. Some scope for the private employment of workers was allowed. The established socialized enterprises were allowed to contract work in the developing private sphere. On a national scale, the CCP established four Special Economic Zones (SEZs) where foreign capitalists were allowed to establish factories, employ local people, export the finished goods, and remit profits. Three of these SEZs were in Guangdong Province adjoining Hong Kong and the fourth was in Fujian adjacent to Taiwan. The SEZs have been very successful and have made a very significant contribution to the overall reorientation of the Chinese economy.

Thirdly, in education and science, the egalitarian stress on mass low-level participation at the expense of more advanced levels was reversed. The pursuit of educational excellence was affirmed and was quickly perceived by the population as a possible route to personal advance. Fourthly, in defence and foreign affairs, a new concern was given to upgrading the armed forces. In particular, new technology was sought and new patterns of arms procurement were initiated, which looked to a modern air force and deep-water navy.

The Chinese leadership also recognized that the only way to pursue these ambitious goals was to attract FDI, which would provide the capital, the management skills, and the technology that was lacking. Chinese officials, furthermore, believed that partnerships with foreign companies could facilitate access to international markets, which would absorb the country's exports and generate the foreign exchange needed to finance China's imports. The promulgation in 1979 of the Law on Joint Ventures Using Chinese and Foreign Investment was the first step. The Regulations for the Implementation of the Law of the People's Republic of China on Joint Ventures Using Chinese and Foreign Investment followed in September 1983. In October 1986, the State Council issued twenty-two Regulations concerning Encouragement for Foreign Investment, which offered foreign-funded enterprises preferential treatment and operational freedom. A further step of improvement for investment conditions was an Amendment to the Law of the People's Republic of China on Joint Ventures using Chinese and Foreign Investment in April 1990.

The open-door policy proved to be very successful. From 1979 to the end of 1994 more than 220,000 foreign-funded ventures were approved with contracted investment of US$300 billion and US$95 billion of utilized investment, making the country the most important recipient of FDI in the developing world. Thus, much of China's economic reform policy guiding the economy's development in the 1990s has been driven by Deng Xiao Ping's theory of developing a 'socialist market economy with Chinese characteristics'. This concept recognizes the need to introduce market economy principles into state policies. The underlying emphasis is to restructure China's economy along lines which are distinctly in tune with the realities and problems of living faced daily by the Chinese people themselves. The 'Decision of the Central Committee of the Chinese Communist Party on Issues concerning the establishment of a Socialist Market Economy' serves as a keystone document for this reform platform. It points out that a socialist market economy requires a healthy macro-control mechanism which is achieved by implementing the following measures:

1. **Restructuring of the banking system** The People's Bank of China independently implements the country's monetary policy under the leadership of the State Council. Whereas the central bank once relied mainly on its control over credit rates, an important initiative in foreign exchange system reform that occurred in 1997 allowed large domestic enterprises to open foreign exchange accounts in state commercial banks. Previously, only foreign-funded enterprises had been permitted to do so. This put domestic enterprises on the same footing as foreign-funded ones.

2. **Intra-regional integration** Another prominent feature of Greater China as an economic entity is the rapid pace of intra-regional 'integration'. Integration is at a more advanced stage between China and Hong Kong than between China and Taiwan. The opening of China has dramatically changed Hong Kong's industrial structure. A massive process of relocating manufacturing plants from Hong Kong to China has taken place.

Over 3 million employees in the Guangdong province of China are reportedly working directly or indirectly for Hong Kong, compared with the total workforce of about 3 million in the territory itself. Hong Kong now handles the traffic of over half of China's external trade, and its container port at Kwai Chung is one of the busiest in the world. Hong Kong is now China's largest outside investor and total contracted foreign investment is over 60 per cent. China's investment in Hong Kong is estimated to be about US$20 billion, second only to that of Britain.

3. **Economic reforms** China's economic reform process is gradual as opposed to what is termed 'shock therapy' or 'big bang' in the context of East European economic reforms. The Chinese leaders named their reform method 'crossing the river by feeling the stones underfoot'. In an effort to revitalize and restructure the economy, the reform leaders in China have focused on reforms of banking, public finance, the legal system and the social welfare system. A comprehensive tax reform programme was introduced in 1994. The main plank of the tax reforms is a value added tax (VAT) at a uniform rate of 17 per cent, replacing other turnover taxes. The split of VAT revenues between the national and local governments is in the ratio 3:1. The tax on corporate profit is standardized at 33 per cent.

4. **Legal reforms** Legal reforms include Chinese standards for the labelling of food showing food name, a list of ingredients in descending order of quantity, net content, production date, and the use by date which became mandatory in April 1996. In September 1997 the Fifteenth Party Congress endorsed a strategy of radical state-owned enterprise (SOE) reforms aimed at clarifying property rights and responsibilites, separating ownership from management, and building up an enterprise system with a diversified ownership structure. Under this strategy the government will (1) corporatize large and medium-size SOEs with the state remaining as sole or majority shareholder for enterprises that are of strategic importance; (2) restructure more than 250,000 small SOEs by means of joint share holding, leasing, contract operation, and employee and management buy-outs; and (3) encourage mergers, bankrupticies, and sell-offs to deal with the worst performing SOEs and to accelerate the reform process. During 1997 the government liquidated 675 SOEs, merged 1,022 SOEs, and took action to increase efficiency by reducing the number of redundant workers in 789 SOEs. The government has offered incentives to SOEs willing to take on the debts, assets, and workers of poorly performing enterprises to make for a more gradual increase in redundancies.

China's Response to the Regional Financial Crisis

China's large foreign exchange reserves have helped insulate it from the worst effects of the crisis. At the end of 1998, China had about $149 billion in total reserves less gold, including about $145 billion in foreign exchange. China also reported external debt of $130 billion in mid-1998. China's debt remains moderate compared to other Asian economies. China thus managed to weather the economic and financial turbulence in East Asia in 1997–98 because of its sound external balances and rising foreign currency reserves, and having only partially liberalized the capital account. The financial crisis in South East and East Asia did not spread to the PRC as quickly as other Asian economies. The renminbi appreciated marginally against the US dollar during 1997. The following factors explain the strength of the renminbi compared to currencies of the PRC's neighbouring countries. First, the PRC's capital account was not convertible. Secondly, the bulk of foreign capital inflows during the first half of the 1990s went into production sectors as direct investment as opposed to portfolio investment. Thirdly, the PRC has adopted prudent policies with regard to external borrowing, with about 82 per cent of its external debt being medium and long term, and its debt to GDP and debt-service ratios being significantly below the thresholds at which the International Monetary Fund expresses concern. Finally, because of massive foreign capital inflows and strong export performance, the PRC maintained a robust external position, with foreign currency reserves exceeding total foreign debt.

The main measures adopted by China to address the Asian crisis, are listed in the APEC home page as follows:

Monetary and Exchange Rate Measures

- Implementation of tight monetary policy in 1997.
- In 1998, monetary policy was moderately lessened to stimulate domestic demand in support of meeting the 8 per cent target growth rate.
- Maintaining stability of the exchange rate.
- Foreign trade enterprises were given the right to control 15 per cent of their foreign exchange.

Banking and Financial Sector Measures

- Interest rates have been adjusted downwards twice in 1998, a unified savings reserve account was established and the central bank's reserve ratio and discount rate were both reduced to stimulate demand.
- Stopping free allocation and introducing a monetary mechanism into the housing area from 1 July 1998 to diversify residents' personal assets.

Trade—and FDI-Related Measures

- Open most industries to foreign direct investment, and encourage foreign business to invest in high-tech industry, infrastructure, and enterprises' technology transformation.
- Cut import tariffs and increase export-refund rates of some products to foster trade.

Fiscal Policy

- Implement moderately expansionary fiscal policy, facilitate structural adjustment, and issue more government securities to increase fiscal revenue.

State-Owned Enterprise Reform

- Accelerating the transformation and reorganization of state-owned enterprises, and encouraging private investment.
- Accelerating the establishment of a modern enterprise system and modern banking supervision system.

As far as the local currency is concerned, since the effective depreciation of the renminbi (RMB) with the unification of China's internal and external exchange rates in 1994, the RMB/US$ exchange rate has remained stable and indeed has even registered a modest appreciation from 8.62 in 1994 to 8.31 in 1996 and further to 8.28 in 1997. The RMB has been supported in this period by four years of continous current account surplus, significant improvement in domestic inflation performance, strong inflows of foreign direct investment (which reflected the high capital demand in the domestic market), and the abundance of foreign reserves. With these fundamentals being sustained, the exchange value of the RMB is expected to remain stable.

Trade and FDI Measures Post-crisis

During the 1990s China was the largest developing country recipient of inward investment. Since 1993 it was second only to the USA as the world's largest host country. In 1994, inward investment amounted to US$34 billion. The general policy of the government continues to encourage foreign investment in China. China is now moving into an export promotion economic model whereby investment is encouraged, particularly in those sectors which will help China's exports. The guidelines for investment by foreign capital are based on a policy of opening wider to the outside world, and actively attracting overseas capital, technology, talent, and management experience. Foreign investors are encouraged to invest mainly in infrastructure projects; primary industries; high technology; the technical transformation of old enterprises; and export-oriented production.

The basic policy direction of the government on foreign investment is to facilitate market access and provide domestic status to foreign firms after their establishment. To this end, the government of China is trying to liberalize and simplify the investment procedures in accordance with overall economic policy. This policy seeks to grant national treatment to foreign investors so that freer and fairer competition can exist between domestic and foreign companies, thereby promoting an efficient free market economy.

Changes in Business Post-crisis

The Chinese government now puts greater emphasis on ensuring that new foreign investments in China are in industries that the government wants to encourage, as well as on their geographic location. Over the past three years, China has implemented policies introducing further incentives for investments in high-tech industries and in inland parts of the country. Policies on restricting and prohibiting foreign investment have for the most part been designed to protect domestic industries for political, economic, or national security reasons.

Changes in incentives illustrate policy-makers' adjustments to deal with changing domestic and global pressures. In April 1996, for example, China eliminated duty and value-added tax exemptions for equipment imported, thereby significantly increasing the costs of foreign investment in joint ventures and wholly foreign-owned manufacturing. These exemptions were for a range of machinery imports for use in foreign investments which the State Development and Planning Commission would certify as 'nationally encouraged projects'. They were introduced particularly for foreign investments that involved technology transfer and appeared on China's lists of 'encouraged' or 'restricted category B' investment projects, as well as foreign investments involving loans from foreign governments or foreign financial institutions. Not only did the government receive complaints about the elimination of these incentives, but it also noted a drop in foreign investment in some of the industries it wanted to encourage. So in January 1998, it reintroduced the duty and VAT exemptions. In addition, the exemptions were extended retroactively to cover many investments made during the period in which the incentive had been eliminated. Imports made by those investments during that period, however, were not covered retroactively.

China has also been gradually relaxing some restrictions on foreign ownership and establishment of businesses. Since 1992, for example, new service sectors including retailing, insurance, and tourism have been opened to foreign investment on an experimental basis. These experiments in the service sector are limited in number and locations allowed. China currently permits a maximum of foreign investments in joint-venture retail department stores in eleven cities and SEZs. So far, only fifteen have been approved, and only ten of these are in operation. More recently, the retail market has also been opening up gradually to foreigners. In late 1996, three years after the authorities announced they would allow a few joint-venture chain stores, two were approved, one involving a Dutch company and the other a Japanese consortium. Each of the two reportedly plans initially to open three retail locations in Beijing. Foreign investment in such joint ventures is limited to a minority stake, and it is still prohibited in wholesaling and distribution.

As the financial crisis in Asia threatened to negatively affect Chinese exports, the Chinese government increased the VAT rebates for exports of certain products, such as textiles, beginning in January 1998. Official Chinese press reports also indicated that similar VAT rebate increases may be in store for even more products, including ships, coal, machinery, electronics, and certain categories of high-technology products and large plant equipment. There have also been changes in the area of foreign exchange controls. China announced full convertibility of its currency on the current account on 1 December 1996 and instituted new, more liberal, regulations allowing foreign invested and domestic enterprises to freely convert currencies for current account transactions such as trade transactions and profit repatriation.

Further changes were made to China's Company Law. Foreign firms can now also open branches in China. Special preferences have been established for projects involving high-technology and export-oriented investments. Foreign investors may also receive benefits by reinvesting profits. They may obtain a refund of 40 per cent of the tax paid on their share of income if the profit is reinvested in China for at least five years, and a full refund if the reinvestment is in high-technology or export-oriented enterprises. As far as acquisitions and takeovers are concerned, the concept as understood in the West is not applicable to the foreign investment environment in China. Under existing regulations, a simple share buy-out could occur, but it would be subject to the approval not only of all the partners in the venture in question, but also of the supervising Chinese government agency. Foreigners can purchase shares in a small minority of Chinese companies listed on Chinese stock exchanges, but foreign portfolio investment is restricted to less than majority ownership. Finally, while China's investment laws and regulations do not require technology transfer, they strongly encourage it and foreign investors are likely to face pressure to agree to it.

Business Opportunities Post-crisis

China has entered its most ambitious and pragmatic reform phase yet. It is now paring down and restructuring the state sector in ways unimaginable only a few years ago. In the mid-1990s China had about 300,000 state companies engaged in manufacturing, trade, retailing, finance, and services. By the middle of the next decade, a much smaller core of strategic industries such as communications and power and heavy industries such as steel and oil are likely to remain entirely in state hands. Although the term is still avoided, privatization is occurring throughout China. Since 1993 more than 6,000 state companies of all sizes have been reorganized as shareholding companies. Although the state usually remains the major shareholder, mergers and acquisitions are quietly increasing the private stake in many. The government is preparing to allow companies with as little as 51 per cent state ownership to be listed on the two domestic stockmarkets, while previously only companies with 75 per cent ownership were allowed to be listed. In an effort to shield companies from political interference, the government has also recently banned government and party offices from running business, which often led to conflicts of interest. It also approved a law to curb fraud on the share markets so they can more effectively channel capital to well-performing companies and it decided to let Guangdong International Trust and Investment Corp. to go bankrupt, signalling a new willingness to let the market discipline badly managed state companies.

The retail business in China is opening up to foreigners. Since 1992, six big cities, including Beijing and Shanghai, and five special economic zones, including Shenzhen and Hainan, have each opened two large Chinese foreign joint-venture shopping centres. So far China has approved some ventures to sell daily consumer goods, such as the Yaohan department store in Pudong, Shanghai; the Yansha shopping centre in Beijing, and a joint venture set up by the Hong Kong Sun Hung Kai properties and Beijing Dongan market. More such approvals are expected soon. At present, however only joint equity ventures are allowed to engage in retail and wholesale operations; foreign-owned commercial retail land wholesale enterprises are still not permitted to set up in China. Opening commercial enterprises to the outside world, according to the Chinese government, can only be achieved gradually. The aim is to upgrade present commercial facilities by importing foreign funds, and advanced foreign managerial and marketing experience and techniques. These would then step up the improvement in the overall strength of state commercial retail enterprises, widen marketing channels, and promote exports through the efforts of overseas partners. China's Ministry of Domestic Trade also believes that conditions have now become ripe for the country to develop chain stores, but for the time being, the development will focus on convenience chain stores. The development of these chain stores will focus on supermarkets, convenience stores, fast food restaurants, and service outlets. To encourage the expansion of these stores, the central government and a number of local governments have adopted preferential policies towards tax and loans such as the ministry plans for chain stores. The Ministry of Domestic Trade has drawn up a plan to develop chain stores on a trial basis in thirty-five big and medium-sized cities. Under the plan, China will have 6,000 chain stores controlled by 300 parent enterprises with total annual sales of RMB 8 billion, or 5 per cent of retail sales nationwide. As of the year 2000, there will be 15,000 enterprises running 60,000 chain stores with total sales of RMB 120 billion making up about 5 per cent of the country's retail sales. Shanghai has been at the forefront of the booming retail industry in China (see e.g. the case study 'Wal-Mart goes to Asia Pacific' in Part IV).

Additionally, China ranks immediately after Japan as the most important pharmaceutical market in Asia. China also offers enormous potential to cosmetics and toiletries exporters. The sector is growing at an extremely high rate, with expansion occurring in both the mass market and in premium product sectors. Chinese consumers, however, have distinct preferences. They tend to look for natural cosmetics products which are perceived as safe and free from side-effects. They also prefer multifunctional and time-saving products. Branded products are increasingly becoming popular as well. Only limited buying power and unavailability of infrastructure such as electricity and roads hold back more purchases of Western and Japanese products. Despite such limits, a significant market for luxury goods is also emerging.

Finally, as 1999 was declared the 'year of getting on the internet', all ministries in China are creating websites. Despite Asia's economic crisis, internet and e-commerce growth rates are among the highest in the world, and often twice as high as that in America (see the Dell case study in Part IV). Napoleon once said of China 'Let China sleep, for when she wakes, she will shake the world'. China is now slowly waking up. Considering its potential market of 1.3 billion customers, this may become the most exciting consumer market the world has ever seen.

Sources

Anon., 'A Funny-Looking Tiger', *The Economist*, 17 Aug. 1996: 17, London.

—— 'Foreign Investment in China: Changing Trends and Policies', *East Asian Executive Reports*, 20(4), 15 Apr. 1998: 8–16.

—— *The Economist*, 17 Apr. 1999: 351(8115), 69–70, London.

Brahm, L., and Daoran, L., *The Business Guide to China*, Singapore: Butterworth-Heinemann Asia, 1996.

Business: Asia online, http://www.apmforum.com/ Capsule Review update, Asia, 30 Mar. 1999.

Dwyer, D., *China: The Next Decades*, Harlow, Essex: Addison-Wesley Longman Limited, 1996.

Kaiser, S., Kirby, D. A., and Fan, Y., 'Foreign Direct Investment in China: An Examination of the Literature', *Asia-Pacific Business Review*, 2(3), Special Issue: Greater China, spring 1996: 44–5.

Koberstein, W., 'Regional structures: A Company Survey', *Pharmaceutical Executive*, 18(1), Jan. 1998: 64–8.

Low, L., and Toh, M. H., 'Regional Outlook: South Asia 1994–1995', ASEAN Institute of Southeast Asian Studies, 1994.

Shu-Ki, T., 'The Political Economy of Greater China', *Asia Pacific Business Review*, 2(3), Special Issue: Greater China: Political Economy, Inward Investment and Business, spring 1996: 23–43.

Slater, J., and Strange, R. (ed.), *Business Relationships with East Asia: The European Experience*, Boston: Routledge Advances in Asia Pacific Business, 1997.

Smith, J., 'State of the Industry: The Asia-Pacific Cosmetics and Toiletries Sector', *Drug and Cosmetic Industry*, 159(3), Sept. 1996: 24–5.

Wilhelm, K., 'China out of Business', http://www.feer.com/Restricted, 18 Feb. 1999.

Wood, A., 'Investment Pace Slows; More Firms Go it Alone, *Chemical Week*, 160(32), 26 Aug.–2 Sept. 1998: 39–4.

Hong Kong

Overview

Hong Kong's strategic location and its excellent communications network and efficient infrastructure have made it a hub for trade, finance, and business services in the region. After Japan, Hong Kong is probably the most developed economy in Asia Pacific. The competitive advantages of Hong Kong include its strategic central location in Asia, its advanced communications network, its solid infrastructure, low tax rate and simple taxation system, free port status, globally acceptable legal system, efficient support services, general efficiency of doing business, and availability of skilled labour. Although small in population, Hong Kong can provide quite a lucrative market in itself, given its very high per capita GNP and its very high propensity to import. Many MNCs have eagerly marketed their products and services in the territory, particularly given the little adaptation they need to undertake. Also, Hong Kong has one of the world's highest proportions of millionaires to population. It is therefore highly attractive for most luxury goods and services.

The Country and its People

Hong Kong consists of the Kowloon peninsula, the New Territories, the business and residential area, and Hong Kong island where most of the financial and administrative facilities are concentrated, as well as over 200 tiny islands, mostly uninhabited. The population is 6 million about double that of Singapore. The vast majority of the population (98%) are Chinese, principally from China's neighbouring Canton province and also from Shanghai. Hong Kong was seized by Britain after the First Opium Wars of 1840–42 and the land was subsequently formally leased to Britain by China in 1898. By the turn of the century, Hong Kong had become the principal distribution centre for British trade with China. In 1949 many hundreds of thousands of Chinese fled to Hong Kong following the communist victory in mainland China.

Hong Kong was a British colony until July 1997 when it reunited with mainland China. China took over the sovereignty of Hong Kong, but promised, under the concept of 'one country, two systems' to keep the capitalist system in Hong Kong running for at least fifty years. The government of Chief Executive Tung Chee Hwa was installed on that date. The Legislative Council was disbanded, but most of the institutions and the vast majority of the senior civil servants who oversee the daily operations of the Hong Kong Special

Administrative Region remained unchanged. The Sino-British Joint Declaration of 1984 provided the framework for this peaceful transfer, stipulating that Hong Kong would become a Special Administrative Region of the People's Republic of China but would retain a high degree of autonomy in all matters except foreign and defence affairs. The Joint Declaration further stated that for fifty years after reversion Hong Kong would retain its political, economic, and judicial systems, and could continue participating in international agreements and organization under the name Hong Kong, China.

The Business Environment

Articles 109 to 113 of the Basic Law of the Hong Kong Special Administrative Region of the People's Republic of China lay down specific provisions relating to Hong Kong's status as an international financial centre, its monetary and financial policies, the status of the Hong Kong dollar and the issuing arrangements, capital movements, and the role of the exchange fund. These principles establish the basic monetary relationship between China and Hong Kong under the principle of one country, two systems. This can conveniently be summarized as 'one country, two currencies, two monetary systems and two monetary authorities' with one sovereign state. The coexistence of two currencies, that is, the Hong Kong dollar and the renminbi, is a clear demonstration of the differences between the economies of Hong Kong and the mainland. It is therefore essential that the two monetary systems should be mutually independent.

The major components of Hong Kong's service sector are shipping, civil aviation, tourism, and financial services. Financial and business services include banking, insurance, real estate, and a wide range of other professional services.

Hong Kong's Response to the Regional Financial Crisis

In 1998, as the Asian financial crisis became progressively reflected in a deep regional economic downturn, Hong Kong's economy slipped into its first recession since the mid-1980s. Hong Kong has addressed the crisis by maintaining its commitment to a market-oriented economic policy and in particular to the linked exchange rate system that ensures stability of the Hong Kong dollar. Fiscal measures have been taken to mitigate the effects of the contraction in private sector spending. The Hong Kong Monetary Authority (HKMA) implements the exchange rate policy by strictly observing the monetary rule of a currency board system under which any change in the monetary base is brought about only by a corresponding change in foreign reserves in the specified currency (i.e. the US dollar) at the fixed exchange (in this case 7.8 to 1). Full transparency is maintained by publishing the reserves and the aggregate balance in the clearing accounts of the banking system. During periods of capital outflow, as occurred from time to time during speculative attacks on the Hong Kong dollar, the monetary base shrank, leading to the higher interest rates that were observed during these periods.

The HKMA introduced a few measures with a view to easing credit tightening amidst the Asian financial turmoil. These included, for example, exempting interest income on deposits placed with authorized institutions in Hong Kong from profits tax and development of the Hong Kong dollar market and schemes to make fuller use of the liquidity available at the Hong Kong Mortgage Corporation. However, in order to offset the impact of the economic slump on the job market, the government also unveiled on 3 June 1998 a series of measures aimed at creating 100,000 jobs over the period to the end of 1999.

Business Opportunities Post-crisis

Hong Kong is highly dependent on imported resources to satisfy both consumer and industrial needs. Demand is particularly strong for agricultural products, fuels, plastic raw materials, and capital-intensive and high-technology goods such as avionics equipment, computer hardware and software, medical equipment, industrial packing equipment, and electronic parts and components. Consumer imports include cosmetics, stereo equipment, sporting goods, and household products. The best prospects for foreign exporters to Hong Kong are as follows:

1. **Air-conditioning equipment** There is significant demand in Hong Kong for air-conditioning equipment, both for the domestic market and for re-export to China. Many private developers have switched to high quality central air-conditioning equipment to meet the demands of Hong Kong's more affluent consumers, but government regulations ensure that room air conditioners will continue to dominate the residential market. Light equipment for small commercial establishments is also one of the fastest growing market segments. The strongest demand within infrastructure projects is for reciprocating chillers of up to 1,000 tons.

2. **Computers and peripherals** Hong Kong's demand for the newest computer technologies and products continues to grow. Industrial, financial, and public sector applications present local sales opportunities for a wide range of suppliers. There is demand for large, medium, and small-scale systems. Besides the financial community, public utilities, telecommunications companies, universities, and government represent a solid base of users of large-scale systems. The principal area of potential growth in sales, however, lies in medium-scale systems for computers that support 15 to 100 users in commercial environments.

3. **Medical diagnostic equipment** Hong Kong medical and health standards have risen considerably in recent years and are now among the highest in the world. Nearly 90 per cent of Hong Kong's hospitals are either government controlled or government assisted, which means that companies intending to enter this market must understand the procedures for selling to the Hong Kong government. For now, the most economical means of market entry is to have an agent or distributor in Hong Kong. Companies that wish to enter China's markets through Hong Kong often establish a regional office. Committed to improving medical services, the Hong Kong government is expected to increase its capital expenditure budget in the next few years. Demand for diagnostic equipment, in particular, is on the rise, and there is currently no domestic production of diagnostic equipment. Exporting opportunities range from cardiac output analysers and computer topography scanners to optical microscopes and ultrasound scanners.

4. **Cosmetics and toiletries** Featuring an increasingly affluent population, a cosmopolitan lifestyle, and over 6 million visitors a year, Hong Kong has become an important market for high quality beauty products. There is also a growing awareness of health

products and products made from organic ingredients. Environmentally friendly products and packaging are also gaining popularity.

So far, Hong Kong has played a role as a gateway to China. Many foreign products made their way into China from Hong Kong, first indirectly by being carried in by visitors from Hong Kong, then directly after demand had been created by the first route. Foreign companies pursuing business in China also depend on Hong Kong to provide or channel technology, capital, management know-how, and ideas. Hong Kong has thus served China in three major areas, namely as its port, marketing outlet, and financier. However, it may see a decline in its relative importance in all three roles in the future, as China's economic strength rises and its direct contact with the outside world deepens.

Sources

Asia Pacific Economic cooperation (APEC), 'APEC Member Economies', http://www.apecsec.org.sg/member/indoec-report.html.

Cragg, C., *Hunting with the Tigers: How to Achieve Commercial Success in the Asian Pacific Rim*, London: Mercury Books, Gold Arrow Publications Limited, 1992.

Gough, L., *The Meltdown: The End of the Miracle*, Oxford: Capstone Publishing Limited, 1998.

Hinkelman, E. G., *Hong Kong Business: The Portable Encyclopedia for Doing Business with Hong Kong*, California: World Trade Press, Country Business Guide Series, 1993.

Mee Kam, M. G., and Wing-Sing, T., 'Land—Use Planning in One Country, Two Systems: Hong Kong, Guangzhou and Shenzhen', *International Planning Studies*, 4(7), Feb. 1999: 7–27.

Shu-Ki, T., 'The Political Economy of Greater China', *Asia Pacific Business Review*, 2(3), Special Issue: The Political Economy of Greater China, spring 1996.

The Banker, 'China: One State, Two Currencies', Nov. 1996.

Republic of Indonesia

Overview

With its 200 million people, Indonesia constitutes the world's fourth most populous country, after China, India, and the USA. Like China, Indonesia is too large a potential market to ignore. The country offers very attractive prospects for MNCs both as a market and in terms of many comparative advantages to investors. It is a vast and fertile country with rich natural resources of oil, tin, natural gas, nickel, timber, bauxite and copper, a large domestic market, and a strategic location. Indonesia, however, was by far the worst hit by the Asian crisis. While it is true that ethnic and religious conflict has escalated with poverty and reduced income during the crisis, this is nothing new. Ethnic and religious conflict has been ongoing for more than ten years in Indonesia, especially in the provincial areas, and during the Sukarno regime. Many investors claim that the Indonesian investment climate is challenged further by a complicated bureaucracy and lack of policy transparency. Investment cancellations have often related to political instability.

The Country and its People

Indonesia is the largest archipelago in the world with more than 3,500 islands of extremely varied size and character, of which some 1,000 are inhabited.

The Indonesians refer to their country as *Tamah Air* (Land and Water), as the Indonesian archipelago covers 3,166,163 sq. km. of water and 1,919,317 sq. km. of land. Stretching from east to west, Indonesia covers a distance of 5,120 km. making it wider than the USA. In terms of sea routes, the country lies strategically along the equator between the south-eastern tip of the Asian mainland and Australia. Its western and southern coasts face the Indian ocean; to the north it faces the Straits of Malacca and the South China Sea; and the remote northern shore of Irian Jaya fronts onto the Pacific Ocean. Indonesia's land frontiers are with Papua New Guinea. Jakarta, the capital of Indonesia is one of the largest cities in the world. It is located on the northern coast of Java. Jakarta was founded in 1527 and now spreads over nearly 580 sq. km. with a population of 6.5 million people, who are predominantly Muslim with Islamic fundamentalist leanings. Most Indonesians are primarily of Malay stock, except in eastern Indonesia. Within the Malay stock, there is a wide variety of different cultures, languages, and ethnic groups known locally as *suku*. The major ethnic groups are Javanese (45%), Sundanese (14%) Madurese (8%), and coastal Malays (8%). Chinese descendants make up 3 per cent of the population. The official language is Bahasa. Bahasa is a dialect of Malay, but English is common for commercial activities and some older Indonesians still speak Dutch from colonial days.

Historically speaking, Indonesia has its roots in Hindu and Buddhist culture in the first century AD. Islamic culture was subsequently introduced to Sumatra in the fifteenth century from where it then spread throughout the rest of the islands. By the sixteenth century, the Portuguese had come hunting for cloves and other spices and imposed their influence. The Dutch then arrived in the early seventeenth century, during which time the area became known as the Dutch East Indies. Next it was Britain's turn to occupy Indonesia unlawfully during the Napoleonic wars.

The Business Environment

Economic Reforms under Suharto Government

A major deregulation programme was initiated in 1993 to encourage private investment. The government also embarked upon reforming the legal and administrative procedures. Changes to regulatory measures introduced since 1993 include the following:

- exemption from import duties, surcharges, and value-added tax for materials imported to be used entirely for exports;
- increasing the allowance for companies operating in bonded zones to sell in the domestic market from 12 to 25 per cent;

- reduction of the number of business areas where new investment is restricted or banned;
- improving the licensing procedures, the stock exchange, and deregulating the pharmaceutical industry;
- streamlining the investment approval procedures;
- waiving visa requirements for businessmen.

Further regulatory changes were introduced in June 1994. These are:

- reduction in tariffs on 739 products taking average Indonesian tariffs to well below Indonesia's 40 per cent Uruguay Round binding;
- removal of non-tariff barriers on twenty-seven products and surcharges on 108 items covering raw materials and intermediate goods used in the livestock industry, textile machinery and components, agricultural machinery, foreign-assembled passenger cars, semi-trailer parts, and components of heavy-duty equipment;
- removal of the entitlement to any tariff escalation for new projects;
- removal of the prohibition on leasing of machinery and equipment by companies in bonded and special export zones to companies operating outside such zones.

The June 1994 announcement also included significant changes in regulations governing foreign investment. The major changes are as follows:

- an increase in the level of permissible foreign capital participation in joint-venture companies from 80 to 95 per cent and lifting of the foreign ownership restriction on Indonesian companies to allow ownership by foreign individuals;
- extension of the period of operation of licence fees from twenty to thirty years;
- abolition of the requirement of a minimum capital investment of US$250,000 on foreign investors;
- easing of the divestment requirement for fully owned foreign companies so that divestment of a token proportion of as little as 1 per cent need only be carried out within fifteen years of the commencement of commercial production, and this can be done by float rather than by finding a suitable local partner;
- opening up to joint ventures of the previously off-limit areas such as ports, electricity generation and distribution, telecommunications, shipping, airways, drinking water, railways, nuclear power, and mass media to joint ventures;
- easing of operating conditions for foreign companies to allow them to establish subsidiaries and acquire other foreign and domestic forms.

The tax system has also been overhauled. The new tax bill introduced in October 1994 reduced rates of the presently existing income brackets and increased the annual tax-free income from 0.96 million to 1.72 million rupiahs. It has also reduced the top rate to 30 per cent for companies as well as individuals and allows for special tax incentives for companies to invest in priority sectors and reinvest their after-tax earnings in Indonesia.

To encourage export competitiveness, the government announced a deregulation package in January 1996. This package reduced tariffs by between 5 to 15 per cent on 428 products, thereby reducing the cost of imported raw materials used in producing exported products. It also allows foreign firms to export forestry, fish, mining, and manufactured products. Furthermore, it permits the involvement of foreign firms in the distribution of goods used by producers in the special export processing zones, for example, in the special Bonded Warehouse Zone. Import duties were also eased on goods supplied to producers in these zones. Also in June 1996 the government announced another deregulation package which schedules tariff reductions, simplifies import distribution systems, and establishes an anti-dumping committee.

Indonesia's Response to the Regional Financial Crisis

In 1998, economic activity contracted sharply in each of the first two quarters, leaving real GDP in the first half 12.2 per cent below its level of a year earlier. With the exception of some agricultural and public utility sectors, almost all sectors of the economy have experienced negative growth since the outbreak of the crisis. The largest output declines occurred in construction, commerce, financial services, and manufacturing. Inflation accelerated sharply due to the sharp increases in the prices of food and other essential items, reflecting the direct effect of the depreciation of the rupiah, the disruption of the distribution system of essential goods, and domestic supply shortages. In the light of these adverse developments, the annual inflation rate reached around 90 to100 per cent in the year to December 1998. The economic crisis in Indonesia has also led to a significant rise in unemployment with approximately 2 million workers losing jobs as companies restructured through mergers and consolidations to increase their efficiency with an additional 2.7 million new job seekers entering the labour market at a time of no job creation.

Indonesia's Measures to Address the Financial and Economic Crisis

The stabilization and reform programme that Indonesia has put into effect following the Asian crisis includes deregulation, trade liberalization, and privatization of state enterprises. Measures adopted by Indonesia to respond to the crisis are listed on the APEC home page as follows:

Monetary and Exchange Rate Policy Measures

- Bank Indonesia has been given full authority to conduct and implement monetary policy.
- A free floating exchange rate system has been adopted.
- The Indonesia Debt Restructuring Agency (INDRA) that provides protection against exchange rate risks and assures availability of foreign exchange for Indonesian debts was established.
- The mechanism of Open Market Operation was revised.

Banking and Financial Sector Measures

- The Indonesia Banking Restructuring Agency (BPPN) was established.

- Liquidation of sixteen insolvent banks, suspension of ten insolvent banks, and the merger of four state banks into one bank took place.
- The Government provided a guarantee for banks' deposit and other claims, such as borrowing, guarantee and letters of credit issued by the banks.
- Restrictions were imposed on property credits for the acquisition and processing of land, except for simple and very simple houses.
- A new facility on swap and forward buy transactions was provided for certain exports, while limitations were imposed on forward sell contracts.
- Statutory reserve requirements for foreign currency deposits were lowered from 5 to 3 per cent.
- The interest rate on Bank Indonesia Certificates was gradually increased.
- Bank Indonesia placed US$1 million within ten internationally reputable foreign banks that will act as confirming banks for Letters of Credit granted by appointed Indonesian banks.

Trade and FDI Related Measures

- Import traffic was lowered for 1,690 items consisting of 1,451 industrial, agricultural, and three product health items.
- There was a deregulation package in the real sector, such as the elimination of soybean, wheat, flour, and onion trading system with increasing import traffic.
- The foreign share-holding limit of 49 per cent in firms other than financial firms in September 1997 was eliminated, and existing foreign ownership in financial institutions was guaranteed.
- Prohibition on FDI, including oil commodities, was removed.
- FDI was allowed in the production and trading sectors.

Fiscal Policy

- More transparency is needed.
- The social safety net was reinforced and subsidies to ensure the availability of food and other essentials at affordable prices throughout the country were extended.
- Reforestation fund to change according to budgetary fund.

Business Opportunities Post-crisis

Indonesia has a free-market economy but the government still plays a significant role through state-owned firms, and the imposition of price controls in selected industries. Japan is the biggest foreign investor in Indonesia, followed by Singapore, Hong Kong, Taiwan, and South Korea. Most approved investment during the last few years has been in manufacturing, especially in textiles, pulp and paper, and chemical industries. The food sector accounts for the largest share of consumption imports. Import requirements include cereals, flour, rice, wheat, chemicals, oil and gas machinery, power generation and supply, pollution control, airport-related equipment, food processing, mining and railway equipment, as well as telecommunications and automotive components and accessories, iron and steel products, machinery and transport equipment, as well as textiles. Financial services and tourism also offer very good opportunities.

Most industries in Indonesia are open to foreign investment, subject to obtaining the required approvals from the Ministry of International Trade and Industry. Those that are still closed to foreign investment include postal services, telecommunications to a certain extent, railway transport, the generation of electricity, and some other public utilities. However, there have been recent examples of the privatization of public utilities, such as the National Electricity Board. Other industries vital to national defence such as those producing arms, ammunition, and military equipment remain entirely closed to foreign investment as well as large sectors of the trading and distribution business, particularly domestic retail trades and exports and imports.

The government has also been trying to liberalize foreign direct investment. For example, in May 1994 the government issued Regulation no. 20, which offered a substantial liberalization on foreign investment. The May package allowed straight 100 per cent foreign ownership either by individuals or enterprises (except in infrastructure and agribusiness), allowing the continuation of foreign majority control, permitting joint ventures (with majority shares by a local partner) in nine vital sectors related to power, telecommunications, nuclear power generation, and public drinking-water—and eliminating the minimum requirement on the amount of capital investment. In September 1997, the government liberalized further to allow MNCs to hold majority control of domestic companies. However, having said that, the Indonesian government remains very sensitive to foreign dominance of key industries. Foreign participation in these sectors can occur only through joint ventures with Indonesian citizens or legal entities. Protection of trade marks and intellectual property remains a major weakness. Indonesia is not a party to the International Community for the Protection of Industrial Property. Consequently, piracy is active in many industries, such as book publishing, video recording, and fashion apparel. Patent protection is also limited. For example, Patent Law no. 6/1080 allows the Indonesian pharmaceutical industry to import and freely copy fifty types of pharmaceutical products, even while the product is under patent protection internationally. The government is currently revising the law to meet the ruling of the Trade Related Intellectual Property Rights (TRIPs) rules of the WTO.

Since July 1998, FDI approvals have increased rapidly following liberalization of the foreign exchange regime. The tertiary sector, and particularly housing, hotels, and restaurants attracted the largest portion. By economy of origin, a large portion of FDI has come from Japan, the United Kingdom, Hong Kong, China, and Singapore.

Finally, Indonesia is noted for its high levels of corruption, ranking forty-third out of the forty-eight country survey in the *World Competitiveness Report*. MNCs will find problematic the relationship between the government and the tight-knit business community. Furthermore, Indonesia exhibits substantial practices of monopoly, oligopoly, and cartels through the mechanisms of coalitions (between government and private players), regulations of entry and exit, and price and distribution controls. Examples of government–business coalitions include: government funds being placed in large private companies that have been chosen as the preferential winners of tenders for large government projects; special licences to specific private companies to produce, buy, import, and sell specific products such as cloves and wheat; and many other transactions lacking transparency between the government and private companies such as in acquisitions of state enterprises by the private sector. Additionally, Indonesia's social tension from uneven income distribution is expected to become even more serious with large-scale unemployment. With the current political tension and corruption of officials exposed by the new 'shame culture' campaign, the country as a whole remains one of the most difficult countries in Asia Pacific to do business in.

Sources

Bhaskaran, M., 'Is Asia Recovering Too Quickly?' *Far Eastern Economic Review*, 162(23), 10 June 1999: 90–1.

Cragg, C., *Hunting with the Tigers: How to Achieve Commercial Success in the Asian Pacific Rim*, London: Mercury Books, Gold Arrow Publications Limited, 1992.

Goodfellow, R., *Indonesian Business Culture: Insider Guide*, Singapore: Reed Academic Publishing, Butterworth-Heinemann, Asia, 1997.

Gough, L., *Asia Meltdown: The End of the Miracle*, Capstone Publishing, Oxford: 1998.

Lim, L., 'Social Welfare', in Kernial S. Sandhu and Paul Wheatley (eds.) *Management of Success: The Moulding of Modern Singapore*, Singapore: Singapore Institute of Southeast Asian Studies, 1989.

Low, L., and Toh, M. H., 'Regional Economic Outlook: South Asia 1994–95', ASEAN Institute of Southeast Asian Studies, 1994: 35–54.

Rowen, H. S. (ed.), *Behind East Asian Growth: The Political and Social Foundations of Prosperity*, London: Routledge.

Savage, V. R., Kong, L., and Neville, W., *The Naga Awakens: Growth and Change in Southeast Asia*, Singapore: Times Academic Press, 1998.

Tongzon, J. L., *The Economies of Southeast Asia: The Growth and Development of ASEAN Economies*, Cheltenham: Edward Elgar, 1998.

Yip, G. C., *Asian Advantage: Key Strategies for Winning in the Asia-Pacific Region*, London: Addison-Wesley, 1998.

Japan

Overview

Japan is currently suffering from low domestic demand and stagnant growth in its domestic economy. The key to Japan's recovery remains hinged on how quickly crony relationships between big business and government can be decreased, and opportunities given to the new management talent in Japan. Despite current economic conditions, the country retains a powerful position in Asia Pacific. Japan's GDP is seven times that of China and twice that of the rest of Asia put together. Its companies play very significant roles in most of the region, and it still provides a huge market for new products in high technology and emerging industries such as personal computers, cellular phones, and other multimedia products. Japan also holds the world's second largest pool of privately held savings. However, the cost of doing business in Japan remains very high and is not expected to come down in the near future.

The Country and its People

Japan is an archipelago whose four main islands comprise approximately 90 per cent of the total land mass. Most of the population live in highly urbanized areas along the coastal plains. Tokyo, Japan's capital, and the surrounding prefectures of Kanagawa, Saitama, and Chiba, occupy the largest flat area in Japan called the Kanto Plain. Together these four prefectures have a population of over 31 million. Tokyo is the governmental, business, higher education, information, media, fashion, and cultural centre of Japan. Kanagawa which includes the cities of Yokohama and Kamasaki is the richest prefecture in Japan with a per capital income of almost 50 per cent above the average Japanese. Kansai is the sixth prefecture region of West Central Japan centring around the cities of Osaka, Kobe, Kyoto, and Nara, with a combined population of over 20 million people. It is the traditional commercial centre of Japan. Chubu is Japan's third largest metropolitan area, after Tokyo and Osaka, and the core of Japan's automotive, aerospace, machine tools, and ceramics industries.

Japan's population is 121 million. The Japanese population is singularly homogeneous in race, religion, values, and language, in striking contrast with other countries in Asia Pacific which are mostly multi-racial, multi-religious, and multi-lingual societies.

The Business Environment

Japan has a fully developed physical infrastructure of roads, highways, railroads, airports, telecommunication networks, harbours, warehouses for distribution of all type of goods and services. The Japanese economy is currently undergoing painful structural adjustments resulting from excessive debt and over-regulation. The Japanese government is strongly promoting a variety of policies in order to revitalize the Japanese economy. As far as recent economic reforms are concerned, institutional changes throughout Japan have in many ways been unprecedented. In March 1999, the Tokyo parliament passed an 81.86 trillion yen ($682 billion) budget designed to steer the economy out of recession. The budget is the largest ever and considered by analysts to be significant enough to inject the stimulus needed for growth. Around the same time, Japan's central bank eased monetary policy by lowering overnight bank-lending rates to zero as a means to push investors into corporate restructuring and also into moving ahead in the form of lay-offs, mergers, and acquisitions. Even the country's Keiretsus are now being pressured to take part in the overhaul. The pressing need to change old management styles, for example, has already prompted the departure of top executives of Mitsubishi, EC, and Hitachi with more high-level changes expected.

The Japanese government is also attempting to de-regulate and stabilize the financial markets. In March 1997, the Deregulation Action Plan was revised. The plan aimed to deregulate the economy, including such areas as land use, construction materials, and medical products, and to strengthen anti-monopoly enforcement, which was weak in Japan. The Deregulation Action Plan contained a number of items related to FDI such as:

- easing of restrictions on foreign capital entry;

- abolishing the international contract notification requirement. Under the old Anti-monopoly Law, the Japan Fair Trade Commission (JFTC) was authorized to screen certain notifiable international contracts—such as joint ventures involving foreigners—and to prohibit specific contracts that, in the JFTC's judgement, might cause unreasonable restraints on trade or involve the use of unfair trade practices. As part of the revised Deregulation Plan, however, the JFTC in June 1997 abolished its contract notification system, under which any Japanese entrepreneur who enters into an international contract that was notifiable under JFTC rules was required to file with the commission within thirty days of concluding such an agreement;

- abolition of thirty-three antitrust exempted cartels by the end of 1998;

- the removal of most legal restrictions on exports and foreign investment in Japan.

Japan's 'Big Bang' Reform of the Financial System

The 'Big Bang' reforms mean new opportunities for Western financial companies to market their products and expertise to a vast market which hold the world's second largest pool of privately held savings. Key features of these reforms are:

1. **Breaking down barriers** The 'Big Bang' promotes competition by lowering, or even eliminating, the barriers separating different sectors of the financial industry. The new law allows financial institutions to establish holding companies. Parent corporations will now be able to offer a range of financial services under one umbrella. Holding companies allow members of the group to cut costs by consolidating overlapping operations. They also allow the group to pursue integrated product development and market strategies. Already the Fuyo group is working to establish a holding company which will offer services in commercial banking, trust banking, and life and non-life insurance. A similar plan is being studied by the Mitsui group. By the end of 1999, banks, trust banks, and securities companies will be able to enter each other's markets. Soon after, insurance companies will be allowed to enter the banking sector, and banking and securities companies will be allowed to enter the insurance sector. Also by the end of 1999, brokerage firms' trust-banking subsidiaries will be allowed to manage pension funds. Brokerage firms would also compete with banks by offering 'wrap accounts', in which customers could deposit paychecks or pay bills.

2. **Freeing prices** Securities companies are now allowed freedom to set commissions on trades of more than 50 million yen ($384,000). Trade had previously been subject to fixed brokerage fees. Auto insurance rates were also liberalized and the Japanese government plans to lift all restrictions on property and casualty insurance premiums in the near future.

3. **Opening Japan to the world** Previously only authorized foreign-exchange banks were allowed to conduct transactions in other currencies. Designated banks were supposed to determine whether a customer's foreign-exchange transactions met Ministry of Finance (Mof) guidelines. Under this protected system the foreign-exchange fees of

Japanese banks were much higher than those of their Western counterparts. This encouraged Japanese multinationals to transfer much of their foreign-exchange operations to subsidiaries in London, New York, Hong Kong, and Singapore. Under the new foreign-exchange law, authorized banks lose their monopoly on foreign-exchange transactions. Now, any business enterprise can enter into foreign-exchange transactions without government authorization. The new foreign-exchange law also allows domestic investors to open accounts in any currency with foreign banks and securities companies without prior Ministry of Finance authorization.

4. **Greater transparency in money policy and bank regulation** The new Bank of Japan Law increased the independence of the monetary authorities. Under the new system, representatives of government agencies cannot be members of the policy board, although they can express their opinions at board meetings. Also greater transparency is expected with the release of the minutes of the policy board's deliberations within only a few weeks.

Protection of intellectual property rights in Japan remains difficult. Obtaining and protecting patent and trade-marks rights can be time-consuming and costly but are essential. Even when intellectual property rights have been acquired, pirating of technology and designs can still occur in Japan. Patents are granted to the first to file an application for a particular invention, rather than to the first to invent. Prompt filing in Japan is therefore important because printed publication of a description of the invention anywhere in the world, or knowledge or use of the invention in Japan, prior to the filing date of the Japanese application would preclude the grant of a patent on the application. It takes an average of four to five years to obtain a patent in Japan. As far as trade marks and service marks are concerned, as with patent applications, Japan's trade-mark registration process is slow. It takes an average of 2.8 years to process a trade-mark registration. Meanwhile, the only protection available is under the Japanese Unfair Competition Law. Under this law, the owner of the mark must demonstrate that the mark is well-known in Japan and that consumers will be confused by the use of an identical or similar mark by the unauthorized user. Copying Western goods, particularly in the fields of sporting goods and clothing, occurs frequently.

Japan's Response to the Regional Financial Crisis

The Japanese economy is in a prolonged slump, owing mostly to fragility in its financial sector and to spillover effects of the Asian financial crisis. Real GDP declined by 0.7 per cent in fiscal year 1997 (April 1997–March 1998) and is projected to shrink further in fiscal year 1998. The government has responded to the downturn of the economy by taking measures with respect to fiscal and monetary policy, the financial sector, and other structural areas in order to revive the economy. Unemployment rose to a historical high of 4.3 per cent in June 1998.

Japan's Measures to Address the Regional Financial Crisis

Since the onset of the Asian financial and economic crisis, Japan has pledged and steadily implemented its assistance measures amounting to US$43 billion based on the following five points of view:

- prompt and effective financial assistance under the IMF-centred international assistance framework;
- assistance for securing domestic liquidity and smooth access to trade finance in order to maintain and promote private sector activity;
- support to the socially vulnerable segment of the population on which the recession and structural reforms have the heaviest impact;
- implementation of a prudent industrial policy to consolidate the economic structure and to build competitive industries;
- development of competent human resources which play a key role in overcoming the current economic turmoil.

Measures to Revitalize the Japanese Economy

Recognizing that the sound functioning of the Japanese financial system and the rehabilitation of the Japanese economy also contribute to the recovery of East Asia economies, Japan is striving to implement the following fiscal and financial policies domestically:

- In November 1997, the government launched a structural policy package including measures such as deregulation, facilitation of land transactions, and promotion of investment.
- In January 1998, the government announced a financial stabilization programme, which made 30 trillion yen (6% of GDP) of public funds available to strengthen the financial position of the deposit insurance system and to inject capital into the banking system.
- In February 1998, a supplementary budget for fiscal year 1997 was approved, which included 23 trillion yen (0.4% of GDP) of income tax cuts.
- In April 1998, a 'Comprehensive Economic Measure' of over 16 trillion yen worth of projects, the biggest such package in Japanese history, was announced in an effort to achieve economic recovery. The package increased social infrastructure investment (8 trillion yen) and implemented additional temporary individual income tax reductions and individual inhabitant tax reductions (4 trillion yen) and tax reductions for special policy purposes.
- Permanent tax reductions, which in total substantially exceed 6 trillion yen, and the fiscal year 1998 supplementary budget of total projects worth over 10 trillion yen, were implemented.
- In order to settle the non-performing loan problems and to revitalize the Japanese financial system, a set of new legislation was passed by the Diet and new schemes were established to prepare for bank failures and to infuse public funds into banks.

Business Opportunities in Japan Post-crisis

Japan's major export industries include automobiles, consumer electronics computers, semiconductors, and iron and steel. Other key industries in Japan's economy are mining non-ferrous metals, petrochemicals, pharmaceuticals, biotechnology, shipbuilding, aerospace, textiles, and processed foods. Despite the recession, a multitude of opportunities exist. Demand for refrigeration equipment has been increasing in line with the high volume of building construction and orders for new residential housing supplies. Import items currently in demand are commercial refrigeration equipment, ice-making machines, freezers, prefabricated refrigeration and cold storage, refrigeration display cases, and refrigeration units for transportation systems.

More recently, the Japanese Ministry of International Trade and Industry (MITI) and the MITI-affiliated Japan External Trade Organization, JETRO, have been promoting the import of high-quality, affordable houses from North America and Europe. The Ministry of Construction (MOC) is trying to cut the cost of housing by 33 per cent, and is encouraging imported houses and building materials. The Huogo Prefectural government has also announced a three-year plan to rebuild 125,000 housing units destroyed in the Great Hanshin earthquake of 17 January 1995.

Japan's consumers are extremely receptive to quality cosmetics imported from Europe and the USA. While European, particularly French, cosmetics have long been admired, US cosmetics are increasingly being well regarded among Japanese consumers. As price-consciousness continues to spread, opportunities improve for intermediate-priced foreign cosmetics. Environmentally sound products, time-saving cosmetics for working women, and products specially designed for women over 40 offer the greatest potential sales. Promising items include perfumes, hair-care products, natural foundations, eye-makeup, lipsticks, and skin-care products.

Business opportunities also exist for foreign mail-order companies with strong brand appeal and distinct character in design and materials. US-based direct selling companies such as Amway, Avon, Tupperware, Nu Skin are enjoying substantial sales of cosmetics, detergents, cleaning supplies, and nutritional products. Metal furniture accounts for 80 to 85 per cent of the office furniture market in Japan. The development of office automation equipment introduces an additional prospect for growth in the office and institutional furniture market.

The gradual introduction of the Regional Medical Care Plan in Japan during the late 1980s has also fostered an emphasis on renovating existing hospitals and acquiring technologically advanced and cost-effective medical equipment. This trend is expected to contribute to a steady expansion of Japan's medical equipment market. Products for the elderly as well as diagnostic and therapeutic products—imaging equipment, sports medicine products and emergency medical equipment—have the greatest potential for growth. The greying of the Japanese population is proceeding faster than in any other country in the world. Today, 12.3 per cent of the Japanese population is over the age of 65. By the year 2025, this segment will increase to 25.7 per cent. Japan's growing senior population and the rising cost of geriatric health care portend a shift from the expensive health care provided in hospitals to less expensive health-delivery systems, typified by nursing-homes. The demand for nursing home equipment in Japan should expand rapidly in the coming years. The best opportunities in this sub-sector include toilet and personal hygiene equipment, bathroom-related equipment used to lift patients, and specialty bedding.

The traditional Japanese diet of rice and fish is undergoing great change, as consumption of meat and prepared foods, as well as dining out gain in popularity. As a result, there is an emerging market for specialized food-processing machinery. Japan's food-processing technology lags behind that of the Western countries except in specialized areas such as rice-cleaning machines and Chinese noodle-making machines. Thus Japan's food-processing machinery industry depends largely on imported technology from North America and Western Europe. Demand for meat-processing machinery is expected to grow. Japanese consumers are interested in specialized meat processing machinery that is hygienic, easy to maintain, and capable of processing foods new to their diet.

The growing popularity of golf, skiing, and other outdoor recreational activities promise a lucrative market for foreign exporters of sporting goods and equipment. Other opportunities exist in high-technology industries such as aviation, computers, semiconductors, software, pharmaceuticals, and medical devices. Sales of premium-priced, consumer-ready food products are also continuing to grow.

Finally, a major effect of the economic stagnation in Japan since 1997 has been to create greater opportunities for alliances. MNCs such as Toyota, Matsushita, Sony, and Toshiba have performed well despite the overall slowdown of the Japanese economy, while Japanese oil companies and other protected companies have struggled to survive. Japanese companies are now realizing that they will not be internationally competitive with high administrative costs. They are now more willing to be flexible in their supplier relationships and are starting to use alliances as viable strategies. This change in mentality of Japanese corporations will bring good opportunities for foreign MNCs that are seeking partnerships with Japanese corporations, not only for the Japanese market, but for the Asia region as a whole.

The Japanese market could represent a strong attraction for foreign MNCs. The obstacles, however, remain formidable. According to a survey of foreign MNCs in Japan, obstacles to Japanese operations include the high cost of land and rent, high prices of goods, too many government regulations, the difficulty of finding good personnel, complex standards and the existence of Keiretsus. Other problems faced by foreign MNCs in Japan are price, the rise in the value of the yen, value-based consumerism, and soaring welfare costs. The unique Japanese distribution system, and close relationships with suppliers also presents a formidable barrier to new entrants, whether foreign or domestic. Japanese companies often form long-term contracts and lasting personal relationships with their suppliers and subcontractors. So new entrants may be at a disadvantage when attempting to conduct business with Japanese wholesalers or retailers, even if their products or services carry a lower price or are of superior quality. Manufacturers often form their own distribution systems, which carry only their own brand. In summary, obstacles making Japan's business environment costly and difficult can be listed as follows:

- a high overall cost structure that makes market entry and expansion expensive for foreign investors;

- corporate practices and market rules that inhibit acquisitions of Japanese firms;

- exclusive buyer–supplier networks and alliances, commonly maintained by the Keiretsus;

- burdensome laws and regulations that directly or indirectly restrict the establishment of business facilities and hinder market access for foreign products, services, and FDI;

- close ties between government and industry as illustrated by the ministries' issuance of informal 'administrative guidance' to Japanese companies, the placement of retired bureaucrats in Japanese companies and trade associations through a practice called *amakudari*, and the delegation of quasi-regulatory authority to trade associations, which are often allowed to devise and regulate their own insider rules.

Despite the range of formal and informal barriers mentioned above, this has not dissuaded foreign corporations from investing in Japan. Most notable was GE Capital Services record of $6.5 billion acquisitions of Japan Leasing in February 1999, a strategy that other multinationals are quickly adopting without much hesitation, thanks to the relative security Japan offers in terms of a highly educated and industrious workforce, incredible purchasing potential, and political stability.

Sources

Anon., 'Japanese Market Barriers', *Nikkei Business*, 6 June 1994: 126–9.

Capsule Review Update: Asia, 30 Mar. 1999.

Gough, L., *Asia Meltdown: The End of the Miracle*, Oxford: Capstone Publishing, 1998.

Hinkelman, E. G., *Japan Business: The Portable Encyclopedia for Doing Business with Japan*, California: World Trade Press, Country Business Guide Series, 1994.

http://www.apmforum.com/research/asia.html

Sowinski, L., 'Asia: Prospects for Japan, South Korea and Taiwan', *World Trade*, 12(6), June 1999: 28–32, Irvine.

Tongzon, J. L., *The Economies of Southeast Asia: The Growth and Development of ASEAN Economies*, Cheltenham: Edward Elgar, 1998.

Whitehill, A., *Japanese Management: Tradition and Transition*, London: Routledge 1992.

Korea

Overview

Korea was known in the past as a country that was difficult for foreigners to do business in. This has changed since the crisis. Korea is now opening up to the external global market, implementing deregulation in all sectors of the economy, conducting business on the basis of market principles. Moreover, Korean businesses are very eager now to restructure themselves and thus offer many opportunities for foreigners to merge and acquire Korean businesses to increase their own competitiveness. The currency has been devalued over the past two years by about 50 per cent so foreign companies can be in a much more profitable position than before. All this in addition to the characteristic Asian merits that are still there like high levels of education, substantial savings rates, and very high worker morale and discipline.

The Country and its People

The name Korea is the English version of *Koryo*, a kingdom which was established in the central region of the Korean peninsula in AD 918. Located in North East Asia, the Korean peninsula borders in the north on China and Russia and extends outwards to Japan. The land area of 221,487 sq. km., making up the entire peninsula, has since 1945 been divided into two: North and South. The Republic of Korea in the south is a little more than twice the size of Switzerland.

Korea was subjected to repeated Chinese invasions and intermittent Chinese occupations. Japan annexed Korea as a colony in 1910. After Japan's defeat in 1945, the USSR administered Korea's northern half and the USA administered its southern half. As the Cold War developed, the two superpowers jockeyed for position. It was not until 1948 that the southern part was granted independence as the Republic of Korea. The Soviets simultaneously set up the Communist Democratic People's Republic of Korea (DPRK) in the North. The DPRK attacked the Republic of Korea in 1950 precipitating the Korean War, 1950–53. The US-led UN forces helped drive the DPRK back. Hostility between the two Koreas has lasted since 1953, despite successive South Korean governments' efforts towards reunification. North Korea to this day has a rigid centrally planned economy.

South Korea is one of the most densely populated countries in Asia Pacific with a population of 44.5 million. Roughly 60 per cent of Koreans are Buddhist or Buddhist-Confucian, 25 per cent are Christian, and almost all of them remain partly Shamanistic. Consequently, a typical Korean is a complex cultural composite: Confucian, Shamanistic, Buddhist, and Christian. Education has been at the heart of Korea's growth, training and supplying the manpower needed for rapid industrial and economic expansion. The national literacy rate is in excess of 95 per cent.

The Business Environment

The unprecedented growth of the Korean economy between the 1960s and the 1990s was attributable to three institutions: government, business, and labour. Of these three, the government has played the most active role in the economic development process.

Relationship between Government and Business Leaders

In the 1960s, straight after taking power in 1961, General Park was strongly anti-business. He imprisoned owners of large business firms and confiscated their wealth, based on the assumption that they could only have accumulated it illegally. Later, however, in an effort to gain political popularity, Park had to seek cooperation from these same businessmen to formulate and implement the first development plan. To gain the support of business leaders, the government granted them immunity from criminal liability for past wrongdoings, respected their property rights and ownership shares, and rewarded firms that participated in the development of basic industries and contributed a share of ownership to the government. As a result of these incentives, business leaders began to participate actively in the government's development schemes. Thus Korean business leaders became pro-government and maintained a familiar and smooth relationship with government officials and influential politicians of the ruling party who controlled economic decisions vital to their activities. Business leaders realized that maintaining a close relationship with government was the best way to survive and maintain maximum growth. The relationship between government and business was thus conducted as a vertical relationship. In order to effectively maintain a vertical relationship with business, the government created policies to favour business, notably limiting workers' rights to organize and negotiate and thus keeping wages low. The government also allocated scarce resources favourably, and at more favourable interest rates, to companies that complied with its policies, thus creating an economic incentive for business compliance. Advancing into the areas selected by the government as strategic industries and achieving targets set by the government enabled businesses to obtain scarce raw materials and financial resources at a time when the national economy lacked productive resources other than unskilled labour. The extent of the powers the government abrogated to itself to guide the economy meant additionally that it could favour compliant firms through tax policy, limits on exit and entry into certain industries, and the conferral of monopolistic or oligopolistic power. At the same time, the government did not hesitate to punish or intimidate firms or business leaders through special tax audits, disruptions of special financial resources, and surveillance of business by its intelligence agency. Only companies that followed government policy and maintained close relationships with the government would succeed in business; those that did not follow this policy perished.

The Korean government began to be active in the economy with the First Economic Development Plan, which was launched in 1961 by the military government after its coup and continued until the 1980s. In an attempt to gain the support of the Korean people, the military government paid close attention to economic prosperity. During the early stages of economic development, General Park's regime considered strong leadership by the central government as necessary for successful development and therefore entrusted decision-making powers to the bureaucrats under the auspices of the president himself. Under the Park regime, a Monthly Trade Promotion Meeting, chaired by the president himself, worked to encourage exports, as this was considered the chief route to Korean economic growth. At such meetings, the president's prime concern was whether export targets were being met; if not, he blamed the authorities concerned. Under the office of the prime minister, an Advisory Committee of University Professors was organized to meet with the president regularly to advise on economic policy. From this brain pool the President filled cabinet posts and other important government positions. Park devoted himself to economic development in collaboration with the established elite bureaucrat group. Bureaucrats thus had great influence on the private business sector in Korea up until the crisis.

In 1961 when the First Economic Development Plan was launched, South Korea began to induce the foreign investment which has made a great contribution to the development of the national economy by way of expansion of production, employment, and improvement of balance of payments. Since then, Korea's industrial structure has been rapidly modernized through the concerted efforts of government and private enterprise to produce technology-intensive, high value-added items, through investment in research and development.

Foreign Investment Policy

The basic policy direction of the government on foreign investment is to facilitate market access and provide domestic status to foreign firms after their establishment. It also seeks to grant national treatment to foreign investors so that freer and fairer competition can exist between domestic and foreign companies, thereby promoting an efficient free market economy. The government has now replaced the Foreign Capital Inducement Act of the 1960s with the new Foreign Investment Promotion Act to attract foreign investors. According to this step-by-step capital liberalization plan, the Korean capital market will be opened to foreigners to invest in stocks and bonds and to issue securities. The High-Tech Industry Cooperation Act of 1995 has been implemented to bring about tangible benefits for direct foreign investors in terms of taxation and financing. Taxation benefits include waivers of up to 100 per cent for the first five years, and a 50 per cent exemption of corporate, income and local taxes for the following three years. Commercial loans for the importation of equipment are allowed up to 100 per cent of the amount invested. Priority is given to investors who build production facilities in industrial zones where land can be leased at an annual interest rate of 1 per cent for twenty years. Restrictive trade barriers in Korea are also in the process of being reduced and eventually dismantled. In response to the growing complexity of the economy, the Korean government promoted the use of market mechanisms to improve the competitiveness of Korean firms, and gradually lowered tariffs and loosened regulations. For example, one of the major trade barriers against Japanese imports was the import diversification regulation. This regulation was intended to block Japanese imports that might have had a direct negative impact on Korean products such as consumer electronics and automobiles. Because of this regulation, Japanese-made Toyotas or Hondas cannot be imported to Korea while American and German cars are freely imported. The only Japanese cars that can bypass this import diversification rule are those made in the USA by Japanese transplants.

Korea's Response to the Regional Financial Crisis

Pursuant to the agreements struck with the IMF, Korea has launched major reforms, unprecedented in its history, to address the structural imbalances exposed by the crisis. Measures already implemented or planned are listed on the APEC home page as follows.

Reforms of the Financial System

- Various steps have been taken to restore health to the Korean financial system through major reform legislation.

- The Financial Supervisory Commission (FSC), pursuant to legislation passed in December 1997, formally began operation on 1 April 1998 with a mandate to consolidate the Banking Supervisory Authority, the Security Supervisory Board, the Insurance Supervisory Board, and the Non-Bank Supervisory Authority; and to monitor and regulate all financial entities in Korea. The FSC will review bank restructuring and recapitalization plans, enforce Bank for International Settlements standards and make recommendations, for example, license revocation, to the Minister of Finance and Economy on the fate of banks that do not meet standards.

- **Korea Asset Management Corporation**: this fund was set up to address the problem of non-performing loans. It has spent 17.7 trillion won (US$13.1billion) to purchase non-performing loans worth 39 trillion (US$20 billion) at face value, in order to accelerate the process of recapitalizing troubled banks.

- **Capital adequacy requirements** All banks are now required to meet the international capital adequacy ratio established by the BIS. Of the twelve Korean banks that currently do not meet these standards, five were ordered to shut down on 29 June 1998 and to merge with other banks; the remaining seven were given conditional approval for continued operation, based on comprehensive management reforms, suspension of international business dealings, and consolidation of operations. The licence of a thirteenth merchant bank was suspended and its ownership transferred while the business of three other merchant banks has been halted. Korea First Bank and Seoul Bank were recapitalized to avoid any systemic risk that might have accompanied their failure and plans called for them to be auctioned in advance of the 15 November 1998 date set out in the agreement with the IMF.

- **Foreign bank entry** Provision has been made to allow foreign banks to establish Korean affiliates, provided they: (1) show minimum assets of 100 billion won in the case of commercial banks and 25 billion won for provincial banks; (2) meet the BIS capital requirements; (3) have no record of business suspension in the past three years, and (4) are qualified to act as majority shareholder of the affiliate.

- **Deposit insurance** The deposit insurance system is being overhauled and strengthened to enhance depositor confidence in the financial system.

- The independence and authority of the Bank of Korea was guaranteed.

- **Foreign ownership** On 25 May 1998 the ceiling on foreign equity ownership of domestic companies was completely eliminated and hostile mergers and acquisitions were fully liberalized, including those by foreign companies.

- **Labour market reforms** The Labor Standards Act was amended to allow lay-offs for the purpose of restructuring. This makes it easier for an investor to acquire a Korean company and to increase its profitability. At the same time, placement services are being strengthened or privatized to promote more efficient manpower allocation across industries. In addition to the new Labor Standard Act, legislation allowing the establishment of manpower-leasing businesses was put into effect in July 1998. This important measure will further help to enhance labour market flexibility by making labour outsourcing an additional option for employment adjustment.

- **Corporate sector reform** A number of measures have been adopted to restructure the industrial sector:

  - The Chaebols have been required to eliminate their existing cross-debt guarantees by 2000 and prohibited from issuing new guarantees since April 1998.

  - To improve transparency and accountability, corporations are required to produce consolidated financial statements in line with international standards by 1999, far in advance of the original schedule.

  - Voting rights of minority shareholders have been strengthened as the representation requirement for class action suits was reduced from 1 per cent to 0.01 per cent.

- Bankruptcy-related laws were streamlined in February 1998 in order to facilitate the exit of viable corporations.
- For their part, the Chaebols have pledged to implement restructuring measures, including steps to (1) enhance transparency; (2) eliminate cross-debt guarantees; (3) improve their capital structure; (4) focus on core business and cooperation with small business; and (5) increase accountability of major shareholders and managers.
- In addition, the five largest Chaebols have agreed to accelerate moves to swap business to help revive the economy.

Korea is currently undergoing a massive restructuring. It is true that there have been only limited asset sales, hardly any manufacturing capacity has been scrapped, and only a handful of owners have had to cede control of their companies. However, business operations have been restructured, with workers across the board accepting wage cuts and lay-offs. Domestic investors are lining up to subscribe to rights issues from companies that have become more transparent or investor friendly than before the crisis. With the International Monetary Fund bail-out, a rise in exports, and a decrease in imports in 1998 because of the devaluation of the won, Korea's foreign exchange reserve soared to an all-time high. Now the won's exchange rate has stabilized and all major economic indicators are showing signs of improvement.

Business Opportunities Post-crisis

Until 1997 Korea was one of the toughest countries in Asia for foreign businessmen because of a myriad of restrictions upon foreign investment that limited access to the Korean market. The Korean government, following the Asian crisis, now believes it necessary to accelerate the economic recovery by attracting more foreign capital. It has invoked a series of measures that were unthinkable in pre-crisis days to greatly open the market with a welcome to foreign investors. The government is actively improving regulations and the climate for foreign investment substantially with the goal of creating the best possible investment climate in the world. President Kim Dae Jung's Big Deal plan is now beginning to pay off. The won has stabilized, interest rates are down to around 8 per cent from a high of 30 per cent; the country's foreign exchange reserves have been replenished; and payments towards the International Monetary Fund's $58 billion loan have begun. Meanwhile, the president's administration has been pushing dozens of bills through the National Assembly aimed at liberalizing and restructuring the economy. Holding companies will be allowed, making it easier for the Chaebols to spin off unrelated subsidiaries and easier for foreigners to invest in Korean companies. Foreigners will now be able to own land and invest more easily in the country. The government has also eased labour laws, thereby making it easier for companies to lay off workers. It has also enhanced the powers of the Fair Trade Commission to permit it to search for and seize company documents, and to monitor the Chaebols to prevent them from amassing huge political slush funds. Chaebol reform alone is viewed by many as perhaps the most critical component leading towards South Korea's economic recovery.

Korea's strategy seems to be paying off. Before the crisis the transfer of management rights from Korean companies to foreign firms was unthinkable. Now domestic firms are hurriedly selling their assets to introduce foreign capital as a way to help restore corporate health. During the first four months of 1999, foreign investment in Korea amounted to US$2.8 billion, representing a 147.4 per cent increase from the same period a year before. Such a result places Korea as primary target for investment in Asia by overseas investors, outplaying such competitors as Singapore, Malaysia, and Indonesia. In 1998, foreign investment hit a record of US$8.85 billion, largely through mergers and acquisitions among domestic companies. Among Asian rivals, Korea is the only country that saw such an increase in foreign direct investment. The USA was the largest investor with US$2.97 billion or 33.6 per cent of the total, followed by the European Union with US$2.89 billion or 32.6 per cent. With the strengthening of the Korean won and the mounting expectation of economic recovery, imports of consumer goods increased 66.3 per cent in January 1999 compared to the same month in 1998. Especially among luxury goods, golf equipment increased by an incredible 212.2 per cent, jewellery by 105.7 per cent and cars by 111.1 per cent.

There has also been a recent growth in the popularity of comparatively new distribution channels in Korea which is reflected in consumers' preferences for cheaper products and substances over those with an excessively overstated appearance. This is why sales at discount stores and home shopping have shown a continuous upswing. For example, total sales through TV home shopping are averaging more than 500 per cent growth annually, amounting to 35.2 billion won (US$29.3 million) in 1996, 157.4 billion won (US$131.2 million) in 1997, and 700 billion won (US$583.3 million) in 1998. As for large discount stores, sales jumped 54.8 per cent to nearly 5 trillion won (US$4.17 billion) in 1999.

The domestic market for refrigeration equipment is also likely to grow due to increased demand for processed food. Korean consumers are showing a preference for all refrigerators with energy-saving features. Rotary compressors, room air conditioners, and heat pumps present additional opportunities for foreign exporters. The Korean market for modern food-processing and packaging equipment is relatively new. But increased local demand for processed food suggests favourable prospects. Significant investments in labour-saving machinery have recently been made to increase food-processing capacity. Korean firms that specialize in food processing are enhancing their production technologies by affiliating with foreign firms through licensing agreements or joint ventures. The most significant imports include cooling and heating machinery, confectionery machinery, line equipment for food containers, and automatic wrapping machines.

Korea is also one of the fastest-growing telecommunications markets in the world. The government has recently lifted barriers to imports of equipment to be attached to the public telecommunications network. The government is now in the process of replacing existing mechanical analogue telephones switching systems and semi-electronic switching systems with fully digital, time-division switching systems. Government plans also call for improving telegraph services, data communication, and other new types of communication services. Demand for laboratory instruments in Korea is likely to be high for several years due to the planned expansion of many research laboratories and hospitals. Private research facilities are also being established by companies that wish to develop and produce their own products locally. All of these facilities require advanced instruments and equipment, much of which can be obtained only from other countries.

Opportunities exist for foreign exporters of sterilizers, laser instruments, and various testing apparatus. Moreover, increased air traffic has placed a strain on South Korea's airports. To relieve congestion and increase air services, many facilities are undergoing expansion and new ones are being constructed. New airport construction projects will provide multi-million dollar sales opportunities for advanced foreign-made ground-support equipment.

Motivated by increasing domestic demand, Korean firms have begun to manufacture high-tech medical equipment. But most firms are able to do so only through technical licensing agreements with foreign firms. Few of the items produced in Korea are considered equal in quality to foreign products. Thus Korea is likely to continue relying on foreign suppliers to meet its medical equipment needs for many years to come. Cardiological equipment, surgical and orthopaedic instruments, respiratory equipment, and diagnostic apparatus are among the primary imports. Foreign investment in Korea's cosmetics industry has been open to foreign wholesalers since July 1991 and has been open to foreign retailers since 1994. Beginning in 1996, the Ministry of Trade and Industry fully opened the retail distribution market to foreigners without any limit on the number or size of outlets. None the less, restrictions on the ownership of land by foreigners and the difficulty and expense of finding appropriate sites may still pose major obstacles for foreign retailers.

Korea's most promising sectors include electrical power systems, aircraft and parts, and security and safety equipment. Non-Korean firms should not overlook the growth potential of the services franchise industry. Accounting, real estate, health, leisure, travel, child-care centres, and janitorial services are among those professional services that are ready for rapid growth. Vocational/educational schools will also do well, as high unemployment has forced many new college graduates to return to school in order to pursue more advanced educational degrees. The automotive and electronics sectors are also ripe for acquisition and consolidation. Many Korean companies burdened by large debt or dollar-denominated obligations, are often those that invested heavily in new production facilities and cannot carry the debt at current interest rates of 20 to 30 per cent. They are now facing bankruptcy unless they downsize.

A further area of opportunity in Korea lies in private equity investments in small to medium-sized Korean companies, with sales of up to at least $500 million. Before the IMF crisis these private equity opportunities were mainly mezzanine equity infusions into companies with up to $100 million in sales. But now the larger companies are seeking private deals. Financial institutions are also an attractive investment as is real estate in any form except plant sites or own-use office buildings which are to be avoided because of regulatory barriers.

Many foreign products are widely known in the Korean market. Foreign firms offering competitive pricing and quality service can take advantage of lucrative prospects, ranging from automotive parts and communications products to videos and cosmetics. Demand is particularly strong for advanced machinery and electronics equipment. Computer hardware, storage units, and input-output devices provide additional opportunities for foreign exporters. Although Korea is capable of developing its own applications software, much of the systems software is imported. A foreign supplier's willingness to modify software slightly to meet the specific needs of Korean consumers will greatly enhance sales prospects. Furthermore, Koreans have had greater exposure to foreign cultures than ever before. As such, consumers, especially the younger generation, are moving in favour of high-quality, Western goods. For example, the total turnover of the eight largest fast-food companies, including Kentucky Fried Chicken and Pizza Hut in 1996, increased by 63 per cent compared to the previous year, and the sales of big department stores have recorded a growth rate of 20 per cent, while general retail stores have shown an increase of only 10 per cent.

By the fourth quarter of 1998 the spending level had climbed to more than 80 per cent of the amount prior to the foreign currency crisis. In particular, the average monthly consumption of education, culture, and entertainment during the period for a wage-earning household totalled 62,800 won (US$52.33). As for eating out, the figure more or less returned to the 1997 level of 140,100 won (US$116,75), while purchases of clothing and footwear jumped to 82,500 won (US$68.75). Korea's location is ideal for foreign businessmen seeking market opportunities in the Asia Pacific region. It has a well-educated and trained labour force as well as a substantial market of 45 million people. Its industries have already reached international standards. The infrastructure is also con-tinuously expanding. The country is now gradually opening up the economy to foreign investors through liberalization and deregulation, especially in the areas of construction, telecommunications, distribution, and finance. Furthermore, in Korea today, the macro-economic uncertainty caused by the economic crisis is gradually disappearing. Since 1998 FDI has improved rapidly. Foreign investment in June 1999 reached US$662 mil-lion, up 24.9 per cent from the same month in 1998. For the first half of 1998, the total amount of foreign investment reached US$2.46 billion, induced by the depreciation of the won.

Sources

Asia Pacific Economic Cooperation, http://www.apecsec.org.sg/member/idoecreport.html

Brook, T., and Luong, H. (eds.), *Culture and Economy: The Shaping of Capitalism in Eastern Asia*, Ann Arbor: The University of Michigan Press, 125–36.

Chong-Tae, K., 'Korea Swings Door Wide Open', *Business Korea*, 16(6), June 1999: 26–8.

Cragg, C., *Hunting with the Tigers: How to Achieve Commercial Success in the Asian Pacific Rim*, Mercury Books, Gold Arrow Publications Ltd., London: 1992.

Goodman, D. P., 'Opportunity from Chaos', *World Trade*, 12(3), Mar. 1999: 96.

Hinkelman, E. G. (ed.), *Korea Business: The Portable Encyclopedia for Doing Business with Korea*, California: World Trade Press, 1995.

James, D., 'Adversity and Opportunity', *Upside* (10)6, June 1998: 60–2.

Ji-Young, S., 'Consumption is Recovering, But is Not the Same', *Business Korea*, 16(5), May 1999: 16–18.

Lall, R., 'Market Surge Signals Recovery', *Far Eastern Economic Review*, 162(24), 17 June 1999: 53–4.

Mason, Edward S., *The Economic and Social Modernization of the Republic of Korea*, Cambridge: Harvard University Press, 1980.

Slater, J., and Strange, R. (eds.), *Business Relationships with East Asia: The European Experience*, Boston: Routledge Advances in Asia Pacific Business, 1997.

Sowinski, L., 'Asia: Prospects for Japan, South Korea and Taiwan', *World Trade*, 12(6), June 1999: 28–32, Irvine.

Republic of Malaysia

Overview

Malaysia offers attractive fiscal incentives, good infrastructure, a trainable workforce, and stable political and legal systems. For MNCs, Malaysia constitutes an attractive market in its own right. In many ways, its relatively small, middle-income population provides a relatively easy market for Western MNCs. Standards of production are sufficiently below most Western ones for MNCs to find it relatively easy in many cases to have a competitive advantage over local producers.

The Country and its People

Malaysia is approximately one-sixth the size of Indonesia, covering 329,744 sq. km. but has only about one-tenth of the population, approximately 16 million inhabitants. It comprises peninsular or west Malaysia, which accounts for roughly 40 per cent of the country's land mass and the former states of Sabah and Sarawak which are situated on the island of Borneo east of the peninsula. Malaysia has one of the best road systems in South East Asia, with over 25,000 kilometres of roads connecting all major towns and ports within Malaysia and connecting Malaysia with Thailand to the north and Singapore to the south. Peninsular Malaysia has three main ports: Penang in the north-west, Kelang in the middle of the west coast, and Johore on the southern tip of the peninsula across from Singapore. They are all serviced by rail and roads.

Modern Malaysia came into existence after gaining political independence from British rule on 31 August 1957. It consists of eleven states in peninsular Malaysia and two states on the island of Borneo. Strictly speaking, Malaysia is a hereditary monarchy, but is composed of a federation of thirteen states, which are collectively ruled by the constitutionally elected King of Malaysia. Malaysia is divided into two distinct areas, peninsular Malaysia and eastern Malaysia. The capital, Kuala Lumpur, is on the western plain of the peninsula. The other main towns in Malaysia are Johor Baharu, Georgetown, Ipoh, Kota Kinabalu, Malacca, Miri, Sandakan, Shah Alam, and Alor-setar.

Malaysia is a constitutional monarchy, nominally headed by the Yang di-Pertuan Agon, customarily referred to as the King, who is elected for a five-year term from the nine sultans of the peninsular Malaysian states. The executive power is held by the cabinet, led by prime minister Datuk Seri Dr Mahatir bin Mohamad who has presided, since 1981, over Malaysia's transformation from a tin and rubber producer at the end of the second World War into a widely diversified economy. In 1981–82 world recession depressed the country's commodity exports and led to a serious increase in debt, from $4 billion in 1980 to $15 billion in 1984. In 1985 Malaysia plunged into a serious recession but was recovering by 1987.

Malaysia is a multicultural society. The Chinese and Indians migrated mainly during the colonial period to work in plantations and mines. In peninsular Malaysia, the Malays constitute about 59 per cent of the population, the Chinese 31 per cent, and Indians 10 per cent. The country's official religion is Islam and all Malays are Muslims. Islam, however, is not the state religion since the constitution guarantees freedom of religious belief for all Malaysians, whatever their ethnic group. Most of the Chinese are Buddhists, Confucians, or Taoists and a few are Christians. Most of the ethnic Indians are Hindu but some are Muslim, Christian, or Sikh. While Bahasa Malay is the national language, English is widely spoken in business. A number of Chinese dialects are also widely spoken including Cantonese, Hokkien, and Mandarin together with Punjabi and Tamil. New legislation is published in both Bahasa Malay and English.

The Business Environment

Malaysia is rich in natural resources and produces 26 per cent of the world output of natural rubber, and 61 per cent of the world output of palm oil. It is also a leading producer of tropical hardwoods, pepper, and cocoa, as well as a net exporter of crude petroleum and natural gas. Rice is the main subsistence crop. Other produce includes coal, coconuts, sugar cane, pineapples, tobacco, vegetables, sago, tapioca, coffee, tea, maize, and groundnuts. Malaysia is also a major producer of timber and timber products including hardwoods.

Under the Promotion of Investment Act 1986, tax incentives are offered by the government for those wishing to invest in the manufacturing, agriculture and tourism sectors. These include pioneer status, that is a tax holiday, ranging from five to ten years as well as an investment tax allowance, export incentives and grants for R & D and training. Since the 1968 Investment Incentive Act, Malaysia has very actively sought to attract foreign direct investment, especially manufacturing activities. Under the sixth Malaysia Plan (1991–95), the Malaysian Industrial Development Authority (MIDA) has been conducting investment briefings in Kuala Lumpur, organizing investment promotions and missions overseas, networking through international industrial cooperation, and placing advertisements in local and international journals, magazines, and newspapers. MIDA is also actively participating in international industrial exhibitions. MIDA also orchestrates industrial cooperation programmes with other countries, such as with the German agency for investment and development. The Malaysian government is now seeking technology transfer. International technical standards are taken seriously. The country also scores relatively high in its commitment to protecting intellectual property rights.

In June 1991, the government announced the New Development Policy (NDP) . The NDP forms the basis of Prime Minister Dr Mahatir's Vision 2020, named for the date by which he intends Malaysia to attain developed country status. Although the Malaysian government is very proactive in its industrial and economic policy, close cooperation between the government and the private sector is an important aspect of the NDP's economic policy agenda. It envisages that the private sector in the new era will play a more leading role. Thus, the government has one of the most comprehensive and broad-ranging privatization programmes in the region. More recently, the Malaysian government has redefined its strategic approach to its policies and reforms. Vision 2020 is the government's long-term goal, that is, to become a fully developed nation in every sense of the word by the year 2020, economically, politically, socially, psychologically, and culturally. The main thrusts of Vision 2020 are:

- to develop a strong science and technology base;
- to develop indigenous technology by increasing the nation's capability to adopt, adapt, and improve technology through R & D;
- to develop a pool of skilled manpower capable of handling emerging technologies;
- to ensure environmental protection and conservation;
- to develop a positive culture based on integrity, discipline, and diligence.

The Malaysian government welcomes foreign investment offering equity participation to investors and is willing to let expatriates fill key positions. At the same time, it continues to privatize state-run industries and is committed to increasing the proportion of business ownership in the hands of the *bumiputras*. A clear challenge is that foreign-owned firms are subject to *bumiputra* policies that tend to favour firms that hire individuals of Malay origin.

Malaysia's Response to the Regional Financial Crisis

The first signs of the crisis for Malaysia emerged in mid-May 1997 when the ringgit came under pressure, triggered by developments in Thailand. In the second half of 1997, the global strengthening of the US dollar and pound sterling and the escalation of the regional financial crisis set the stage for the depreciation of the ringgit to unprecedented levels. The depreciation was concentrated in the last four months of 1997 when adverse market reaction to a series of events pushed the ringgit to a year-end close of US$1 = RM 4.88 on 7 January 1998. In January, the ringgit closed at US$1 = RM 4.5674 and subsequently fell to the 3.8 to 3.9 range for the balance of the first half of 1998. The government then fixed its value at US$1 = RM 3.8, effective from 2 September 1998. At the same time, trading in Malaysian shares and currency outside Malaysia was halted and selective capital controls were put in place. The impact of the financial crisis in the region began to have a significant effect on the level of domestic economic activity in 1998. The government introduced adjustment measures that it deemed appropriate to maintain financial stability and business confidence as well as to minimize the impact of the crisis on the economy and support an early recovery and sustainable growth over the medium term.

Malaysia's Response to the Regional Financial Crisis

The government of Malaysia flatly refused to seek the assistance of the IMF during the crisis. Instead, the government has undertaken its own adjustment policies and implemented financial reforms to reduce the risks and vulnerabilities to external developments. These are listed on the APEC home page as follows:

- Monetary policy has been adjusted as necessary to reflect developments.

- In the initial period there was a pronounced tightening of monetary policy to respond to rising inflationary pressures following the depreciation of ringgit.

- The monetary policy response was subsequently directed to restoring stability and to overcoming the disruptions to economic activity caused by uncertainties in the foreign exchange and stock markets.

- Monetary policy has also focused on addressing the tight liquidity situation and inefficiencies in the financial intermediation process that has emerged in the banking system.

- The government remains committed to maintaining fiscal discipline while strengthening the social safety nets to protect lower-income groups, and implementing counter-cyclical measures, including fiscal stimulus, to support economic recovery and to contain the contractionary impact of the financial crisis, due to the limited capacity of the private sector. In the 1999 budget, the government changed its fiscal stance from a surplus to a deficit budget, with an overall deficit of 3.7 per cent of gross national product (GNP) compared with the surpluses registered for the past five consecutive years since 1993.

- The government remains committed to the liberalization of investment restrictions in order to deepen competition and to accelerate the revival of capital flow. The policy will aim to:

  - introduce more competition in key domestic trading activities particularly for products subject to price controls; and

  - reduce investment restrictions (domestic and foreign) in the financial sector as well as in other key sectors.

- The exchange rate for the ringgit has been quoted at RM 3.80 against the US dollar for foreign currency transactions effective from 2 September 1998. Measures adopted during this period were aimed at:

  - limiting the contagion effects of external developments on the Malaysian economy;

  - preserving the recent gains made in terms of policy measures to stabilize the domestic economy;

  - ensuring stability in domestic prices and the ringgit exchange rate and creating an environment that is conducive to a revival in investor and consumer confidence and facilitating economic recovery;

  - promoting good corporate governance;

  - enhanced disclosure of corporate information;

  - closer scrutiny for corporate governance;

  - enhanced standards of corporate governance to boost investor confidence.

Business Opportunities Post-crisis

Until the early 1960s Malaysia's economy was primarily based on the production and export of primary commodities. Although Malaysia remains the world's largest supplier of natural rubber, palm oil, tin and tropical hardwoods, since the 1970s the manufacturing sector has become increasingly important. This economic restructuring is the basis of the New Development Plan which is designed to span over three decades from 1990 to 2020. Under Malaysia's policy of Vision 2020, the objective is that Malaysia will be a fully developed country by the year 2020. The NDP aims to eradicate poverty and to attain a more equitable distribution of wealth.

Malaysia is now the world's leading exporter of integrated circuits and the third largest exporter of air conditioners. The industries most highly encouraged in Malaysia are the high-technology, capital-intensive industries, which do not require much labour. Among the favoured and priority products are steel, machinery, electronics, office equipment, and medical equipment. Although substantial progress has been made in achieving the manufacturing objectives of the NDP, agriculture remains an important factor in the Malaysian economy. The electronics sector dominates manufacturing employment with some 100,000 workers and 200 companies. Of these nearly one-half are US or other foreign companies. Malaysia is also the world's third largest importer of transistors, tubes, and valves after the USA and Germany.

One of the main issues facing the Malaysian government is how to improve the economic power of the Malay majority while maintaining racial harmony with the economically dominant Chinese minority. A policy favouring *bumiputra* (Malay) owned enterprises has been in place for many years. Freedom from exchange controls and a liberalized economy have brought a flood of foreign investment into Malaysia, along with its thirteen free zones. Ten FIZs offer investors duty-free importation of raw materials, parts, and machinery and feature minimal customer control and formalities. One FCZ (Free Commercial Zone) is designed for establishments engaged in training, breaking bulk, grading, repackaging, relabelling, and transit. The other two free zones are for trading in export products. The government has instituted a large number of attractive incentives for foreign manufacturers and high-tech workers. Most industries in Malaysia are open to foreign investment subject to obtaining the required approvals from the Ministry of International Trade and Industry.

The adjustment measures introduced in December 1997 and in March and July 1998, coupled with emerging signs of restoration of regional financial stability, have had a positive effect in restoring investor confidence. However, a number of risks remain. They include the possibility of sharper-than-expected moderation in world output and trade, a more prolonged regional crisis and increased uncertainty in the performance of capital flows, more intense competition, slower growth in regional trade, and an uncertain outlook for exports of electronic and electrical goods. Malaysia's young, educated, and highly productive workforce remains one of the country's key attributes.

Sources

Cragg, C., *Hunting with the Tigers: How to Achieve Commercial Success in the Asian Pacific Rim*, London: Mercury Books, Gold Arrow Publications Ltd., 1992.

Davidson, Paul J., and Ciambella, Franca, *Investment in Southeast Asia: Policy and Laws*, Singapore: Butterworth-Heinemann, Asia, 1997.

Gough, L., *Asia Meltdown: The End of the Miracle*, Oxford: Capstone Publishing, 1998.

Lemaire, D., 'Malaysia: Vision 2020', *Canadian Business Review*, 23(2), summer, 1996: 44–7.

Low, L., and Toh, M. H., 'Regional Outlook: South Asia 1994–95', ASEAN Institute of Southeast Asian Studies, 1994: 35–54.

Singapore

Overview

On 3 June 1959 when Singapore attained self-government after nearly 140 years of British colonial rule, it had a population of 1.58 million that was growing at the rate of 4 per cent annually, an economy based on entrepôt trade and an unemployment rate of 5 per cent. Housing was a serious problem, with half of the population living in squatter huts and only 9 per cent in public housing. Today, Singapore is so transformed that it has received the status of an advanced developing country. It has had phenomenal economic growth since becoming an independent republic in 1965, transformed from a poor sea port into the cleanest, safest, and most prosperous city-state in the world.

The Country and its People

The republic of Singapore consists of a main island and fifty-four smaller islands at the southern tip of the Malay peninsula. It has a total land area of approximately 622 sq. km. and a population of approximately 3 million. Singapore is situated at the southern tip of the Malay peninsula to which it is connected by a causeway carrying a road and railway. The city of Singapore, which is the commercial and financial centre, is located in the southern part of the island. Singapore has virtually no natural resources, other than its deep-water harbour and its strategic geographic location. Singapore's port acts both as the trading and distribution hub for the economies of South East Asia, as well as the major trans-shipment point linking the region to the rest of the world. In addition to trade, it also acts as a financial centre for the region as a whole. Singapore was originally established as an entrepôt trade centre and this trade is still important although its nature has changed from an activity dominated primarily by commodities such as rubber and foodstuffs, to one where capital goods such as machinery and equipment are becoming more important.

Founded in 1819 by Stamford Raffles, Singapore rapidly became an important trading centre in the region. From 1963 to 1965 the country was part of Malaysia, but was expelled from the federation when it refused to implement Malaysian laws intended to favour ethnic Malays or ethnic Chinese in business. Singapore is a melting-pot for fifteen ethnic groups. Of its estimated population of 2.9 million, about 78 per cent are Chinese, 14 per cent Malays and 7 per cent are Indians. There are four official languages, Mandarin Chinese, Malay, Tamil, and English. However, the Chinese speak many dialects. English is the language of the government. Unlike Indonesia, the government in Singapore has been successful in maintaining racial harmony and is keen to protect traditional Eastern values against the influence of individualistic Western philosophy. It promotes core values of Confucian morality, family loyalty, placing society before self, frugality, and regard for education, and has put a great deal of emphasis on creating a uniquely Singaporean culture. At the same time, each of the main racial groups has retained a specific identity, with its own traditions and languages carried over from the homelands of the original arrivals. The Malays are the only ones who can claim to have always called Singapore home, being the indigenous people of the island.

The Business Environment

Singapore has a planned economy in which the government closely monitors developments and constantly revises and updates its economic policies to adapt to changing world conditions. Basic policies include the encouragement of private enterprise; co-operation among government, business, and labour; modernization of the infrastructure; expansion and upgrading of education, particularly technical and engineering; and incentives for investment.

The Swiss-based International Institute for Management Development (IMD) ranked Singapore as the second most competitive economy, two years in a row, after the USA in their *World Competitiveness Report* with a highly effective government ranked first, sound financial structure third, and good performance in management fourth. The World Economic Forum that prepares the *Global Competitiveness Report* ranked Singapore as the most competitive economy in the world, up from second place the previous year, with strengths in finance, trading, and as a multinational hub. The US-based Business Environment Risk Intelligence Inc. (BERI) in 1996 similarly granted Singapore top ranking on its government proficiency measure. The government dominates all external links in Singapore by providing infrastructure (such as utilities, telephone and post, port and airports, industrial estates, television, sanitation, all education, three-quarters of the housing, and medical services); engaging in production (through government-linked companies or GLCs, state airlines, state shipping lines, shipyards, banking and many joint ventures); holding an estimated 75 per cent of Singaporean land with mandates to acquire the rest if necessary; directing the capital markets (via the Central Provident Fund's or CPF's compulsory savings, and the POS banks; the development bank of Singapore's and the monetary authority of Singapore's holdings). It offers various incentives to guide private investment and shapes labour markets through extensive regulation of work conditions and labour, in addition to enforcing a housing policy (through the Housing Development Board's or HDB's extensive social, economic, and political role). It requires compulsory national service in the Singapore Armed Forces for all male citizens; emphasizes education (which it often portrays as social engineering); improvement of health; seems to affect the position of women (through family policies); increase of savings and pensions (through the CPF); foreign workplace and labour laws (via regulation and co-opted unions); supports community centres; but the government also constrains political and social campaigns and controls the press.

Government and Business Relations

Singapore Incorporated began in the 1960s when a United Nations Survey Mission, led by Dr Albert Winsemium, recommended an industrialization programme. Singapore's Economic Planning Unit used Dr Winsemium's unpublished document to prepare the first State Development Plan. Singapore's need for funds from the World Bank, and a demonstration of rationality and legitimacy from this newly independent state, prompted the plan. The first State Development Plan covered the years from 1960–64. The plan provided the blueprint for industrialization and also paved the way for the government's central and dominant roles as agenda-setter and agenda-achiever. The government, furthermore, favoured cooperation with the labour unions and forged strong alliances with them. In 1972 Singapore Inc. moved into wage settlements: it established a tripartite National Wages Council to ensure that wages and labour's shares grew to maintain Singapore's competitive edge. In 1979 the government adopted a corrective high-wage policy to orchestrate belated economic restructuring. Labour costs rose by as much has 10.1 per cent between 1979 and 1984 compared to productivity growth of 4.4 per cent. The Skills Development Fund levy and other fiscal incentives encouraged automation, mechanization, and robotics to emphasize efficient labour utilization and productivity. In 1982, the introduction of levies for foreign workers dampened the demand for unskilled foreign labour, relieving some of the economy's heavy dependence on labour sources.

Singapore Government and FDI

Foreign direct investment came to Singapore in electronics, computer peripherals, aerospace and biotechnology. Singapore Inc. responded with a ten-year indicative economic plan for the 1980s. This indicative plan aimed to develop Singapore into a modern industrial economy based on science, technology, skill, and knowledge. The 1980s left industrial restructuring in its wake. Singapore Inc.'s competitive advantages since then have shifted from labour intensive to service oriented. Unlike other countries, Singapore actively encourages its companies to invest abroad. In 1991, government-led regionalization started with a pilot project: labour-intensive, lower-skilled, and technology-intensive industries moved from Singapore to the Riau Island in Indonesia and to Johore in Malaysia. By 1993 this area had evolved into the Indonesia–Malaysia–Singapore growth triangle, an area of focused investment, expanded in 1995 to include West Sumatra, Malacca, Negri Sembilan, and Pahang.

Singapore's Response to the Regional Financial Crisis

Singapore measures to address the regional financial crisis were listed on the APEC home page as follows:

- After the financial crisis, the trade-weighted exchange rate was allowed to fluctuate within a wide range.
- The benchmark 11 month inter-bank rate rose significantly from 3.86 per cent in July 1997 to 10.05 per cent in January 1998, but has since fallen to about 5 per cent.

Fiscal policies were predicated on the following principles:

- maintain a healthy balanced budget in the long term, while supporting growth in the near term with modest deficits;
- maintain an internationally competitive tax structure;
- promote healthy investments and growth through elective use of tax incentives;
- maintain strict control on government spending;
- after the crisis, investment has tended to be cautious due to tighter liquidity and higher interest rates; overseas investment has been transferred to strategic fields and regions with sound financial systems.

Stress has been placed on prudential and transparent guidelines. After the crisis, banks have put much emphasis on information disclosure and Singapore's standard of banking disclosure is under consideration.

Business Opportunities Post-crisis

Singapore's corporatism differs significantly from states like Japan, the USA, or Germany. Drawing on Confucian beliefs of governmental paternalism and omnipresence, the government also sees itself as the only decision-maker in the business environment.

For a small city-state like Singapore, market protection does not make much economic sense. Protective tariffs have been few. The ability to import machinery and intermediate inputs at world prices has been an important factor in export competitiveness. Generally the Singapore government encourages foreign investment, particularly if such investment involves high technology and is export-oriented. There are no restrictions on the amount of capital investment in Singapore nor on the repatriation of capital or remittance of profits. There are also no percentage restrictions placed on the foreign ownership of enterprises operating in Singapore. However, there are certain restrictions on foreign investment in certain sectors. Sectors closed to foreign investment include the manufacture of arms and ammunition, the supply of public utilities such as electricity, gas, and water and the supply of telecommunications service. Licences are required from the monetary authority of Singapore to engage in banking, financing, and insurance businesses. In addition there are restrictions on equity participation in locally incorporated banks by non-Singapore citizens. As far as property ownership is concerned, due to housing shortages in Singapore in the past, government approval is required for foreign ownership of certain residential property or commercial real estate.

Singapore has import duties on only a small number of items. Notable among these are duties of 45 per cent on automobile imports, designed to alleviate traffic problems on the crowded island. In addition, there are substantial import duties on tobacco products, alcoholic beverages and petroleum products, and minor tariffs on a few items including furniture and garments. Franchising is a very popular and explosive concept in Singapore, particularly in areas such as food, health, recreation services. American fast-food restaurants such as McDonalds, Burger King, Kentucky Fried Chicken, and others have established more than 200 outlets on the tiny island. The government's efforts to foster entrepreneurial endeavours and to increase per capita output, combined with Singapore's high per capita income, have provided a well-spring of franchise opportunities such as the recent success of the California keep-fit franchises (illustrated in Chapter 11).

Sources

Chia, Siow-Yue, C., 'The Economic Development of Singapore: A Selective Review of the Literature', in Basant K. Kapur (ed.), *Singapore Studies: Critical Surveys of the Humanities and Social Sciences*, Singapore: Singapore University Press, 1986.

Cragg, C., *Hunting with the Tigers: How to Achieve Commercial Success in the Asian Pacific Rim*, London: Mercury Books, Gold Arrow Publications Ltd., 1992.

Haley, U. C. V., and Low, L., 'Crafted Culture: Governmental Sculpting of Modern Singapore and Effects on Business Environments', *Journal of Organizational Change Management*, (11)6, 1998: 530–3.

—— —— and Toh, Mun-Heng, 'Singapore Incorporated: Reinterpreting Singapore's Business Environment through a Corporate Metaphor', *Management Decision*, (34)9, 1996: 17–28.

Murray, G., and Perera, A., *Singapore: The Global City-State*, New York: St Martin's Press, 1996.

Quah, S. R., and Quah, J. S. T., *Friends in Blue: The Police and the Public in Singapore*, Singapore: Oxford University Press, 1987.

Taiwan

Overview

Taiwan is an economic powerhouse with the world's third largest foreign exchange reserves and over $235 billion in two-way trade. The economy is expanding at a rate of 6 per cent per annum, with full employment and low inflation, while other economies in the region are shrinking. Taiwan is poor in resources. The island imports nearly all of its energy needs, most of the raw materials needed to maintain industrial production, and a diversity of manufactured and agricultural goods. Today, Taiwan is opening up several areas of its economy that were previously closed to foreign investors. According to the US Department of Commerce, over 90 per cent of Taiwan's demand is supplied by imports.

The Country and its People

Taiwan is situated in the Pacific Ocean approximately 160 km. off the south-east coast of the Chinese mainland. It is about mid-way between Korea and Japan to the north and Hong Kong and the Philippines to the south. Taiwan includes Taiwan Island, a number of surrounding islands, as well as the archipelago in the South China Sea. Taiwan has a land area of 36,000 sq. km., which is mostly mountainous, and only about 25 per cent of the land is cultivated. Taiwan has an estimated population of 21 million and an average density of 581.8 person per sq. km., which is one of the highest in the world. The original inhabitants of Taiwan were tribes of Malayan origin. Over 2.6 million people live in Taipei, the capital and business centre. Koahsuing in the south has a population of 1.4 million, is a major industrial centre, and the primary port of Taiwan. Taichung in the centre of the island is the seat of the provincial government, and has a population of over 1 million. Eighty-five per cent of Taiwan's population are descendants of mainland Chinese, and the main ethnic group is Han Chinese. Mandarin is the official language. Japanese is also spoken in the south as a result of Japanese occupation from 1895 to 1945. English is spoken by most people in government, business, and tourism. The majority of people in Taiwan are Buddhist Taoist. Confucian influence is also strong. Less then 5 per cent of the population is Christian.

Taiwan was returned to China after the surrender of the Japanese in 1945. At that time, it had been a Japanese colony for fifty years. Taiwan declared itself an independent country in 1949 following the victory of the communist army in the civil war, and the establishment of the People's Republic of China. Taiwan's relationship with the People's Republic of China has been problematic since then. Both parties have long asserted that there is only one China. The Taiwan authorities seek recognition as one of what they claim are two legitimate political entities, each governing part of China, while the PRC regards itself as the sole legal government of all of China, and Taiwan as a renegade province.

The Business Environment

The Taiwanese economy has gone through three distinct phases of development. In the 1950s, agricultural growth and import-substituting industries were encouraged. In the 1960s, export-oriented industries involving mainly low-technology light industry and the assembly of imported raw materials and parts for consumer goods and machinery were promoted. In the third phase of development, industries became more capital intensive with the main emphasis on high-technology areas. Taiwan is aiming at further developing its technology-based industries. Taiwan today is the world's third largest supplier of computer hardware, and is placing greater emphasis on software development. The manufacturing sector is dominated by the production of machinery, telecommunications equipment, petrochemicals and plastics, electronics and personal computers, including notebook computers and accessories (keyboards, scanners, computer mouse sets, PCB, motherboards, UPS, CD-ROM, and monitors).

Direct foreign investment in Taiwan is encouraged by the government for projects which are considered strategic or vital to economic development. Emphasis is placed on export oriented, heavy industry, and high technology. Investment incentives usually take the form of tax concessions, which are available to foreign and local investors without discrimination. Most foreign companies will find it advantageous to have Foreign Investment Approval (FIA), although such approval is not required in order to operate or invest in a business in Taiwan. The incentives accorded to government-approved projects include a five-year tax holiday, accelerated depreciation of equipment used for research and development, subsidies to offset loan interest, provision of government land and exemption from import duties. FIA has some important benefits:

- The firm may obtain foreign exchange for repatriation of invested capital, net profits, or interest earned from equity and loan investments.

- The firm is exempt from the requirement that stock be offered to the public or employees, provided that the investor owns at least 45 per cent of the company.

- The firm is exempt from nationalization or expropriation within twenty years of the start of business operations, provided that the investor owns at least 45 per cent of the company.

- The income tax payable by foreign investors who derive dividends from such firms is withheld at a rate of 20 per cent.

- The firm receives a waiver of the normal domicile, nationality, and capital stock requirements for shareholders and officers.

- The firm receives treatment and protection equal to that extended to domestic firms.

Limitations are generally not applied on the percentage of foreign equity, except in the case of some government-owned projects. The only prohibited foreign investment is in government monopolies (including most agricultural sectors), public utilities, and specified strategic industries, and is restricted in service industries including the financial sector.

Business Opportunities in Taiwan

With Taiwan's application to join the World Trade Organization, barriers to trade will come down further and Taiwan is expected to become a large export market for goods and services. Taiwan needs a wide range of agricultural and industrial raw materials, intermediate components, and specialty items to feed its active industry. Both the upgrading of that industry and Taiwan's large public and private sector development projects require materials, capital goods, and services. Taiwan has relied on Japan for many goods, but the strength of the yen has made Japanese products less competitive, opening up opportunities for new suppliers. Taiwan is in the process of opening up additional areas of its economy that had previously been off-limits to foreigners, including its growing service and financial sectors. It particularly encourages foreign participation in its emerging high-technology industries and the development of key technologies and targeted product groups, offering tax breaks, exemptions, and incentives. A multitude of brand-name items produced abroad, including automobiles, household goods, cosmetics, and processed foods, are widely known in the Taiwan market. In addition, demand for such capital-intensive and high-technology goods and services as pollution control equipment, computers and peripherals, scientific instruments, and advanced electronic components is particularly strong. Two of the most important considerations for foreign exporters to Taiwan are price competitiveness and solid customer service.

Taiwan's current six-year development plan places great emphasis on environmental protection, and this emphasis has stimulated rapid growth in the market for pollution control equipment and services. Between 1992 and 1997, 68 public environmental protection projects budgeted at US$37 billion were initiated. Water quality protection, waste-water control, air pollution control, monitoring systems, toxic and solid waste management, and noise-control devices and materials have been highlighted. The growing demand for technologically advanced products means that foreign firms should continue to dominate Taiwan's market for pollution control equipment. Rapid computerization of the private and public sectors in Taiwan has also created a strong demand for sophisticated computers and peripherals. Twenty-nine national computerization projects are now being planned by various public agencies, and additional projects are envisaged under the ten-year 1991–2001 information industry Sector Development Project.

In Taiwan, there is at present a sharp increase in demand for sophisticated scientific laboratory instruments. Virtually all must be imported. Some of the most promising products are analytical instruments, electronic laboratory instruments, medical instruments, optical instruments, clinical treatment equipment, metal-testing equipment, and measuring instruments. US firms currently maintain the largest share of the market, followed by Japanese, German, and UK firms. Major efforts to introduce new and upgraded products and services suggest that demand in Taiwan for telecommunications services and equipment will grow rapidly throughout the 1990s and beyond. As the dominant public monopoly, the Directorate General of Telecommunications (DGT) is the principal buyer of key technology-based products. DGT purchases, mainly from foreign firms, are estimated to account for approximately 80 per cent of the telecommunications products sold to Taiwan. These purchases include network switching systems, local distribution electronics, and long-haul transmissions. The private sector is the largest user of private branch exchange systems, facsimile machines, and mobile phones. As the telecommunications market gradually opens to direct sales, foreign exporters can expect many more opportunities in this industry.

Taiwan is also one of the best markets for foreign automobile manufacturers in the world. Future prospects for automobiles, parts, and accessories should remain positive, as proposed tariff reduction programmes are implemented. Small-engine sedans, sports and utility vehicles, light commercial vehicles, and trucks are currently the best-selling motor vehicles. The steady increase in the number of automobiles in Taiwan is bolstering demand for foreign parts and service equipment. Such equipment includes radial tyres, diesel engines, fuel nozzles, and compression engine parts, as well as computer diagnostics, body-repair equipment, and mechanical tools and equipment. Strong market position in the auto accessories market also exists, accounting for about 80 per cent of domestic sales. As the automotive market continues to expand, demand for high quality imported automotive accessories, including high quality car waxes, floor mats, waxing sponges, wipe cloths, and cup holders, will increase. Imports of such items as garbage disposals, filters, microwave ovens, and washers and dryers are expected to continue to expand.

Changing consumer preferences and rising living standards are expanding the market for imported cosmetics and toiletries. Given a strong preference for foreign products, such international brands as Lancôme, Elizabeth Arden, and Clinique currently enjoy lucrative sales of high-end products, including facial creams, foundation, lipstick, eye make-up, face cleansers, nail polish, and perfumed soaps. Steady growth is also projected for perfumes, shampoos, and powders. A relatively new phenomenon in Taiwan is the specialty chain store. US-based chains such as Pearl Vision Center and Toys R US have set up outlets in Taiwan, as have firms from other foreign countries such as Aoyama Suits and

Joshin of Japan. These chain stores, with product specialization, are gaining market share rapidly. In addition to department stores and specialty chain stores, hypermarkets are proliferating in Taiwan. The largest hypermarket chain on the island is Carrefour. It is estimated that about forty new hypermarkets will open in the next three to five years. New supermarkets are also being opened. A variety of franchise arrangements also exists in Taiwan. In recent years, franchise operations have shifted from fast-food restaurants such as McDonalds, Kentucky Fried Chicken, Pizza Hut, and Burger King, to non-food store services such as Cosmed, Tower Records, JaniKing, and Midas. As the establishment of shopping malls takes off, greater opportunities for franchise operations will abound. Finally, the opening of the Type One Fixed Telecommunications Network Service market to private companies and the liberalization designed to break the current monopoly enjoyed by the state run Chunghwa Telecom Co. and promote free competition are expected to induce further massive growth in the telecom sector.

Resource-poor Taiwan will continue to rely on imports of raw materials necessary to sustain industrial production, and a wide range of manufactured and agricultural goods. Imports of industrial process controls, laboratory scientific instruments, computers and peripherals, and electronic components have all been targeted for expansion. Furthermore, Taiwan is the fifth largest importer of US agricultural products. Although economic growth in Taiwan in 1998 was measured at 4.83 per cent, the slowest rate of increase in sixteen years, the country still managed to stay ahead of the other Asian countries hit by the crisis. Economic figures are now pointing towards a modest recovery. For instance, the country's export orders for January and February 1999 rose by more than 2 per cent over the same period in 1998, while its industrial output was up 4.4 per cent during that period.

Sources

Country Profile—Taiwan Trade NZ, http://www.tradenz.govt.nz/

Hinkelman, E. G. (ed.), *Taiwan Business: The Portable Encyclopedia for Doing Business with Taiwan*, California: World Trade Press, Country Business Guide Series, 1995.

Sowinski, L., 'Asia: Prospects for Japan, South Korea and Taiwan', *World Trade*, 12(6), June 1999: 28–32, Irvine.

Taiwan Commercial Guide, 1999, www.state.gov

Taiwan—Country Profile, http://www.exportaust.com.au/

Thailand

Overview

While the crisis is still hurting Thailand, opportunities still abound for foreign investors and economic participants. Thailand is a global source for customers seeking cheap labour or material inputs. The country is rich in natural resources, and is also a major source of agricultural products. Thailand also has an abundant supply of low-skilled labour with high participation rates in the workforce. The Thai government, since the crisis, has cooperated closely with the IMF. Thai Prime Minister Chuan's recent negotiation with the IMF has resulted in great compromises on the part of the latter, providing for the release of more funds with fewer restrictions.

The Country and its People

Unlike other countries in Asia Pacific Thailand has never been colonized and is known as the 'land of the free'. Thailand lies in a central position in the South East Asian mainland. It has a land area of some 513,115 sq. km. It is located in the centre of the Indo-China peninsula in South East Asia with Myanmar to the west, Laos to the north, Kampuchea to the north-east, and Malaysia to the south. The country is divided into five distinct regions: the central plain along the Chao Phraya river with its fertile alluvial soils; the northern mountains with their heavy forests and mine deposits; the north-eastern sandstone plateau; the eastern seaboard; and the southern peninsula with coastal lowlands rising into a ridge of low forested mountains.

Thailand has a population of 57 million. The indigenous Thai people came from the mountainous areas of the Yunan province in China and gradually spread southward into the present-day Laos. The first Thai kingdom was established along the river Chao Phraya in AD 1238 and was called the Kingdom of Sukothai. Approximately 85 per cent of the population is comprised of ethnic Thais, 12 per cent are Chinese, and the remainder are of Malay, or Indian extraction, or are of the indigenous hill tribe minorities. The country has also provided a refuge for large numbers of people from neighbouring countries which have been beset by wars for the last fifteen years. The national language is Thai but Chinese and English are fairly widely spoken. English is the second language in the larger urban centres. The vast majority (95 per cent) of the population is Buddhist with a Muslim minority of 4 per cent concentrated in the four southern provinces. The remainder of the population belong to the Christian, Hindu, Sikh, or other faiths. Because of the emphasis in the Buddhist religion on tolerance, there is an almost complete absence of religion friction. The country has one of the oldest monarchies in the world.

The Business Environment

Thailand's economy is export-oriented with a free market philosophy. The economy has now changed from being primarily based upon agriculture, with some light industries, to one dominated by manufacturing and services. Wholesale and retail trade now accounts for about two-thirds of Thailand's GDP. Thailand is the world's largest exporter of rubber, canned pineapple, and fresh orchids and the fourth biggest exporter of cane sugar. A large-scale food-processing industry is now fast replacing the production of agricultural commodities like rice, cassava, sugar, cane, maize, and rubber. Agro-industry has been designated in Thailand's National Economic and Social Development Plan as the linkage between the traditional agricultural society and the expanding industrial base. Thailand is also a major producer of chickens. The CP Group (Charoen Pokphand) of Thailand is one of the world's largest chicken producers, and animal feed millers with extensive international operations.

The most important industrial sector in Thailand is computer parts and integrated circuits, followed by textiles, garments, and motor vehicle production. The food industry is also an important sector contributing 15 per cent of total industrial output. There is also a growing petrochemical industry based on gas from the Gulf of Thailand.

Despite a history of frequent changes in government, political violence, and military intervention, economic policies have always remained friendly to foreign business throughout all domestic difficulties. The government has liberalized the foreign exchange system and banks to allow private individuals to hold accounts in foreign currencies. Repatriation of investment capital is allowed and reporting requirements have been reduced. The government has consistently recognized the importance of the private sector and has played a supportive rather than an interventionist role. At the beginning of 1997 the number of tariff rates were reduced from thirty-nine to six with the following spread: 0 per cent on such goods as medical equipment and fertilizer; 1 per cent for raw materials, electronics components, and vehicles for international transport; 5 per cent for primary and capital goods; 10 per cent for intermediate goods; 20 per cent for finished products; and 30 per cent for goods needing 'special protection'. To promote foreign investment in the provincial areas, the government offers special rights, benefits, and supports to help reduce production costs. In general, rights and benefits will be granted to projects that are labour-intensive, export-oriented, and agro-based—transit sector as well as in telecommunications. Since the mid-1980s the government has been encouraging the private sector to take a leading role as it embarked on a programme of privatization. In addition, the Telephone Organization of Thailand has entered into joint ventures for mobile phones, fibre optics, communication networks, and pagers. The Thai government's eighth Five-Year Plan (1997–2001) places emphasis on the following areas:

- development of the private sector, industry, and the services sectors;
- further deregulation in trade, finance, and industry with tax revisions to encourage domestic competitiveness;
- national policies on environmental protection and pollution;
- increased government expenditure on infrastructure development and health care;
- land reform, improved education, and government decentralization.

Piracy, however, remains a serious problem in Thailand. The US pharmaceutical, film, and software industries estimate lost sales at over $200 million annually. Despite new and improved laws, judicial proceedings remain slow and the fines actually imposed are light.

Thailand Response to the Crisis

The crisis of confidence in Thailand's economy, which set the Asian crisis in motion, occurred against the background of financial sector exposure to an over-extended property market, a weakening equity market, a slowdown in export growth, and a deep current account deficit. The initial defence offered by the Bank of Thailand against this selling pressure (interest rate increases and direct intervention) actually pushed the baht to a thirteen-year high. However, with pressure on foreign exchange reserves continuing, on 2 July 2 1997 the central bank dropped the thirteen-year-old pegged rate system and adopted a floating exchange rate. Wide-ranging structural reforms were adopted to address these as part of the IMF-led US$17.2 billion support package. Thailand has generally been acknowledged to have made good progress in implementing these reforms and has seen the baht stabilize, inflation contained, and policy-determined interest rates return to pre-crisis levels.

To address the financial crisis, the Thai authorities have taken the following measures as listed on APEC's home page:

Monetary and Exchange Rate Policy

- Monetary policy has been kept tight in order to stabilize the exchange rate, as the first order of priority, and remains prepared, in view of continued unsettled international financial market conditions, to implement necessary monetary measures if there were to be renewed pressures on the exchange rate. The exchange regime continues to be a managed float.

- With the external value of the baht stabilizing, lower than anticipated inflation, and a deeper than anticipated real economic contraction, the Bank of Thailand has cautiously eased monetary policy, allowing greater scope for reserve money expansion and increasing the broad money (M2A) growth target for 1998 from 5 to 9 per cent.

Fiscal Policy

- In 1997, the government's fiscal position recorded a cash deficit for the first time since 1988. The overall public sector deficit target under the economic reform programme for 1997/98 has been raised from 2.0 per cent to 3.0 per cent of GDP, in light of the deepening of the real economic downturn.

- Concrete measures have been developed to strengthen the social safety net and to increase spending on well-targeted public works programmes: the 1997/98 budget has allocated funds equivalent to an additional 0.5 per cent of GDP for this purpose.

Economic Policy

- Foreign investors have been allowed to acquire major stakes in bank and finance companies.

- Privatizastion policy has promoted corporate reconstruction.

Business Opportunities Post-crisis

In line with its World Trade Organization Uruguay Round commitments, Thailand has opened its market to a wide range of products. Following the economic crisis, demand for Western products has decreased, particularly in the area of processed food products, beverages, and the wine market. However, in line with the upgrading of Thailand's telecommunications system, there is scope for the supply of telecommunications equipment and expertise. There is also a demand for customized business software packages. Thailand's shortage of trained managers and technicians creates a wide spectrum of specialized training opportunities varying from tourism management to nursing to airline pilot training.

Sources

Capsule Review Update: Asia, 30 Mar. 1999.

Cragg, C., *Hunting with the Tigers: How to Achieve Commercial Success in the Asian Pacific Rim*, London: Mercury Books, Gold Arrow Publications Ltd., 1992.

Gough, L., *Asia Meltdown: The End of the Miracle*, Oxford: Capstone Publishing, 1998.

http://www.apmforum.com/research/asia.html

Low, L., and Toh, M. H. 'Regional Outlook: South Asia 1994–95', ASEAN Institute of Southeast Asian Studies, 1994: 35–54.

The Philippines

Overview

Although the country has a history of frequent changes in government, political violence, and military intervention, economic policies have remained friendly to foreign business throughout all domestic difficulties. However, the Philippines government involvement in the economy and consequent corruption has been a major disincentive for MNCs. Political instability has also been a deterrent to foreign investors. Although the government has now successfully phased out direct involvement in business, it does remain a significant customer for many products and services that are related to national defence, peace and order, health, education, and public works.

The Country and its People

The Philippines has a land mass of approximately 300,439 sq. km. and a population of approximately 70 million. It is located at the centre of South East Asia off the south-east coast of the Asiatic mainland and is an archipelago comprising over 7,000 islands and islets which stretch over 1,600 km. northward from the north-east corner of Borneo in the south to Taiwan in the north. There are three main groups of islands: Luzon, Mindanao, and Visayas which together cover roughly 66 per cent of the territory. Another 26 per cent is accounted for by the nine next largest islands, Samar, Negros, Palawan, Panay, Mindoro, Leyte, Cebu, Bohol, and Masbate. The capital, Manila, is located on Luzon. The Philippines has the world's largest coastline which is dented with numerous bays, harbours, and gulfs. There are sixty-one natural harbours, several landlocked straits, and hundreds of rivers, bays, and lakes. Manila is situated on the west coast of the island of Luzon and has one of the finest natural harbours in the world with a coastline of approximately 200 km. and an area of approximately 2,000 sq. km.

The people of the Philippines come basically from the same racial group as Malays, but there is very extensive ethnic mixing with Chinese, Indian, Spanish, and American influence prevalent throughout its peoples. These are divided according to language, religion, and ethnic groups. The Philippines lacks a common language and about eighty languages and dialects are spoken in the islands. However, Filipino, a Malay dialect, is the official language of the Republic. Both Spanish and English are widely used for government and commercial purposes. The country is predominantly Roman Catholic, making it the only country in the Asian Pacific Rim where a majority of the population is Christian. Protestant churches are quite common too in larger cities. Less than 15 per cent of the population is Buddhist and, in the southern regions of the country, especially Mindanao, there is a large number of Muslims.

The Business Environment

Prior to the Second World War economic activities centred around agriculture, primarily plantation crops and related industries. At the conclusion of the war massive imports to rebuild the war-torn country and to support industrial development led to enormous foreign debt with the result that trade and exchange restrictions were imposed. This, along with the government's import-substitution industrial policy, led to the growth of light and capital-intensive industries, such as fabrication, assembly, and packaging. During the 1950s manufacturing recorded a 10 to 12 per cent annual growth rate. Although the economic system is based primarily on private sector initiatives, government regulates business, and the state has taken over a number of enterprises. For example, the state has become involved in areas ranging from banking and finance to sugar trading, oil refining, steel making, transport, power generation, and hotel operation. This growing government participation has led to a certain amount of uncertainty among investors.

Manufacturing in the Philippines is dominated by electronics, garments, footwear, food manufacturing, petroleum and coal products, and basic metals products. The Philippines is also rich in land resources of gold, copper, and nickel. The Philippines is among the world's top ten gold producers. The country is also the largest copper producer in Asia and is among the top ten in the world. It has been successful in developing its light industries and has gained footholds in the major world markets; the manufacture and exports of semiconductors and electronics, garments and textiles, footwear, processed food and beverages, furniture and woodcraft products, metal products and machinery, ceramics, gifts and household goods, marine and agriculture, and computer services are increasing.

With a view to encouraging foreign investment, the Ramos administration broadened the Foreign Investment Act of 1991 by removing foreign equity restrictions in enterprises exporting at least 60 per cent of their total products. Under the changed regulation, 100 per cent foreign ownership in enterprises serving the domestic market is also allowed, except in areas identified in the negative list. The negative list is reviewed continuously and the areas of exemption are reduced. The government is also planning to remove the current minimum capital requirement for foreign investors and to open up retail trade. The Ramos government also initiated a privatization programme of the nation's telecommunications, telephone systems, utilities, transportation, and shipping ports. In

1992, the government invested $1 billion in modernizing the electrical power sector. By 1994 this had resulted in an 18 per cent increase in electrical supply. These improvements to the infrastructure enabled Filipino companies to borrow far more abroad and began to attract capital back into the country. This liberalization resulted in a vibrant tele-communications industry. The market for telecommunications equipment and services is predicted to take off with the implementing of a national information highway. Electrical power, construction, and chemical manufacturing are all well established.

Between 1992 and 1998 the government succeeded in implementing important reforms to:

- liberalize the trade, foreign exchange, and investment regimes;
- privatize state-owned enterprises;
- eliminate or reduce entry barriers into important industries such as banking, insurance, telecommunications, aviation, and petroleum products;
- address urgent infrastructure concerns under a build–operate–transfer programme;
- restore effective monetary management through the financial restructuring of the previously insolvent central bank;
- improve longer-term fiscal stability through the passage of a comprehensive tax reform programme.

While substantial reforms have been made in recent years, significant problems remain with intellectual property rights protection. Piracy of computer software and motion pictures continues to be a serious problem in the Philippines. The Philippines government has committed itself to eliminating the use of pirated software within government agencies, but video and cable piracy continue to be widespread and the Philippine courts have been reluctant to impose substantial penalties.

Country's Response to the Regional Financial Crisis

The Philippines' policy framework and adjustments/response to the regional economic and financial crisis are listed on the APEC home page as follows:

Monetary/Financial Policy

- The Philippines monetary authority has adjusted its key overnight interest rates and gradually raised liquidity reserves.
- The Monetary Board adopted the following measures on 21 January 1998 to effect a reduction in bank lending rates:
  (a) opening of a thirty day lending window;
  (b) opening of a swap window for banks without government securities holding; and
  (c) outright purchase of government securities at market rates.
- Banks were required to observe loan ceilings and exposure limits as follows:
  - single borrower limit of 25 per cent of a bank's unimpaired capital and
  - a ceiling on equity investment that varied across types of bank.

Fiscal Policy

• Fiscal policy was directed towards improving the efficiency of revenue collection and the tax system, maintaining prudence in government spending, improving the government's financial management system, and further rationalizing the government corporate sector.

• Fiscal policy was likewise focused on reducing and reviewing financial subsidies, reducing the budget deficit, improving the quality of public services through careful selection of projects and strictly carrying out the Reform Act introduced in December 1997.

Exchange Rate

• On 11 July 1997 the BSP allowed the peso–dollar rate to move within a wider band to facilitate more timely adjustment in light of the more difficult conditions in regional currency markets. It also intensified dollar sales and adjusted upwards its key overnight interest rates.

• New banking regulations were implemented to rationalize foreign exchange trading.

• A new volatility band was initiated and implemented by the BSP on 7 October 1997 in an attempt to stabilize the foreign exchange market.

• Foreign exchange rules were further liberalized to encourage overseas Filipino workers and investors to remit dollar earnings through the banking system.

Corporate Governance

• As part of its full disclosure policy, the Securities and Exchange Commission is requiring all publicly listed firms to include a summary of the effects of the peso depreciation and the current economic crisis as part of their regular financial report to the Commission.

Business Opportunities Post-crisis

The entire service sector, which includes transport and communication, trade, finance, real estate, and private and government services is an important element of the Philippines economy, contributing around 45 per cent to annual GDP. The major growth areas within this sector are tourism, computer services, advertising, financial services and institutions; transport and communications services, housing, and trade. Private firms, both local and foreign, are now being encouraged by the government to invest in transportation, communications, tourism, and financial services.

With the increasing awareness by both the government and private sectors of the importance of improving and preserving the environment, environmental consultancy services are needed. Consultancy services in the energy and telecommunications and airports development sectors are also sought by the government. These two major infrastructures have been prioritized by the government and are in need of improvement. Other sectors offering great potential for foreign investment are: electronics/semiconductor assembly; energy, including the gas and power generation industries, and information technology.

The Philippines was late in joining the miraculous pre-crisis growth and thus received less foreign capital than its neighbours, and thereby was less affected by the crisis. The crisis had a mainly social impact on poverty, education, health, and nutrition. These social impacts will impede Philippine economic development in the longer run.

Sources

Alburo, F., 'The Asian Financial Crisis and Philippine Responses: Long Run Considerations', *Developing Economies*, 37(4), Dec. 1999: 439–59.

Country Commercial Guide for year ending 1999, Philippines, http://www.state.gove/

Cragg, C., *Hunting with the Tigers: How to Achieve Commercial Success in the Asian Pacific Rim*, London: Mercury Books, Gold Arrow Publications Ltd., 1992.

Low, L., and Toh, M. H. 'Regional Outlook: South Asia 1994–95', ASEAN Institute of Southeast Asian Studies, 1994: 35–54.

Gough, L., *Asia Meltdown: The End of the Miracle*, Oxford: Capstone Publishing, 1989.

Socialist Republic of Vietnam

Overview

With a population of nearly 76 million, where 70 per cent are under 35 years old, Vietnam provides a cheap and capable labour force and a wide market for consumer goods. After strong growth between 1993 and 1994, the country experienced a considerable slowdown in economic activity due to the spillover effect of the Asian crisis. Moreover, since Vietnam was not directly hit by the Asian crisis, it has not implemented such stringent recovery measures, so the return to prosperity is predicted to take longer. Frustration with Vietnamese bureaucracy and government interference in business has also put off many investors.

The Country and its People

Vietnam stretches over 1,600 km along the eastern coast of the Indo-China peninsular, and has a land area of 329,566 sq. km. Westerners often separate Vietnam into two parts, The Red River Delta in the North and the Mekong Delta in the South. However, the Vietnamese divide their country into three geographical areas: Bac Bo (the north), Trung Bo (the central region), and Nam Bo, the south. The majority of people in Vietnam are Buddhists, with six and a half million Roman Catholics and close to 600,000 Protestants.

Ho Chi Minh declared Vietnam independent of French rule on 2 September 1945, after Japan's surrender in the Second World War, but the French returned to rule Vietnam until their defeat in Dien Bien Phu in 1954. The Geneva Agreement divided Vietnam at the Ben Hai river into the Republic of Vietnam (the south) with Saigon as its capital, and the

Democratic Republic of Vietnam (the north) with Hanoi as its capital. For the next nine years, fighting between the Soviet and Chinese-supported communist north and the US-backed south intensified. In 1965, the USA committed its armed forces to the war in Vietnam until the 1973 Paris Peace Agreement. But the fighting between Vietnamese forces continued until 30 April 1975 when communist troops captured Saigon and reunified the country. Since the north's victory in 1975, Hanoi has been the capital city, although Saigon, renamed Ho Chi Minh City, remains the centre of business. The Socialist Republic of Vietnam came into existence in July 1976 as a communist country modelling its political system after those of the Soviet Union and China.

With 76 million inhabitants, Vietnam is the second most populated nation in South East Asia following Indonesia (196 million) and the third most populated nation in East Asia, including China. The country is already in the top fifteen most populated countries in the world. Even though Vietnam was essentially part of mainland China, it is wrong to think of her people as simply Chinese. Vietnamese have a strong sense of national identify developed over a decade of struggle and warfare. Eighty-four per cent of the population are ethnic Vietnamese, 2 per cent ethnic Chinese, and the remainder are Khmers, Chams, and members of some sixty ethno-linguistic groups each with its own language and culture. The predominant language is Viet.

The Business Environment

Vietnam began adopting an open-door policy after the collapse of the USSR. Facing a deteriorating economic situation and international isolation, Vietnam's Communist Party introduced free-market reforms in the late 1980s. Vietnam has now mended relations with China. In February 1994, Washington lifted its nineteen years' economic embargo against Vietnam and in July 1995 the two countries restored diplomatic relations. Vietnam became the seventh member of ASEAN in July 1995.

The economic restructuring programme, *Doi Moi* or 'open door', was adopted in December 1986. *Doi Moi* aimed to achieve three main reforms: restructuring the economy, stabilizing a new socio-economic management system, and expansion of foreign economic relations. To transform the centrally planned economic system into a system that is highly decentralized, operationally efficient, and market-oriented, the reform process was implemented as follows:

- 1976–79: unifying the country after the 'liberation of the south' and turning the economy into an integrated whole in accordance with central planning principles;
- 1980–86: experimenting and readjusting economic policies orientated the country towards trade liberalization;
- 1986–96: affirming the principle of economic renovation with the *Doi Moi* Reform

The key elements of *Doi Moi* are:

- decentralization of state economic management and autonomy to state-owned enterprises;
- the replacement of administrative measures and controls by more economic and market-oriented monetary policies;

- the adoption of an outward-oriented policy in external relations;
- the promotion of agricultural policies, allowing greater freedom in the marketing of products;
- the development of private sector enterprises as an engine of growth.

Despite the implementation of several of these reforms, the Vietnamese government still has not completely created a business-friendly environment. The Vietnamese government, faced with the task of remodelling communist bureaucratic structures, which are no longer in tune with the new economic system of *Doi Moi*, has been forced to create new institutions for its new economic model. For example, Vietnam dramatically lacks a comprehensive legal framework, business skills, and accurate marketing information.

Business Opportunities Post-crisis

In Vietnam there are substantial underdeveloped reserves of natural resources, including plentiful coal, oil, gas, hydroelectric potential, and so on for commercial development. However the country has a serious shortage of business skills. The poor state of the Vietnamese infrastructure is a major constraint on the country's economic development. Major areas of concern are transport, telecommunications, energy, and the water management infrastructure.

In 1987 Vietnam promulgated a Foreign Investment Law in order to attract international entrepreneurs, but this law has been modified on several occasions. Manufacturing, especially in light industry, is widely encouraged by the government. Major products include processed foods, textiles, cement, chemical fertilizers, glass, and tyres. The government is also giving high priority to the development of food processing, thus opening investment, consulting, and supply opportunities.

Foreign investors in Vietnam regularly complain about the lack of a legal framework, the economic risks, the mediocrity of infrastructures, and corruption, in addition to public deficit, social instability, the inadequate business environment, and low levels of savings. Vietnam is therefore deemed less attractive by foreigners than China or Singapore in terms of capacity to attract direct foreign investment. Transformation of Vietnam will indeed take several decades. Recent surveys have heightened the sense of caution towards Vietnam's business prospects. Three polls by the Political and Economic Risk Consultancy (PERC) in the first quarter of 1996 found Vietnam as the most stressful country to live and work in Asia, ranking ahead of India, China, South Korea, Indonesia, the Philippines, Taiwan, and Thailand. A similar survey of corruption levels in Asia ranked Vietnam the second highest after China, and ahead of Indonesia, the Philippines, India, and Thailand. Vietnam is also judged to be the riskiest place to do business in Asia, among those countries included in a survey of Japanese investors in Vietnam, conducted by Daiwa Research Institute which also found disappointment among those polled, citing various problems in enacting investment after having received approval to invest.

Sources

Freeman, N., 'Realism Reigns', *The Banker*, June 1996: 65–6.

Islam, I., and Chowdhury, A., *Asia Pacific Economies*, London: Routledge, 1997.

Vernard, B., 'Vietnam in Mutation: Will it be the Next Tiger or a Future Jaguar?', *Asia Pacific Journal*, 15(1), Apr. 1998: 77–99.

Part II

Asian Management: Theory and Practice

Introduction

As shown in Part I, the Asia Pacific economies in general are bottoming out and moving towards a recovery. The potential for doing business in the region post-crisis is huge. The failure of some Western firms in the region is often related to their inability to adapt to the different managerial cultures and business practices in the region. Asian business culture and managerial practices are often very difficult for Westerners to understand. Furthermore, the subject of Asian management itself is not only enormous and complex, but is also changing rapidly. The aim of Part II is to provide a general understanding of the business culture in Asia Pacific, to learn about the main principles and operations of Asian management, its strengths and weaknesses, and to find ways to profit from that knowledge. The question inevitably arises as to what can be learned that might be useful for Western firms doing business in the region, and what might be usefully applied or adapted for the management of Western firms themselves.

In addition to the complexity of the relationship between business and culture in Asia Pacific discussed in Chapter 4, Asian management theories and practices differ to a great extent from those applied by Western firms. The Japanese and Korean management philosophies and practices have been selected in Chapters 5 and 7 because they have been, on the one hand, the dominant forces in the regions and behind their respective country's economic growth post-Second World War, and, on the other, they are currently experiencing difficulties, in the post-crisis context. In Chapter 7, Chinese management practices are introduced. These are significant, not only because they have contributed largely to the pre-crisis booming economies of Taiwan, Hong Kong, and Singapore, and to a certain extent Indonesia and Malaysia, but they are currently central to mainland China's efforts to develop and reform its own state-owned enterprises, and to create a new generation of corporations to assist its further development and entry into world markets. China is potentially the future major player in the Asia Pacific region.

Chapter 6
Culture and Business in Asia Pacific

Once upon a time there was a great flood, and involved in the flood were two crea-
tures, a monkey and a fish. The monkey, being agile and experienced, was lucky
enough to scramble upon a tree and escaped the raging waters. As he looked down
from his safe perch, he saw the poor fish struggling against the swift current. With the
very best of intentions, he reached and lifted the fish from the water. The result was
inevitable.

(Adams, 1969: 22–4)

It is mistaken to assume that people from different cultures think, feel, and act in the
same way. Ignorance of cultural differences could have fatal consequences, as dramatized
so vividly in the story of the monkey and the fish. Sensitivity to cultural difference is
crucial to successful business dealings in Asia Pacific. Asian business is not only very
difficult for Westerners to understand but ignorance of the cultural differences could
have fatal consequences. The failure of many Western firms in the region is often related
to their inability to adapt to Asian management philosophies and business practices. In
Asia Pacific, culture affects not only social norms, but also government policies, business
transactions, management practices, and labour relations. Although the region is at the
crossroads of a variety of languages, races, religions, and cultural traditions, it is possible
to identify many characteristics that are more or less common across the region. This
chapter aims at providing a basic understanding of those cultural characteristics which
are specific to Asia Pacific and are necessary for succeeding in the region.

Cultural Analysis in Asia Pacific

Culture is an extremely broad concept and very difficult to define. It touches and alters
every aspect of human life. There is no general agreement on its definition either. To
some, culture refers to the distinctive way of life of a particular group of people, or a
complete design for living. Others refer to culture as a pattern of behaviour transmitted to
members of a group from previous generations of the same group (Hall, 1977: 16–17).

Culture is not simply a product of conditioning acquired, learned, or transmitted from one generation to another (Gross and Kujawa, 1992: 322). Culture also shapes people's values, attitudes, beliefs, and behavioural patterns (Terpestra and David, 1985). It is therefore crucial for business managers to understand fully not only how people in different cultures behave but why they behave in the way they do. Knowledge about culture is achieved by a combination of factual knowledge and interpretive understanding. Factual knowledge is acquired through an accumulation of the characteristics or observable facts about a particular culture. Interpretive understanding requires a deeper insight and understanding of the 'nuances of different cultural traits and patterns, which require more than factual knowledge to be appreciated, such as learning the meaning of time, of life, of attitudes towards others, of gender, and of business itself' (Cateora, 1990: 69–70).

There is no best method of cultural analysis that is appropriate for doing business in Asia Pacific. Given the cultural diversity in the region, an appropriate approach would be to break down the broad area of the region's socio-cultural environment into its various elements and to study each element in detail. It should be noted, however, that these elements, although representing different facets of Asian culture, are all intricately intertwined and must be viewed as an integrated complex whole. In Asia Pacific, it is not enough for business managers to learn about the various cultural elements existing in the region, such as, for example, language, religion, social structures, education, aesthetics, attitudes, moral values, and so on. It is also essential to understand the reasons and motivations behind such behaviours and cultural norms. Consequently, a systems approach to the analysis of the cultural environment in Asia Pacific is needed. A systems approach is one where culture is understood as a system composed of parts that are related to other parts which mutually influence and adjust to each other, through a process of cooperation, competition, conflict, and accommodation (Parsons, 1951).

Social Norms and Asian Values

There are many elements of the cultural environment in Asia Pacific. To describe any one of them fully would require a discussion of greater length and depth than we can undertake in this chapter. We shall therefore focus only on those dimensions that have been found to influence Asian business practices substantially, mainly religion, social norms, and 'Asian' values.

Major Religions in Asia Pacific and their Influence on Asian Culture

In Asia Pacific, religious beliefs shape many kinds of individual behaviour, whether economic, political, legal, or social. Understanding the major religions existing in the region, therefore, can provide business managers with a better insight into Asians' values, cultural attitudes, and work ethics. Ignorance of differences in religious beliefs could lead to frustration and misunderstanding, poor productivity, and a drastic reduction in the sales of products, or even cause the ultimate failure of a business. The following survey intends merely to identify and describe the core values of the major religions, which may affect business in the region.

The Asia Pacific region is at the crossroads of several cultural and religious traditions. As a result, the region as a whole has developed some unique norms and values where geography plays only a minor role in the cultural make-up of Asia. The region may be divided into distinct cultural spheres, which do not follow national or geographic boundaries (Engholm, 1991: 24–7). The ethical and religious philosophies have left a legacy of behaviour, attitudes, and beliefs that have a deep and constantly evolving impact on Asian business culture. These are: Confucianism, Shintoism, Buddhism, and Islam. Each one of these influences business practices in some distinctive ways. Western business people need to be acquainted with all of them, to effectively conduct business across commercial borders in Asia Pacific. In addition, there are elements of Taoism, Hinduism, and Christianity in the region. However, these do not appear to have nearly as much impact upon the culture of business and will not be dealt with in any detail.

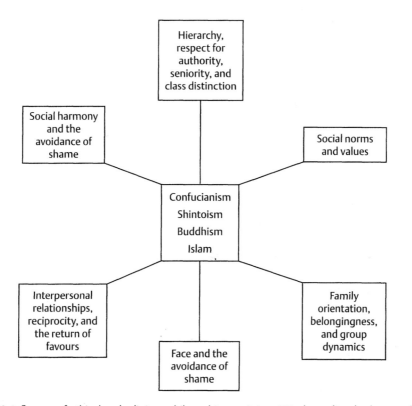

Fig. 6.1 Influence of ethical and religious philosophies on Asian attitudes, cultural values, and work ethics

Confucianism

Confucianism is more a social code for behaviour, a general approach to life, than a religion. Thus it does not preclude other formal religions from existing side by side with it. The Japanese, Korean, Chinese, Taiwanese, Hong Kong, and Singaporean cultures are all rooted in the social ethic espoused by Confucius and his disciples. The influence of Confucianism is also evident in Indonesia, Malaysia, and the Philippines although in these latter cases Islamic values are dominant in Indonesia and Malaysia, while the Philippines, with its large majority of Roman Catholics, is an unusual exception in the whole region.

A traditional starting-point for understanding Confucianism is the work of its founder, the philosopher Confucius (551–479 BC), who was a contemporary of Socrates in ancient Greece. Like Socrates, Confucius spent most of his life as a teacher. According to legend, Confucius had 3,000 disciples, 72 of whom later became 'sages': men of erudition and wisdom. Born in feudal China, Confucius witnessed anarchic feudal wars destroying what had been a peaceful land in his youth. He concluded that stability was the most important goal for society and taught that it could be achieved through the correct management of interpersonal relationships and the relationship between individual and society. In order to rule a state, Confucius preached, one first needed to have one's house and family in order. And in order to manage a household correctly, one needed to look continuously within oneself in search of faults that could be improved, if not corrected, through learning. This Confucian philosophical approach to life is embodied in the principle of the Golden Mean, or *zhongyong zhidao*, which dictates that one avoid extremes by taking the middle road, or compromising (Chen and Pan, 1993). One of Confucius's followers, Hsu-tzu saw that conflict arising from innate bad human nature could be avoided only through education via learning the *li* (rituals and ceremonies to emphasize proper conduct according to status). Confucius did not believe that man's passions and impulses must be wholly suppressed but that they should be regulated in order to achieve personal harmony. Confucius preached that social harmony must be maintained above all. He also asserted that to maintain harmony, the community's well-being must supersede that of the individual, should the two come into conflict. When the community is a state, Confucius prescribed that the people respect and obey the ruler, who should in turn be benevolent to his subjects (Kindel, 1983). Confucius therefore concentrated on creating a set of guidelines for living properly and harmoniously. Although non-religious, he tolerated those who worshipped a god, and even gave them advice by saying 'When you worship God, you should think he is there with you' (Chen and Pan, 1993: page 4). This tolerance of religious belief, or non-religiousness, had prevented religion from becoming a political issue of any importance in Asia, at least until the recent period of crisis, in spite of considerable assimilation of religious cultures from other parts of the world such as Buddhism, Islam, and Christianity.

The most important virtues of Confucianism include: loyalty to the state or emperor, respect for elders, filial piety, faith in friendship, reciprocity in human relations, and education and cultivation. These virtues are reflected in the five cardinal relationships identified by Confucius (Hinkelman, 1994: 153–5):

1. **Ruler to people** In the Confucian view, the ruler commands absolute loyalty and

obedience from his people. They are never to question his directives or his motives. In return, the ruler is to be wise and work for the betterment of his people. He should always take their needs and desires into account.

2. **Husband and wife** The Confucian husband rules over his wife just as a Lord rules over his people. The wife is to be obedient and faithful, and she has a duty to bear her husband sons. The husband has the duty of providing his wife with all the necessities of life.

3. **Parent to child** Children must be loyal to their parents and obey their wishes without question. While the parents must raise and educate their children, the children must care for their parents in old age and always love and respect them.

4. **Older to younger** Respect for age and obedience to all older family members is a key element of the Confucian ethic. Grandparents receive deferential treatment from grandchildren as well as from children.

5. **Friend to friend** The relationship between two friends is the only equal relationship in Confucianism. Friends have a duty to be loyal, trustworthy, and willing to work for each other's benefit. Dishonesty between friends is a social crime and demands punishment.

Thus, in brief, the basic tenets of Confucian thought are obedience to and respect for superiors and parents, duty to family, loyalty, humility, sincerity, and courtesy. Confucianism, moreover, inculcates servility, frugality, abstinence, and diligence. It also recognizes hard work, patriarchal leadership, entrepreneurial spirit, and familial devotion.

The Confucian ethic transfers easily into the business environment in Asia Pacific. China, Taiwan, and Hong Kong share a common Confucian cultural heritage. Despite forty years of communist rule in mainland China, Confucian norms are still a visible and viable part of life there. The spirit of communalism, for example, which requires the submission of the rights and interests of individuals to the family, and those of the family to the state, is omnipresent. The mentality of modern Chinese is still shaped largely by the teachings of Confucius. In modern Hong Kong too, where Westernization and competing philosophies have diluted Confucianism somewhat, its ethics are still manifest in its inhabitants. Characteristics of Hong Kong's culture that result directly from the continuing influence of Confucianism can be seen, for example, in the organization structure and management of Hong Kong companies, where the boss is a ruler and father to his subordinates, and where workers have a duty to obey the boss and work diligently to help the company succeed. In return, the boss must concern himself with the daily affairs of his workers and make sure that all their basic needs are met.

Largely, the teaching of Confucius also still shapes the mentality of modern Koreans. In fact, Korea is more deeply imbued with Confucian elements than any other country, including China. Confucianism is so pervasive that Koreans unconsciously behave in Confucian manner. 'To be Korean is essentially to be Confucian' (Hinkelman, 1995a: 138). In a typical company, the boss is a ruler and father to his subordinates. Workers have a duty to obey the boss and work diligently to help the company to succeed. They are expected to make great self-sacrifices by working overtime without additional pay. In return, the boss must concern himself with the daily life of his workers and their families, and make sure that all their basic needs are met. Among co-workers, those of greater status and age command the respect of their juniors. Younger people are expected to defer to their elders in speech and manner by opening doors, being polite, and so on. In return, elders are expected to reward their juniors for work well done and to ensure that their subordinates benefit from any personal successes or promotions that they receive.

Shintoism and Buddhism

Although Japan's state religion was traditionally Shintoism, early rulers did not suppress Buddhism or Confucianism. Most Japanese are a Buddhist–Shintoist–Confucian blend, in their religious outlook. Prince Shotoku of the Imperial family developed a way to reconcile the different religions in Japan. He compared the religions of Japan to a cooking pot on a tripod, the legs of which are Confucianism, Shintoism, and Buddhism: 'Let Shintoism be the trunk from which Buddhism spreads its branches, luxuriant with the etiquette of Confucianism to achieve a flourishing in the real world' (Schütte and Ciarlante, 1998: 20). The Japanese people thus came to follow existing Shinto rituals and to believe in Buddhism at the same time.

Shintoism, also known as 'the way of the gods', is Japan's only indigenous religion. It is not widely practised today, but its traditional teachings still influence Japanese thought. Traditionally, Japanese believed themselves to be children of the gods and their origin to be totally different from and superior to that of the rest of humanity. Shintoism stresses the harmony of the earth and the spiritual powers of natural features. Mountains, trees, rivers, large rocks, and weather are all believed to be imbued with spirits called *kami*. Homage is paid to them in annual rites of fertility, harvest, and the like. Shinto holds further that the Japanese race is descended from *kami* (Hinkelman, 1994: 153–5). Another important Shinto belief is that the spiritual world, mankind, and nature are all bound together and that they should exist in complete peace and harmony. This element is very much alive in the Japanese business environment and Japanese society at large, where the highest premium is placed on maintaining harmony at all costs in Japan. Shintoism, furthermore, contributes the idea of loyalty to one's clan, group, or company. In the tradition of the Shintoist Samurai warriors, the Japanese value sacrifice for the sake of their leaders, whether in government or business, and apologies and atonement for one's mistakes or breaches of responsibility (Engholm, 1991: 25).

Buddhism came to Japan from China more than a thousand years ago, and at one time the Japanese aristocracy embraced a mixture of the two beliefs in what the West knows as Zen Buddhism. Zen reinforces the Shinto belief in harmony, but it is a much more active philosophy than other Asian religions. In ancient times the warrior caste of Japan, called Samurai, practised Zen to make themselves better fighters. Zen stresses meditation and concentration. Meditation is not restricted to the kind you do sitting down. Zen practitioners learn to concentrate intensively on every detail of whatever they do, whether it be walking, working, fighting, or negotiating a business deal. Zen is one source of the very intense way in which some Japanese do business. Japanese businessmen, in fact, have often been referred to as modern-day Samurai (Hinkelman, 1994: 153–5). Buddhism's lifestyle affects spiritual, cultural, and political identity. It stresses tolerance and spiritual equality and focuses on wantlessness and contemplation rather than upon consumption and work. The ultimate goal of Buddhism is nirvana: the achievement of an ethical state marked by the absence of desire and suffering. Human suffering for a Buddhist is caused by the desire for possession and selfish enjoyment of every kind. This suffering will only cease when desire ceases. It would therefore be difficult for international business managers to motivate workers to increase their productivity and acquire greater wealth. Marketers might also face great difficulties in selling products because of the lack of enthusiasm for new products and material possessions. Buddhism also believes in reincarnation and the cyclical nature of life and teaches of the brevity and impermanence of all things in life. Since there is more than one chance at life there is less pressure on business people to be 'doing' orientated (Theravaada, 1972).

Other forms of Buddhism are also present in Japan. The most popular of them is Pure Land Buddhism. Pure Land Buddhism resembles Christianity in its belief that people who are good in this life will go after they die to a heavenly place where they can live in bliss. Pure Land ensures a degree of ethical consideration in daily affairs, and people are reluctant to be unethical for spiritual, as well as for temporal reasons. Buddhism's five major commandments are:

- do not take life;
- do not steal;
- do not commit adultery;
- do not tell untruths;
- refrain from intoxicants (Engholm, 1991: 25).

Like Japan, Thailand is also overwhelmingly Buddhist. However, Buddhism there is summed up in one simple belief: 'All life is suffering'. The interpretation given in Thailand is that everyone should be tolerant and easygoing, because material things and personal achievement don't matter much in the grand scheme of life. One's well-being is more important than one's career position. One's economic status is the result of *karma* accumulated over the course of past existences. Because of their Buddhist values, Thais are frugal and they see time as cyclical, which diminishes any reason for rushing. Thais enjoy more personal freedoms than Koreans, Chinese, Taiwanese, and most other Asians. If a task isn't a pleasant one, it is not considered worth doing; one's well-being is more important. Nearly all Thais are devoted Buddhists, which makes them almost inhumanly tolerant. No one seems to be in a hurry in Thailand. Like Buddhism's Wheel of Life, time itself is cyclical rather than linear. Thais accept the authority of those in positions of power, believing that these people must have acquired the merit to deserve such power, through successive past lives in which they progressed to a state of karma closer to nirvana. Thai business people are thus humble, patient, good-humoured, and tolerant and they live austerely without ostentation. They eschew conspicuous displays of intelligence, wealth, or talent. They accept their lot in life. Passing through this life is, after all, an experience that will be repeated for them many times before they enter nirvana (Engholm, 1991: 36–51).

Islam

Collectively, the countries of South East Asia make up the largest concentration of Muslims in the world with an approximate total population of more than 200 million. Muslim traders introduced Islam into South East Asia from the seventh century onwards. Muslim Asians in Indonesia, Malaysia, and Singapore pride themselves on their loyalty and devotion to Allah and see themselves as part of the 'brotherhood' that makes up the Islamic world. They are committed to the protocol of Islam, which has two forms. As individuals they observe *adab*, the responsibility to show courtesy in word, deed, and action to all people at all times. As members of society, they observe *rukun*, acting in ways that encourage social harmony in the family, community, and society as a whole.

Islam is a word that means resignation or submission to God. Accordingly, Islam is based upon the belief in one God whose power and knowledge are infinite. Islam is not simply a religion but also a way of life promoting equality and brotherhood of every Muslim, of whatever race or colour. The Koran contains a system of Muslim law that encompasses every aspect of life, be it ritual, personal, family, criminal, or commercial. The Sharia, or Islamic Law, regulates all facets of life, including political, social, and legal justice. Western firms must be familiar with the five pillars of Islam because of the serious implications some of these might have for the conduct of business. These are:

(1) A declaration that there is no one worthy of worship except Allah, and that Mohammed is High Messenger to all human beings until the Day of Judgement (Koran 3: 17, 2: 119–29).

(2) The performance of daily prayers at the times and in accordance with the code set out in the Koran and the traditions of the Prophet. All Muslims are required to pray five times a day. Any work must be interrupted during these periods to allow individuals to conduct their religious duty. Work schedules, meeting times, sales calls, and production schedules must be planned accordingly.

(3) The payment of Zakat, a religious tax or alms-giving. Alms-giving refers to the sharing of wealth. It is an annual tax of 2.5 per cent collected from all individuals and used for charity.

(4) The observance of fasting during the month of Ramadan. Muslims are required to fast for thirty days during this holy month. Fasting includes complete abstention from food, drink and smoking from dawn to sunset. This obviously reduces workers' productivity to a great extent. Working hours are drastically reduced during that month. Public consumption of food during Ramadan would be an insult. Foreign expatriates are expected to show some respect and refrain from drinking coffee or smoking in offices.

(5) The obligation to make a pilgrimage to the holy city of Mecca, in Saudi Arabia, at least once during one's life, if one is able to do so.

Islam furthermore forbids the consumption of alcoholic drinks as well as eating pork meat. These are considered *haram*. Many foreign firms have responded to this by producing all-beef hot dogs, beef bacon, and non-alcoholic beer, wine, and even champagne to be sold in those particular markets. In Indonesia, for example, the word 'ham' does not appear anywhere on McDonald's menu. Big Mac burgers is the popular name. Smoking, eating crabs and shellfish are *makruh* (allowed but not encouraged).

Islam is a way of life. Unlike the West, where there is both a distinctive and deliberate separation of religion from other activities, such as politics or economics, Islam provides integrated guidance for daily living. This includes guidelines for what constitutes sound economic practice. In addition to the Koran, a more detailed form of guidance can be found in a number of other sources, such as the *Ahadith* (traditions of the Prophet Mohammed) through the work of Muslim religious scholars.

As far as Islamic economic values are concerned, these are of major importance in the Koran. Positive values include an instruction to be just and fair, to value generosity or magnanimity, to demonstrate honesty and cooperation. Negative values include cheating, lying, depriving others of their due rights, malice and hatred, amassing wealth or hoarding, greed, niggardliness, and excessive indebtedness. Islamic banking is another important and distinctive aspect of Islam. Islamic banks, like other banks, are essentially financial intermediaries, which bring lenders and borrowers together, manage risk, and provide a range of peripheral services, including the transfer of funds and international exchange. However, Islamic banks cannot charge interest. The fee charged is not interest, because the amount is not connected to the market price of money but to the value of the service provided. The reason for the prohibition of usury or the charging of interest *per se*, is because it is believed by Muslims to be unjust in the Eyes of Allah. 'Deal not unjustly by asking more than your capital sums and you shall not be dealt with unjustly by receiving less than your capital sums.' In stating the Islamic prohibitions against usury or *riba*, it is interesting to note that the practice was also unacceptable according to the philosophies of Plato and Aristotle as well as the early Christian church. Aristotle condemned it as an improper use of money and an illegitimate method of becoming wealthy. The early Christian church also voiced its strong opposition to the practice. In addition to the prohibition on charging interest, Islamic prohibitions on other economic activities include hoarding in order to increase the price of certain goods or to satisfy greed, any form of gambling; the sale of *haram* or prohibited goods or alcoholic drinks, and finally unjust brokerage (Goodfellow, 1997: 65).

Ignorance of Asia's diverse value systems and business cultures has often been at the root of the clash between Asian and Western business practices. Acceptance into Asia's diverse business cultures, and forming strong relationships with business people there, are advantages that equal, or even outweigh, many of the traditional factors in a firm's competitive advantage, such as lowest price, after-sales service, and quality of products. For the majority of busy foreign executives, the pressure of their jobs often prevent them from acquiring a deep and sensitive understanding of the multicultural diversity that exists in Asia Pacific. Consequently, their familiarity with their individual host country's culture is often superficial. While not denying the existence of certain distinctive and country-specific cultural characteristics, it is nevertheless possible to identify some values commonly shared in the region as a whole, as detailed next.

Social Harmony and the Avoidance of Conflict

The ultimate goal of all personal interaction in Asia Pacific is harmony. For example, in China, in order to establish or achieve social harmony, Confucius first prescribed practicing *li* (rite) as a means of achieving *jen* (man). *Jen* is the central substance of man as a social and cultural being and it cannot be achieved without applying *li* in one's interactions with fellow human beings. *Jen* is an essential element of Confucianism and represents an ideal state in which an individual maintains harmonious social relationships with his fellow men. Thus, the Chinese individual thinks foremost of himself in relation to other people and the way in which they are connected. The principles of *li* guide the individual in his interactions with others by spelling out the proper way to behave in various social situations, and towards various individuals with whom he has interpersonal relationships. Thus *li* guides one to achieve the ideal state of *jen*. The principles of *li* require an individual to behave not according to his desires or for self-centred reasons but to follow what is prescribed by ritual, constantly monitoring his own behaviour to ensure that it is socially acceptable on any occasion (Hsu, 1971).

In Indonesia, *Mmsyawarah*, or the cooperative village harmony, is embedded in Indonesian character and culture. Tens of thousands of Indonesian villages are organized according to the tradition of mutual assistance, a system based on an ancient model of joint responsibility and cooperation known as *gotong royong*. When a person, family, village, or state is in trouble or need, the people nearby drop their own work to give needed assistance without pay or coercion. This emphasis on harmony in Indonesia permeates social, commercial, and national affiliations (Engholm, 1991: 36–51). The Javanese culture is also characterized by the avoidance of all forms of direct confrontation. There is in fact an official formula for avoiding unnecessary and inflammatory arguments. This is known by its abbreviation *SARA* standing for *suku* (tribe or ethnicity*)*, *agama* (religion), *ras* (race), and *antar golongan* (inter-community rivalry). This is government policy. In the past year the formula has expanded to *SARA plus G* for gender—an indication that the issue of women's rights in Indonesia is a sensitive one (Goodfellow, 1997: 34).

Harmony and peace are also the pre-eminent concerns of Japanese society. This belief is summed up in the traditional concept of *Wa*. *Wa* literally means circle, but it can be understood as the ethic of harmony, unity, peace, and wholeness in a social group. The ethic of *wa* implies a set of social gestures where the group is greater than the sum of its individual members. In this belief, an individual standing alone is incomplete and can find fulfilment only by lending his personal will to the needs of the society in which he lives. Whether stated or implied, *wa* is the guiding philosophy for the Japanese in the family, the company, and even during leisure activities, such as baseball (Hinkelman, 1994: 155). Company managers point to *wa* as the secret of Japan's business success. When top executives, middle managers, and production-floor employees all embrace *wa*, the result is unparalleled trust, cooperation, loyalty, and even love between all parties involved. Productivity is increased, responsibility is shared, and management–labour relations are smooth.

Closely related to *wa* is the concept of *amae*, which can be interpreted to mean unquestioning love between people. In business circles, *amae* means trust and loyalty between associates, and it is the foundation for a working relationship. It is difficult for foreigners to understand the importance of trust in business, but it may be more difficult for them to conceive of the degree of trust implied in *amae*. *Amae* has been likened to the love between a child and its mother. To hold *amae* for another person is to be able to trust him with your life, family, or possessions. In corporations, managers make an effort to foster the spirit of *wa* through *amae*. Group-centredness is supported by company slogans, songs, and philosophies that employees recite in unison every morning before work begins. Workers may also assemble in a yard on the company grounds to engage in group exercises at the start of the day. For those in subordinate positions, *amae* entails a child-like trust and devotion to senior leaders and the company as a whole. A worker may expect the company to take care of all aspects of his life, ranging from housing to health care as well as salary. A superior in the organization must play the role of a parent to his subordinates and take a deeply personal interest in their well-being. *Amae* is developed among members of the same sections and departments in the company, and in smaller companies. All employees may develop shared feelings of fraternity and camaraderie. Japanese have a strong desire to belong to a group, and this desire carries over from business into other activities. Co-workers routinely spend time together relaxing in bars after work or at company-sponsored picnics at weekends (Hinkelman, 1994).

In the process of protecting group harmony and politeness, Japan has evolved into a society where the visible surface of a situation, the *tatamae*, may be quite different from the true state of affairs, or the *honne*. In business, this means that if you are not very close to a Japanese, he is more likely to tell you the official company policy concerning a subject than to let you know what individuals in the group are really thinking. In Japanese society, both *honne* and *tatamae* are considered to be valid points, of view, and you should not interpret misunderstandings as the result of intentional deception (Hinkelman, 1994: 155–6).

Koreans too place the highest premium on harmony and the maintenance of good feelings—*kibun*. *Kibun* is a sort of intuitive feeling for social balance and correct behaviour. Koreans always try to maintain a harmonious environment in which a person's *kibun* can stay balanced. They try never to do anything that could upset another person's *kibun*. Social etiquette and behaviour are centred on respect for *kibun*. *Kibun* also plays an important role in the Korean business environment (Hinkelman, 1995a: 139–40). For this reason, Koreans are very formal in business relations. On the surface, polite Koreans will always appear to be good-natured and friendly. They will try hard to neither say nor deliver bad news. Foreigners interacting with Koreans can have problems if a project runs into difficulty, because no one may want to confess that a problem exists. Instead, managers must learn to read between the lines or interpret subtle hints that a problem has developed. The good-natured appearance can also be misleading. Koreans are also people with strong convictions. These characteristics conflict with the social demand for harmonious relationships. As a result, personal grudges or dislikes can be kept beneath the surface. An unwitting foreigner could mistake everyday courtesy for true friendliness and work with or confide in someone who really wishes his downfall.

Asians often try to avoid conflict and direct confrontation. In Vietnam, for example, a direct refusal or negative answer is considered impolite and crude. This often leads Vietnamese to agree to something even when they have no intention of carrying it out. From a Vietnamese perspective, this is not considered to be untruthful; it is simply the means for maintaining a harmonious relationship. This Vietnamese attribute offers great potential for cross-cultural misunderstandings with Western businessmen for whom disagreement and negative responses are merely a part of the negotiating process and have nothing to do with interpersonal relationships (Smith and Pham, 1996).

Interpersonal Relationships, Reciprocity, and the Return of Favours

Interpersonal relationships in Asia Pacific are strongly influenced by the typically collectivist orientation of these cultures. It is absolutely essential to build a network of personal friends in Asia. In fact, the engine of Asian business is built largely on personal contacts. Who you know assumes great importance in achieving success or failure in business negotiations. Asians are networkers *par excellence*. Their networking extends beyond the Western concept across all their business deals and into their personal relationships.

In Japan, for example, networking is a never-ending process. The term *jinmyaku* means a web of human beings, and this network is relied upon in almost all management actions (Hinkelman, 1994). For example, to work effectively through the complex Japanese distribution system requires close and long-standing relationships with individuals at all levels. It takes many years to build such a network. This creates obvious limitations for foreign business executives who simply cannot create the necessary web of intimate contacts during relatively brief overseas assignments.

Personal connections are the key element for doing business in Korea too. As in other Asian countries, little or no distinction is made between business and personal relationships. To succeed in Korea, you must cultivate close personal relationships with business associates and earn their respect and trust. Attempts to establish long-term businesses in the country have often failed because foreigners did not recognize that business relationships were also personal relationships. It must be noted that many Koreans will return trust, respect, and honour only for those people whom they count as personal friends. Foreigners working in Korea tell stories of contracts broken and promises reneged on simply because the Korean had no qualms about cheating someone foolish enough to enter into a business relationship without having first established a personal relationship. Westerners may have a hard time understanding this attitude (Hinkelman, 1995a: 137–40).

Personal connections are also a key element of doing business in Hong Kong. However, this might be a difficult process for foreigners because the Chinese possess a clan mentality under which those inside the clan work cooperatively and those outside the clan are seen either as inconsequential or as potential threats (Genzberger, 1994).

Furthermore, interpersonal relationships in Asia Pacific are based on reciprocity and return of favours. But the rules concerning reciprocity and the ways in which reciprocity is conceived in Asia reveal distinct differences from Western cultures. Norms of reciprocity in Asian cultures tend to be far more formalized and binding than those in the West.

In China, the principle of *pao* (doing favours) signifies one's honour to another

(Schütte and Ciarlante, 1998: 38). Every Chinese is brought up to be highly aware of this principle for its application has a tremendous influence on social and business relationships. The application of *pao* signifies a sort of social investment for which the donor expects repayment. In the business context *pao* is used to foster *guanxi* (connections) in order to build one's network of business relationships that are imperative for success in China (for further details related to *guanxi* see Ch. 8).

In Japan, *on* represents the concept of reciprocity. *On* has been described as a 'relational concept combining a benefit or benevolence given with a debtor obligation thus incurred'. *On* represents both the social credit that is conferred upon the donor and the social debt accepted by the receiver. Similar to Chinese *pao*, the recipient is obligated to repay *on* in order to restore balance to the relationship. *On*, however, is different from the Chinese *pao*. The most important component of *on* is the gratitude, deep sense of obligation and guilt that an act of *on* confers upon the recipient. The giver of an act of *on* must in no way imply expectation of repayment. This is in contrast to the pragmatic Chinese who pay strict attention to the balance between debts and credits. In the Japanese context, the desire is to appear purely altruistic with no apparent expectation of repayment. Reciprocity may take the form of immediate and symmetrical repayment as is the case on prescribed occasions for giving, such as life-cycle ceremonies relating to birth, marriage, death, seasonal gifts. *On* is, however, not created merely through gift-giving, but also through acts of kindness and generosity. As such, *on* cannot be economically calculated or repaid. Instead, its significance lies in the creation or maintenance of a social relationship (Lebra, 1976: 73–7).

Vietnamese society is also characterized by an interconnected network of personal relationships, all of which carry mutual obligations on both sides. A similar strong bond among friends exists in the Korean business world, where those who have established mutual trust and respect for each other will work hard to make each other successful, and where favours and gifts are constantly reciprocated.

Family Orientation, Belongingness, and Group Dynamics

Asian culture places extreme importance on familial relationships and their implicit responsibilities and rewards. Ideally, the Chinese family acts as a refuge for the individual against the indifference, the rigours, and the arbitrariness of life outside (Bond, 1991: 6). The Chinese individual is ready and willing to make sacrifices for his family and, in exchange, expects his family to be there as his support, comfort, and safety net. A Chinese person never grows out of this intense relationship with the family. It is a lifelong affair and extends to aunts, uncles, grandparents, cousins, and so on (Schütte and Ciarlante, 1998: 48). Moreover, Chinese individuals consider themselves as part of a web of relationships with other members of society. The closest knit group of all is the Chinese family in which complete devotion to parents is expected. *Xia*, filial piety, and *ti*, fraternal love and respect, are expected of all children in Chinese families (Chen and Pan, 1993: 5). As with the Chinese, the Japanese family also plays a key role in maintaining social stability, dependence, and mutual support.

In Indonesia, Indonesians are Indonesian first and members of their ethnic groups second. Instilled in Indonesia's population are the values embodied in the *Pacscilla*, a five-point manifesto for Indonesian politics and social life: belief in one supreme god (any god is fine); a just humanity; the unity of Indonesia; democratic rule by representation; and social justice for all Indonesians regardless of ethnicity. Responsibility to family, friends, and community takes precedence over economic advancement. People are more important than possessions and the deepest sentiment is reserved for kin and other close relationships. Obligations towards blood relatives (*darah* meaning blood) are primary, especially in the parent–child bond, under Islamic law (Engholm, 1991: 36–51).

For the Koreans, individuals are part of the collective family as a whole. The family is the source of identity, protection, and strength. In time of famine or war, the Korean family structure was a bastion against the outside world, where no one and nothing could be trusted, As a result, trust was reserved for family members and extremely close friends.

The Vietnamese also consider themselves part of a larger collective, generally centred on the family or clan. Individual needs are considered subordinate to those of the family organization. These differences in values and outlook can have significant implications for business transactions. Praising or singling out an individual for attention or to be rewarded in public, for example, is embarrassing to the individual concerned and is likely be counterproductive. Public rewards are best given to groups, not individuals.

Thus, while most Asian cultures are strongly collectivist in orientation, Western cultures, on the other hand, are highly individualistic, believing in the primacy of the individual as a highly valued ideal.

Among the Chinese, the kin group is the most important and long lasting of any membership group. As with the Chinese, ties to the family in Japan include both present members and those of past and future generations. Thus the term *ie* (house) refers to the family as a whole, including ancestors and future descendants (Schütte and Ciarlante, 1998: 33). To be lonely, to be a stranger, to be isolated from one's group—these are constant dreads among Japanese people. Therefore groupism, in the sense of total commitment and identification to the group, is a treasured cultural value. This groupism starts at an early age with very close family ties. Japanese familialism, *Kazokushugi*, is a basic value which is reflected in many aspects of management such as the so-called lifetime employment. In contrast to Western individualism, Japanese groupism requires subordination of self to the goals and norms of a collectivity. This may be one's family, class in school, university, corporate department or section, or Japan itself. It is considered right and proper to be dedicated and loyal to such groups and to be satisfied with basking in the glories and accomplishments achieved through collective efforts (Schütte and Ciarlante, 1998: 53–4).

Face and the Avoidance of Shame

No understanding of culture in Asia is complete without a grasp of the concept of face. It might be argued that the concept of face is in fact a cultural universal. To the Italians it is '*honore*', to the Spanish '*dignita*', to the French it is '*amour propre*', to the Anglo-Saxon '*self-respect*'. In Asia, however, having face means having high status in the eyes of one's peers, and it is a mark of personal dignity. One's self-image and self-respect depend very much on how one is viewed by others. Although the terms used to describe face and the exact way in which it operates vary somewhat from society to society, the underlying dimensions are consistent across Asian culture.

The Chinese, for example, distinguish between two types of face, *lien* and *mien-tsu*. *Lien* refers to the moral integrity of an individual's character. Every individual is entitled to *lien* by virtue of being a member of society. Thus one thinks in terms of losing *lien* rather than gaining it. Should a person's behaviour cause him to be cast out of society, he has lost his right to *lien* (Yau, 1994: 71–5). *Lien*, moreover, implies the presence of *ch'ih* (shame) which is one of the fundamental requirements of being human. *Mien-tsu*, on the other hand, represents a form of face involving prestige or reputation based on personal effort. It can be obtained through personal qualities or derived from non-personal characteristics such as wealth, social status, level of education, occupation, or authority. *Mien-tsu* may be lost or gained when the quantity or quality of such characteristics decreases or increases. Since the standards and requirements are set by the social expectations of the group, one is highly dependent on the evaluation of others for enhancing one's *mien-tsu* (Kindel, 1983: 99).

Lien and *mien-tsu* are interwined with one another. *Mien-tsu* cannot exist without *lien*, but also *lien* cannot exist without *mien-tsu*. In other words, when we talk of loss of face, it means losing not only *mien-tsu* but also *lien* (Lee, 1990). Thus a person has no option but to meet the social requirements to gather status to his name and maintain *mien-tsu*. Failure to do so would jeopardize his standing in society, cause him to lose *mien-tsu*, and cast into doubt his moral integrity—*lien*—in the eyes of society. Thus Chinese individuals are very conscious of showing due regard for the *mien-tsu* of others. They are careful not to cause others to lose face and expect the same regard in return. To cause a person to lose face is regarded as an act of aggression, while to protect another person's face is seen as an act of consideration (Yau, 1988). Compromise is a means of allowing all parties in a situation to save face. Indirect language is also employed to avoid confrontation, embarrassing situations, and direct rejections. The Chinese try to avoid saying 'no' when asked to express an opinion in order not to embarrass or offend others. Other common strategies used to save face for others include avoidance of criticism of anyone, but especially superiors, and the use of circumlocution and equivocation when criticism of another's performance is unavoidable.

In the Japanese context, face is the individual's badge of respectability and the source of self-confidence. For an individual to keep his *ame* and reputation unsullied is, in a sense, a duty and one type of *giri* (Zimmerman, 1985: 65–6).

The concept of face is also present in other South East Asian cultures. In Indonesia and Thailand, dignity and smoothness of behaviour are highly valued and form one of the key sources of respect. It is considered a deep insult to lose face, in front of others—and is more damaging than material loss. Indonesians usually conceal negative feelings such as jealousy, envy, anger, and even disappointment. They also suppress or down-play positive feelings. The suppression of strong emotions is a virtue instilled from childhood. Indonesians are trained to cope with stressful interpersonal situations in an entirely different way to Westerners, who, for the most part, are encouraged to externalize their thoughts, opinions, or frustrations. Indonesians, on the other hand, are typically non-assertive. They internalize their feelings (Goodfellow, 1997: 97). The use of the word feelings is significant, because the Javanese, in particular, usually describe their thought processes in terms of feelings. It is also worth remembering that if you ask a Javanese Indonesian what *they feel* about a certain situation, that is, as opposed to asking them what *they think*, you will usually get a more comprehensive response (Schütte, 1974: 62).

In Asia, 'Yes' Can Mean Either 'Yes' or 'No'

In Indonesia, if you do get a positive response to an enquiry, this may not necessarily mean 'yes'. Indonesians generally, and the Javanese in particular, cannot say 'no'. A negative response is believed to invite conflict. In order to avoid a confrontation, it is considered to be not only prudent but also polite to say 'yes' when in fact you mean 'no'. This can be both confusing and frustrating, until you learn that 'yes' can mean either 'yes' or 'no' (Goodfellow, 1997: 97). The Japanese too believe that declining a request outright could cause embarrassment and loss of face. If a request cannot be met, the Japanese may say that it is inconvenient, or under consideration. Such expressions generally mean 'no'. Another way of saying 'no' is to ignore a request and pretend that it was not made. Sometimes a Japanese will respond to a request by saying 'yes'. To a Westerner, this response may seem to be affirmative, but in Japan it may well mean 'no' or probably not. If a person says 'yes' to a question and follows it with a hissing sound made by sucking breath between his teeth, the real answer could be 'no' (Hinkelman, 1994: 155).

There are thus, four levels of meaning for the word yes in Asian countries. These levels are:

1. *Recognition*
The first level acknowledges that you are talking to me, but I don't necessarily understand what you are saying. In many societies politeness demands that we recognize the words of the speaker either through a nodding of the head or uttering the word 'yes' more out of instinct and focusing on the conversation than any real affirmation.

2. *Understanding*
The second level acknowledges that you are talking to me and adds that I understand you perfectly, but I may have no intention of doing what you propose. This is similar to tacit agreement in Western culture. The 'yes' means that your words and meaning are clear to me. Whether I agree with what you are saying cannot be determined unless it is specifically asked.

3. *Responsibility*
The next level of yes conveys that I understand your proposal, but I must consult with others and secure their agreement before your proposal can be accepted

4. *Agreement*
The final level of yes means that I understand, we are in total agreement and your proposal is accepted. (Ruthstrom and Matejka, 1990)

Avoidance of shame is also widespread in Japan. The Japanese value system includes an absolute obsession to avoid bringing shame to themselves, to their families, to their company and immediate work group, or to their country. Nothing must ever be done which will cause disgrace and tarnish the reputation of oneself or of others. The Japanese thus have a habit of telling a person what they believe he or she wants to hear whether or not it is true. They do this as a courtesy and rarely with malicious intent, although it can be a problem, especially in the workplace. If bad news needs to be told, Japanese will be reluctant to break it. They may use an intermediary to communicate it, or they may simply imply that the news is bad without ever saying so bluntly. For these reasons, it is best in a situation of uncertainty to stick to gentle questions and prolonged discussion in order not to upset the harmonious atmosphere that the Japanese prize so much.

To Filipinos, a sense of self-esteem, or face, is essential. *Hiya* refers to shame, the loss of face. Filipinos avoid conflict to avoid *hiya*, and they go to great lengths to protect others from *hiya*. Filipinos have a deep respect for fellow humans, regardless of rank or status. The Filipinos regard for self-esteem is mirrored by their code of personal honour. Filipinos honour their guests with hospitality and do not accept open criticism passively. To confront or accuse is to attack a Filipino's sense of *amor-propio* (love of self), a serious affront that often results in violence. Filipinos avoid people who do not reciprocate a favour. They feel a profound patriotic duty to their nation, and they are willing to sacrifice for it (Engholm, 1991: 36–51).

Vietnamese culture also considers face as an extremely important individual public image. Any overt public criticism or disparaging remarks can result in a loss of face and cause extreme embarrassment. For this reason, criticism is best handled privately and, if possible, indirectly.

In Singapore, the word most often used to describe the concept of face is *kiasu*, a Chinese Hokkien dialect word that roughly translates into 'being afraid to lose' which in recent years has taken on a far broader local connotation of 'always wanting to be number one' and 'always wanting bargains', or 'an obsessive desire for value for money' (Ho *et al.*, 1998). *Kiasu-ism* has also been dubbed the 'negative complement of competitiveness'. Competition breeds a sense of drive and commitment, while *kiasu-ism* stems from greed and promotes envy and selfishness (Kagda, 1993: 2). *Kiasu-ism* is a topic for discussion and laughter in local literature, television and theatre, in comedy clubs and cartoon strips, and even in schools (Lim, 1995; Seah, 1995). Despite the generally negative connotation of *kiasu* behaviour, there is also a positive side to it, one which surfaces as diligence and hard work in order to be on top of any situation (Chua, 1989). Consequently, Singaporeans are totally afraid of failure, of making a mistake, or failing in some way that could be career-damaging. And this is directly at odds with Westerners, who, in general, believe it's acceptable to take risks and make mistakes from which valuable lessons can be learnt for the future. This can be something of a problem for the Western employer of Singaporeans to deal with (Murray and Perera, 1996).

Koreans, on the other hand, have suffered a long and violent history of humiliating foreign invasions and occupations. They are consequently euphemistically known as a 'people of many sorrows'. If one fundamental aspect of Korean character were to be singled out, it would be the ingrained value called *hahn*, the deep-seated feeling of rancour, frustration, shame, and insecurity, bred of centuries of oppression, that has given Koreans a national sense of inferiority. The Korean language has a word for the pent-up energies and frustrations that develop in the human psyche under conditions of extreme oppression and hardship—*hahn*. *Hahn* is one of the forces that have led the Korean people to regain their face and their present prosperity (Engholm, 1991: 36–51).

Hierarchy, Respect for Authority, Seniority, and Class Distinction

A distinctive and common feature in Asia Pacific is the development of a strictly hierarchical working environment. In Indonesia, the Western business person can learn a lot about Indonesian culture from *bapakism*. It demonstrates that Indonesians culturally and socially interpret their world in a hierarchical fashion. At a very basic level this means that in business you must attract the attention of the 'head of the clan'. While many business activities and projects are controlled by the children of Indonesia's leading and established business, political, and military leaders, it is the founding fathers, particularly from the time of the Indonesian Revolution against the Colonial Dutch in 1945–49, who still hold real power and make most of the crucial decisions in business as well as in politics. *Bapakism* operates at every level of Indonesian, and in particular Javanese, society. It manifests itself in many ways. First, many Indonesians who are lower down in the social hierarchy are afraid, or are perhaps psychologically incapable, of taking personal initiatives, unless they first obtain direct permission from a superior. In any case this is not initiative, but rather social programming with pre-set boundaries. Western people find this frustrating. Individuality and personal initiative are encouraged and rewarded in the West. But when one does find a person who is authorized to make a decision, and this can sometimes be difficult, especially when dealing with the Indonesian bureaucracy, there are a number of useful things to remember. *Bapakism* can thus be seen in the complex system of relationships: between men and women, between the old and the young, and between the powerful and powerless (Goodfellow, 1997: 29).

Seniority is very important in the Indonesian coporation. Indonesians highly esteem their company seniors in a way that is difficult for Westerners to understand or appreciate. In Indonesia, seniority is measured not only by position or length of service but by age, status, and title, authority structure and education, and by family, political, and corporate connections.

Similarly, Japanese society has a hierarchical structure in which most relationships are unequal. In ancient Japan, every person was categorized as belonging to a distinct class based on family background and occupation. Class structure ranked from lowest to highest, beginning with menial labourers and ending with the Emperor and his family. Within each class, there was another system of rank, often with the youngest and least skilled people in a particular occupation at the bottom and the oldest and, presumably, most skilled and experienced members at the top. Although modern Japan is officially egalitarian and based on Western concepts of political as well as social equality, it is still based largely on a traditional social system that relies on unequal relationships to maintain harmony and order. In business environments, seniority within a group is determined more by age and length of service than by individual skill or initiative. The words *kohai* (junior) and *sempai* (senior) are used to express hierarchical relationships in both business and education. The world *doryo* (equal) is seldom used in business circles, because the Japanese often find it difficult to work in a personal situation without clearly defined levels from junior to senior roles. A person's educational level and former school are also important in determining status within the group. Family connections are somewhat limited for social leverage at work. Even if a person is from a well-known and powerful family, he will nominally still be junior to any group members who graduated from a more prestigious university or who graduated before him. In the event that two employees in the same work group have nearly identical credentials, their rank may be determined by personal, social skills and talents. Businessmen in Japan are so concerned about status that they cannot be sure of how to behave at their first meeting until their relative status has properly been established. For this reason, they exchange name cards before bowing. If the name cards are too vague, they may ask each other their age, company position, or Alma Mater. They bow only after they have determined who is the superior. The junior person bows lower. Afterwards, they continue to behave as superior and subordinate. The junior person is exceptionally polite (Hinkelman, 1994).

The Vietnamese have a similar attitude towards age. Respect for the elderly in Vietnam is a cardinal virtue. Age carries experience and wisdom. Often, the oldest member of a foreign delegation is treated with great deference, regardless of his official position or rank. The Koreans, on the other hand, are extremely class and status-concious. They divide themselves along class lines; the elite occupy bureaucratic, business, and academic positions. Social stature is based largely on education and family ties, and fits into a hierarchy of dependent relationships based on loyalty. Moreover, a militaristic discipline pervades all levels of Korean commercial endeavour. Upward mobility usually depends on nepotism or personal affiliations, yet everyone strives to gain top positions of power and influence. Tenacity, talent, and hard work are needed to get anywhere.

Belief in Fate

Among Asian cultures, there is a much stronger belief in fate, external forces, and pre-determined events compared with Western cultures. The majority of Asian cultures regard man as part of nature and believe that man should not try to overcome or master nature but should learn to adapt to it harmoniously. A person must accept his or her fate in life (Schütte and Ciarlante, 1998: 23).

The concept of *yuarn* refers to predetermined relationships with other things or individuals, which are beyond one's control. It is believed that the existence or absence of relationships such as friendship and marriage is predetermined or governed by a powerful external force. In Japan, the individual places faith in fate, destiny, and *innen*. *Innen* is a combination of *in*, the inner, direct cause, and *en*, the outer, indirect facilitating cause, that produces an effect. This belief in fate serves a similar purpose to *yuarn* in the Chinese context in that it encourages individuals to be resigned to their fate when things do not happen as hoped for. One cannot change one's *innen* since it comes from one's previous life. The Japanese refer to fate as *un* and attribute a large part of success or failure to having good or bad *un*. A person who is unsuccessful is consoled by the thought that he simply did not have good *un* and there is nothing that can be done. One can influence one's *un* by planning carefully and taking precautions, but there is no use in having regrets as things, once done, are regarded as irreversible. Once something has happened, fate will take its course. This may explain to some extent the Japanese desire to plan to the minutest detail (Lebra, 1976: 165).

The Thais, as Buddhists, are also believers in the philosophy of karma, that is, that good and bad things happen as a consequence of one's actions in present and past lives. While fate for Muslims, known as *Kadr*, simply means that life is predetermined. Good or bad things happen as a consequence of God's wish and should be accepted without questioning.

Thus, to succeed in Asia Pacific, business relationships must be based on the following cultural norms dominant in the region:

- Social harmony and the avoidance of conflict should be the ultimate goal of all personal interactions.
- It is absolutely essential to build a network of personal friends and relationships as the first part of doing business.
- Reciprocity and the return of favours is binding in business relations.
- Conformity to families or clan must be respected.
- Understanding of the 'Asian' concept of face is crucial. You should avoid causing others to lose face at all costs.
- Finally, show respect for hierarchy, seniority, and status.

Review Questions

1 Why do Western firms face greater cultural problems when operating in Asia Pacific?

2 What are the key characteristics of the main religions in Asia Pacific? In your opinion, what are the commonalties between them?

3 What is so unique about Asian cultures and norms?

4 To what extent have 'Asian' values and religious philosophies contributed to the Asian Miracle and to the crisis?

Exercise: Culture and Business in Asia Pacific

Aim This exercise aims at improving students' research skills, updating their knowledge, and developing their cultural awareness of Asian cultural attitudes, beliefs, and norms.

Assignment As an assistant to the managing director of a multinational firm wishing to expand its operations in Asia Pacific, you have been given the task of choosing a particular country in the region of interest to you as a possible market for one of the company products. Outline the major cultural problems that the company might face and suggest steps that might be taken to overcome these problems.

Cross-Cultural Training Exercise: Role Play: Negotiating a Business Deal in Asia Pacific

Aim The aim of this exercise is to stimulate students' awareness of the problems faced by multinational firms while conducting international negotiations in Asia Pacific, and to develop their skills in cross-cultural communications and negotiations.

Assignment The class is assigned to various countries in Asia Pacific. Students in each group are asked to investigate fully the business practices, communications, negotiation tactics of their assigned country and become as familiar with them as possible.

Role play Representatives from each group are then given a deal to negotiate between a Western and an Asian firm and are asked to conduct a cross-cultural negotiation exercise in front of the class representing their own country and company. The rest of the class is then asked to comment on their performance, based on their knowledge of the cultural and business practices of those countries.

Further Reading

Engholm, Christopher, *When Business East Meets Business West: The Guide to Practice and Protocol in the Pacific Rim*, New York: John Wiley & sons, 1991.

Goodfellow, Rob., *Indonesian Business Culture: Insider Guide*, Reed Academic Publishing, Butterworth-Heinemann, Asia, 1997.

Hinkelman, Edward, G. (ed.), *Hong Kong Business: The Portable Encyclopedia for Doing Business with Hong Kong*, Country Business Guide, California: World Trade Press, 1993.

—— (ed.), *Japan Business: The Portable Encyclopedia for Doing Business with Japan*, Country Business Guide series, California: World Trade Press, 1994.

—— (ed.), *Korea Business: The Portable Encyclopedia for Doing Business with Korea*, Business Guide Series, California: World Trade Press, 1995.

—— (ed.), *Taiwan Business: The Portable Encyclopedia for Doing Business with Taiwan*, Business Guide Series, California: World Trade Press, 1995.

Chapter 7
Japanese Management

Japanese management is in a state of flux today. At the time of the Japanese economic 'miracle', Western, especially American, fascination with Japanese management was very strong. Japanese companies were praised for their management styles and production techniques. Their employees were admired for their good morale, cooperation, high quality, and hard work. Foreign business managers and academics flew to Japan to see how they were doing it and what could be learned from their experience. However, by the end of 1989, and following the burst of the 'bubble economy', with the subsequent stagnation and recession, this positive interest has changed. Japan's human resources management system is being more severely criticized for its traditionalist approach, inflexibility, rigidity, and bureaucracy. Although some of the most distinctive features of the 'classical' Japanese model of management are nowadays undergoing continuous evolution and deep changes, other Japanese characteristics will remain. These have already made valuable contributions to the competitiveness of global firms and have become universalized. Before introducing and evaluating the Japanese management system, it is important to acquire some basic understanding of the structure and organization of Japanese business firms.

Inside the Japanese Business Organizations

Japanese business groups can be divided into two major categories: Zaibatsus and Keiretsus. Zaibatsus began in the late nineteenth century but were dismantled by the Allied Forces Suprème Command after the Second World War while the Keiretsus were first formed in the 1950s.

Key Features of the Japanese Zaibatsu

There is no precise definition of a Zaibatsu. It is generally understood to be a diverse group of large industries controlled by a single family usually through a central holding company. The Zaibatsu ownership structure resembled a pyramidal model in which Zaibatsu families owned a large portion of the stock of the holding company, which in turn owned a large portion of the stocks of the subsidiary and affiliated companies.

Zaibatsus played an important role in the rapid modernization of Japan from the late nineteenth century until the Second World War. The four largest Zaibatsu groups were Mitsui, Mitsubishi, Sumitomo, and Yasuda. Together they accounted for about 25 per cent of all Japanese business. Mitsui was formed in 1876. It initially concentrated on textiles. By the end of the Second World War, the Mitsui family virtually owned the entire Mitsui group. The family, however, gradually dissociated itself from direct participation and delegated the running of the Zaibatsu to professional managers from non-Zaibatsu families. Mitsubishi was formed in 1893. It expanded from shipping business into other areas by diversifying its products. By 1945 the Kwasaki family owned 55.5 per cent of the Mitsubishi holding company, which in turn owned far more than 52 per cent of the subsidiary and affiliated companies. Sumitomo made wealth from copper refining and mining businesses. In comparison with Mitsui, the Sumitomo family commanded a lower ownership percentage in 1946. Like Mitsui, the Sumitomo family gradually dissociated itself from direct management, with the exception of the head of the Sumitomo family, Domonari, who assumed the office of president. His role, however, was nominal, and the group was actually managed by professionals. After the Second World War ended, Japanese Zaibatsus became the target of the Allied Forces Supreme Command. Many Zaibatsus, with the support of the Japanese government, owned over half of Japanese industry, and had been responsible for the success of Japan's war machine during the 1930s and 1940s; hence MacArthur's decree that they should be disbanded (Lorriman and Kenjo, 1994: 34). Their dissolution was focused on depriving them of their ownership interest in banks, subsidiaries, and affiliated companies (Bisson, 1954). However, in 1951, when Japan regained its independence, the post-occupation Japanese government immediately allowed the former Zaibatsus to re-establish relations with the banks of their former groups. Old familiar names like Mitsui, Mitsubishi, and Sumitomo began to re-emerge in the form of postwar Keiretsus.

Key Features of the Japanese Keiretsu

The word Keiretsu does not translate neatly into English, and that is the beginning of the problem. The most common Japanese meaning is something close to the English verbs 'link', 'affiliate with', or 'connected to' (Miyashita and Russel, 1994: 7). Keiretsus are different from pre-war Zaibatsus in many respects (Okumura, 1976: 20–5). The pattern of ownership changed from a hierarchical system in which the owning facilities controlled the stocks of the holding company which in turn owned the stocks of affiliated companies, to an interlocking ownership pattern with the member companies cross-owning the stocks of others within the group. Each group of firms within a Keiretsu now has at least 20 to 30 per cent or more of its equity residing with other member firms. Such cross-shareholding is an important means for promoting and maintaining group cohesiveness. Additionally, each Keiretsu has an organized research group to promote joint development. This joint business among members within the group not only allows members to participate in large projects but it also helps build mutual trust, communication, and personnel development among the group member companies (Chen, 1995: 172–5). Finally, each Keiretsu is now organized around a general trading company and a major bank that help in financing member companies, which consist of their own subsidiary and affiliated companies.

There are different types of Keiretsu ranging from horizontal, vertical, to bank-centred and non-bank-centred. A horizontal Keiretsu (*yoko*) is a group of very large companies with common ties to a powerful bank, united by shared stockholdings, trading relations, and so on. The Mitsubishi group of companies is one example. A vertical or pyramid Keiretsu (*tate*) is made up of one very large company and hundreds of thousands of small companies subservient to it. A good example is a large manufacturer like Toyota, with twin vertical Keiretsus within its total group, Hitachi, NEC, and Toshiba. One pyramid produces goods and the other pyramid distributes and sells those goods. Bank-centred Keiretsu (*kinyu keiretsu*) are descendants of the Zaibatsus such as Mitsui and Sumitomo. These are financial groupings that have a more horizontal inter-industry linkage with complex financial ownership. Non-bank or industrial group Keiretsus (*kigyo shudan*) include corporations such as Toyota, Hitachi, Matsushita. These have vertical or pyramid structures in which the subsidiary and smaller companies are subservient to the companies higher up the pyramid. The subsidiaries and smaller companies in vertical Keiretsus generally have less autonomy than those in the bank-centred horizontal Keiretsus (Kienzle and Shadur, 1997). Sometimes, however, an overlap across these groups might exist with some industrial groups being closely related to a bank-centred grouping. Toyota, for example, is associated with the Mitsui group.

The Sogo Shosha

Each Keiretsu group is supported by a Sogo Shosha, or trading company. The Sogo Shosha however is not an ordinary firm and the definition of general trading company gives us a very poor idea of what it actually does. A Sogo Shosha offers a broad and changing array of goods and services. Therefore it cannot be defined by the products it handles, nor even by the particular services it performs (Miyashita and Russell, 1994: 53–5). Sogo Shoshas were originally started during the post-Meiji restoration period, when the government acted to recover the rights of trade from foreigners. They were developed as offshoots of the major industrial groups such as Mitsui and Mitsubishi, and provided an invaluable service as the marketing arm of the manufacturing companies that formed the groups. The members of manufacturing companies relied on the trading companies with which they were affiliated, not only to develop markets but also to purchase goods for them. By representing these member companies, the Sogo Shosha took all the risks and financial responsibilities related to the businesses. (Chen, 1995: 250–1).

However, unlike their pre-war predecessors, postwar Sogo Shoshas are more diversified and trade with a much lower margin. They perform various functions. The first one is trade—especially the import of raw materials and energy. They procure raw materials and self-finished products throughout the world. In the process, they serve as the eyes and ears of their major clients, providing them with global market information and analysis. They help smooth out the difficulties their clients would otherwise face in dealing with foreign languages, foreign currencies, and foreign governments. They also provide assistance in the export of manufactured products of the heavy and chemical industries. The second function is financing trade, with their own money or money borrowed from

Mitsui & Co.: The Changing Sogo Shosha

Mitsui & Co. is Japan's largest Sogo Shosha, or trading company. The company has two principal roles: to facilitate its clients' international trade-related activities and—making use of its substantial information, human, financial, and other resources—to create new trade flows, new enterprises, and new industries around the world.

The original Mitsui & Co. was founded on 1 July 1876 and was dissolved in 1947 under the orders of the Allied occupation forces to dismantle Japan's Zaibatsus, or industrial conglomerates. The Mitsui name was later adopted by a new company, created in 1959 by the merger of several new companies which had been established in the postwar period. As of 31 March 1999, Mitsui has 283 domestic subsidiaries and 271 overseas trading subsidiaries. Its associated companies include 161 in Japan and 185 overseas: a total of 900 companies employing around 10,957 people, with a paid-in capital of 192,487,084,922 yen.

1. **Market information provision** Mitsui's fundamental activity is providing transaction services, more specifically, acting as an intermediary between buyers and sellers who want to import, export, or engage in offshore or domestic trading activities. It provides a broad range of useful information services to clients to assist them in identifying and taking full advantage of business opportunities. It provides updates on business trends, market conditions, and individual commodities and products as well as advice on legal matters and local business customs to assist clients in realizing the full potential of their products.

2. **Credit supervision** Often impeding the development of international trade is a lack of credit information on potential buyers and sellers. Mitsui overcomes this obstacle, while sharing a portion of the risk of trade transactions, by monitoring trading partners on a regular basis with the aim of preventing the performance of contract obligations and thus ensuring the smooth implementation of transactions.

3. **Financing** To facilitate trade transactions, Mitsui utilizes a range of financing schemes. These include assisting clients in making use of letter of credit financing, providing goods on credit to buyers while paying sellers on delivery, offering instalment payment arrangements, and devising barter and counter-trade financing schemes for clients in countries where hard currency financing is difficult to obtain. Mitsui also offers financing schemes for large-scale business transactions. It has a broad range of experience in making arrangements for multinational joint financing schemes to facilitate major contracts between developing and developed countries. It thus plays a leading role in organizing the consortium of international engineering and plant construction companies.

4. **Market risk management** Mitsui assists its customers in hedging against market risks through the use of derivatives. It provides a variety of derivative products related to such commodities as metals, petroleum, and grains and can offer support for its customers' asset and liability management. It can also arrange commodity swaps and options for its customers as tools for managing market risk. Besides such services, Mitsui also helps its customers hedge against the risks associated with fluctuations in interest rates, exchange rates, and stock prices as well as other market risk factors.

5. **Transportation logistics** Another key aspect of Mitsui's transaction services is its logistical know-how, which allows the company to arrange for the most efficient and economical transportation of goods. Depending on customer needs, Mitsui can ensure the physical distribution of products from and to virtually any point on the globe.

6. **Assisting in global expansion** Mitsui provides assistance in relocating production

facilities overseas. The range of services here include providing advice on taxation, legal matters, local business practices, and potential tie-up partners. Its services also extend to assisting in the establishment of joint ventures and in recruitment and employment matters.

7. **Assisting foreign companies in building strong positions in Japanese markets** Mitsui organizes joint ventures for importing into and marketing consumer goods in Japan. It is also closely involved in assisting many foreign companies in expanding their exports to Japan, licensing technology, and setting up manufacturing facilities. Mitsui activities also extend far beyond facilitation of existing trade flows. Mitsui acts in the following capacities as well: distributor of goods and services, transfer agent for technology, financier, investor, project organizer, market developer, resource developer, and consultancy.

From Conventional Sogo Shosa to 'Solution Provider'

During the fiscal year ended 31 March 1999, Mitsui reported declines in consolidated total trading transactions and net income. This was mainly due to the weak economic conditions in Japan and other Asian countries following the Asian crisis. Mitsui is now considering moving from a conventional Sogo Shosha, described as a business enterprise that handles everything, to a more consolidated management system.

The new Long Term Management Vision was released in April 1999. A most significant change is the introduction of a new human resources management system, of which the basic principle is 'pay for performance', which breaks the traditional system in Japan of seniority-based payment. Another key element of the Management Vision is greater concentration on IT and FT (financial technology) and the introduction of a global consolidated management system. This system will have four elements: a consolidated accounting system, a risk management system, systems for associated companies in Japan and overseas, and an electronic data interchange system. The purpose of this system is to provide quick access to information related to overall corporate and risk management on a consolidated basis and to enhance efficiency by reducing Mitsui's accounting and financial costs. The key concept of the system, according to Seiichi Shimada, senior executive managing director and chief information officer, will be 'one input point—multiple output points'. The consolidated management system, it is hoped, will make available accurate information on net income generated by various operational units and will allow Mitsui to make allocation decisions to take optimal advantage of the vast network of offices and associated companies that Mitsui has developed over the years. The system, Shimada asserts further, 'will greatly enhance our capabilities as a "solution provider" for our clients, offering them not only trading and procurement services but also providing business process reengineering services to enhance their competitiveness. Making the transition from a conventional Sogo Shosha to a "solutions provider" will be a key factor in Mitsui's survival and continued success'.

Sources: Mitsui & Co. Website *http://www.mitsui.co.jp*
'Setting the Stage for the 21st Century', *Mitsui in Action*, 35(6) Nov.–Dec. 1998.
'Long Term Management Vision', *Mitsui in Action*, 36(4), July–Aug. 1999.

banks at low interest rates. Sogo Shoshas have close relationships with in-house banks and other commercial banks. They provide finance for manufacturers in return for an export agency and for importers' access to the market. The third function is information collection through their offices all over the world. The fourth general function is overseas investment (Yoshino and Lifson, 1986: 57–8). Sogo Shoshas not only buy and sell but also invest overseas, particularly in fields that provide a steady supply of critical raw materials such as mining and oil and gas exploration and in large-scale industrial projects where few other companies have the resources to compete with them (Miyashita and Russel, 1994: 55).

Japanese Management Philosophy and Techniques

Nihonteki Keiei, or Japanese-style management, has become a popular phrase in the West. It refers to what people see as substantially different between Japanese management techniques and those widely practised in the West (Whitehill, 1991). The differences often cited are: lifetime employment, job rotation, promotion-based seniority, group consensus, just in time, quality circles, *Kaizen*, and the suggestion system. Most of these techniques have become well known across the world. However, a successful implementation by Western firms requires a critical understanding of their basic principles and operations, while some of the elements need to be critically assessed in the light of the structural problems of the Japanese economy since 1989.

Lifetime Employment (*Shushinkoyo*)

The main objective of offering lifetime employment or a job for life is to provide workers with a sense of security and identity. Once recruited, lifetime employees become members of the corporate family, which will have to take care of them for their entire career. The corporation promises to provide them with employment for life along with cheap housing, health plans, pensions, education, and recreation facilities for their families in return for loyalty and commitment. Such a system, it was strongly believed, would assist the corporation in building and maintaining a strong sense of belonging among the workforce, increase harmonious relationships, and reduce staff turnover. In Japan, groupism or the total commitment and identification to the group is a treasured cultural value. It starts at an early age and is known as *kazokushugi* or very close family. Japanese familalism is a basic value underlying many aspects of lifetime employment (Whitehill, 1992: 53–4).

Lifetime employment is usually offered to full-time male employees. These are hired directly from high schools or universities and are expected to stay with the company for a lifelong period. The recruitment and selection procedures for candidates who are being considered for lifetime employment are more complex that those used in recruitment for standard employment. In addition to the standard collection of documentation from each applicant, such as personal curriculum vitae, technical skills, official family registry record, physical examination report, and letters of recommendation, the Japanese firm assembles information related to political orientation, family background, finances, home ownership, and general characteristics and abilities of potential candidates (Chen, 1995: 188). In some cases, private investigators are sent to the applicant's neighbourhood to check on the truthfulness of the applicant's claims, on his general lifestyle, and to talk with friends and shopkeepers to make sure this individual is worthy of employment (Whitehill, 1992: 137).

When forced to cut the number of lifetime employees, such as witnessed recently during the recession following the Asian crisis, Japanese firms usually encourage early retirement. Management engages in what is known as 'shoulder-tapping' (*kata-takaki*) by urging senior individuals to resign voluntarily. Another option often used is the lending of these employees to other companies or sending them to a subsidiary or subcontractor, often with a more prestigious title but harder work and less pay (Whitehill, 1992: 132). *Shukko* is the Japanese term for transferring staff to other companies (subsidiaries and suppliers). This option has two forms: *Zaiseki Shukko* 'where staff are temporarily transferred to the other companies but retain their employee status in the company' and '*Iseki Shukko* where staff are actually released by one company to be employed by the other company' (Kenkyujo, 1995). Surplus workers could also be sent home 'on call' and still get paid about 60 per cent of their base pay for a fixed period of time. In all these cases the expectation is that such workers will return to their earlier position when conditions improve.

Commitment to the security of lifetime jobs has significantly declined in Japan since the recession. Japanese corporate executives are increasingly acknowledging that they have 'to make a break with the past to survive in the next century' (Nishumuro, 2000). Matsushita, the epitome of traditional Japanese management, has recently introduced short-term contracts to attract young graduates. The old lifetime system was enshrined in the pay system and amounted to iron links that chained employees to their employer. Workers could not leave because rises were limited during their employment until they reached their mid-fifties when they received a huge lump sum. Under the new system of short contracts, wages can be drawn from this fund each month. It is up to the workers to decide whether they invest it in a private pension scheme, use it to improve their skills, or spend it. According to Atsushi Murayama, personnel director at Matsushita Electric, this new system was introduced because they realized that, under the old system, people were loyal to the company even after they lost interest in their actual work. They did not want a half-hearted workforce. They want their workers to stay with them because they share a common interest with the company. This, they believe, would create a more active and conscious loyalty among their staff. Of the 800 graduates recruited each year since the introduction of the new system, 40 per cent of the graduates have already taken this option (Nishumuro, 2000; see also the Matsushita case study in Part IV).

Subcontracting, and the reliance on part-timers is also increasing in Japan. Part-time workers do not receive any social insurance, pension, union rights, or paid holidays. They help reduce labour costs and provide needed flexibility when there are seasonal fluctuations. Temporary contract employees (*rinjiko*), who work full-time for limited periods, are another pool of so-called non-ordinary workers available to Japanese companies. These individuals are usually not recruited on the open market but are sent from sub-contractors and subsidiaries. Low wages, unskilled work, and lack of union protection are all characteristics of such temporary employment status. When business slackens, these temporary workers are the first to go (Whitehill, 1992: 143). This change in the employment system is now causing serious social unrest among the Japanese. Because large firms used to take care of their employees, there is very little state aid for those who are losing their jobs. Many are having great difficulties keeping their dignity in a culture where redundancy is still equated with incompetence and laziness. Managers who have recently lost their jobs are choosing to become homeless rather than losing face with their families (Bubble Trouble, BBC, 2000). Recruit, one of Japan's leading personnel and information-technology businesses has recently introduced a novel approach (for Japan) to take the pain out of downsizing.

Taking the 'Ouch' Out of Restructuring: Recruit in Japan

It is no secret that Japanese companies—no matter how pressing the need for staff cuts—are loathe to retrench workers. Recruit has managed to achieve the same result without pain by introducing the IO system.

'IO is a name that symbolises the constellation Jupiter', says Sonoe Shimizu, a public relations officer at Recruit. Just as the Jupiter constellation is known for its independence, the IO concept was developed to symbolize the position's independent spirit. People who take up the IO position are hired on a contract basis and are allowed to follow their own job schedules. In addition, they must make clear contributions to the company's development and are chosen for their special skills. IO workers, however, do not receive housing or transport allowances and are not entitled to the bi-annual bonuses.

In addition to the IO concept, Recruit has also devised Opt and Fellow positions as part of its new management system. The Fellow carries the highest status and is coveted for its high salary, though bonuses are not included. The Fellow is chosen on the basis of his or her exceptional performance. The position is not easy to attain. There are only five Fellows in the company. One Fellow is Japan's famous female marathon runner Yuko Arimori, a former Recruit employee. She quit the company and was re-employed on contract as a Fellow. 'As long as she keeps winning her races, she provides an excellent example of a Fellow because she puts the spotlight on Recruit', says Shimizu. Arimori runs with a large Recruit banner stitched onto her T-shirt.

The Opt system, on the other hand, is designed for Recruit employees who are not satisfied with their jobs and want to resign and start new projects of their own. These people are given a US$90,000 golden handshake from the company. Since the Opt system was introduced, more than 100 employees have taken the option, and as Shimizu explains, the Opt scheme has trimmed excess staff, helping the company in its restructuring efforts. As a result, Recruit's 5,000 personnel, including its 1,200 part-time workers, will have to prove themselves by what they can offer to the company rather than their loyalty, a big move from the traditional hallmarks of old Japan: loyalty and seniority.

Source: Taken from S. Kaukuchi, 'Problems and Pills—The Soft Touch', *Asian Business*, 1 Dec. 1999.

Job Rotation

Japanese firms are often regarded as a *dojo*, a training place where one practises the martial arts of life (Whitehill, 1992: 162). Job rotation is valued as the best means of increasing the motivation of the workers, improving their performance, and thus achieving better efficiency and productivity. During the first ten years, the employee is put on a job rotation scheme. Under this scheme, management trainees are expected to learn and acquire considerable expertise in a number of areas of the firm. Those identified as potential top management candidates are rotated through key departments on a regular schedule to increase the breadth of their knowledge and experience (Keys *et al.*, 1998). After ten years, the first real threshold is reached and the employee may be promoted to *kakari-cho* (sub-section chief) or *kacho* (section chief). The third threshold is reached after a total of twenty years or more of employment—perhaps at about age 45. It is at this time that promotion may be made to *jicho* (deputy department head) or directly to *bucho* (department head). Those individuals who have built up impressive records of accomplishment through the years, at about age 52–5 will be promoted to a directorship (Whitehill, 1992: 163–4). Job rotation, it is argued, enables companies to create a well-rounded company man and allows the senior manager trained in this manner to understand the company as a holistic system. Additionally, since knowledge and skills are shared among all the workers, the company's dependence or reliance on a few highly specialized workers can be minimized. It may also be argued that workers, under such a scheme, are constantly learning and acquiring new skills. The drawback of such a system, however, is the potential de-skilling of the workforce itself. Workers may be gaining new expertise in various fields, but these are often limited to the company's specific operations and production techniques and may not be valuable for employment elsewhere. Thus, workers' chances for a career move outside the firm become seriously restricted.

Promotion Based on Seniority

Traditionally, Japanese society has a hierarchical structure. This is a direct effect of Confucianism, which describes the natural order of human relations as hierarchical. According to Confucianism, one of the most important values is respect for elders. In business environments, seniority within a group is determined more by age and length of service than by individual skill or initiative. The words *kohai* (junior) and *sempai* (senior) are used to express hierarchical relationships in both business and education. The word *doryo* (equal) is seldom used in business circles, because the Japanese often find it difficult to work in a personal situation without clearly defined levels of junior–senior roles (Hinkelman, 1994: 164–165).

Entering employees are usually paid a standard base rate with no great difference related to company size. Added to the base rate is overtime pay earned by ordinary employees for work beyond the normal working week or at night or during holidays. In addition, a position allowance is typically paid to employees holding formal supervisory posts in the firm. Additional work-related allowances paid each month may include those for special assignments and skills. Special assignments include overseas positions and other temporary assignments of a non-recurring nature. In addition to the basic pay, and overtime, there is also a wide variety of allowances designed to meet individual personal needs. Each person's total situation will influence the amount of his income. The number of family members, his housing needs, the distance from his home to the plant, and other person-centred factors are given consideration. This leads to the payment of special allowances depending upon individual needs. These person-centred allowances are not related to the work performed, and include family allowance, housing allowance, commuting allowance, and allowance for non-absences. But there are many others, with several companies reporting the payment of a 'dating allowance' for single, young, male employees in need. Japanese employees also receive bonuses twice a year, in December and in July, in addition to their monthly compensation. The amount of the employee's bonus is determined, at least in theory, by overall corporate profitability. This is a discreet means of rewarding outstanding individuals without compromising the seniority-based wage system. The annual amount of the bonus can average the equivalent of between four and five months' pay. These provide a somewhat flexible link with overall organizational performance and thus provide motivation for group and individual efforts to improve market share and profitability. From management's point of view, it is really a deferred wage payment, which provides a substantial amount of 'free' working capital for the company. Also the bonus is, of course, a flexible cost item that can be reduced in difficult times without cutting the total labour force (Whitehill, 1992: 179). Other benefits and services include many recreational, educational, and cultural programmes, excursions, seaside and mountain resorts, as well as nursery and child-care facilites.

Today, Japanese management's primary emphasis upon length of service in promotion is under the greatest pressure. While seniority and years of service are still a component of wage/salary calculations, many Japanese companies are making determined efforts to eliminate the seniority principle completely. They have become increasingly aware of the dysfunction of reward systems based on seniority and have been gradually introducing merit as a factor in pay rises. Merit ratings nowadays are increasingly being used in conjunction with a seniority coefficient to calculate rises. Seventy-five per cent of Japanese companies are now administering pay by competency (Mroczkowski and Hanaoka, 1998). Many companies are shifting to a policy called *noryokushugi kanri*, or ability-based management, with a greater emphasis being placed upon such meritorious criteria as personal trust of colleagues, knowledge and skills, practical experience, contribution to productivity increases, and sense of responsibility. At Mazda, for example, the traditional respect for age was first challenged in 1996 following its take-over by Ford by the appointment of the youngest-ever Japanese director below the age of 45. Older managers felt resentful and found it very difficult to report to a younger director, thus jeopardizing their incentive and pride in working hard (Nishumuro, 2000).

Japanese Decision-Making Process (Ringi)

Harmony and peace are the pre-eminent concerns of Japanese society. These have had a direct effect on Japanese decision-making. The *ringi* system of decision-making is one of the most important features of Japanese management (Fukuda, 1988: 65). (*Rin* means submitting a proposal and requesting a decision, and *gi* denotes deliberations and actual decisions.)

The *ringi* system comprises two methods: *nemawashi* and *ringi seido*. *Nemawashi* refers to dealing with the roots of trees. In Japanese gardening, the transplanting of a tree requires much skill and meticulous effort. Business decision-making involves a similar process, with careful attention being given to the preliminary stages of the process (Chen, 1995: 184). *Nemawashi* is thus the practice of preliminary and informal sounding out of employees' ideas about a proposed course of action or project. *Nemawashi* also implies the activities that take place below ground level and describes the nature of the sounding out, in which contacted persons remain anonymous and feel free to talk about their ideas. *Ringi seido*, as opposed to *nemawashi*, is a commonly used formal procedure of management by group consensus. A *ringisho* is a proposal that originates in a section, and is forwarded to all relevant sections on the same level, the section heads, the managers, the directors, and eventually the president of the company. Upon receiving the *ringisho*, each will make comments on a sheet attached to the back of the proposal. The decision will be made by top management based on the comments from all people involved in the process. The purpose of this roundabout way of making decisions is to eliminate dissension, as many are given a chance to change a decision before it is actually made.

Thus under a *ringi* system, the Japanese think an issue over thoroughly, define the question, put it all down on paper, and pay immense attention to all aspects of *nemawashi*. And because the views of many are sought, with consensus management and group consciousness, the decision is likely to be sounder and later implementation made easier because it has already been pre-sold and employees are committed. Consequently, when the proposal reaches the president he can, in theory, pass it back and say: this is your idea, get on and implement it. With this collective method miscalculations are rare and it suits the Japanese sense of values. It also helps to boost morale, generate harmony, and strengthen loyalty and cohesion among staff. Group decisions tend to be bolder than those made by individuals and better represent a long-term view (Waters, 1991: 36). Another main advantage of the Japanese form of decision-making is that employees at lower levels can initiate proposals or work out plans, which are then transferred upward to higher levels of management. The power lies in the joint responsibility of all employees for the successful implementation of the new idea since they have all been involved in the process. Also the infusion of many different individuals in the decision-making process tends to reduce the danger of a decision being manipulated by certain individuals (Chen, 1995: 187).

Some would argue, however that consensus in the Japanese decision-making system is not a virtue, but a weakness since, traditionally, Japanese are led to believe that there is always one right answer to a question and that authority should not be challenged (Nishumuro, 2000). Another flaw with the system is that it can be a slow, cumbersome process. Too many meetings are held, with many unnecessary questions and suggestions raised, thus delaying business decisions, which often require a swift response. By the time a decision is reached, the deal may already have been clinched by competitors. Spontaneity, personal initiative, and entrepreneurial spirit are thus automatically eliminated from the process.

Just in Time (JIT)

Just in time (JIT) is a Japanese management philosophy which has been applied in practice since the early 1970s in many Japanese manufacturing organizations. It was first developed and perfected by Tai-chi Ohno, Toyota vice-president. The concept is that one should supply parts, as they are needed. The main objective is to meet consumers' demand with minimum delays. Tai-chi Ohno drew the original inspiration from the operational logic of the American supermarket, where empty shelf space or gaps constituted the 'trigger mechanism' for shop assistants to replace products (De Gruyter, 1989: 211–18). JIT gained extended support during the 1973 oil embargo and the increasing shortage of other natural resources, and was later adopted by many other organizations.

Today, JIT has evolved from being a method of reducing inventory levels within Japanese shipyards into a management philosophy containing a body of knowledge and encompassing a comprehensive set of manufacturing principles and techniques. A benefit associated with JIT manufacturing is that the system has the capacity, when properly adapted to the organization, to strengthen the organization's competitiveness in the market-place substantially, by reducing waste and improving product quality and efficiency of production. JIT can also be used as a means of obtaining the highest levels of usage out of the limited resources available. Furthermore, JIT allows companies to filter out waste in the production process, improve upon quality, and satisfy consumer demands in an efficient and reliable manner. Finally, JIT principles and objectives are universal. They can be applied and adapted to a diversity of organizations within industries that differ greatly from one another. JIT helps to increase the organization's ability to compete with rival firms and remain competitive over the long run. Organizational competitiveness is enhanced through the use of JIT since it allows organizations to develop an optimal process for manufacturing their products. JIT can offer organizations a competitive advantage which can take the form of offering consumers higher quality products than those offered by rival firms, or providing a superior service, or developing a superior means of production which allows the organization to become increasingly efficient or productive. JIT, thus, would be most suitable for application in organizations that need to respond quickly to changes within the environment and are willing and able to adjust their manufacturing processes to the changes in order to remain competitive (Suzaki, 1987).

However, in order for JIT management to work and be profitable, it must be fully adapted to the organization. Since every organization is unique in its production processes and the goals it aims to achieve, and taking into consideration the different stages of development within the organization, the goals of JIT may be useful in assisting the organization to define, direct, and prepare for implementation. There exist short and long-term goals, which include the following:

• Identifying and responding to consumer needs. This goal will assist the organization in focusing on what is demanded by customers and required of production. The fundamental purpose of the organization is to produce products which its customers want, therefore, developing a manufacturing process which produces quality products will ensure the organization's viability.

- Aiming for the optimal quality/cost relationship. Achieving quality should not be done to the point where it does not pay off for the organization. Therefore, emphasis should be placed on developing a manufacturing process that aims for zero defects. This may seem like an unrealistic goal; however, it is much less costly to the firm in the long run as it eliminates redundant functions such as inspection, rework and the production of defective products.

- Eliminating unnecessary wastes. These are wastes that do not add value to the product. Different categories of waste are identified, some of which are more concern in the waste elimination processes than others.

- Aiming for the development of trusting relationships between the suppliers. Also, relationships with just a few or even one supplier, if possible, should be focused upon. This will assist in the reaction of a more efficient company in terms of inventory and materials, timeliness of deliveries and reassurance that the materials will be available when required.

- Designing the plant for maximum efficiency and ease of manufacturing. This involves the use of machinery and labour that are absolutely essential to the manufacturing process.

- Adopting the Japanese work ethic of aiming for continuous improvement even though high standards are already being achieved. This will ensure that the organization remains competitive by continually striving for means of fulfilling consumer demand. (Cheng and Podolsky, 1996: 11)

Finally, JIT is a long-term process which cannot be implemented in a short period of time, nor can its rewards be realized overnight. It took Toyota ten years to perfect the JIT technique within its plants. Other limitations might be related to the loss of safety stocks, which usually act as a buffer for companies to fall back on to offset inaccurate demand forecasts. Loss of individual autonomy is also often reported as well as the greater amount of stress and pressure placed upon the worker to perform, and the resistance of the workforce to change.

Total Quality Control

Total quality control (TQC) was initially developed by Professor William Deming of New York University, but was not popular in the USA. The Japanese adopted it as a way to revive their war-torn economy and considered quality and productivity as one and the same. In the TQC concept, quality by inspection, scrapping, and reworking are unacceptable. The corrective measure must be built into the entire productive process. Each individual employee is exhorted to try his utmost to guarantee the total quality of his own products and also to help improve the overall quality of the company's product (Cheng and Podolsky, 1996: 206).

In the West, TQC is often understood as part of separate QC activities and it has often been thought to be a job only for quality control engineers. By contrast in Japan, TQC is a movement centred on the improvement of managerial performance at all levels including quality assurance, cost reduction, meeting production quotas, meeting delivery schedules, new product development, productivity improvement, supplier management and safety. More recently TQC has come to include marketing, sales, and service as well. TQC also deals with such crucial management concerns as organizational development, cross-functional management, policy deployment, and quality deployment. In other words, Japanese managers have been using TQC as a tool for improving overall performance (Masaaki, 1986: 14). The 'quality' refers to improvement in all of these areas. Japanese managers have found that seeking improvement for improvement's sake is the surest way to strengthen their companies' overall competitiveness with the belief that 'If you take care of the quality, the profits will take care of themselves'. TQC related activities in Japan are thus conducted with the customers' needs in mind. A core element of the total quality control concept is the use of quality circles.

Quality Circles (QC)

To understand the role QCs have played in Japan's history, one must first understand the concept of quality as it applies to the Japanese and the rest of the world. After the Second World War, the Japanese were faced with limited resources and a need to regain economic security. Elsewhere the focus was on mass inspection and the Americans exported their expertise to the Japanese who were ready and willing to learn. Western companies began to adopt the idea in the 1970s. Although these functioned in the same way as for the Japanese, North American firms often referred to them as 'employee participation groups' or 'focus groups' or simply quality circles, with many organizations developing their own customized name (for an illustration, refer to the case study on Rover in the UK in Part IV).

Quality circles are small groups of employees doing similar or related work, which meet regularly to identify, analyse, and solve product-quality and production problems, and to improve general operations. Quality circles also deal with issues like personal training, job enrichment, and leadership development. Participating employees are encouraged to make suggestions, which are put into a handy box and examined by specialists. If these suggestions prove to be appropriate, they will be put into practice and the originators of the accepted proposals will receive some sort of reward (Cheng and Podolsky, 1996: 206). There is no unified formula for scheduling and for payment of participants. If the meetings take place during normal working hours, no additional payment is offered, for participation is so high that even long meetings after work do not provide overtime pay. Membership in the quality circles is usually voluntary for all members (Werther *et al.*, 1990). Training is provided to the members of each group to assist with problem-solving. Group members, through consensus, select problems for consideration by the QC. Employees are given freedom to choose and select potential problems, as through this process they are more likely to be motivated to find a solution and remain within the group.

The success of a QC requires a leader, coordinator, facilitator, and other members who function together to achieve objectives. The objectives of the circle are to identify and solve quality problems and improve processes within their immediate area or work cell. All the circle members receive training related to problem-solving skills. Meetings between members occur at least once a week. The identification of a problem and formulation of a solution then allows the circle members to present their ideas to management who must then provide the circle members with authorization to implement the suggestion. Approximately 80 per cent of a circle's suggestions are in most cases accepted by management. Failure to accept a suggestion requires management to offer valuable feedback, in order to ensure the continuing success of the quality circles. The leader, coordinator, and the facilitator each play a unique role in the function of the QC. The QC leader assumes a key position in the success of the QC, which depends upon how well the leader is able to promote group problem-solving success while the circle's coordinator assumes the responsibility of administrative duties and supervises the facilitator. The circle's facilitator is responsible for coordinating and directing the activities of the circle members, maintaining documentation, training circle members, providing the link between management and the circle, monitoring and assessing programmes, and facilitating communication (Ross and Ross, 1982).

QCs do not provide quick-fix solutions to all organizational problems but the potential benefits an organization can experience through their use outweigh the costs. Some of the benefits include:

- increased employee commitment through participation and consensus decision making;
- increased sense of employee ownership and control;
- a mechanism to realize employee potential;
- improved communication between employees;
- increased motivation and employee morale; and
- effective means of training (Werther *et al.*, 1990).

Common costs and problems associated with the implementation of QCs are (Ross and Ross, 1982 and Werther *et al.* 1990):

- cost of training employees;
- union concerns. Unions may express some reservations to management regarding the implementation of QCs and their use. Objections may include the following: the use of the QC as a means of eventually eliminating the union; increasing productivity levels to the point where this will produce adverse effects on the workforce and reduce the size of the workforce through increased productivity levels;
- resistance to change. The implementation of QCs represents a change to the established work methods. Resistance is likely to be directed at management from superiors and employees. Common concerns frequently address the increased level of responsibility of workers and reduced supervisory control;
- failure with previous attempts to increase the level of employee involvement. Success with QC implementation requires a positive attitude, commitment from all involved, and a well-defined plan of action;
- failure to provide sufficient training to members of the circles. This will result in incorrectly identifying cause, effect, and formulation of solutions;
- lack of management support. Circle members need management support from provision of the necessary tools for problem-solving to feedback on suggestions;

- setting unrealistic expectations for the QC. The most effective approach to managing QCs is to allow them necessary time to develop and grow on their own. Expecting too much too soon will result in a group of frustrated and defeated employees;
- failure to establish specific, quantitative measures.

To assist in the problem-solving process, the following techniques are often used:

Brainstorming

Brainstorming can be defined as a group of people using their collective imaginative power to create ideas and solutions. The objective of the regular meetings of the QC members is to identify problems and develop solutions. The process demands participation by all group members to avoid being guided by the opinion of a select few. Although this represents the ideal practice, in actuality, there will always be some group members who are hesitant to offer their suggestions. The actions of members can be directed towards creating an open and positive environment, which encourages participation. Members should:

- offer encouragement on a consistent basis;
- attempt to generate as many ideas as possible without being judgemental;
- foster a positive attitude towards suggestions;
- attempt to make everyone feel welcome and involved in the process (Cheng and Podolsky, 1996: 173).

The Silent Idea-Generation Process

The silent idea-generation process can be used to identify problems, inadequacies in training, and so on. The process commences with a group of employees, managers, or superiors who privately list on a piece of paper possible causes of problems or solutions. The ideas are then shared with the group without being criticized or judged, until each person within the group passes or runs out of ideas. Clarification of ideas occurs and group participants vote on the five ideas deemed to be the most important. This process is often regarded as superior to brainstorming as it tends to encourage all members to develop ideas through the sessions.

The Five Whys

This can be applied to any problem to determine its real cause. The underlying purpose of asking why five times is to avoid attributing a false cause to the problem. The tendency for most people is to assign the first symptom or cause identified to be the root of the problem, whereas there may be several causes or symptoms.

Pareto Charts

Pareto charts assist in problem identification and analysis of the percentage of each cause that contributes to the problem. The method of constructing a Pareto chart involves the following steps:

- Collect data for a specified period of time for the causes or defect identified.

- The data is then categorized as it relates to each cause or defect identified.
- Construct the graph:
  - (a) draw the horizontal X axis, then two vertical Y axes, one on the left and one on the right;
  - (b) place the causes or defect categories along the X axis, starting from the left in order of largest to smallest;
  - (c) place the number of occurrences for each cause or defect on the left Y axis; and
  - (d) place percentages on the right Y axis.
- Plot the data in bars of equal width.
- Study the graph to understand the relationship between the cause categories and percentages.

Other techniques include the use of histograms, check sheets, and flip-charts (Japanese Human Relations Association, 1988).

The assumed values and benefits of QCs spread quickly from Japan to the Western advanced political economies. However, the outputs from this replication varied greatly from place to place, even though the underlying objective remained the same. The adoption of QCs in Land Rover in 1998 is a good example of frustrated ambitions (see case study, 'Quality Circles at Land Rover: The UK Experience' in Part IV).

The Concept of *Kaizen*

After a day-long discussion on the *Kaizen* concept William Manly, senior vice-president of the Cabot Corporation, said: 'I thought they had two major religions in Japan: Buddhism and Shintoism. Now I find they have a third: *Kaizen*' (quoted in Masaaki, 1986: 40). *Kaizen* is one of the most important concepts in Japanese management and the main key to Japanese competitive success. It constitutes the basic philosophical underpinning for the best in Japanese management. Japanese managers devote at least 50 per cent of their attention to *Kaizen*. Normally the driving forces for competition are price, quality, and service. In Japan today, Japanese companies are even now competing in introducing better and faster *Kaizen* programmes (Masaaki, 1986: 16). Once the *Kaizen* movement has been started, there is no way to reverse the trend. *Kaizen* is an ongoing process.

Kaizen is generic and can be applied to every aspect of everybody's activities. The *Kaizen* philosophy assumes that our way of life—be it our working life, or social life, or our home life—deserves to be constantly improved. In any business, an employee's work is based on existing standards, either explicit or implicit, imposed by management. Maintenance refers to maintaining such standards through training and discipline. By contrast, improvement refers to improving the standards. Improving standards means establishing higher standards. Improvement can thus be broken down into *Kaizen* and innovation. *Kaizen* signifies small improvements made in the status quo as a result of ongoing efforts while innovation involves a drastic improvement in the status quo as a result of a large investment in new technology and/or equipment (Masaaki, 1986: 16). *Kaizen* also means ongoing improvement involving everyone—top management, managers, and workers.

Underlying the *Kaizen* strategy is the recognition that management must seek to satisfy the customer and serve customer needs if it is to stay in business and make a profit. Improvements in such areas as quality, cost, and scheduling (meeting volume and delivery requirements) are essential. *Kaizen* is thus a customer-driven strategy for improvement leading ultimately to customer satisfaction.

Kaizen is also people oriented and is directed at people's efforts. This contrasts sharply with the result oriented thinking of most Western managers where the individual's contribution is valued only for its concrete results. *Kaizen* does not necessarily require sophisticated techniques or state-of-the art technology. Often all that is needed is common sense. It does not necessarily call for a large investment to implement it. However, it does call for a great deal of continuous effort and commitment. Unlike innovation, which is technology and money oriented, *Kaizen* is people oriented and calls for a substantial management commitment of time and effort, rather than capital (Masaaki, 1986: 24–7). Thus investing in *Kaizen* means investing in people. *Kaizen* and the Japanese 'suggestion system' work in concert. An important aspect of the suggestion system is that each suggestion, once implemented, leads to a revised standard. Through the suggestions, employees can participate in *Kaizen* in the workplace and play a vital role in upgrading standards.

Suggestions System — Japanese Style

The suggestion system was brought to Japan by Training Within Industries (TWI) and the US Air Force. In addition, many Japanese executives who visited the USA straight after the war learned about the suggestion system and started it at their companies. Whereas the American style stressed the suggestion's economic benefits and provided financial incentives, the Japanese style stressed the morale-boosting benefits of positive employee participation. Although the suggestion scheme was transferred from the West, the phenomenal success of the Japanese suggestion system is in its transfer from being a mode, merely waiting for suggestions, to an active programme for educating personnel concerning all aspects of the plan (Whitehill, 1992: 236). In addition, a major factor contributing to the success of the suggestion system in Japan, is that generally speaking Japanese managers have more leeway in implementing employee suggestions than their Western counterparts do. Japanese managers are willing to go along with a change if it contributes to any one of the following goals: making the job easier, removing drudgery from the job, removing nuisance from the job, making the job safer, making the job more productive, improving product quality, saving time and cost. This is in sharp contrast to the Western manager's almost exclusive concern with the cost of the change and its economic payback (Masaaki, 1986: 114). Also, most Japanese companies which have a suggestion system, incorporate incentives into it: whenever a suggestion yields savings, management provides rewards in proportion to the savings realized. Such rewards are paid both for suggestions made by individuals and those made by groups such as QC circles.

The suggestion system, the Japanese way, has a span of five to ten years. It involves three stages. In the first stage, management makes every effort to help the workers provide suggestions, no matter how primitive, for the betterment of the worker's job and the workshop. This stage is usually used to help the workers look at the way they are doing their jobs. In the second stage, management stresses employees' education so those employees can provide better suggestions. In order for the workers to provide better suggestions, they should be equipped to analyse problems and the environment. This requires education. Finally, in the third stage, after the workers have become both interested and educated, management starts to be concerned with the economic impact of the suggestions (Masaaki, 1986: 113–14). Workers, under a suggestion system, are expected to make daily suggestions for improvement in Japanese companies (Keys *et al.*, 1998: 131). The Toyota suggestion system, for example, produces a legendary 47.7 suggestions per employee per year (Young, 1992). The success of the Toyota suggestion system is more understandable when the company's internal suggestion response procedures are examined. Every suggestion receives a response within 24 hours from the employee's direct supervisor. Suggestions of merit are rewarded with medals or with membership of a Gold Idea Club. The most important proof of the success of this programme is the percentage of suggestions implemented. In 1986 Toyota reached an implementation rate of 96 per cent of the suggestions submitted, a percentage that is indicative not only of the higher calibre of suggestions but also of the sincerity and commitment of management to using them (Chang *et al.*, 1992). In a recent interview Toyota Motor Chairman Eiji Toyota said: 'one of the features of the Japanese workers is that they use their brains as well as their hands. Our workers provide 1.5 million suggestions a year, and 95% of them are put to practical use. There is an almost tangible concern for improvement in the air at Toyota' (Masaaki, 1986: 14–15).

Review Questions

1 Most surveys of Western companies operating in Japan identify human resource management as one of the most complex and difficult challenges for their operations. To what extent do Western management practices differ from the Japanese?

2 Identify and evaluate the most valuable contributions of Japanese management principles and practices to the competitiveness of global firms.

3 'What other nations need to learn from the Japanese is not how to modify their economy, nor even how to organize management practices similar to theirs, but rather how to learn and to fuse practices learned into a cohesive, integrated whole.' Discuss.

4 Japan's human resources management system is now being severely criticized for its traditionalism, inflexibility, rigidity, and bureaucracy. Do you agree?

Exercise: The Virtual Keiretsu

Aim This exercise should assist students in familiarizing themselves with various search engines available on the internet. It should also develop their internet surfing skills in locating up-to-date and reliable sources of information and the latest news related to their case study.

Assignment Japanese management is facing transformation brought about by several forces. Attitudinal change is taking place among the younger Japanese who are disenchanted with the standard of living and quality of life forced on them by traditional standards. Using the internet, company websites, and various databases, trace some of the recent changes being introduced by Japanese organizations in response to the economic crisis and the changing needs of society, and evaluate their effectiveness.

Students are asked to choose a Japanese Keiretsu of interest to them, trace its management practices and development since its establishment, the problems it has been facing since the economic crisis in Japan, changes in the attitude of its workforce, reforms so far introduced, and report their findings to the class.

Relevant Cases Studies (in Part IV)

- Matsushita: Putting the Employee First
- Quality Circles at Land Rover: The UK Experience

Further Reading

Chen Min, *Asian Management Systems*, London: Thomson Business Press, 1995.

Cheng T. C. E., and Podolsky, S., *Just in Time Manufacturing: An Introduction*, 2nd edn., London: Chapman and Hall, 1996.

De Gruyter, Charles J. Walter, *The Japanese Industrial System*, New York: Macmillan, 1989.

Ross, J. E., and Ross, W. C., *Japanese Quality Circles and Productivity*, New York: Restow Publishing Company Inc., 1982.

Whitehill, Arthur, *Japanese Management: Tradition and Transition*, London: Routledge, 1992.

Chapter 8

Korean Management

Korean children are told the story of a Duke Chuang, who had difficulties governing his district. The wise sage, Master Mu-Sun, used the analogy of comparing fire and water to analyze the Duke's predicament. Although the fire whilst it is burning is seemingly invincible, it does eventually burn out. Whereas water, starting only as a small stream in the mountains, permeates every crack in the land and humbly touches and fills every crevice. So in terms of leadership, Master Mu-Sun explained, it is not always the most thrusting and dynamic managers who succeed, but frequently the humblest of leaders, who are closer to the common people.

(Quoted in Ju-Choi and Wright, 1994: 57)

Understanding Korean management style is important for foreign companies looking for business partners in Asia Pacific. Korean management is at present undergoing a massive change as a result of the Koreans' corporate restructuring efforts. However, despite the current movement towards the so-called 'Westernization' process, Korean management still remains unique. A good place to begin understanding how Korean firms are organized and managed is to consider the Chaebols, how they evolved and developed, what made them unique competitors in the international market-place during the 'Asian Miracle', and how they are now riding the Asian crisis through to recovery.

The Rise and Growth of the Korean Chaebols

The first Chaebols were formed in South Korea in the 1920s and 1930s when the country was under Japanese colonial rule. Japan planned Korea's economic development to feed its own markets and set up a series of companies which were privately owned and run, but strictly controlled by the central government—through credit, the approval or not of trading licences, and a host of other measures (OTN, 1998). This system was then massively developed during President Park Chung Hee in the 1960s and 1970s by selecting a few companies to prosper and grow by granting them all kinds of preferential treatment. These Chaebols then became the engines of growth behind Korea's economic development. Between them they employed over half a million South Koreans and controlled the jobs of millions more. They have also used their dominating size to enjoy monopolistic profits in the markets of the various fields of business they have moved into, and thus acquired an excessive concentration of economic power. This concentration of economic power can be divided into four types: general concentration, complex concentration, market concentration, and ownership concentration. General concentration is economic power based on the proportion of the national economy accounted for by all conglomerates. Complex concentration is economic power based on the degree of conglomerate diversification. Market concentration is economic power based on the level of monopoly or oligopoly that Chaebol affiliates hold in the markets of their respective areas of business. Ownership concentration is economic power based on the distribution of enterprise voting right equity (Dohyung, 1999: 493).

Organization Structure and Operations

A Chaebol can be defined as a business group consisting of large companies that are owned and managed by family members and relatives in many diversified business areas (Sangiin and Sang, 1987). The term, Chaebol, itself means a financial clique created by talented entrepreneurs consisting of varied corporate enterprises engaged in diverse businesses that produce a wide range of product lines for global consumption. This large corporate entity is typically owned and controlled by one or two interrelated family groups (Ungson et al., 1997). The major difference between Korean Chaebols and the Japanenese Keiretsus is that Chaebols do not all have their own financial institutions. This has traditionally made them much more dependent on government approval, especially after the nationalization of the South Korean banks in the mid-1970s. They do, however, hold shares in each other. Also, unlike the Japanese Keiretsus, which are vertically integrated in the same industry, Chaebols spread across various industries. They also have a more formal structure and centralized control than the Keiretsus.

Chaebols, furthermore, are more family based and family oriented than their Japanese counterparts. Indeed, a fundamental difference in the concept of 'family members' between the Japanese and Koreans exists (Lee and Yoo, 1987). The Japanese concept of family consists of two meanings. One is the concept of family based strictly on blood relationship. The other is the concept of the household or clan which is not only based on blood relationship but also on adoption. The Korean concept of family, on the other hand, is strictly based on a blood relationship. This difference in concept has important implications for family inheritance and for the ownership structure. In Korea, the inheritance is carried out strictly on the basis of blood relationship, with the eldest son enjoying priority and other members of the family having their due shares. This family ownership of Korean Chaebols, according to Hattori, can be classified into three types (Hattori, 1984). The first is direct and sole ownership, where the founder or his family members own all the business. The second is the domination of a holding company in which the founder or his family members own the holding company, which in turn owns the affiliated companies. The third is interlocking mutual ownership, where the founder or his family members own the holding company and/or some kind of foundation, which in turn owns the affiliated companies. Consequently, family members of the founders play very important roles in the management of most Chaebols. This explains why children of the founders often hold key positions in Chaebols. In Japan, by contrast, the main objective of succession is to protect and expand the wealth of the family through the leadership of a capable individual rather than to bequeath the wealth only to blood-related family members. Therefore the family wealth can be bequeathed to an adopted son with no blood relationship.

Another factor which distinguishes the Korean Chaebols from their international counterparts is their fervent commitment to entrepreneurship. 'I can smell money everywhere even in bleak, economically bankrupt North Korea', Daewoo Chairman Kim Woo-Choong observed in 1992 (Kraar, 1995). This strong entrepreneurial orientation which has encouraged risk-taking on a grand scale has largely contributed to the rapid growth of the Chaebols during the 'Asian Miracle', but also to the sudden collapse of some during the crisis. Chaebols are also substantially smaller than the Keiretsus. They can move more quickly and decisively than their Japanese counterparts because they devote less time to consensus-building among people at various levels of the organization (Ungson *et al.*, 1997: 43). This characteristic has proved valuable in riding the Asian crisis through the introduction of swift measures of restructuring and reforms.

Inside the Korean Chaebols

Korean companies have developed their own management system known by some as K-type management. Inspired by Confucianism, Japanese, and American influences; Korean management represents a unique blend of Western and Eastern management philosophies and practices.

Koreans have a tradition of working extremely hard. This attitude towards work can be traced to the Confucian value system. The term for this attitude is *eui-yok*. Roughly translated, it means 'will' or 'ambition' (Ungson *et al.*, 1997: 170–1). A person with *eui-yok* has an internal drive to succeed, to accomplish something important, not so much for the financial reward as for the spiritual reward. This ambition and achievement-oriented drive in Korea, however, is different from the Western conception. While achievement-oriented individuals exist in both East and West, the basis, or focus of their behaviour is quite different. In Korea, reflecting a 'Confucian' work ethic, an employee's work effort is primarily group oriented. Hard work is done so that the group—that is, the company—will succeed. In the West, reflecting the Western Protestant work ethic, a person's work effort is primarily focused on individual advancement and achievement. The worker generally puts himself or herself first in striving for success. The main traditional requirements of Confucianism have a deep influence on the conduct of Korean workers. These are as follows:

- absolute loyalty to the hierarchy within the structure of authority, be it family, community, organization, or nation;

- trust between friends and working colleagues. This is deemed to be an important virtue;

- allegiance and respect to parents, incorporating love and gratitude;

- orderly and clearly defined conduct between children and adults. All children were taught to be respectful to their parents and grandparents. They spoke only when spoken to, bowed when expected, and only used respectful language;

- separation of husband and wife. They conducted their lives almost in total exclusion from one another. Men conducted their business affairs and women were responsible for running family matters (Ju Choi and Wright, 1994: 41).

Respect for ancestors, grandparents, and elders remains a key element in creating and demonstrating the right attitude. Relationships as a result tend to be vertical, related to age and position within the hierarchy. This then clearly explains the basic principles behind K-type management which includes: top–down decision-making, planning, and coordination; authoritarian and paternalistic leadership; *inhwa* (harmony-orientated cultural values); centralized management; flexible lifetime employment, compensation based on seniority and merit rating, and high mobility of workers (Lee and Yoo, 1987).

Authority and Paternalistic Leadership

Confucian tradition favours regimentation and authoritarianism. Thus, authority in the Korean firm is concentrated at senior levels of managerial hierarchies. The hierearchy starts with the chairman, followed by the president, vice-president, senior managing director, managing director, department manager, section manager, and continues down to the foreman and blue-collar workers. This is then strongly supported by functional control from staff departments like planning, finance, and personnel (Chen, 1995: 214). The Chaebols are managed by one central paternalistic figure. The chief executive, or the founder, typically assumes personal responsibility for the performance of every aspect of the firm. The relationship between superiors and subordinates in the Chaebols is characterized by a high degree of paternalism. It is expected that a supervisor or manager will assume personal responsibility for the development of his subordinates and that these subordinates will respond by showing proper respect and obedience. These are mutual commitments and obligations. A manager will take an active interest in his subordinate's personal and family life, attending funerals and birthday parties, giving gifts on certain occasions, and so forth. This practice stands in stark contrast with the Western norm that clearly separates work life from home life. In the West, superior–subordinate relationships tend to be more distant and less personal, governed largely by the responsibilities laid out in a detailed job description, with employment and promotion based solely on merit and qualification. In the West this paternalistic behaviour has often been resented and resisted, viewed as either a form of favouritism or an invasion of one's privacy (Ungson *et al.*, 1997: 173).

Centralized Planning and Coordination

Most Chaebols have a planning group, known variously as the planning and coordination office, the central planning office, or the office of the chairman. The role of the central planning function is to work closely with the group chairmen in reaching decisions and developing strategic plans for future corporate actions. The central planning office collects, analyses, and presents useful information to the chairman for future decision-making. The planning group also plays a major role in personnel decisions. It is mainly responsible for screening, hiring, and assigning all new college graduates hired by the company, thereby ensuring continuity and quality across the various units. It is also responsible for transferring personnel between the various companies and for overseeing the overall salary and bonus system.

Top–Down Decision-Making

Decision-making, especially financial decision-making, is therefore centralized and tightly controlled by top executives who make decisions either unilaterally or in small groups after consultation with the various parties involved. The general preference is for quick actions rather than detailed planning, usually dominated by the 'go for it first and fix it later' mentality (Chen, 1995: 232). A *pummi*, or proposal submitted for deliberation, in theory appears similar to the Japanese *ring-sei* decision, but is seldom followed in any systematic fashion. Instead the *pummi* system serves mainly to provide documentation for all company programmes and new ventures, and to diffuse responsibility for implementation of the decision. Once a decision is made, the responsibility for its implementation is decentralized. Subordinates are not expected to question the decision, rather, their job and their future career rest on making the venture successful, against any and all odds (Ungson *et al.*, 1987: 175–6).

This authoritarian style, however, is not despotic. Corporate leadership in Korean companies is heavily influenced by a key value of *inhwa*, or harmony. *Inhwa* emphasizes harmony between unequals in rank, power, and prestige. Another aspect of *inhwa* is that each party has responsibility to support the other. Managers tend to make decisions with the consultation of subordinates. The process of informal consensus formation or *sajeon-hyupui*, is similar to the Japanese *nemawashi*, but Korean subordinates are usually reluctant to express their opinions (Byung-Nak, 1995: 29). Subsequently, managers are often expected to understand the feelings of the subordinates before making appropriate decisions. Managers maintain various interactions with their subordinates on an informal basis as an important way to achieve harmony-orientated leadership, which is based on mutual trust and benevolent authoritarianism.

Flexible Lifetime Employment and 'All-Round Person' Management Training

Individual jobs are not clearly structured in many Korean companies and usually do not have clear-cut job descriptions. The responsibilities of individual employees tend to be decided by the supervisor according to the needs of the occasion. Although it is argued that such a system of poorly defined job assignments can bring about low efficiency from ill-distributed workloads in adjusting to changing conditions (Chen, 1995: 215), this has proved most useful during the crisis, as shown later in this chapter.

As far as mobility of workers is concerned, Korean firms can lay off employees at all levels if the business encounter a downturn. South Korean employees also change jobs fairly frequently. As the concept of loyalty in Korea is based on individual relationships, the loyalty of employees is often devoted to a specific superior. When a manager moves to another company for a better job, he may often bring many of his subordinates with him. Employees, thus, move jobs quite freely (Byung-Nak, 1990: 95).

Like their Japanese counterparts, Korean firms take considerable pains in the development of their employees at all levels. However, instead of the Japanese system of job rotation, the Koreans' focus is not so much on gaining new job-related knowledge or skills as it is on moulding current and future managers to fit into the company's corporate culture. Emphasis is placed on developing positive attitudes rather than professional skills, on the assumption that loyalty, dedication, and team spirit are more important than current job skills. The company's aim is to develop what is often called the 'all-round person'. The all-round person possesses general abilities but is not a specialist. His commitment to the company and his co-workers is unquestioned, and above all, he fits into the group. Training is seen as one means of instilling this attitude in employees across the corporation (Ungson *et al.*, 1997: 197).

Compensation Based on Seniority and Merit

Most large Korean corporations classify their employees into three categories: core (top management), basic (permanent employees), and temporary. Most of them also have their own employee-training centres. With regard to rewards and promotion, traditionally this was based on seniority. It is strongly believed that the seniority system contributes to the maintenance of group harmony and reduces competition between co-workers. Some Korean companies have gradually combined seniority with performance in distributing rewards. Wages remain generally based on seniority, but bonuses may also be awarded based on performance (Hookeun, 1985). Performance appraisal, however, is rather a difficult task in Korean firms. In addition to job performance, appraisers are expected to evaluate employees' personal qualities such as sincerity, loyalty, and attitude towards their work, which are difficult to measure. Since subjective judgements may hamper an objective evaluation of job attitude and special ability, many managers are often unwilling to give their subordinates too negative an evaluation to save face. Also, because of the emphasis placed on harmony between unequals (*inhwa*) in prestige, rank, and power, a negative evaluation may undermine harmonious relations. Another Korean value *Koenchanayo* or 'that's good enough' also hampers critical evaluation, as it urges tolerance and appreciation of other people's efforts. The key part of *Koenchanayo* is that 'one should not be excessively picky in assessing someone else's sincere efforts' (Kang, 1989: 12).

Korea Inc.: Business–Government Relations

Observers have often described the close business–government relationship between the Chaebols and the Korean government as Korea Inc., but a clear distinction exists between Korean Inc., Singapore Inc., and Japanese Inc., In Singapore, the government sees itself as the main agenda-setter and agenda-achiever while in Japan the relationship between business and government is typically one of mutual consensus among relative equals on policy decisions. Most major Japanese firms have their own banks as part of their organizational structure and are thus assured of a reliable source of credit; they do not require government financing (Ungson *et al.*, 1997: 72). In Korea, by contrast, the government sets the policies and businesses have to follow. Firms have not been allowed to own banks until recently. As a result, the government has traditionally controlled firms' access to capital. The government in Korea, furthermore, dictates the operations of the Chaebols on an unequal basis. (Ungson *et al.*, 1997: 43). A key to the Chaebols' success during the 'Asian Miracle' has been their usefulness to the government as an instrument for economic development. The government used its power through preferential loans and interest rates, through licensing authorizations, and through the inclusion of certain companies in its economic development plans to select and guide those chosen for success. To be successful, it was thus essential for the Chaebol to be well connected. The Chaebols' existence depended on having to support the incumbent political party, make donations to the right causes, and succeed with the government-sponsored ventures. Failure to do any of the above could and sometimes did lead to a termination of financing and sometimes bankruptcy. As a result, it is sometimes said that Korea represents an unusual blend of free enterprise and state direction (Lee and Yoo, 1987: 95–110).

Prior to the Asian crisis, the four super Chaebols were: Samsung, Hyundai, Goldstar, and Daewoo.

Korea's Top Four Chaebols

Samsung Means Three Stars in Korean

Before the Asian crisis, Samsung was rated as the eighteenth largest firm in the Fortune Global 500. Its businesses were so diversified that they included electronics, heavy industry, insurance, chemicals, trading, construction, financial and information services, and consumer products and services.

Samsung was established by Lee Byung-Chull (known as B. C. Lee) after the Korean War. Initially, the company focused its efforts on providing basic necessities to resupply a war-torn country. As Korea's standard of living began to rise in the 1960s, Samsung moved into the service sector with such businesses as insurance, broadcasting, securities, and department stores. By the end of the 1960s Samsung had an annual turnover of $100 million. In the 1970s the company entered electronics and heavy industries. By the end of the decade, Samsung's combined turnover had reached $3 billion. Between 1976 and 1980, Samsung expanded its foreign branches in New York, Tokyo, and Frankfurt, and from 1980 onwards, more emphasis was placed on high-technology ventures and globalization of its production in Europe, South-East Asia, Latin America, South Africa, and the Middle East. During the 1990s, Samsung expanded further into socialist countries such as China and Vietnam, and into Eastern Europe. Further investments were made in South-East Asian countries.

Hyundai: Means Modern in Korean

Chung Ju-Yung formed Hyundai Engineering and Construction Company in 1947, focusing on the construction of dams, roads, harbours and housing projects. In 1968 Chairman Chung decided to enter the automobile industry and established Hyundai Motor Company to assemble Ford passenger cars to be sold locally. With technical assistance from Mitsubishi, Hyundai designed and produced Ford's first integrated passenger car, the Pony. In 1973 Hyundai Heavy Industries Co. was formed as a major shipbuilding enterprise, one of the largest in the world.

Many units were spun off as independent companies: Hyundai Engine and Machinery Co., Hyundai Electrical Engineering, Hyundai Rolling Stock. Hyundai also acquired Inchon Iron and Steel Co. and Aluminum of Korea. In 1976 Hyundai Corporation was formed as the corporate groups' general trading company, and in 1980, Hyundai Electronics Industries Co. was formed, followed in 1984 by the establishment of Hyundai Offshore. Hyundai embarked on its first overseas assignment in Saudi Arabia in 1970. It then expanded its international operations into countries like Thailand, South Vietnam, Australia, Singapore, and the USA. Up until the Asian crisis, Hyundai consisted of 47 companies, with 83 branch offices in forty-six countries, employing more than 161,000 employees worldwide. Its annual sales reached $49 billion in 1996.

Lucky-Goldstar

Lucky Chemical Company was founded by Koo In-Whoi in 1947. The company initially manufactured cosmetics. The company then branched out into plastics. After the Korean War, toothpaste and laundry detergent were also being produced. A trading company was established in 1953 followed by the creation of Goldstar Co. in 1958 to produce radios, refrigerators, and televisions. In 1967, an oil refinery was also founded. International expansion began in 1982 when LG became a major manufacturing plant in Alabama, USA, manufacturing 1 million colour televisions. A second facility was opened in West Germany in 1987. In 1989 Goldstar built a television manufacturing facility in China and in 1995 LG bought 58 per cent of Zenith Television. Up until the Asian crisis the LG group consisted of 39 affiliated companies, 39 joint ventures, and 130 branch offices around the world, employing around 100,000 people with sales reaching $35 billion by 1996.

Daewoo: Means Great Universe in Korean

Daewoo was founded by Kim Woo Choong in 1967 as a small textile trading company with an investment of $18,000 and four employees. It has since grown into a 100,000 employee organization with 19 domestic companies and 135 overseas subsidiaries, with sales reaching over $35 billion by 1996. A detailed case study of Daewoo growth strategies before and after the Asian crisis is provided in Part IV.

Note: Most of the information provided above was accessed through the companies' home pages.

The Asian Crisis and the Chaebols

The Chaebols were considered the engine of growth behind Korea's economic development. Korea's impressive growth during the 'Asian Miracle' was largely attributed to its Chaebols. Although their assets and sales increased over the years, their financial structure was seldom improved. Most Chaebols, in fact, suffered from poor financial structure. In the early 1980s, the average debt ratio was high and the stockholders' equity ratio to assets was low. Chaebols chronically depended on bank loans to supply capital. For example, between 1980 and 1984, while Korean companies could supply only 43.7 per cent of capital for themselves, US, German, Japanese and Taiwanese companies supplied 93.7, 71.1, 66.5 and 67.4 per cent, respectively of capital for themselves. Even between

1986 and 1988 when Korea enjoyed a trade surplus, companies could either have decreased the debt ratio or increased the stockholders' equity ratio. Instead, they invested their surplus capital in purchasing real estate and bonds, or deposited it in secondary financial institutions such as insurance companies and short-term financing companies, which would provide a higher rate of interest (Yeon-Ho, 1997: 37).

The Korean government's preferential allocation of bank credit and easier access to foreign loans greatly contributed to the Chaebols' economic expansion under the Park regime. Korean firms were highly dependent on external borrowing, and their dependence deepened rapidly as the Korean economy developed. Government commercial and foreign loans had two attractive conditions: they were relatively long term and were at low interest rates. The loans were provided at favourable terms, and a period of grace for their repayment was sometimes granted, with significantly low interest rates. Another factor that caused the high debt-equity ratio of the Chaebols was the government's taxing policy. In the 1960s, 1970s, and early 1980s, the government intentionally applied a low tax rate on interest on financial capital deposited with banks, for the purpose of promoting savings. Hence the Chaebols tended to use profits to expand their business rather than improve their companies' financial state (e.g. the debt-equity and the stockholders' equity ratios, (Yeon-Ho, 1997: 39). Chaebols speculated in real estate, which was not directly related to productive activities, by using cheap bank loans acquired by the government's special favour, rather than make an earnest effort to improve their poor financial status. As of 1989, the thirty largest Chaebols owned 438.3 sq. km. of land, which accounted for 9.7 per cent of the 4,496 sq. km.; of land owned by all domestic corporations. In terms of currency, this was equivalent to approximately US$16.8 billion. The reason the Korean Chaebols invested heavily in real estate was that it was regarded as an important source of capital gain. The Chaebols' possession of real estate for speculative purposes rose by an average of 18.9 per cent per annum. The years from 1986 to 1989, during which time Korea made a trade surplus, were largely the period when the Chaebol invested their profits in purchasing real estate instead of redeeming the debt (Yeon-Ho, 1997: 59).

When the South Korean economy entered a recession in 1990, the Chaebols were criticized for having expanded their assets by investing in real estate and financial business instead of improving the competitiveness of the manufacturing industry by reinforcing R&D. The Korean government has, since then, reduced loans and payment guarantees directed to the Chaebol enterprises. The Chaebols were forced to dispose of their non-business-purpose real estate. Radical measures to restrict investment in real estate by the Chaebols have also been introduced. The government banned the Chaebols from purchasing real estate until the end of June 1991. The ban was extended twice on 24 January 1991 and in May 1992 (Ju Choi and Wright, 1994: 65).

Another major weakness perceived to characterize all Korean Chaebols is that they are far too diversified and dabble in every conceivable business sector, from aerospace to cars, to construction, to textiles, and to foods. In future, they will need to specialize in the core business and focus their individual strengths, if they are to continue their phenomenal success in world markets. Following the Asian crisis, President Kim presented a bold plan to restructure the Chaebols, aiming to transform them from highly diversified export-driven conglomerates into lean, highly focused international competitors. Kim

Dohyung's article entitled 'IMF Bailout and Financial and Corporate Restructuring' provides an interesting discussion of the main issues involved. The main structural reforms listed are as follows (Dohyung, 1999: 460–513):

(1) enhancing the transparency of management and the dissolution of the cross-debt guarantee through the appointment of external auditors and the early introduction and submission of consolidated financial statements;

(2) abolishing cross-debt guarantees and the reduction of debt-equity ratios. From 1 April 1998 the conclusion of any new cross-debt guarantee was prohibited, and existing guarantees would have to be terminated by March 2000. Also financial institutions were prohibited from demanding cross-guarantees from corporate borrowers;

(3) improving the corporate financial structure. The government decided to exempt enterprises from excise taxes on assets when these were sold to repay debts to financial institutions, effective until 1999. In April 1998, the government called on the sixth to sixty-fourth ranking conglomerates to conclude a Capital Structure Improvement Agreement with their main creditor banks whereby they would promise to reduce the ratio of their debt with these banks to 200 per cent or less by the end of 1999, including a request to submit plans for corporate improvement plans;

(4) determining core business areas. The five top Chaebols were expected to designate the areas of business where they had comparative advantages and draw up proposals to concentrate their core competence in these areas. According to the 7 December 1998 Big Deal, the five Chaebols were to designate three to five areas as their primary businesses and were to concentrate their core competence in these areas. This specialization has already begun, with corporations such as Samsung concentrating on such growth industries as electronics and aerospace, LG on chemicals and energy, and Daewoo on automobiles, machinery, and distribution transportation;

(5) institutionalizing the accountability of management and controlling shareholders. The government required enterprises listed on the stock exchange to appoint and empower outside directors;

(6) closing insolvent companies and stimulating mergers and acquisitions. Fifty-five companies were designated for closure, including twenty affiliates of the five largest Chaebols, and banks stopped all new lending to these firms. These were considered as the opening steps towards reforming the conglomerates' propensity for excessive borrowing and lax management.

Daewoo represents a good case illustration of how a Korean Chaebol has globalized its operations in a short span of time. It also illustrates how this Chaebol successfully penetrated the European car market which was already saturated with a large number of competitors. However, following the Asian crisis and the Korean government's pressure towards downsizing, Daewoo Motor faced the challenge of restructuring itself (see detailed case study in Part IV).

Review Questions

1 It is often argued that promotion based on seniority contributes to the maintenance of group harmony. Do you agree?

2 How can the Chaebols succeed in world markets with less support from their government and a more specialized structure, without destroying their essential strengths?

3 Are the Korean Chaebols 'engines of growth' or 'engines of destruction'? Identify and evaluate their strengths and weaknesses.

4 What are the key principles behind Korean management, and how do they differ from the Japanese?

Exercise: Confucianism versus Capitalism

Aim This exercise is designed to illustrate the complexity of Confucian ethics and modern society. It aims to improve students' skills in conducting a debate, in choosing the main issues to be discussed, and in reaching an acceptable position between the different points of view involved.

Assignment It is often claimed that Confucian values such as education, work ethics, endurance, harmonious interpersonal relationships, respect for the elderly, group solidarity, and discipline have played a major role in Korea's economic development. Others argue that many facets of Confucianism, such as its rigid ethical codes, disdain for democracy and equality, might be regarded as retarding economic and technological progress and innovation. Confucianism is in fact inherently incompatible with capitalism and modernization.

The class should be divided into two groups. The first group should explain the benefits of Confucian values and their implications for business. The second group should argue against it by highlighting the negative contribution of Confucian values for business. Both parties should support their points of view with empirical evidence taken from the experiences of various Korean and Western firms known to them.

The class debate should then focus on discussing whether Confucianism is in fact inherently incompatible with capitalism and modernization.

Relevant Case Studies (Part IV)

- Daewoo: 'The Chaebol you Never Heard of'
- An Emerging Regional Manufacturing Network in South East Asia: The Case of Samsung Group of Korea

Further Reading

Chen, M., and Pan, W., *Understanding the Process of Doing Business in China, Taiwan and Hong Kong. A Guide for International Executives*, Lewiston, NY: The Edwin Mellen Press, 1993.

Dohyung, Kim, 'IMF Bailout and Financial and Corporate Restructuring in the Republic of Korea', *The Developing Economies*, 37(4), Dec. 1999: 460–513.

Ungson, Gerardo R., Steers, Richard, M., and Park, Seung-Ho, *The Korean Enterprise: The Quest for Globalization*, Boston: Harvard Business School Press, 1997.

Chapter 9

Chinese Management

Doing business with the Chinese requires a thorough understanding of their management philosophy and practices. Their management style is in many respects different from mainstream Western management and is characterized by a combination of a paternalistic approach and an intuitive, entrepreneurial, and fast decision-making style. Founders of Chinese businesses often make decisions to invest, grow, and compete almost solely on the basis of business sense, experience, and their individual propensity to take risks.

Inside the Overseas Chinese Family Business

A significant part of Chinese management styles and practices is located not so much in mainland China, but among the vast numbers of 'Overseas Chinese' settled in many locations throughout the Asia Pacific. Wherever they have settled, they have come to have a major impact upon their host economy, and upon business practices within it. It is still reasonable to assert, however, that the essential elements of Chinese management are related to the longer history of China, prior to the communist revolution of 1949. Consequently, this chapter begins by focusing explicitly upon those characteristics of business and management to be found in the activities of the so-called overseas Chinese. However, as the People's Republic of China (PRC) moves more and more towards the marketization and privatization of its economy, and loosens the constraints of centralized state planning, we can expect that the specific cultural, social, and historical elements that together allow us to identify the distinctive nature of Chinese management in general, will re-emerge and assert themselves more and more within business and management in China. This is bound to be facilitated by the return of Hong Kong to the PRC in 1997, and the noticeably increased investment from overseas Chinese into the mainland economy. Since China implemented its open-door policy in 1978, the local market has experienced a huge inflow of foreign direct investment. Since 1993, the FDI flow to China has been the second largest in the world each year. By the end of 1996, an estimated US$283 billion of foreign capital had actually been invested in China. Of this, 45.2 per cent had come from overseas Chinese firms, including those from Hong Kong (39.5%), Taiwan (5.5%), and other overseas Chinese communities outside China (0.2%) (Li *et al.*, 1999: 447).

The overseas Chinese family business networks in Asia Pacific extend from Taiwan, Hong Kong, through South East Asia to Australasia and the Pacific. There are two main types of overseas Chinese family business: the core family business and the clan business. The core family business is normally very small and employs only family members and close relatives. The clan family business hires non-family members, but the core family still controls the ownership, and key family members hold the most important positions of management (Chen, 1995: 85). Both types have common distinctive features such as patriarchal, centralized, and autocratic leadership, informal structures and the compartmentalization of activities, a network of personal contacts or *guanxi* and Chinese deal-making, and use of different financial levels.

Patriarchal, Centralized, and Autocratic Leadership

The major characteristic of Chinese management is the father-figure role of Chinese manager, which is based on Chinese cultural values (Ching, 1998). As a consequence of this paternalistic approach to management, leadership in the Chinese family business is highly centralized and heavily personalized. The business owner tends to wield all the power in his own hands and makes all his decisions on his own. The leadership style is thus authoritarian. In order to maintain his power, the business owner controls information and transmits it piecemeal to subordinates so that they become dependent and unable to outperform him. The amount of information given to a specific subordinate depends on the degree of trust that the leader has for that individual. Without the control of information, the subordinates frequently have to ask the leader for instructions.

The decision-making process is also often limited to a kind of deal-making mentality limited to the business owner. Decisions are usually made by the business owner himself based largely on his own intuition and/or experience. Subordinates are in no position to challenge his authority directly. They are expected to anticipate what he is thinking and tailor their ideas accordingly. Dissenting opinions or proposals may be conveyed to him only through private and personal channels, with a duly respectful tone (Chen, 1995: 68).

Informal Structure and Compartmentalization of Activities

Up until the early 1980s the organization structure of the overseas Chinese family business used to be small and simple. Most of them concentrated on production, sales, or services. Even in larger businesses very few developed large functional departments. The overwhelming majority of Chinese family businesses did not have ancillary departments for R&D, labour relations, public relations, or market research. All employees were expected to be involved in the main products or services of the company, which directly created profits. Staffing the overseas Chinese family business was simplified by its reliance on familial relationships. In addition to family members, the extended Chinese family includes close relatives, distant relatives, and long-term non-related employees. There is thus an extensive network from which to choose. Key family members usually filled top management positions in the family business. The chief financial officer is typically either the boss himself or a key member of the family, often the son or wife. Secondary key management positions were often reserved for close relatives and those who have worked for the family for an extended period and were qualified as quasi-family members (Chen, 1995: 86). This classic method of centralized management was modelled on the ancient Chinese principle of the secretariat. The director of the enterprise is surrounded by a handful of trusted advisers without defined positions who are expected to oversee the operations of what can be a vast array of subsidiaries. Virtually all decisions of any strategic or operational importance are filtered through these advisers and passed back up to the director (Lasserre and Schütte, 1999: 105).

Also overseas Chinese family businesses did not have rigidly defined job classifications. Roles are not always clearly assigned and career paths are potentially quite broad. The level of specialization is very low. Individuals may engage in many different activities over the course of their employment. Few routine work procedures in fact exist. Employees can be assigned to various jobs at the wish of business owners. Promotion ladders likewise are not clearly defined. Due to the lack of structure and rules, the authority and responsibility of each position are not clearly defined. Therefore, it is difficult for managers at different levels to make objective assessments of employee performance. Training is also often seen as a cost with unclear future benefits. Job evaluations are not typically used, and the wage system consequently is not very complex. Fringe benefits are relatively few. Top management usually pays special attention to the degree of 'managers' loyalty'. Those highly loyal to top management and capable of special skills integral to the business are usually rewarded by the business owner with substantial personal rewards in the form of year-end bonuses and/or a 'little *rebagbag*', or bag containing money (Chen, 1995: 89). These incentives, however, are largely at the whim of the business owner. Other rewards may be distributed on special occasions such as during the Chinese New Year celebration.

Since the introduction of the new reforms in 1978, the management and operations of overseas Chinese family business have been undergoing some changes. Chinese economic reforms have put more pressures on enterprises to improve. An increasing number of overseas Chinese firms are beginning to engage in more complex and bigger manufacturing operations and financial services (Li *et al.*, 1999). In a recent survey, Li *et al.* (1999: 445–53) report significant changes in the strategic postures of overseas Chinese firms making investments in China. According to the study, overseas Chinese firms have begun to enter the industries which the traditional Chinese firms tried to avoid, such as those sophisticated manufacturing industries. They have also begun to compete with Western firms in such high-tech industries as electronic product manufacturing. Overseas Chinese firms in the electronics industry have even outnumbered foreign non-Chinese firms in China's electronics industry. Furthermore, the study suggests new competition that Western firms is likely to face in the near future in major emerging Asian markets. Asian Chinese firms are catching up and will soon challenge the dominance of Western firms in industrial sectors, including high-tech industries (Li *et al.*, 1999: 445–53). Other studies have also indicated a change in recruitment policy, with some overseas Chinese firms beginning to hire more and more professionals for the top management positions from outside their families, while others are gradually introducing more decentralized decision-making systems (Dumaine, 1997). However, it is important to note that while traditional values of filial piety, authoritarian attitude, male superiority, fatalism, and self-restraint and control are weakening, progress remains relatively slow. Chinese management is deeply rooted in cultural traditions and norms that will take a long time to change.

Guanxi or Network of Personal Contacts

A key difference between Chinese and Western business practices lies in the utmost importance of *guanxi*. For firms interested in operating in Chinese society, understanding the crucial role of *guanxi* and how it affects all the major dimensions of firm performance, and knowing the ways of creating and maintaining *guanxi* networks are essential for corporate success (Punnett and Yu, 1990). China is in fact a land of *guanxi*, where nothing can be done without it. Regarding the complexity and importance of *guanxi* in Chinese society, Fox Butterfield, a former *New York Times* journalist in Beijing, has made the following observations:

Guanxi provides the lubricant for Chinese to get through life. In a society, which for millennia had no public law, as we know it in the West to enforce impartial justice, people depended on their *guanxi*, their personal relationships, and particularly their contacts with those in power, to get things done. It was a form of social investment. Developing, cultivating and expanding one's *guanxi* became a common preoccupation. The advent of the Communists has not fundamentally changed that. As a result, the Chinese have turned the art of personal relations into a carefully calculated science. There are people who live entirely on their *guanxi*. (Butterfield, 1983: 80)

Definition and Nature of *Guanxi*

The Chinese word *guanxi* itself consists of *guan* and *xi*. *Guan* originally meant a door, and its extended meaning is 'to close up'. Thinking metaphorically inside the door you may be 'one of us' but outside the door your existence is barely recognized. Today *guan* is often used to mean a pass into various kinds of economic life, from social activities to organization names such as, for example, customs, *hai guan*. In addition *guan* can refer to 'doing someone a favour'. The Chinese world *xi* means to tie up and extend into relationships, such as kinship. It implies the formalization of hierarchy. While the word primarily applies to individuals, the concept is also used equivalently with organizations (e.g. department *xi* can also be used to refer to maintaining long-term relationships). *Guanxi* thus refers to the concept of drawing on connections in order to secure favours in personal relations (Yadong, 1997). The concept therefore contains implicit mutual obligation and governs Chinese social and business relationships.

Guanxi also often refers to a special relationship two persons have with each other. It can best be translated as friendship with implications of a continual exchange of favours (Pye, 1992). According to this conception, two people enjoying a *guanxi* relationship can assume that each is consciously committed to the other. This kind of relationship, however, does not always have to involve friends, and often tends to be more utilitarian than emotional by bonding two persons through the exchange of favours rather than through sentiment. The moral dimension functioning here is that a person who fails to observe a rule of equity and refuses to return favour for favour loses face and looks untrustworthy (Chen, 1995: 53). *Guanxi* relations that are no longer profitable or based on mutual exchanges can be easily broken.

Guanxi Base

Whether *guanxi* exists between two people depends on the existence of a *guanxi* base. People having such a base share an aspect of personal identification that is important to them as individuals (Jacobs, 1979). *Guanxi* bases are divided into blood bases and social bases. The former includes only one's family members, relatives, and members of the same clan; the latter includes other *guanxi* bases, which mainly arise from social interactions (Tsang, 1998).

Main Characteristics of *Guanxi*

Guanxi is transferable. If *A* has *guanxi* with *B* and *B* is a friend of *C*, then *B* can introduce or recommend *A* to *C* or vice versa (Yadong, 1997). This is a rather popular tactic used by foreign companies in China. For example, cosmetics manufacturer Avon initially failed to convince the central government of the workability of its direct marketing methods. Avon later obtained the assistance of David Li, the head of the Hong Kong Bank of East Asia. Li was well known for his cordial *guanxi* with the Chinese communist government. He successfully introduced Avon to the Bureau of Light Industry in Southern China. An arrangement was worked out in which Li became a partner with a 5 per cent equity because of the services that he rendered (De Keijzer, 1992). *Guanxi* thus is a reciprocal obligation to respond to requests for assistance. In this sense, it is also a liability, 'a double-entry system', a continued exchange of favours between the two parties involved. When one party receives a favour from the other, it is expected that the former will reciprocate at some time in the future; otherwise the *guanxi* cannot be sustained. The reciprocation is morally binding and is related to the elements of trust and credibility. Therefore, whenever a favour is obtained by means of *guanxi*, an entry should be made on the liability side (e.g. as payable) as well as on the asset side (Tsang, 1998). A person who does not follow a rule of equity and refuses to return favour to favour will lose his face and will be defined as untrustworthy.

Guanxi is therefore intangible. It is established with overtones of unlimited exchange of favours and maintained in the long run by unspoken commitment to others in the web. People who share a *guanxi* relationship are committed to one another by an invisible and unwritten code of reciprocity and equity. Disregarding this commitment can seriously damage one's social reputation, leading to a humiliating loss of prestige or face (Yadong, 1997). *Guanxi* is also virtually personal, and not based on corporate relations. *Guanxi* between organizations is initially established by and continues to build upon personal relationships. When the person leaves, the organization loses that *guanxi* as well. In other words, *guanxi* does not have to have group connnotation; the relationship is personal.

Finally, *guanxi* is a social capital. It is an investment in a relationship and should be clearly distinguished from the Western conception of networking that is virtually associated with commercial-based corporate-to-corporate relations. Many Western business people are often in danger of overemphasizing the gift-giving and wining-and-dining components of a *guanxi* relationship, thereby coming dangerously close to bribery. *Guanxi* is not, however, similar to a fee for service. It is given to strengthen personal relationships. A second distinction with the Western networking is the focus on personal rather than corporate relations. Whereas Western networking focuses on organizational commitment in the assessment of the partner firm's effort to develop the relationship, *guanxi* emphasizes personal relationship creation and development. When the personal relationship is devoted to and used by the organization for whatever purposes, *guanxi* then plays a role at the organizational level (Yadong, 1997).

Organizational *Guanxi*

Guanxi usage is sometimes elevated from an individual to an organizational level. Loosely speaking, a social *guanxi* base exists when there are regular transactions or a formal collaboration agreement between two organizations. The relationship can be supplier–purchaser, producer–customer, banker–client, or one of the various types of strategic alliance. A blood *guanxi* base exists where there is an ownership connection between organizations, for example, when one organization is a subsidiary of the other, or both are subsidiaries of a third organization. Under this classification, the parent companies of a joint venture are said to have social *guanxi* while the venture has blood *guanxi* with the parents (Tsang, 1998).

Since all business transactions are initiated and implemented by individuals, organizational *guanxi* has to be based on individual *guanxi*. Companies suffer when their Chinese staff leave because they take their valuable *guanxi* with them. A Chinese general manager of a wholly foreign-owned company in China once said that his company used to suffer when some of his Chinese staff left the company and took with them their valuable *guanxi*. To prevent such a loss, he designed a strategy to transform individual *guanxi* into organizational *guanxi*. When he employed a local staff member who possessed some valuable *guanxi* with, say, a senior manager of a state enterprise, he and other senior staff would try to get involved in the *guanxi*, not only with that senior manager but also with other key decision-makers in that state enterprise. This was achieved through organizing regular meetings and social activities for the staff of the two companies. Organizational *guanxi* was thus strengthened by the multiple personal *guanxi* among the staff. He also added that, whenever possible, he would try to formalize the relationship between the two companies by signing some agreement or memorandum of understanding. Since *guanxi* is a crucial company resource, it is therefore worthwhile for senior management to audit their company's *guanxi* with its outside stakeholders, such as customers, suppliers, and government bodies. Such an audit would allow management to analyse the progress that the company has made in playing the *guanxi* game and to identify the strengths and weaknesses of the current *guanxi* network (Tsang, 1998: 69–70).

The Development and Maintenance of *Guanxi*

As illustrated in Figure 9.1, the development and maintenance of *guanxi* depends on two main elements: face and *renqing*.

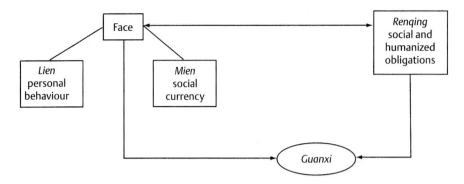

Fig. 9.1 The development and maintenance of *guanxi*

Face

'Face' is a major element of *guanxi*. Simply put, face is an individual's public image, gained by performing one or more specific social roles that are well recognized by others (for further details see Hu, 1994; Ho, 1976; Redding and Ng, 1982). The central goal of Confucianism is not only to achieve social harmony which depends on the maintenance of harmonious relationships among individuals but also on the protection of an individual's 'face' or dignity, self-respect, and prestige. If a Chinese loses his or her face, he or she might as well feel according to tradition, as if he or she had lost eyes, nose, or mouth (Chen, 1995). 'Face' can be classified into two dimensions: *Lien* and *mien-tsu*. The former is associated with personal behaviour whereas the latter is something valuable that can be achieved. A Chinese individual is socially criticized if he has no *lien*. *Mien-tsu* is a social currency and a Chinese individual is deemed unsuccessful and low in status if he has no *mien-tsu* (Hu, 1994). One has to have *mien-tsu* in order to build one's own network. Normally, one who holds higher social position or is materially richer has greater *mien-tsu*. The Chinese interact with each other to protect, save, add, give, exchange, or even borrow 'face'.

Renqing or the Social or Humanized Obligation

The cultivation and development of *guanxi* requires a social or humanized obligation known as *renqing*. This obligation, however, is not similar to emotional feelings. Emotional feelings are more personal than social, whereas *renqing* is more social than personal. In a way, *renqing* can be interpreted as 'human feelings' which cover not only sentiment but also its social expressions such as the offering of congratulations or condolences and the making of gifts on appropriate occasions (Yang, 1957). *Renqing* is thus a kind of favour with the inclusion of a sentimental element. If one fails to follow the rule of equity in exchange of *renqing*, one loses face, hurts the feelings of friends, and appears morally bad (Chen, 1995: 55).

How to Handle the Face-Saving Element of the Chinese Culture

- At all times try not to make the Chinese feel as if they are losing face. Use any method available that can save their 'face'.

- Give the Chinese a way out. The emphasis is on giving the Chinese an opportunity to extricate themselves from an awkward position. In other words, when a conflict occurs and you are in an advantageous situation, a wise way to solve the problem is to give the Chinese a chance to get out without making them lose face.

- Do not miss an 'out' that may be given from the Chinese. When both parties are in a deadlock or a negotiation has reached an impasse, at a point when the Chinese people are not very willing to take the final step, they usually give a final chance of an out to their opponents. This chance may be offered obviously or just by a hint; the opportunity may last a while, or may be just fleeting. If you do not want to take the final step either, you need to pay attention to every signal from the Chinese side.

- Do not cast aside all considerations of 'face' unless you desire conflict with the Chinese.

Source: Adapted from Quanyu *et al.*, 1997.

Chinese Deal-Making and the Use of Different Financial Levels

A further key to understanding Chinese management is their deal-making skills (Engardio, 1991). Chinese business owners generally like to seal a deal as soon the opportunity presents itself. Deals here refer to business activities practised to correct sudden and unexpected deviations in the market-place, such as abrupt changes in government trade and industrial policies. Since deals cannot be programmed in advance, Chinese business owners are usually obsessed with retaining liquidity. They realize that to seize a business opportunity they must keep some cash on hand or be capable of raising cash at short notice. An understanding of the Chinese cash-generation cycle is thus important. For a Chinese businessman involved in a business deal, cash metaphorically falls asleep until it is awakened into cash again. This sleeping period is the most dangerous part of the cycle, because due to political uncertainties in the country, the cash may never awake from its deep slumber. Thus, in order to get quick cash, a good Chinese businessman focuses on accelerating the cash-generation cycle by trading a smaller margin for a shorter sleeping period, thus achieving a fast turnover. The Chinese businessman recognizes that, by being satisfied with a lower price and a smaller margin, he can sell much faster, thus reducing the slumber period. For these reasons, he would rather get a margin of 10 per cent than a margin of 20 per cent. If the business deal requires a long slumber period, the Chinese businessman would demand much higher rates of return to justify his risk. This mentality of 'fast-in and fast-out' is prevalent among Chinese businessmen (Chen, 1995: 107).

The Chinese businessman, furthermore, does not follow the Western management practice of separating marketing from financing (Limlingan, 1986). For example, when a Chinese trader offers a cash advance to a coffee grower, he is not interested in separating the income from financing the farmer, the income from transporting the coffee, the income from extending receivable finance to the coffee manufacturer, and the income from the sale of the coffee. His sole concern is to generate an amount of cash at the end of the cycle large enough to compensate for the sleeping period of his money (Chen, 1995). The ability to simultaneously conduct several deals at different stages of completion is another distinctive skill of Chinese deal-making. By treating these deals as sub-deals of a larger deal, the Chinese businessman is able to manipulate them to enhance his benefits. He may sell some goods at a loss in order to generate badly needed cash in another sub-deal, thus considering voluntary losses as financing losses. Those who are not familiar with these tactics may easily sustain losses. Many Chinese businessmen, for example, took advantage of the liberal credit terms of Western multinational corporations by 'dumping' their products in the market for cash. Sometimes Chinese businessmen may even borrow from a non-Chinese bank, only to put the cash straight back in again on deposit with the same bank. They are willing to absorb the cost of the interest differential if such a practice assures them of instant access to ready cash (Engardio, 1991).

These deal-making skills are also reflected in the formation of alliances with indigenous businessmen favoured by the government. This is the so-called *Ali Baba* relationship in which *Ali*, the Indonesian or Malay, becomes the 'sleeping' or 'blind' partner of a business but gives it a 'native' front, while *Baba*, the Chinese businessman, runs the actual business, enjoying *Ali*'s protection. Since *Ali* obtains financial benefits from the deal, the alliance can be very solid (Clad, 1989: 52–3). Chinese companies adopt this approach when they invest in countries where the overall political environment is not transparent and stable.

Finally the entrepreneurial style, intuition, and personalities of Chinese business leaders play a major role in their deal-making activities. They make swift decisions on the basis of gut feelings while at the same time keeping close control over all aspects of the operation. Chinese managers also approach business from a pragmatic stance rather than a moralistic one. In a culture where personal relationships are paramount, pragmatism may mean telling people what they want to hear or taking actions that may appear less than optimal from a strict business perspective (Saunders, 1992).

The Chinese State Enterprises[1]

Since the inception of the People's Republic of China, the Chinese State Enterprises (CSEs), especially large and medium-sized ones, have been at the centre of China's

---

[1] This section draws heavily on Chen (1995: 113–18).

economic development (Naito, 1991). Owned by the State Council, Chinese State Enterprises adopted the Soviet centralized system of macro-management organized around a network of several branches of industry. A hierarchy of authorities, starting with the central governmental ministries, to provincial bureaux, to city government, still manages each industrial branch. Under the old state planning regime, there was no recognition of the law of value or the principle of supply and demand. Various measures were taken to de-marketize or restrict the development of the market. Apart from some markets for consumer products, all the markets for production materials, capital, labour, technology, and information ceased to exist. Even the market for consumer products was fragmented and limited in coordinating power. With regard to pricing policies, there was only one form of price, that is, the state-set price, except for those agricultural products sold in free markets. Most products were bought and sold by the state. CSEs were simply considered as subsidiaries of government institutions without any managerial autonomy. Under such a system, the director of a CSE had neither independent management power nor managerial responsibility. Managers were officials appointed by the government. Technicians and workers were allocated by the state according to state plans, and the government set their wage standards according to region and profession. CSEs' managers had no power to allocate income on the basis of performance or job quality.

Since 1979, an ambitious reform programme has been introduced in China that has greatly changed the operational environment of the CSEs. In order to clarify the relationship between the government and these enterprises, the state gradually separated ownership from the power of management in many CSEs. Although the state still enjoys ownership, CSEs now have more managerial autonomy. The system of supply and demand has also improved greatly. While before 1989 it was basically a seller's market, after 1989 it has turned into a buyer's market. Enterprises have basically obtained control of the right to set prices. In addition, except for the few products still under the imperative plans, most goods can be freely purchased and sold in the market since the original state-controlled wholesale channels no longer exist. Also there have been fundamental changes in personnel policies. Contract systems have been instituted for both cadres and workers and the traditional lifelong employment system has been significantly weakened.

Today, the operational environment of the CSE is still undergoing rapid changes as China's economic reform continues to develop with full force. In addition to the decentralization of decision-making from the planning authorities introduced in the early 1980s, China has in recent years embarked upon an intensive programme to modernize every aspect of its economy and society. The programme for the so-called four modernizations—of agriculture, industry, science and technology, and national defence—envisages the complete transformation of the economic life of the country over a period of several decades. The prime mover behind the modernization campaign was China's vice-premier Deng Xiao Ping, who was determined that ideology must be set aside and the country must modernize at all costs (Brown and Porter, 1996).

Table 9.1 Comparative table of Asian and Western management styles

Japanese management	Korean management	Chinese management	Western management
Keiretsus	Chaebols	Family business	Multinationals
group of industries	large conglomerates	small firms	
Human resource management			
• lifetime employment	• flexible employment	• family/relatives	• short-term contracts
• job rotation	• all-round person in-house training	• no training provided	• career development
• promotion based on seniority	• promotion based on seniority and merit	• only family members in high positions	• promotion based on merit
Recruitment			
• selected schools and universities	• combination of back-door selection, and universities	• family and extended family members	• open market
Decision-making			
• consensus	• *inhwa*	• autocractic	• democratic
• bottom-up (*ringi*)	• top–down decisions	• top–down decisions	• participative
• quality circles	• central planning	• intuition of business owner	• management by objectives
• group harmony	• loyalty to supervisor	• loyalty to the business owner	• individualism, conflict, and confrontation

Review Questions

1   Each of the four management styles mentioned in the above table has its own strengths and weaknesses. Evaluate each one of them, and identify the circumstances under which they could be used most efficiently.

2   Management in China is facing transformation brought about by several forces. Attitudinal change is taking place among the younger population who are disenchanted with the standard of living and quality of life forced on them by traditional standards. Using the internet, company websites, and news, trace some of the recent changes being introduced and evaluate their effectiveness.

3   What can Western business learn from Asian management systems (Japanese, Korean and Chinese)?

4   Which Asian management practices are most suitable for application in Western firms? Illustrate your answer with examples taken from real-life case studies.

End of Unit Exercise: Human Resource Management in Asia Pacific

Aim Most surveys of Western companies operating in the Asia Pacific region identify human resource management as one of the most complex and difficult challenges to business development. For this major exercise, students need to integrate all the skills and knowledge covered in this unit.

Assignment Managerial failures in Asia Pacific not only cost firms a vast amount of money, but can also change their relationship with the host country, lose their market share abroad, or affect their employees' performance. It is therefore essential for business managers to be aware of the various problems of managing their human resources in the Asia Pacific region, and how to deal with them.

Students are asked to prepare a report identifying the main factors that should be taken into consideration when staffing, recruiting, and training for overseas subsidiaries in Asia Pacific. Students are free to choose any country in Asia Pacific, of particular interest to them.

Further Reading

Chen, Min, *Asian Management Systems*, London: Thomson Business Press, 1995.

—— and Pan, *Understanding the Process of Doing Business in China, Taiwan and Hong Kong. A Guide for International Executives*, Lewiston, NY: The Edwin Mellen Press, 1993.

Li, J., Khatri, N., and Lam, K., 'Changing Strategic Postures of Overseas Chinese Firms in Emerging Asian Markets', *Management Decision*, 37:5, 1999: 445–56.

Part III

Strategic Planning for Asia Pacific after the Crisis

Introduction

The Asian crisis has significantly changed the business environment in the region. Business firms are quickly discovering that if you want to play in Asia, you must play on Asia's terms. As shown in Part I, the region is slowly recovering, but the coming years will not be a smooth ride. Nevertheless, the crisis has opened many strategic opportunities, provided the big players are ready. For businesses that aspire to grow, these markets represent opportunities that cannot be ignored. The Asia Pacific region remains one of the world's largest markets, with enormous growth potential. Many economic analysts believe the region's long-term economic outlook after 2002 is good. Needs are still there and they are not going to go away. Opportunities exist in almost every line of business and the size of Asia's consumer market is still growing. In order to realize the potential of these markets, it is no longer enough for Western firms to understand and adapt to different managerial cultures, business practices, and enterprise cultures. They need to understand the unique opportunities opened to them and the different competitive climates created by the crisis. The core question is no longer how to exploit this vast market with a billion potential consumers, but how foreign firms should reorganize themselves to compete for new business in Asia. The current tough market environment in Asia following the crisis will impose severe conditions on all participants. It will allow only the most competitively advantaged to survive. Additionally, Asian competitive approaches will force foreign firms to re-evaluate and, in some cases, adapt their own traditional business strategies and concepts to the changing business environment in the region. Success in Asia Pacific will depend to a large extent on their capacity to 'learn' new repertoires and new approaches to doing business in the region. This requires not only a complete transformation of Western management practices and business strategy, but also long-term effort, commitment, and the ability to invest cash, time, and people.

Given the wide disparities in the levels of economic recovery in Asia, the existence of different political regimes, the variety of local culture and customs, there is no single strategy applicable across the region. Furthermore, following the crisis, foreign firms' promotional tactics, competitive pricing, product quality, and sales and distribution networks will become ever more critical in gaining or retaining market share in Asia. This is why Part III is filled with interesting examples rather than systematic theories. It aims to provide an insight into the region's new business environment and the change occurring within it, and the new rules of the game. An introduction to the strategic process is provided in Chapter 10. This framework is then used in Chapter 11 as a basis for formulating strategies for Asia Pacific, using examples drawn from the experience of both Western and Asian multinational firms operating in the region. Chapter 12 then examines the various international business operations available for doing business in Asia Pacific and Chapter 13 concludes by providing an insight into 'Asian' marketing principles and practices.

Chapter 10
The Strategic Process

There is no universal definition of strategy. Some writers include the purpose of the organization as part of strategy, while others make a firm distinction between purpose and actions. Corporate strategy is concerned with an organization's basic direction for the future: its purpose, its ambitions, its resources, and how it interacts with the world in which it operates (Lynch, 1997, ch. 1). A firm's business strategy can be defined as the action managers take to attain the goals of the firm. For most organizations, a principal goal is to be highly profitable. To be profitable in a competitive global environment, continual attention must be paid to both reducing the costs of value creation and to differentiating product offering so that consumers are willing to pay more for the product than it costs to produce it. Thus, strategy here is often concerned with identifying and taking actions that will lower the costs of value creation and/or will differentiate the firm's product offering through superior design, quality, service, functionality, and the like (Hill, 1999: 380).

There are four stages in the strategic process: defining the corporate overall strategy, strategic approach, strategic formulation, and strategic choice, followed by the strategic implementation plan. These are outlined in Figure 10.1.

Developing the Corporate Strategy

The starting-point in any business strategy formulation is defining the corporate strategic decision and determining its overall mission. There are four overall strategies available for firms to compete in the international environment: an international strategy, a multi-domestic strategy, a global strategy and a transnational strategy (Bartlett and Ghoshal 1989).

An *international strategy* is used when firms create value by transferring valuable skills and products to foreign markets where indigenous competitors lack those skills, and products developed at home for new markets overseas. Such a strategy can be profitable if the firm concerned has a valuable core competence that indigenous competitors in foreign markets lack and if the firm faces relatively weak pressures for local responsiveness and cost reduction.

A *multi-domestic strategy* is used when firms face high pressures for local responsiveness

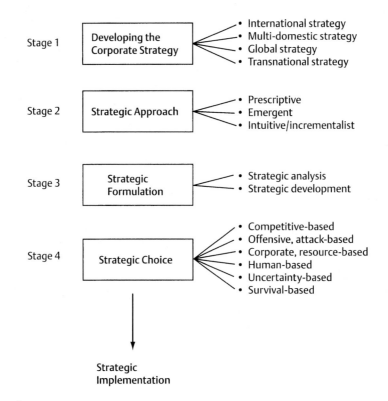

Fig.10.1 The strategic process

and low pressures for cost reductions. Under such a strategy, firms orient themselves towards achieving maximum local responsiveness by extensively customizing both their product offering and their marketing strategy to match different national conditions. They also tend to establish a complete set of value-creation activities including production, marketing, and R & D in each major national market in which they do business.

A *global strategy* is usually adopted when there are strong pressures for cost reductions and where demands for local responsiveness are minimal. Firms pursuing a low cost strategy mainly use such a strategy. Their main focus is on increasing profitability by reaping the cost reductions that come from experience-curve effects and location economies. Their production, marketing, and R & D activities are therefore concentrated in a few favourable locations. They prefer to market a standard product worldwide so that they can reap the maximum benefits from the economies of scale.

Finally, a *transnational strategy* is used when a firm faces high pressures for cost reductions and high pressures for local responsiveness. Firms that pursue a transnational strategy are trying to simultaneously achieve low-cost and differentiation advantages. According to Bartlett and Ghoshal, in today's environment, competitive conditions are so intense that to survive in the global market-place firms must exploit experience-based cost economies and location economies. They must transfer core competencies within the firm, and they must also do all this while paying attention to pressures for local responsiveness. Since core competencies do not reside just in the home country but can be developed in any of the firm's worldwide operations, the flow of skills and product offerings should not be all one way, from home firm to foreign subsidiary as in the case of firms pursuing an international strategy. Rather, the flow should also be from foreign subsidiary to home country and from foreign subsidiary to foreign subsidiary, a process Bartlett and Ghoshal refer to as global learning. A transnational strategy however is not easy to pursue. Pressure for local responsiveness and cost reductions place conflicting demands on a firm (Hill, 1999: 393). Once the firms' overall strategy has been identified, the next stage is deciding which specific approach to adopt.

Strategic Approach

There are two main Western approaches to corporate strategy formulation. These are the prescriptive approach and the emergent approach. Each complements the other, and both are relevant to the strategy process. The two approaches can be used to develop models for the corporate strategy process (Lynch, 1997: 25–6).

Strategic formulation in the West favours the *prescriptive approach* where planning typically cascades in logical steps from broad mission statements to more specific objectives like the enumeration of tasks, the assignment of responsibilities, and the fixing of a time schedule. All these tasks are linked together sequentially. Western firms, for example, first match their strengths and weaknesses against opportunities and threats in the market environment to formulate an appropriate strategy. They then implement the strategy by combining the competitive advantages of the firm into an optimal marketing programme that positions the product in the pre-selected target market segment.

The *emergent approach* takes a much more experimental view of the strategy choice and its implementation. It seeks to learn by trial, experimentation, and discussion as strategies are developed. There is no final, agreed strategy but rather a series of experimental approaches that are considered by those involved and then developed further. Strategies will then emerge during a process of crafting and testing. There is therefore no clear distinction in the emergent approach between the two stages of developing the strategy and its implementation. Moreover, there is no need to identify a separate stage of discussion involving the leadership, culture, and organization, since all these will occur initially during the strategy development and implementation phases.

The Asian approach to strategy uses a combination of the prescriptive and the emergent approaches. Companies such as Sony or Matsushita, for example, are known for their long-range planning, including grand schemes for the future of their organizations and their country. In marketing, however, they tend to be less strategic and less technical than Western business. In foreign markets in particular, where they face a great deal of uncertainty, they tend to shun grand schemes and formal planning techniques and rely on trial and error, learning gradually from small steps, and constantly adjusting decisions and objectives. They are what you might call: *intuitive incrementalists* (Johansson and Nonaka, 1996: 61).

This *intuitive incrementalism*, particularly prominent in Japanese companies, means essentially experience-based learning. It involves a lot of initial information sharing, agreeing to do something relatively small, getting quick feedback, pondering it and discussing it, then doing something small again. The main benefit of such an approach is in its speed of execution. When market conditions change rapidly, competitors need to adjust their strategies quickly. Prices might have to be reduced, advertising campaign themes shifted, in-store promotions implemented, and new product introductions delayed or speeded up. Whether it is the entry of a new competitor, a new product, or some exogenous factor such as an unexpected oil crisis or the eruption of a war, if the demand or supply conditions change, the company might have to quickly adjust or even abandon its planned strategy (Quinn, 1980: 66). The Western prescriptive approach might help pinpoint exactly where the target is at the beginning of the strategy formulation. However, Western firms in general tend to wait for their strategy to be off-target by some some magnitude before adjusting it. Given the rapidly and consistently changing environment in Asia Pacific, this may not be a good planning strategy. The Japanese incremental approach of consistently introducing small adjustments might be quicker in responding to changes in market demands. In the light of the rapidly changing business environment in the Asia Pacific region, the immediate execution advantage of the incremental approach makes it much more suitable for doing business in Asia Pacific post-crisis, where speed and flexibility are at a premium.

Thus, the main difference between the Western approach and the Asian approach to strategic planning, as illustrated in Figure 10.2 is that in the Western approach, the setting up of goals and actions are geared to achieving the goal. Chains linking alternative actions to the ultimate objective are clearly spelled out, directions are given, and so on. The Western strategist always keeps the objective firmly in view, sees the path to the top, and focuses all efforts on reaching the summit. The Japanese counterpart looks

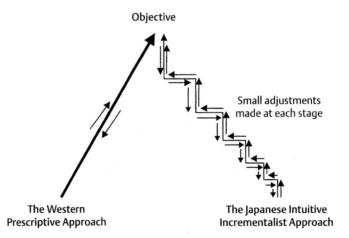

Fig.10.2 Western versus Japanese strategic approach

at the path itself, assumes that there is a peak to reach, and is not stopped by a clouded objective. 'For the Japanese, celebration does not hinge on reaching the top. The Climb itself is the raison d'être—from the top you see only higher mountains to climb' (Johansson and Nonaka, 1996: 160–1).

Strategic Formulation

There are two core areas in corporate strategy formulation. These are: strategic analysis and strategic development.

Strategic Analysis

This is the first stage in corporate strategy formulation where the organization, its mission, and objectives have to be examined and analysed. Corporate strategy provides value for the people involved in the organization and its stakeholders, but it is often the senior managers who develop the organization's overall objective in the broadest possible terms. The first step in strategic analysis is to determine the overall goal of the company, its vision and mission. For example, this could be maximizing profit, control of a market, production of a higher quality product, expansion of existing activities, entry into a new business, elimination of present activities, take-over of a rival firm, or expansion into new geographical markets. This stage is also known as identifying the overall vision of the company: in other words, deciding what the company hopes to achieve.

This is then followed by an evaluation of the current position. This must be done in relation to the identified overall company objectives. It involves analysis of the external and internal environment of the organization. Analysis of the external environment is achieved through an initial external environmental scanning, particularly of those factors over which the company has little or no control such as economic, social, political, and cultural factors and any changes in them. Analysis of the internal resources includes a financial appraisal, for example, profit contribution, return on investment, cash flow, budget, return on investment, used to determine the relationship of profit to invested capital and cash flow. A SWOT analysis is also useful at this stage to identify the organization's strengths, weaknesses, opportunities, and threats. These SWOT analysis findings can then be grouped into a TOWS matrix. This matrix was developed by Weihrich and is proposed as a conceptual framework for a systematic analysis that facilitates matching the external threats and opportunities with the internal weaknesses and strengths of the firm (Weihrich, 1982: 59). The analysis starts with the external environment by listing the external threats (T) which are of immediate importance to the firm, followed by a list of the opportunities (O). These threats and opportunities are usually related to economic, social, political, and demographic factors, products and services, technology, markets and competition. The firm's internal environment is then assessed for its strengths (S) and weaknesses (W). These factors are found in management and organization, operations, finance, marketing, and in other areas. A

	S(strength)	W(weakness)
O(opportunity)	SO	WO
	MAXI-MAXI	MINI-MAXI
	• Maximize strengths • Maximize opportunities	• Minimize weakness • Maximize opportunities
T(threats)	ST	WO
	MAXI-MINI	MINI-MAXI
	• Maximize strengths • Minimize threats	• Minimize both W and T • Fight for survival

Fig.10.3 SWOT strategic analysis
Source: Adapted from Weihrich (1982: 59)

combination of these SWOT factors often requires distinct strategic choices as illustrated in Figure 10.3.

Once the SWOT analysis is completed, it should be followed by a review of the organization structure and human resource allocation and management.

Strategic Development

Based on the above-mentioned internal and external analyses and in line with the company's objectives and mission, it is at this stage that the strategy needs to be formulated. This process involves examining the options available to achieve the agreed objectives and finding the strategic route forward. This is then followed by an evaluation of strategy options proposed, assessing each one of them and selecting the most appropriate to the company. To be successful, the strategy should be built on the particular skills of the organization and the special relationships that it has or can develop with those outside: suppliers, customers, distributors, and government. According to Ohmae, in the construction of any business strategy three main players must be taken into account. These are the corporation itself, the customer and the competition, which have come to be commonly known as the strategic three Cs (Ohmae, 1983). Two more Cs must be added at the international level. These are: country and currency. The volatility of current exchange rates, explains Ohmae, can severely affect international business operations. A sudden fluctuation in trade policy of exchange rates could cause an 'irreparable hemorrhage of cash' (Ohmae, 1990: 2). To neutralize the adverse effects of currency fluctuations, many firms are now trying to achieve a 'currency-neutral' position by moving more deeply into foreign markets (Ohmae, 1990: 8–9). This requires a deeper knowledge of foreign countries, not simply in terms of political risk analysis and attractiveness in terms of market size, growth, and local competition, as was the case in the 1960s and 1970s, but to serve the needs of their customers in global markets. The role of the governments in the internationalization process is also changing. Contrary to the claims made by classical theories of international trade, the prosperity of countries nowadays does not depend simply on the abundance of resources. Shortage of supplies, for example, may put greater pressure on finding or developing alternative supplies (Ohmae, 1990: 11). Small land area and few natural resources characterize all Switzerland, Singapore, Taiwan, Korea, and Japan. They have achieved economic development and prosperity not through husbanding resources and technologies but through developing a well-educated workforce (Ohmae, 1990: 12).

In addition to the five Cs, a competitive analysis is needed. Michael Porter, of the Harvard Business School, identifies five major forces in his competitive advantage analysis, each of which threatens an organization's ventures into a new market. According to Porter, it is the company strategist's job to analyse these forces and propose a programme for influencing or defending against them. These five forces are: the threat of new entrants, the threat of substitute products, the bargaining power of suppliers, the bargaining power of buyers, and rivalry among existing competitors. Analysis of these five factors can contribute to an evaluation of the company's strengths and weaknesses. The strengths of these five forces vary from industry to industry and determine the long-term industry profitability, because they shape the prices that firms can charge, the costs they have to bear, and the investment required to compete in the industry. The threat of new entrants limits the overall profit potential in the industry, because new entrants bring new capacity and seek market share, pushing down margins. Powerful buyers or suppliers bargain away the profits for themselves. Fierce competitive rivalry erodes profits by requiring higher costs of competing, or by passing on profits to customers in the form of lower prices. The presence of close substitute products limits the price competitors can charge without inducing substitution and eroding industry volumes (Porter, 1990: 34–5).

To assist students and business managers in their construction of a comprehensive and detailed strategic analysis based on Porter's five forces, the following questions have been developed by Gore *et al.* as useful guidelines (Gore *et al.*, 1992: 172–3).

Threat of New Entrants

- Is the customer base, present and potential, sufficient to support new entrants?
- How heavy is the capital investment requirement in the industry, and is finance available?
- Is there a strong brand image to overcome?
- How costly would access to distribution channels be?
- What operating cost advantage might existing competitors hold (experienced staff, patent protection, and so on)?
- Is there governmental/legislative protection for existing players?
- How vigorously will existing operators be expected to react against entry attempts?

Threat of Substitute Products

- Do customers perceive other products/services able to perform the same function as ours?
- Do substitutes offer higher value for money?
- Do substitutes offer higher profits?

The Bargaining Power of Suppliers

- Is there a concentration of suppliers?
- Are the costs of switching from one supplier to another high?
- Is a supplier likely to integrate forward if it does not obtain the price, profits, and performance it seeks from us?
- What is or would be the extent of any countervailing power we might be able to employ?

The Bargaining Powers of Buyers

- Is there a concentration of buyers?
- Is product/service information easily available?
- Do customers have bargaining 'will and skill'?
- Is there a threat of backward integration if customers do not obtain satisfactory supplies and prices?

Rivalry Among Existing Competitors

- How intense is rivalry now and what is it likely to be in the future?
- Are market rivals seeking dominance?
- Is the market mature and subject to 'shake out' activity?
- Do high fixed costs provoke users to maintain capacity?

There are usually many strategic options available and one or more will have to be selected.

Strategic Choice

Without competition there would be no need for strategy. The sole purpose of strategic planning is to enable a firm to gain, as efficiently as possible, a sustainable edge over its competitors (Ohmae, 1983). A good business strategy is one that assists a firm in gaining a competitive advantage over its competitors at an acceptable cost to itself. There is no single best strategy. It is up to business managers to choose which market to contest, and to decide which strategy to adopt for competing in that market. The following is a basic introduction to the different strategies formulated by various schools of thought.

Competitive-Based Strategies

These are strategies for optimizing functional performance. Profit maximization is the clear goal of such strategies. Competitive-based strategies can be constructed by looking at possible sources of differentiation in functions ranging from purchasing, design, and engineering to sales and services (Ohmae, 1983: 126). Firms can also create competitive advantage by perceiving or discovering new and better ways to compete in an industry and bringing them to market, which is ultimately an act of innovation (Porter, 1990: 45). Some competitor-based strategies include the power of an image, exploiting functional strength, capitalizing on profit, and cost-structure differences.

There are various sources of competitive advantages. These are as follows: (Lynch, 1997: 167).

- **Differentiation** This is the development of unique features or attributes in a product or services that position it to appeal especially to a part of the total market. Differentiation occurs when the product of an organization meets the needs of some customers in the market-place better than other competitors. When the organization is able to differentiate its product, it is able to charge a price that is higher than the average price in the market- place. Underlying differentiation is the concept of market segmentation, or the identification of specific groups who respond differently from other groups to the product. In order to differentiate a product, it is necessary for the producer to incur extra costs. The differentiated product costs will therefore be higher than those of competitors (Porter, 1980, 1990). Branding is an example of this source of advantage.

- **Low cost** The development of low-cost production enables the firm to compete against other companies either on the basis of lower prices or possibly on the basis of the same prices as its competitors but with more services being added. Low-cost leadership in an industry is achieved when a company has built and maintains plant, equipment, labour costs and working practices that deliver the lowest costs in that industry (Porter, 1980, 1990).

- **Niche marketing or focus strategy** A niche strategy occurs when the organization focuses on a specific niche in the market-place and develops its competitive advantage by offering products especially developed for that niche. Hence the focused strategy selects a segment or group of segments in the industry and tailors its strategy to serve them to the exclusion of others (Lynch, 1997: 489). Companies may select a small market segment and concentrate all their efforts on achieving advantages in this segment. Such a niche will need to be distinguished by special buyer needs.

- **High performance or technology** Special levels of performance or service can be developed that simply cannot be matched by other companies, for example, through patented products.

- **Quality** Some companies offer a level of quality that others are unable to match.

- **Service** Some companies have deliberately sought to provide superior levels of service that others have been unable or unwilling to match.

- **Vertical integration** The backward acquisition of raw material suppliers and/or the forward purchase of distributors may provide advantages that others cannot match.

- **Synergy** This is the combination of parts of a business such as that the sum of them is worth more than the individual parts, that is, $2 + 2 = 5$. This may occur because the parts share fixed overheads, transfer their technology or share the same sales force.

- **Culture, leadership, and style of an organization** The way that an organization leads, trains, and supports its members may be a source of advantage that others cannot match. It will also lead to innovative products, exceptional levels of service, fast responses to new market developments, and so on. This is more difficult to quantify than some of the other areas above, but this only adds to its unique appeal (Lynch, 1997: 167).

Offensive or Attack-Based Strategies

An attack-based strategy is a concerted effort involving attacking competitors in their own market. There are four main possibilities for attack, developed from military strategy: head-on attack, flanking manoeuvres, occupying new territory, or guerrilla warfare (Dudley, 1992).

1. **Head-on attack strategy** is when the firm decides to attack its main competitor's market leader in another country head-on. It is a very expensive process, needing sufficient resources for a sustained campaign to be successful. It can take a long time, perhaps several years for branded goods, or more than six years for capital goods. Sony, Hitachi, and Toshiba have all taken on the European TV industry head-on. When Western companies enter foreign markets, they usually come with a new product or new technology, and their task is to create a new segment or market. The marketing challenge is the development of latent demand, often where domestic competition is simply non-existent. Asia Pacific companies do not usually face this situation. The Western approach emphasizes new entrants' uniqueness, a new feature or two, and then targets open and undefended niches in the market. The new entrant stresses its uniqueness and avoids head-to-head battles with the market leaders. The Japanese approach is quite different. The Japanese adopt in mature foreign markets a target-the-leader strategy to overseas entry. They aim for a well-established brand, perhaps the market leader; benchmark and reverse-engineer that product and develop a similar alternative, choose a position indistinguishable except for price, and then attempt to replace the leader. Rather than trying to test the waters in a low position, the Japanese firm will go head-to-head against the best (Johansson and Nonaka, 1996: 92).

2. **Flanking manoeuvres** refer to an attack on a specific part of the leader's market that is relatively undefended, or currently holds little interest for the major multinational firm. This requires investment for some years before gaining a foothold and then to keep it and prevent others from getting in. Great attention and care should be given to pricing, performance, and service in a flanking operation. This is also known as a loose-brick approach, by which an entrant exploits the weak strategic position of a firm or sector.

3. **Occupying totally new territory** requires the creation of a totally new sector or niche market, choosing a small area that the leaders are simply not interested in or geared to handle. Prices play a major role here. A company will need to operate at a premium price, and launch on a modest scale in specialized outlets where the targeted group is located. Innovation is the key to success in this strategy, while improving existing products would lead nowhere.

4. **The guerrilla approach** refers to when a company decides to produce one-off machinery designs or limited-run fashion products, launched to take advantage of a gap left by market leaders. Guerrilla tactics need reliable, up-to-date information, and the ability to respond to market opportunities quickly, regardless of location. The company must also be prepared to withdraw rather than to stand and fight if a larger company moves in.

Corporate or Resources-Based Strategies

These have the functional aim to maximize the company's strength relative to the competition. The role of functional strategy, according to Ohmae, is to design and deliver a cost-effective function, which is done in three ways. The first method is to reduce costs much more effectively than the competition. The second method is simply to exercise selectivity in terms of orders accepted, products offered, or functions to be performed. The third method is to reduce functional cost and to share a certain key function among the corporation's other business or even with other companies: it assumes that the source of competitive advantage lies in the organization's resources (Ohmae, 1983: 91–162). Internal resources, analysis consists of core competence skills, core resources, and benchmarking.

Core competence underlies the leadership that companies have built or wish to acquire over their competitors. It is defined as a group of production skills and technologies that enable an organization to provide a particular benefit to customers. Core skills are a basic fundamental resource of the organization and cover an integration of skills, knowledge, and technology (Hamel and Prahalad, 1994). These then build into core products, which then form the basis of the business areas of the company. This combination can then lead to competitive advantage. There are three areas that distinguish the major core competencies:

- **customer value** Competence must make a real impact on how the customer perceives the organization and its products or services;

- **competitor differentiation** Competence must be competitively unique. If the whole industry has the skill, then it is not core unless the organization's skills in the area are really special;

- **extendible** Core skills need to be capable of providing the basis of products or services that go beyond those currently available (Hamel and Prahalad, 1994).

In analysing the *core resources* of an organization, Kay identifies architecture, reputation, and innovative ability as being important company resources (Kay, 1993). Architecture is the network of relationships and contacts both within and around the firm. Its importance lies in its ability to create knowledge and routines to respond to market changes and to exchange information both inside and outside the organization. Reputation, on the other hand, allows an organization to communicate favourable information about itself to its customers. It is particularly concerned with long-term relationships and takes a lengthy period to build up, for example a reputation for good quality work, delivered on time and to budget. Finally, there is innovative ability. Some organizations find it easier to innovate than others because of their structures, procedures, and rewards.

Benchmarking is the continuous process of measuring a firm's goods, practices, and services against those of its toughest competitors and leading firms in other industries. Through benchmarking, a firm can find the best way to do something and implement it. Firms no longer compete on a local regional or national basis. They compete on a global basis. Therefore remaining competitive in this environment is a major challenge facing managers. Benchmarking is a strategy to survive the globalization of business. It allows a firm to establish operating goals and productivity objectives based on the best practices in the industry. Successful benchmarking requires three fundamental activities:

- Know your operation and assess its strengths and weaknesses. This involves documenting work-process steps and practices and defining the critical performance measurement used.
- Know industry leaders and competitors. Capabilities can be differentiated only by knowing leaders' strengths and weaknesses.
- Incorporate the best and gain superiority. This involves emulating and surpassing the strengths of the best (Camp, 1992).

Human-Based Strategies

These emphasize the personnel element in strategy development and highlight the motivation, the politics and cultures of the organization, and the desires of individuals. Organizations consist of individuals and groups of people, all of whom may influence or be influenced by strategy. Therefore the human resource aspects of strategy development is fundamental to the strategy process itself. They assume that strategy will benefit from an element of learning and experimentation that empowers individuals.

Uncertainty-Based Strategy

Uncertainty-based strategies regard prediction as impossible because of the inherently unstable nature of business and its environment. The underlying assumption here is that it is not possible to predict sufficiently accurately many years ahead (Gleick, 1988). Strategies therefore must be allowed to react to the changing environment and emerge from the chaos of events. Uncertainty-based strategy uses mathematical probability concepts to show that corporate strategy development is complex, unstable, and subject to major fluctuations, thus making it impossible to undertake any useful prediction in advance. Because of these difficulties, the development of long-term strategic planning is regarded as having little value.

Survival-Based Strategy

Survival strategies are based on the survival of the fittest in the market-place. Corporate strategy, accordingly, is about how to survive in an environment which is shifting and changing (Lynch, 1997: 66). The market-place is more important than a specific strategy. Survival-based strategies aim to rely on running really efficient operations that can respond to changes in the environment. Hence the optimal strategy for survival is to be really efficient. Beyond this, companies can only rely on chance. Since the environment matters more than a specific strategy, then survival-based strategists have argued that the optimal strategy will be to pursue a number of strategic initiatives at any one time and let the market-place select the best (Hannan and Freema, 1988).

Strategic Implementation

The final stage in strategic planning consists of developing an action plan for implementation. This includes the following:

- strategic implementation: choosing an appropriate strategy for competing;

- market-entry strategy: reviewing the various methods of entry available and choosing the most appropriate strategy for the firm to adopt;

- marketing strategy: evaluating the various marketing strategies available and choosing the one most suitable to the firm.

These are discussed with a specific Asia Pacific dimension separately and consecutively in Chapters 11, 12, and 13.

Review Questions

1   Outline the benefits and limitations of a prescriptive approach to strategy formulation. Illustrate your answer with examples taken from organizations known to you.

2   Why does the Asian approach to strategy use a combination of the prescriptive and the incremental approach? Evaluate the strength and weakness of such an approach.

3   'Without competition there would be no need for strategy' (Ohmae, 1983). Explain and evaluate this statement.

Exercise: Business Strategy Formulation

Aim This exercise is designed to illustrate the complexity of strategic formulation and its implications for business. It aims to improve students' research skills and critical examination of issues considered.

Assignment Take an organization with which you are familiar. Find out whether it has been following prescriptive, emergent or intuitive incrementalist strategies, or any combination of strategic approaches and critically evaluate its benefits and limitations.
    Each group in the class should be assigned a different region in the world: Europe, USA, Africa, Middle East, and Asia Pacific.

Further Reading

Hamel, G., and Prahalad, H. K., *Competing for the Future*, Boston: Harvard Business School Press, 1994.

Hill, C., *International Business*, New York: McGraw-Hill, 1999.

Lynch, R., *Corporate Strategy*, London Pitman Publishing, UK, 1997.

Ohmae, K., *The Mind of the Strategist: Business Planning for a Competitive Advantage*, London: Penguin, 1983.

Ohmae, K., *The Borderless World: Power and Strategy in the Interlinked Economy*, London: Collins, 1990.

Porter, M., *The Competitive Advantage of Nations*, Basingstoke: Macmillan, 1990.

Chapter 11

Post-Crisis Strategies for Asia Pacific

The post-crisis environment in Asia Pacific poses many challenges for business. The Asian economic crisis and the resulting catastrophic loss of investors' confidence in Asian currencies and institutions has reduced many strong and weak companies alike to financial ruin. Given the dynamic and rapidly changing environment, it is best to experiment with different approaches as mentioned in the previous chapter and see which emerges as the best through natural selection. Firms which have already invested in Asia need to look ahead to see how they can achieve competitive positions in the post-crisis environment. Similarly, those considering entry into Asia after the crisis need to present strong arguments of future growth to justify acquisitions or partnerships in such a volatile market. As the economic crisis in Asia continues to evolve and move towards recovery, business firms should seek strategies that target long-term success, as well as short-term survival.

Rising import prices for materials and components, increasing financial difficulties, and especially the fall in regional demand affected most firms in Asia Pacific during the crisis. Firms have used different approaches to address the crisis. However, although the individual situations and objectives of each firm differed, their experiences reveal the emergence of a set of common short-term reactions such as: reducing working time, freezing salary increases, forcing vacation leave, laying off personnel, and the temporary or final closure of single plants. Some provided support for suppliers and dealers by extending payment terms, shouldering the cost of raw material purchases or offering letters of credits and so on. The onset of the economic crisis has also caused a wave of corporate regional consolidation, downsizing, and outsourcing. Others, on the other hand, embarked on long-term strategies such as the introduction of 'new strategies' for riding the crisis by either changing the rules of the game entirely, introducing new game opportunities, developing their localization and good citizenship strategies, or increasing their global/local flexibility and regional production and price cutting.

Changing the Rules of the Game

Competitive strategy generally assumes that existing players in the market will work according to a mutual understanding of how competitors are engaged—the rules of the game. Innovatory-based strategies are mostly concerned with rewriting the rules of the game, achieving technological innovation, or higher levels of service. In the case of smaller players, it may be essential to introduce some form of innovation in order to take market share. This does not mean that this is the only way to enter a market and survive, but in certain types of industry, it may represent a viable route. In some cases where, for example, technology may not be a dominant feature, achieving a higher level of service might be more appropriate. Dell, the world's third biggest PC maker, enjoyed phenomenal success in Asia. Despite the heightened risk and turmoil in the region, the company managed to keep expanding its operations in Asia by subverting the traditional models of selling through dealers and retailers outlets, with its famous direct-sales strategy and its innovative concept of 'relationship marketing'. It not only redefined the computer industry rules on how to sell a personal computer, but also pioneered what the company describes as its direct business model (For further details, see Dell's case study included in Part IV). A number of US competitors like IBM, Compaq, and Hewlett Packard are now considering going direct in Asia. But there is no evidence of it yet. Only Gateway, a smaller competitor, is a direct supplier in some parts of Asia (Weldon, 1999). The Fast-Food Business Model introduced by the Taipei-based ACER group is another inspiring example of how the computer industry is changing the rules of the game.

New Game Opportunities

Another strategy newly introduced following the Asian crisis is the practice of pursuing what is called 'new game opportunities'. This strategy begins with an awareness of the nature of the change triggered by the crisis causing, for example, severe contraction of local market demand; high interest rates and crashing equity markets; extreme exchange rate differentials; the break-up of monopolies and cartels; reduction in tariffs; liberalization of foreign ownership restrictions; and companies making pre-emptive strikes to secure advantaged positions. The result is a fundamental change in who can play the game, how they can play it, and how much it is worth. Faced with these changes, firms must now ask three questions: what will the game look like in the future; what are the crown jewels I will need to win; and how do I get them (Boulas *et al.*, 1999). The first step in evaluating 'new game opportunities' is to identify the product or marketplace that offers the greatest potential for both the near and long-term plan. This involves determining which geography and product or market segments offer the greatest value-creating opportunities, and developing a vision of how the company can take advantage of those opportunities by leveraging its own strengths. Once the attractive product or market-place

---

ACER'S Fast-Food Business Model

ACER's 'Fast-Food Model' of computer supply is based on the example of the uniform quality with which McDonald's produce hamburgers worldwide. The approach is mainly to assemble ACER products locally while still maintaining consistency. The assembly process is spread to thirty-five sites around the world. While tight controls are prescribed to ensure workers everywhere follow the same testing procedures, components are prepared in large mass manufacturing facilities, then shipped to assembly sites close to local customers. Retail buyers of ACER computers are thus guaranteed the 'freshest' ingredients . . . the latest technology—because ACER made them itself and sped them from Taiwan and Malaysia to its assembly sites: motherboards are flown in directly, while CPUs (central processing units), hard drives, and memory were purchased locally to fill individual user requirements. In addition to achieving standardized quality, customizable products, and lower inventory costs, ACER was able to drop the turnaround time from idea to market to only one or two months from the six months for old ideas and specifications. As a result, ACER was able to turn over its inventory more than seven times per year. This high turnover aided ACER to achieve a 35 per cent return on equity, as against an industry average of 15 to 20 per cent.

Source: Clyde-Smith, D., The Acer Group; 'Building an Asian Multinational', Fontainebleau, France: INSEAD-EAC, 1997 Case 397-1-5-1.

---

have been identified, approaches to gain access should be developed and valued. Depending on the industry-specific differentiators, this can involve gaining access to raw materials, control over distribution, buying into customer or product franchise, extending networks, or building scale (Young, 1998). An example of a company that pursued the 'new game opportunities' successfully is Pioneer International, the Australian cement company. In Malaysia, Pioneer Int. gained access to raw materials by purchasing the quarries of local conglomerate, Sungei Way. Pioneer Int. has thus changed the game by obtaining the dominant quarry position in Malaysia and operating the quarries in an integrated fashion, gaining a competitive advantage over other players in the market. Another example is British Telecom, which leveraged an opportunity to extend its network by partnering a local Malaysian telecommunications company (Boulas and Fryling, 1999). The Asian financial crisis, the currency devaluation, companies closing down or merging provided a number of opportunities for Wal-Mart to expand inexpensively in the region. Unlike a number of other retailers, Wal-Mart devoted a great deal of time and effort to maintaining growth as opposed to putting out fires, by opening several outlets in Indonesia (1996), China (1998), and South Korea (1998) (for further details, See Wal-Mart case study in Part IV).

Timing is another crucial element in pursuing a 'new game opportunities' strategy. The timing for the new competitive game depends on the country's stage of development, the industry environment, and local competitive dynamics. The limited set of available opportunities places great value on making a pre-emptive strike to beat the competition when the game changes. As Chipper Boulas, vice-president with Booz Allen & Hamilton in Hong Kong, and Ian Buchanan, vice-president of Booz Allen & Hamilton in Singapore put it: 'It is essential for an MNC to equip itself to influence the course of the game where it is advantaged today and has significant value at stake. Advance preparation also provides a map to ensure the company doesn't get stuck in the routine of business while others move to put it at a disadvantage in its key markets' (Boulas *et al.*, 1999).

Localization

The crisis in Asia has prompted many firms to rethink the importance of their local relationship both with government and other players in the region. Localization involves planning local national managers in all key managerial positions. Although governments in Asia are now actively opening up their markets to foreign investors, it is important to note that they are still particularly concerned that the benefit of this process goes to their own people. Partnerships with local nationals are still favoured. You can no longer expect to penetrate these high-rise markets exclusively from an exporting factory in the UK, for example. In these emerging markets you have to establish a local presence whether by setting up sales, liaison, technical or service offices, or by manufacturing part or the whole of the product locally. Today, more than ever, Asian markets want local service and support.

Local partnership in Asia Pacific can be difficult, but local relationships both with government and other players still remain important. Although the time when these relationships were sufficient in and of themselves to make a deal succeed has certainly passed, they remain an invaluable tool for building trust (Young, 1998). Furthermore, establishing a local presence is crucial not only to gain recognition but also to build personal relationships. Foreign firms are thus strongly advised to establish a permanent base in the region. Substantial investment in establishing an office is viewed by the Asian business community as evidence of a company's sincerity and commitment to the region. Alcatel, a French firm and one of the world's biggest makers of telephone switches, found itself on the right side of the Chinese government following the Tiananmen Square killing. Along with several other foreign switch-makers, Alcatel had begun selling to China in the mid-1980s. But, alone among the competition, Alcatel invested in a switch-making factory in China. When the Tiananmen Square killings took place in 1989, everyone else scampered; Alcatel, because of its factory, decided to stay put. By the time the others began returning in the early 1990s, Alcatel was well ahead in the race for government contracts thanks to the long-term view of China's prospects that it took (Rohwer, 1995: 218–19).

The base must be permanent, and the executives involved must be stationed there for a long time and must be willing to live in the region on a long-term basis. In addition to their understanding of the corporate strategy and their ability to promote the company's products and services, they should also understand and be comfortable in the local business environment. Furthermore, in Asia Pacific, because of the respect and importance given to seniority, these executives must have positions of real authority within the company. Foreign companies often tend to send personnel that have never been used to the Far East. They should recruit locally and make use of the wealth of local experience and personal relationships. The so-called overseas Chinese are often excellent expatriate choices because they are able to combine Western training with local understanding and sensitivity. Another valuable group consists of Western-trained Chinese (Wong and Maher, 1997).

Global/Local Flexibility

Firms operating in Asia Pacific after the crisis are now facing two types of competitive pressure: pressure for cost reductions and pressure to be locally responsive. These pressures place conflicting demands on firms. To reduce unit costs, for example, they have to base their productive activities at the most favourable low-cost location. This may also necessitate offering a standardized product to ride down the experience curve as quickly as possible. On the other hand, to be locally responsive, firms have to differentiate their product offering and marketing strategy from country to country in an attempt to accommodate the diverse demands that arise from national differences in consumer tastes and preferences, business practices, distribution channels, competitive conditions, and government policies (Hill, 1999: 386–7).

Global/local flexibility will be the winning strategy for multinational enterprises doing business in Asia Pacific, in the future. Honda, the Japanese car manufacturer, provides an interesting illustration.

In Asia Pacific, pressure for local responsiveness arises from a number of sources:

- differences in consumer tastes and preferences;
- differences in infrastructure and traditional practices;
- differences in distribution channels;
- differences in host government demands;
- different national standards and regulations;
- the importance of being an insider, as in the case of customers who prefer to buy local such as in Japan;

This might seem an enormous challenge but not for McDonalds. Their formula seems to work all over the world by providing their customers with a basically identical eating experience everywhere, but also paying close attention to local tastes and expectations. Some examples are useful here.

In Indonesia: Big Mac Burgers

Indonesia is one of the world's most populous Muslim countries. Under Islam, eating pork meat is prohibited. Therefore any reference to the word 'ham' might offend some customers. Few Jakartans would be likely to know that the world 'hamburger' is actually derived from the German city of Hamburg and that it is supposed to contain only beef—

Honda: The Global/Local Firm

Andrew Mair, in his book, *Honda's Global Local Corporation*, provides us with an inspiring insight into Honda's efforts towards 'glocalizing' the organization (Mair, 1994).

Mass Manufacture for Mass Markets, Niche for Niche

Honda introduced a flexible mass-production system, tailored to its mass markets in North America. Niche markets in Japan and North America are supplied from the niche base in Japan.

Global/Local Parts Sourcing

Honda operates a complex global networking pattern. Some parts are built strictly locally for inclusion in local cars. Others are brought in from Japan to Marseille, Swindon, and so on, and still others flow from Europe to North America or from North America to Japan. The vehicles, in which these parts end up, are then sold in any market.

The Global/Local car

Timing and flexibility are the keys to Honda's global factory network. Timing refers as much to synchronizing internal organizational changes—for instance, bringing new products on-line, or new production capacity—as to predicting external events. Flexibility means the ability to respond to environmental changes, to move with the flow of markets and tastes at the same pace as they change. To deal with the unstable global market environment, Honda introduced the 'total car behaviour' concept by creating appropriate overall images such as safe cars, prestige cars, and environmentally oriented cars. The goal in this approach is to introduce variations in the design of a basic and single global model to the appropriate 'total car behaviour' for each market. The key to making this approach work is to retain the same major mechanical parts, the same body frame, and many other parts such as exterior lights, for instance. The exterior bodies, however, hence the styles, can vary, and likewise the interiors, seats, and suspensions, to suit differing fashions and driving conditions. In essence, that means reversing one traditional solution to the problem of meeting diverse needs with basically the same car, which was to keep the same bodies but to vary trim like lights and bumpers.

Global Centralization

The key here is organizational speed, timing, and flexibility, the ability to respond quickly, at the right moment, and with sufficient variation to meet local needs and all the while mass producing cars at sites across the globe. To achieve this, basic research and fundamental product research—new engines, new mechanical and electronic components—are kept in Japan. That allows economies of scale in these areas. The global/local car does not vary from region to region along these lines, so global centralization makes sense.

Global/Local R & D

Honda's strategy for global/local R & D has developed a high degree of complementarity between variations in the global/local car, that is, what is shared, what is different locally, either in variations in the types of parts locally sourced and in which R & D are localized. The global/local corporation thus emerges as a coherent whole, an enterprise that retains some activities at home base but decentralizes others. The process is governed in a carefully coordinated way in which the centralization/decentralization combination runs in parallel for R & D, car design, models made, parts sourcing, and manufacturing.

Americanization versus Japanization

Americanization, for Honda, does not mean adopting traditional American managerial approaches. Instead, it means incorporating a new culture and social structure, reinterpreting the Honda Way in terms judiciously selected from the elements that make up American culture and ideology, terms which are able to mesh closely with the production system Honda wants to implant and to motivate the people to play the roles Honda wants of them. In this regard, Honda may have been blessed with particular insight precisely because of its stress in Japan on non-traditional ideas like individuality and breaking down status barriers.

Japanization, for Honda, is to do with adaptation and the skilful creation of new behaviour, not imitation of Japanese cultural practices, and this is so for Honda's worldwide operations too. Paradoxically then, true Japanization does not mean adopting Japanese behaviour in a concrete sense, but an approach aimed at finding fruitful combinations of the cultural dualist opposites.

Learning, Global/Local Style

The ultimate goal of learning at Honda is a global learning network with no necessary primacy of one direction for knowledge transfer over another. To begin with, there is the flow back to Japan. A great advantage for Honda of having a large Japanese staff stationed in North America is the build-up of a significant cadre back in Japan with several years of experience of working in California, Ohio, or Ontario. The process gives fresh, Westernized impetus to thinking in Japan. Rather than the overseas appointment signalling disfavour as it used to do in Japan, at Honda it becomes a positive advantage to career prospects. The Americans on long-term secondment to Japan will carry the same knowledge of the American production facilities with them to Japan. So great is the influence of Honda North America in Japan now, that Japanese Honda engineers working in Europe complain that the European viewpoint is swamped by North American ideas, and they can hardly get themselves heard in Japan.

Such horizontal learning at Honda means spreading the innovations that are developed in each factory, with carefully organized study visits, and with people at appropriate, that is, low hierarchical levels taking part. And the process need not be limited to personal visits. By the early 1990s, for instance, the Americans were busy making videos and developing training modules to increase their technical competence, which they expected might later be used at Honda facilities around the world. Japanese staff were developing ways to ensure that manufacturing innovations developed in North America could be passed back to Japan. So the global/local corporation can seize the opportunity not only to utilize the different environments in which it operates to complement each other, but to systematically swap and learn the innovations developed independently within each local production complex. Moreover, the very process of comparison and exchange itself can lead to further fertilization of the innovation process.

Global/Local Management

Honda has pioneered the idea that a posting in the West is a positive advantage from a career viewpoint. It has become systematic strategy to run almost all the top management through North American posts before they are promoted in Japan; and not just at an early stage in their careers for the experience, but in high-level postings as well.

Global Identity/Local Citizenship

Far from wanting to lose its original national identity as a Japanese company or to adopt a 'nationality-less', stateless character, Honda is in fact trying to gain several new identities: American, Canadian, British, European even. And that means more than just 'acceptance' by the host country as a local corporate citizen. Adopting a new citizenship role also means adopting new habits and practices within the corporation, real habits and real practices, in tune with the national culture.

Source: This case draws heavily from Andrew Mair, *Honda's Global Local Corporation*, St Martin's Press, New York: 1994.

no pork products. Consequently, in Indonesia the word hamburger does not appear anywhere on McDonald's menu. Big Mac burgers is the popular name.

In Singapore: Kiasuburger and Rendang Burger

In Singapore the Sausage McMuffin served for breakfast time is made from spicy ground chicken rather than pork, again out of respect for the Muslim religion. Also in Singapore they developed the 'Kiasuburger', an oversized sandwich whose name derives from the Hokkien word meaning 'afraid to lose out'. The Kiasuburger was designed to assure Singaporean gourmands that they would not leave the place hungry. McDonald's Singapore menu also includes curried chicken and the Rendang Burger: slices of beef simmered in a hot and spicy sauce

In Japan: Teriyaki Burger

As a response to a recent trend back to more traditional Japanese tastes, teriyaki burgers often appear on the menu alongside the Big Mac. Mild curries, rice dishes, and rice balls have been added from time to time in an attempt to cut back tough local competitors such as Mosburger.

Other examples of adjusting to local consumer tastes include the case of Kentucky Fried Chicken dropping their mashed potatoes and gravy and adding chicken curry with rice. In Singapore, Pizza Hut offers special toppings. The *Singapura* has beef with onion and chilli flakes, the *Kelong* features sardines, onions, and fresh chilli and the *Merlion* is loaded with mutton and chillies. Meanwhile, for Thai customers they add pineapple to the toppings and place little bowls of hot sauce on the tables. In China, under government pressure, Coca-Cola are developing other soft drinks for the local market. So far they have come up with *Tian Yu Di*, a soft drink in three flavours, lychee, mango, and guava. In Hong Kong, Coca-Cola's beverage assortment includes soymilk and flavoured tea drinks. In Japan *Oolong* tea seems to be one of the local favourites.

Good Citizenship

In Asia, according to Andrew Liveris, president of Asia Pacific at Dow Chemical Asia, and especially following the crisis, Western firms should be aiming to build a business, not an asset (Young, 1998). Companies must not only put down local roots but also take steps on the road to becoming a respected member of the local business community in order to be considered a serious player. Projecting the image of a caring company, for example, has been an essential part of BASF's successful expansion drive in South Korea. While most foreign firms were doing their best to avoid the Korea debt-laden companies, when Hannam Industrial was on the verge of bankruptcy in April 1998, BASF rescued its suppliers by increasing their orders from Hannam and paying premium prices in cash. 'We cannot turn a blind eye to the misfortune of Hannam. We have maintained ties with the company for the past 15 years', says Kang Chi-Oh, deputy general manager of raw material purchasing at BASF. Despite the crisis, Hannam is now receiving more orders and the factory is operating at full capacity. 'This is thanks to BASF, who quickly came to our aid', says Lee Jong-Gi, president of Hannam Industrial (Mi-Young, 1999). These actions of BASF are helping to change perceptions in South Korea about foreign multinationals that, traditionally, have been seen as foreign marauders quickly devouring the 'local underdog'.

Foreign firms are also strongly advised to establish close links with their host government and local community. They should be able to analyse the local 'investment climate', understand the host government's development intentions, and set themselves an agenda for assistance. Foreign firms should also act as diplomats and must be able to work with local politicians, understand them, search for common goals and areas of mutual interest, brief them on the company's contributions to the local economy, and establish a long-lasting relationship based on mutual trust. Good citizenship, however, involves much more than building contacts in the political society. It should also include active contributions to local, social, and economic goals of the host country. Foreign firms should not only be good diplomats in Asia, but also need to be culturally aware and able to deal with local issues effectively, and cultivate many local allies from the social groups. When Asia Brown Boveri (ABB) established Asia Pacific as a target region, it soon realized that the complexities of the region could cause differences of opinion leading to friction. To succeed in the region, ABB realized that it had to adopt customer-based strategies. It needed to understand local requirements and strengthen its relationships with local customers, governments, and communities. According to Alex Fries, managing director of ABB 'the important issue to succeed in Asia was not become a local citizen but to act like one. A pre-requisite for gaining such a recognition is through the adaptation of local employment, local management, local supply base, local business practices and recognition of local social responsibility' (Fries, 1995). Nike's experience in Asia Pacific between 1997 and 1998 is also quite inspiring. After suffering a wave of accusations by human rights groups about its use of cheap labour in factories in South East Asia and its labour practices in the Asia Pacific region in general, and seeing its market share dropping considerably, Nike immediately revised its code of ethics, improved the working conditions in its factories in China, Indonesia, and Vietnam and joined the World Bank's Global Alliance for Workers and Communities (for further details, see case study in Part IV).

Regional Production Strategy

A shift to a regional production strategy is clearly under way among all multinational firms active in Asia Pacific. Following the crisis, many Western and Japanese firms have started to feel the need for a regional corporate strategy to be built around regionally oriented production activities. A regional production strategy consists of three main elements: concentration of production, regional R & D, and regional headquarters. A first step towards this transformation process is illustrated by Matsushita Electric Industrial. In the 1960s this company had established the so-called Mini-Matsushitas in most Asian countries to serve local markets. The local affiliates, however, lost their competitive edge in the 1990s and are now regarded as negative assets by Matsushita. Up until 1998, Matsushita still had several affiliates in Asia excluding Chinese produced television sets. In 1998, Matsushita started converting its Mini-Matsushita in Thailand into a holding company with eight independent firms each specializing in different products. Western European car makers like Volvo and Volkswagen also decided recently to concentrate their production in Thailand. Ford and General Motors, too, have recently returned to Thailand (Legewie, 1999).

Another relatively new development is the emphasis on the development of products tailored for regional markets and consumers. The best-known examples of this new trend towards regional products are probably the so-called Asian cars City and Soluna that were developed by Honda and Toyota in Thailand for sales only in Asian markets outside Japan. The Japanese food company Kikkoman is another telling example. For the first time in its history, this company decided to alter the formula for its 'Asia Taste'. In spring of 1999 this product was launched on the Singaporean market from where it will be exported to other neighbouring countries. Additionally, the establishment of regional headquarters stands out as a clear indicator of a shift to regional strategies requiring a functional and regional coordination of production activities. Japan, the USA, and Western European firms are leading the trend with most of them building up regional headquarters not only in the South East Asia region but also in neighbouring countries including Taiwan and Korea. These regional headquarters, however, are rarely in charge of China, which is still regarded as a market and a region of its own (Legewie, 1999).

Time-Based Strategy

Hardly a new concept, time-based strategy is probably worth considering as a way to survive the post-crisis storms. Today, timely response to the crisis in Asia Pacific means survival; it could even mean competitive advantage. Many executives believe that competitive advantage is best achieved by providing the most value for the lowest cost. This is the traditional pattern for corporate success. Providing the most value for the lowest cost in the least amount of time is the new pattern for corporate success in Asia Pacific after the crisis.

In their book, *Competing against Time*, although written in 1990, George Stalk Jr. and Thomas M. Hout provide an interesting idea for dealing with the Asia Pacific post-crisis business environment (Stalk and Hout, 1990). Time, they argue, is the cutting edge. It could be used as a strategic weapon equivalent to money, productivity, quality, and even innovation. Reducing elapsed time can in fact make the critical difference between success and failure. Give customers what they want, when they want it, or the competition will. Time-based companies can offer greater varieties of products and services, at lower costs, and with quicker delivery times. They operate with flexible manufacturing and rapid-response systems, and place extraordinary emphasis on R & D and innovation. The old, cost-based strategies require managers to do whatever is necessary to drive down costs; move production to, or source from, a low-wage country; build new facilities or consolidate old plants to gain economies of scale; or focus operations down to the most economic subset of activities. Such tactics reduce costs but at the expense of responsiveness to customer needs. In contrast, strategies based on the cycle of flexible manufacturing—rapid response, expanding variety, and increasing innovation—are time based. Factories are close to the customers they serve. Organization structures are designed and managed to enable fast response rather than low costs and control. Time-based competitors concentrate their efforts on reducing and eliminating delays and on using their response advantages to attract the most profitable customers. By compressing the time required to manufacture and distribute the products, these companies are then able to offer a broader product line, to cover more market segments, and to rapidly increase the technological sophistication of their products. Although more and more Western companies are pursuing time-based advantage, many of the early developments and leading practices in the use of time as a competitive weapon have been pioneered by leading Japanese companies. The experiences of these Japanese companies are instructive, not because they are necessarily unique, but because they best illustrate the stages through which today's leading companies have evolved—from advantage first based on low wages; next on scale, then on focus; and now on flexibility, variety, speed, and innovation (Stalk and Holt, 1990). Japanese firms, by adopting time-based strategies, have become two to three times faster than the best Western companies. They also provide fresher product offerings that have a higher degree of technological sophistication. An example of these time-based competitors in Asia are Sony, Matsushita, Sharp, Toyota, Hitachi, Canon, Honda, Sharp, and Toshiba. Western time-based competitors include Benetton, the Limited Federal Express, and Domino's Pizza.

Companies that become fast innovators benefit from many advantages both internal and external. Internal advantages include the following:

- the latest technology can be used closer to the time of introduction;
- faster realization of cost reductions as new products with more cost-effective designs displace older, less effective designs;
- dramatically improved quality;
- lower development costs because programmes are completed sooner with less money being lost to reworking, waiting reviews, and so on;
- improved working environment;
- a very much improved sense of control of one's destiny since with faster development times, vicious cycles are broken and customer needs can be forecast over shorter time horizons.

The external benefits include:

- taking the position as technological or idea leader;
- higher price realization in the market from having a fresher product or service offering that customers find more desirable;
- a position in the minds of customers as innovator that is reliable and responsive, even while products or services are adjusted through successive introductions to get closer to the optimum definition;
- the ability to attract and lock up the most attractive channels of distribution, which like to be able to differentiate themselves by offering the latest innovation;
- the ability to set standards by being the first with innovations and to use market response to establish the standard;
- improved market share;
- new approaches to marketing new products and services. While companies with long product development and introduction cycles depend on extensive market research and testing to define the feature, performance, and cost specifications before marketing a new product or service, companies with rapid development and introduction cycles can experimentally market new products or services, and, if successful, introduce them broadly (Stalk and Hout, 1990).

Furthermore, time-based strategies can be used to achieve competitive advantage as follows (Stalk and Hout, 1990: 139).

- by using the reduced cost of development to provide more value for less cost to the consumer than competitors can provide;
- by flanking competitors either by making obsolete their previous product or service design with a new design, or by using innovations to quickly draw customers *en masse* away from their competitors' offering and towards their own. Most Japanese companies base their growth on flanking strategies—intending to roll up their competition in a wave of new product introductions. Sun Microsystems has used and is using fast innovation to flank the former leader in engineering work stations;

- by breaking new life into mature businesses by increasing the technological or fashion content of a business so as to reinvigorate consumers' interest in the product or service;
- by changing the shape of a company to escape an industry where the future may be irreversibly bleak.

Finally, fast innovation can enable management to change the shape of its business. Sometimes certain products or services are no longer profitable and the firm has to find something else to do with its resources. Honda changed from the manufacturer of small motors to motorcycles to cars; Fujitsu changed from a machine tool controller manufacturer to a computer company; Brother changed from a sewing machine manufacturer to a manufacturer of typewriters, then of printers, and then of small computers.

Canon is a good example of the use of innovation to change shape as well as sustain growth in mature markets. Canon used to be just a camera manufacturer. Cameras are a product that seems to mature, then grow and then mature again. In the second-to-the-last maturing cycle, in the mid-1970s, Canon launched itself into the plain paper copier business in search of growth. Canon found growth, but it was not long lived. By the early 1980s Canon found itself in two slow growth businesses, cameras, and copiers—deriving over 80 per cent of its revenues from these two lines of products. The remaining 20 per cent included calculators and portable typewriters. By 1988 sales of cameras and copiers were less than 60 per cent of total Canon revenues. Virtually all of Canon's growth came from products other than cameras and copiers. These new products include high speed and resolution facsimile machines, and later, laser computer printers. Both these products have double-digit growth rates that, if

---

Primefield Group: The New Time-Based Innovators of Singapore

The IT industry is one in which decisions and changes must be made very quickly. Primefield Group was founded by Florence Tay, one of Singapore's early entrepreneurs. The company prospered as a distributor of big PC brands. Through its distribution arm, Landmark Technologies, Primefield helped Compaq become the best-selling brand in Singapore and Indonesia, and had also for years put ACER and Toshiba PCs into the hands of eager Singapore consumers. However, during the Asian crisis, big brand names started to change their strategy and sell their products direct to consumers. Compaq, for example, acquired Digital, which is well known for its direct selling, and Dell was achieving phenomenal success with its web-based selling. Realizing that the distribution system might soon die, Tay decided it was time for Primefield Group to change. The company's strength was management and marketing. Since in the IT business, managing inventory, product positioning, customer relationships, and internal processes are very important, she decided to review the company's business and identify areas where it could be improved. Furthermore, after the crisis, customers in Asia have become more cost conscious. Instead of paying a premium for foreign PC brands, she decided it was time for Singapore to have its own brand of quality desktop and notebook PCs. The Whitebox PCs were offered at a PC show in January 2000, and consumers carried off the entire stock during the show (Jordan, 2000).

they continue to grow as expected, will eventually propel Canon out of the camera and copier business. As Fujio Mitair, president of Canon USA says 'Saturated markets don't matter because innovation can break through to new markets' (Stalk and Hout, 1990: 146).

Competitive 'Churning'

The term 'churning' was first proposed in a 1990 speech by Kevin Jones during his presentation at the YPO (Young Presidents' Organization) International Conference in Nagoya, Japan (Johansson and Nonaka, 1996: 81). The churning phenomenon involves quick imitations of new product entries by some competitors adding new features, the pioneering firm responding by upgrading the first entry, and competitors renewing the attack. The effect is a type of vicious high-speed tit-for-tat circle of new and modified product entries, intense proliferation of models, and continually lowered prices.

Examples of Japanese churning are almost unlimited. The churning practised by the Japanese usually endorses the newest technology and goes one step further to improve it. And then another step. And another. This is why churning does not have only one winner—and also why the game never ends. In fact you could almost say that the Japanese recreate the same competitive conditions in mature markets as are the rule in fast-moving high-tech markets, with new innovations constantly introduced to the market. Because of churning, being first in the Japanese market-place may not yield the typical first-mover advantage. The first entrant is caught rapidly by imitative competitors, whose new features may wipe out an early advantage. It is a common pattern of experience for Western innovators in Japan, such as Procter & Gamble's Pampers, Braun's coffee-makers, and Unilever's Timotei shampoo, which all quickly lost large initial market shares to Japanese firms (Johansson and Nonaka, 1996).

Rapid imitation requires close monitoring of market developments. It also requires rapid mobilization of company personnel and know-how to reverse-engineer the first-mover's new product and develop a clone. The flexibility of the Japanese incrementalism helps here, as does the fact that the technical know-how is usually already diffused. How can companies in Japan continue to innovate under this pressure? According to Kozo Ohsone, who was lead developer of the Discman, the portable compact disc player, the answer is simply to run faster, and keep adding features. There is considerable truth in the joke told about the American and the Japanese on a safari together in the African bush. Suddenly they are confronted by a man-eating lion. The American turns and starts running, but notices that his Japanese colleague instead bends down and takes a pair of running shoes from his knapsack and proceeds to put them on. 'You will never outrun that lion' shouts the American. 'I don't have to', replies the Japanese, 'I only have to outrun you!' (Lorriman and Kenjo, 1994a).

The first-mover advantages can only be sustained by proliferation of new products. Sony simply adopted the philosophy that it must churn against its own products and not

---

Churning at Toshiba

The laptop market was a great success for Toshiba despite—and perhaps because of—the entrance of several competitors. Toshiba had a first-mover advantage in brand recognition, and had managed to establish the dominant design for the new product category. Its ability in flat-screen technology had finally been sufficiently advanced to produce a picture resolution that made laptops a viable complement or even alternative to a desktop computer. The other key components—portability for ease of carrying, and battery operations for use away from home and office—came from intensive development work both within the company and with outside vendors. The portability, in particular, relied on the rapid diffusion of miniaturization technology throughout the Japanese consumer electronics industry. It became possible to produce laptops weighing only a little more than 10 lbs, quite acceptable for carrying during travel. The imitators had to retool to get up to speed on a product many had written off because of the screen resolution problems. Zenith, then still American owned, introduced its own unit in 1987, retailing for about $1,800 compared to the $2,300 required for the Toshiba in the American discount outlets. Because of its lower price and comparable performance characteristics, it was quickly dubbed the 'Toshiba killer'. The first Japanese manufacturers entering the market, NEC and Epson, concentrated on compatibility with the NEC operating system and were not direct competitors of Toshiba. As in desktops, NECS's dominance in Japan was a double-edged sword. It allowed the company easy access to existing local customers, but the incompatibility between its operating system and MS-DOS hampered the company and its Japanese compatriots overseas.

Toshiba never looked back. Realizing the benefits of having caught their Japanese competitors unawares, and not worried about the American competitors, they realized that the key was to grow the market, especially in the USA. The company embarked on a strong product-line proliferation strategy of quickly introducing new features and new models and adding additional processing capacity. This strategy served multiple purposes. First, it grew the market by making the laptops realistic competitors to the desktops, and by increasing the range of applications. Further, it forced prices down without introducing lower-priced models by antiquating previous or original models. Thus, it opened up the lower end of the market without aiming new products directly at it. At the same time, this strategy eroded the profit potential of Zenith's Toshiba killer, which could not keep up with the product churning. Soon Zenith was forced out of the market.

Source: J. K. Johansson and I. Nonaka, *Relentless: The Japanese Way of Marketing*, Oxford: Butterworth Heinemann 1996: 91–2.

---

worry about cannibalizing existing winners with newer variants. Toshiba's strategy in laptops illustrates how competitive churning helps a first-mover develop and expand a new market.

The Japanese Imitative Strategy: Me-Too and Me-Too-Plus Strategy

The main advantages of the Japanese me-too-plus strategy is that first the technology necessary to build a me-too product is known and available, or at least obtainable. Secondly, with an imitative strategy there is no need to spend a lot on advertising to educate buyers about product features: you need only to show the new features added. And there is less need to spend on expensive market research with uncertain outcomes. Additionally, local sub-assemblers, component manufacturers, and parts suppliers might hesitate to invest in new and costly machines to tool up for a new design. The company might have to guarantee order quantities greater than would be prudent and assist its suppliers' conversion in other ways. If the parts used are those in the market leader's dominant design, then the risks to all parties are much lower. Immediately after entry, the competitive rivalry becomes intense as the churning gets under way.

The main advantages of churning can be summarized as follows:

- shifts in the production positioning maps;
- rapid extensions of product lines;
- immediate imitation of new features that prove to sell;
- promotion with an emphasis on brand names;
- unprecedented and free service to create and sustain loyalties (Johansson and Nonaka, 1996: 95).

Furthermore, given the market uncertainties and lack of knowledge of the Asian market, it is better for foreign firms in Asia to 'shoot many arrows and hope one will hit, rather than aim carefully at one—and miss' (Johansson and Nonaka, 1996: 160).

Late Entrants Strategy

Liberalization and deregulation are slowly opening the economy to foreign investors in Asia Pacific, after the crisis. For these late entrants, Ragu Gurumurthy, a principal in Booz Allen & Hamilton's Communications, Media, and Technology practice in New York offers the following basic guidelines (Anon., 1 Aug. 1999):

(1) Reduce price to penetrate an existing market. By introducing a product at a lower price than the first mover, a latecomer can attract new customers who would not otherwise have purchased such a product. A reduced price can also induce the first mover's current customers to switch.

(2) Improve a product or service, with focus on a niche market. Companies can compete by being innovative in the marketplace. The innovation may be radical or incre-

mental. One example of incremental innovation is an enhanced version of an existing product. The enhanced product can compete directly with existing products, or it can be positioned to attract a smaller segment of the existing market. In addition, the improved product or service can sometimes attract new customers that are not the current target for the existing product or service. For example, potential satellite-based wireless service providers are currently offering a new feature called global coverage. This service could both complement and replace options available to current customers.

(3) Target new geographic markets for existing products. As markets mature in the home base, companies traditionally look outside to more lucrative markets. Most consumer goods companies, for instance, are setting their sights on China.

(4) Develop new channels of distribution to access new markets or better penetrate existing ones.

(5) Determine the timing of the introduction of any new product. This is especially true in high-tech industries, in which product life cycles are short and it is difficult for late entrants to catch up and extract reasonable returns.

(6) Differentiate yourselves substantiallly in the mind of consumers. Such positioning can be accomplished through substantial changes in the product or in promotion strategies. In other words, late entrants should position themselves as variety enhancers rather than as replacements or substitutes.

(7) Late entrants can also succeed by attacking high-growth markets, particularly when there is a significant shift in the industry. Such shifts can be due to changes in regulation, technological breakthroughs that improve the product, or breakthroughs that improve the process of manufacturing and delivering the product.

(8) A final strategic option for the later entrant is micro-segmenting the customer base to target high-value customers who are able and willing to pay a higher price for the product or service relative to the cost incurred in catering to that segment.

Review Questions

1   Asian Pacific business philosophy, enterprise cultures, and competitive approaches have often forced Western companies to re-evaluate and, in some cases, adapt their own traditional business strategies and concepts. Using company websites and other sources of information, describe and evaluate some of these changes.

2   What are the lessons to be learned from all the case examples presented in this chapter? What would you suggest are the best strategies for competing, or simply surviving, in Asia Pacific after the crisis?

3   What is meant by competitive 'churning'. In your opinion, does it improve or inhibit the international competitiveness of the firm?

4   As a consultant working for an international consulting firm, you have been approached by a small local firm wishing to expand its operations in Asia Pacific. Write

a report to the director-general briefing him on the various post-crisis strategies available. Which strategy would you advise him to adopt and why?

Group Project Post-crisis Strategic Planning

American cosmetics giant Avon gathered all its Asian Pacific country heads for an urgent meeting in Hong Kong a few weeks ago, just as the region's currency crisis was heating up. But they weren't there to plan lay-offs or production cutbacks. Instead, Avon's Asia Pacific president Jose Ferreira Jr. exhorted his team to focus on the opportunities offered by the gathering economic slowdown. Two Avon managers from Brazil, both veterans of Latin America's chronic financial instability, had some advice for their Asian colleagues: the downturn would give Avon the chance to expand its customer base, as women who once bought upmarket cosmetics scaled down to less expensive brands—like Avon. And when growth picks up again, the firm should have a larger market share than before (Rahul, 1997).

Using this chapter as a guideline on doing business in Asia Pacific, and the above case as an illustration of a firm's reaction to the crisis, collect as much current information as possible on one particular company operating in the region, and evaluate its experience post-crisis in terms of success or failure.

Relevant Case Studies (Part IV)

- P.B. BIT: An Indonesian Textile Case Study
- Coca-Cola Indochina Ltd.
- Nike: Ethical dilemmas of FDI in Asia Pacific
- Daewoo: The Chaebol You Never Heard Of
- Telecommunications in Thailand: The Mobile Phone Sector

Further Reading

Boulas, C., Fryling, J., and Buchanan, I., *Asian Business*, 1 Jan. 1999.
http://web3.asia1.com.sg/Timesnet/data/ab/docs
http://web3.asia1.com.sg/Timesnet/data/ab/docs_

Johansson, J. K., and Nonaka, Ijujiro, *Relentless: The Japanese Way of Marketing*, Oxford: Butterworth Heinemann, 1996

Stalk, G. Jr., and Hout, T. M., *Competing against Time: How Time-Based Competition is Reshaping Global Markets*.The Free Press, New York: a division of Macmillan, Inc. and London: Collier MacMillan Publishers, 1990.

Chapter 12

Methods of Entry into Asia Pacific Countries

The Asian crisis has prompted business firms to adopt or even in some cases to formulate new survival strategies for their operations in Asia Pacific. Once the appropriate strategy has been selected, the next stage is choosing the appropriate method of market entry. The choice of entry mode into Asia Pacific markets depends upon the company's prior experience and capabilities and the particular strategic attractiveness of an industrial sector or country in the region. It is often argued that depending on the volume of its sales, a firm starts by exporting; then proceeds to either a licensing agreement or a joint venture. In the case of Asia Pacific, licensing and joint venture have been traditionally in many cases the first step of an entry strategy for Western firms. However, following the Asian crisis and the trade liberalization and marketization efforts undertaken by local governments in the region, joint ventures are no longer a requisite in most Asia Pacific countries. The choice of an optimum control mode is now an open question. Choices for entering the region now include franchising, exporting, FDI and wholly owned operations, build–operate–transfer (BOT), management contracts, barter, and counter-trade, in addition to the old methods adopted in the past such as joint ventures, licensing, and long-term contractual agreements. However, it must be noted that despite the introduction of several liberalization measures, foreign firms in the region will still experience difficulties, particularly with governments' industrial policies, governments' pressures requiring firms to transfer technology and expertise to Asian producers, and in some cases, pressures to increase the amount and level of employment for nationals of the host country.

Modes of Entry into Asia Pacific, Before the Crisis

Until the Asian crisis, licensing, joint ventures, and long-term contractual agreements were considered more important for Asian governments than any other type of international business operations.

International Licensing

Governments in Asia Pacific have always favoured international licensing, particularly those involving technology transfer. This mode of entry was considered for many years as the easiest and quickest way of expanding into the region's most closed economies. International licensing is the process whereby one firm—the licensor—provides certain resources, for example technology, brand-name use, the right to use certain patents, copyrights, or trade marks to another firm—the licensee—in exchange for a fee or a royalty or any other form of payment according to a schedule agreed upon by the two parties. International licensing can be negotiated for intellectual properties such as patents, know-how, trade marks, copyrights, brand names, and technical production. Cross-licensing agreements are often found in industries in which R & D and other fixed costs are exorbitant, but where aggressive competition is needed to maintain industry-wide discipline and innovation. The pharmaceutical and chemical industries are replete with cross-licensing agreements.

There are a number of internal and external circumstances where international licensing seems appropriate. Some of these are:

(1) when the cost of entry into a foreign market is too expensive, due to high rates of duty, import quotas, prohibitions or technical barriers, and the firm lacks the capital, managerial resources or knowledge of foreign markets, but wants to earn additional profit with minimal commitment;

(2) when a firm needs to test its product in a foreign market before deciding on foreign direct investment;

(3) when the host country is politically unstable and the risk of nationalization or expropriation is high. International licensing provides some protection against political risk. It also protects the firm's intellectual property in some countries where they ignore trade marks and patent rights, at the risk of patent litigation;

(4) when the licensor wishes to exploit a secondary market for its technology, but where the smaller market does not justify large investments (El Kahal, 1994: 12).

International licensing is often used as a first step for entering a new market and to gain knowledge of the foreign environment before the firm establishes foreign plant and service facilities. It also provides a relatively quick, low-cost, low-risk means of penetrating new markets. It allows new firms to test foreign markets for their product, and to become associated with locally established firms. International licensing provides the firm with additional revenues in the form of fees or royalties in return for information or assistance that the company can provide at very little cost to itself. Finally, international licensing does not require heavy investment in the production and marketing facilities required in the foreign environment.

Although international licensing may seem the easiest, cheapest, and quickest way to enter the market in Asia Pacific, there are several disadvantages and risks involved in international licensing agreements that foreign firms need to be aware of. First, the licensor's profit is limited to receiving royalties, and it cannot share in the licensee's profits. Secondly, the licensor might create its own competitor in the foreign market. Since the licence is usually limited to a certain period of time, and may not be renewed after the expiry date of the licence, foreign manufacturers may still be able to produce the product using the licensor's technology acquired over the previous years. Thirdly, the international licence is usually drawn under the local laws of the host nation, and thus comes under its local jurisdiction. The licensor may also lose control over the quality of its products, due to the possible difficulties of controlling and ensuring the maintenance of quality and service standards for foreign licensees. The use or misuse of the international licence might damage the corporate reputation and corporate image. Fourthly, the licensor may face difficulties in receiving royalties under the agreement, especially in countries where there are strict foreign exchange controls or other restrictions on royalty payments, such as withholding tax on royalty payments to non-resident licensors (Beamish *et al.*, 1991: 61–5; Stitt and Baker, 1985).

Licensing in Asia Pacific remains as good as the enforcement system behind it. Despite the issuance of several laws, the protection of intellectual property is still hazardous and notably inadequate. The theft of intellectual property rights (IPR), copyrights, trade-mark patents remains a large and growing problem in the region. In 1995 the Washington-based International Intellectual Property Alliance estimated that US industries had lost almost US$15 billion in revenues to IPR pirates globally. Of this amount, countries in Asia Pacific accounted for over 41 per cent. Within Asia Pacific, China emerged as the largest manufacturer of illegal products from counterfeit motion pictures, compact discs, CDs, software, and books for both domestic consumption and the export market. Japan is the next largest manufacturer of pirated goods, followed by South Korea, Indonesia, Taiwan, and India. Thailand, Hong Kong, Singapore, Malaysia, and the Philippines are also major regional counterfeiters (Strizzi, 1998).

In China, for example, trade-mark rights can only be protected by registration. In this regard, it has adopted the first-to-file rule. This means that the first applicant to file and register a trade-mark is the one who receives rights and protections in that mark. The applicant does not have to prove ownership or prior use. Consequently anyone can register a trade-mark, even if a different company somewhere else in the world registers that mark. Under Chinese law, only the holder of a trade-mark who has received registration approval can be the legitimate proprietor of that mark, and only the legitimate proprietor can be protected. When an application for trade-mark registration is approved, it automatically becomes impossible for another applicant to gain approval for the same or a similar mark on the same or similar goods. Therefore, if a trade-mark proprietor does not bother to apply for registration in China, someone else, even if he is not the legitimate owner, can apply and receive legal protection for that mark (Brahm and Daoran, 1996: 167). Following the Asian crisis, the Chinese government has introduced tougher measures. However, such measures have only forced intellectual property rights pirates to shift their production capacity to neighbouring countries with weaker legal and regulatory regimes. It is estimated that pirate plants in Hong Kong, Macao, Malaysia, and Singapore can manufacture around 550 million illegal CDs annually. In Hong Kong alone, illegal CD production capacity has reached 330 million units annually and 100 million each in Macao and Singapore (Strizzi, 1998). Computer software piracy by retailers in Indonesia remains a problem where piracy is also active in book publishing, video recording, and fashion apparel. In Thailand, enforcement of protection over intellectual property rights remains poor. Piracy of computer software and motion pictures is also a serious problem in the Philippines. Protection of intellectual property in Japan is difficult and time consuming. Thus, Asia Pacific in general remains a major source of illegal production, distribution, and export of high-tech and entertainment-based products. Business firms will need to adopt heightened vigilance to protect their assets and people from theft of proprietary information and advanced technology.

Techniques for minimizing the pitfalls of international licensing and increasing its potential advantages (taken from Stitt and Baker, 1985) include the following:

• capability, reliability, and trust are absolutely crucial in the selection of the licensee;

• a draft agreement with the licensee must be carefully put together. The licence agreement should make explicit reference to the product, a description of the two parties to the agreement, their reasons for entering into the agreement, and their respective roles;

• the duration of the agreement, and any necessary provision for its automatic extension or review, should be clearly specified;

• details regarding the royalties, methods of payments, and the percentage rate of the royalty must be explicitly defined;

• control and monitoring. Minimum performance requirements must be specified. Penalties for lack of diligence, rights of inspection, and number of visits permitted per year, together with inspection of the licensee's accounts, should be determined;

• agreement on arbitration methods, in case of infringement of the licence agreement and the type of appeals permitted, with details of specific reasons for termination by licensor or licensee must be determined;

• requirements for the training of technical personnel must be set out.

International Joint Ventures

In the past, succeeding in Asia Pacific without a local partner, because of the different cultural, legal, economic, and political viewpoints involved was difficult. A joint venture with a well-connected Asian partner has often been considered as the best or indeed the only way to enter the region. In China, it was, and still is almost impossible to succeed without a Chinese partner. The freedom of choice was often restricted (Wong and Maher, 1997). The major contributions of the Asian partner, however, were limited primarily to labour and local facilities, while foreign firms have had to provide capital, training, technology, specialized equipment, and know-how. With such outlays, the time required to reach a payback position could be very long. Western firms interested in the region should be willing to invest and have long-term objectives.

Before considering the various motivations for establishing joint ventures in Asia Pacific, a brief overview of what international joint ventures are is necessary. International joint ventures are business partnerships or alliances jointly owned by two or more firms from different countries, foreign multinational firms and local governments, or foreign multinational firms and local business people. In an international joint venture, each party contributes capital, assets, or equality ownership, but not necessarily on a fifty-fifty basis. Peter Killing identifies four basic purposes for establishing international joint ventures. The first is to strengthen the firm's existing business, the second is to take existing products into new markets, the third is to obtain new products which can be sold in the firm's existing markets, and the fourth is to diversify into a new business (Killing, 1982).

Establishing international joint ventures can have many advantages. These include, for example, the opportunity for a firm to share its risks, to learn about a partner's skills and proprietary processes, and to gain access to new distribution channels (Lei and Slocum, 1991). Joint ventures are also less exposed to the danger of expropriation. Unlike wholly owned foreign subsidiaries, international joint ventures also enable the firm to utilize the specialized skills of local partners, together with their knowledge of local markets, culture, and government contacts. They provide wider access to the local partner's distribution system, particularly when the company lacks the capital and personnel capabilities itself to expand overseas (Habbib and Burnett, 1989). A further advantage of using international joint ventures is that they are less expensive. One party may provide the technology and management skills needed, and the other might raise the capital (Beamish *et al.*, 1991; Hamel and Prahalad, 1994; Killing, 1982).

Firms considering entering a joint venture in Asia Pacific should make sure that this is the best option available to them. International joint ventures are difficult to maintain. A company should determine clearly its objectives and its partner's objectives before forming the venture. What type of partnership, in terms of management role—dominant role, degree of independence of operations, or share management—needs to be established (Beamish *et al.*, 1991: 66–71). International joint ventures carry risks and problems as well. Successful operations could become a target for nationalization or expropriation by the host government. The transfer of management skills to the other partner might create a local competitor in the foreign market by providing greater access to information and technological know-how. Different parties might also have different objectives for the joint venture. A local partner might be more interested in long-term profit. There could be a wide difference in management styles, corporate cultures, and missions between the two partners. The joint venture between Daewoo and General Motors is quite illustrative (for details, refer to the Daewoo case study in Part IV).

Joint Ventures Motivation in Asia Pacific

Due to the high cost of offshore sourcing and the need for quality, foreign firms felt that joint ventures were the best vehicle to use in Asia. By converting to local sourcing, they have been able to bring in their overseas suppliers to China, for example, and develop them into local suppliers. Another major reason why Western firms have traditionally chosen to enter into partnerships in Asia is to gain access to contracts for important government infrastructure projects (Lasserre and Schütte, 1999; 173–4). Partnerships with local government in Asia are harder to deal with than joint venture partners, but winning their trust can be rewarding. Even in free-trading Hong Kong and Singapore, government connections and often outright government ownership have given a big boost to politically favoured firms, although such firms in both city-states have been held to strict performance standards by world prices and practices. In Japan too, as in most of Asia, foreign firms need to market themselves heavily to government officials and regulators. Additionally, until recently, most countries in Asia Pacific particularly Japan, China, and Korea, did not generally authorize foreign equity of over 50 per cent, with the exception of high-tech or export-oriented investment. Foreign firms were also not authorized to own land, and needed to find a local partner in order to secure land rights.

Foreign enterprises also looked for a partner with a suitable distribution network or other specific assets. In Korea, for instance, a local partner may also offer a link to an industrial association and a channel to the banking system. As stressed by the president of the European Chamber of Commerce, 'it is very difficult for a foreign company to persuade a Korean bank to lend. Even a big company has to go through the local branch managers who have never heard of you and a local partner enables a foreign firm to minimize its transactions costs in the domestic market' (European Chamber of Commerce in Korea, White Paper, 1993, quoted in Chaponniere and Lautier, 1995).

Managerial and human resources have often been the most critical resources that can be obtained from an Asian joint-venture partner such as his ready-made distribution networks or production facilities. Furthermore, Western firms have sought out local partners in Asia Pacific in order to reduce the risk of their financial investment or human resource commitment to a particular Asian market. The French tyre manufacturer Michelin, for instance, entered three separate partnerships, in Japan (with Okamoto), South Korea (with Wuon Poong), and Thailand (with Siam cement), although the Michelin company has never engaged in such partnerships in other parts of the world. Finally, partnerships with the Japanese, Korean, and Taiwanese firms have often assisted Western firms to reduce production costs, and to increase their market share by providing an easier access to markets too difficult to enter unilaterally.

Having established the motivations for establishing joint ventures with Asia Pacific partners, the question arises as to why the number of unhappy joint-ventures stories in the region is accumulating, and what are the conditions for their success.

Problems with Joint Ventures in Asia Pacific

The creation and management of a joint venture in Asia Pacific is a dynamic process in which many factors, not only political, legal, and economic, but also social and cultural, will contribute to its success or failure. Many partners in Asia are increasingly realizing that their partnership is not working anymore. Some common problems for all Western firms so far have been closely related to differences in cultural backgrounds, corporate culture, industry culture, and national or ethnic culture. Another major problem faced is with the differing objectives between partners. While the domestic market is the main objective of the foreign entrant, the Asian partner often considers the joint venture as a tool to upgrade his technology and export competitiveness. He is often reluctant to share his domestic market. Once his objective is reached, his need for a foreign partner diminishes and the joint venture is bound to run into difficulties. Another major problem for managing successful joint ventures in Asia is the difficulty of making the right choice of partner. The choice of a local partner can mean life or death for a foreign firm. In an interview with an executive of Nissan, Japan's second biggest car maker, about his company's prospects in the rising market of Indonesia, the executive shrugged his shoulders, more or less admitting that Indonesia seemed lost. Nissan had a market share there of 1 per cent. The reasons: 'we linked up with the wrong guy' (Rohwer, 1995: 218–19).

Sometimes, the local government imposes the choice of partner. Western firms have to deal with whatever the government has to say rather than with what the firm is trying to do. Volkswagen has been one of the most successful foreign investors in China. Its joint venture with Shanghai Automotive Industry Corp. has been making money on its Santana Sedan since a year after opening in 1986. But things have gone very wrong at VW's second joint-venture plant, First Auto Works, in the north-eastern city of Changchun. Here VW had a partner forced upon it. The Authorities dictated that the factory should have a massive 150,000-unit capacity to roll out the Jetta. As a result, production has been less than one-third of capacity. The two sides have quarrelled over everything, from distribution rights to accounting. While VW enjoyed healthy margins with the Santana, Beijing set the price of the Jetta at $16,750, not enough given the small production runs and high content of imported parts. According to VW, the venture has lost at least $100 million. The partner, using its own accounting, insisted it was breaking even (Anon., 26 May 1997).

Another area of conflicting perceptions and expectations is technology spillover. Indeed, this is perhaps the greyest of many grey areas of doing business in Asia Pacific, particularly in China. The desire for technology is one of the reasons China opened its markets in the first place, and foreign firms are expected to share what they know with emerging Chinese companies (Vanhonacker, 1997). Western multinationals do not usually devote the same amount of time and resources to partner selection. Successful partnering in Asia must begin with a thorough investigation of potential partners. Ideally, the Western firm should establish a representative office in Asia far in advance of any investment commitment, and staff it with at least one full-time Western expatriate manager, whose task is primarily to collect information on market opportunities and potential candidates for partnership and acquisition.

One method often used by companies willing to test a partner before embarking on a joint venture is to establish some sort of 'pre-marital' arrangement either in the form of a manufacturing contract, a limited distributorship, or a licensing agreement. This allows partners to experiment with their working relationship on a small scale (Lasserre and Schütte, 1995: 179). Trading houses are often the most suitable partners in Asia, such as the Japanese Sogo Sosha, discussed in Chapter 6.

Dissolving equity joint ventures in Asia, however, is difficult. Same bed, different dreams—but in Asia Pacific divorce is difficult. The Asian business culture is mostly characterized by relationships based on trust and confidence. These constitute the basic fabric of Asian society. Western firms seeking closer cooperation with Asian firms are strongly advised to share swap. The Asians believe it is the right structure for building trust (Rohwer, 1995: 128–9).

Selecting the appropriate partner is therefore a vital decision that will have considerable influence on the effectiveness of a joint venture. Lorange and Ross (Lorange, and Ross, 1995) identify four key criteria for successful selection. These are complementary assets, compatible business and management cultures, commitment and trust, and termination.

- **Complementary assets** If a company needs market access, for example, it must not only find a partner that can supply the necessary access, but that partner must also require something in return, that is, technology or product, if an alliance is to flow. Firms tend to seek a partner whom they perceive to have complementary assets for which synergies can be realized. The goals between the two partners may be different, but they should be complementary.

- **Compatible business and management cultures** Most failed joint ventures cite incompatibility as a key reason for their failure. This does not mean, however, that business and management cultures between the joint venture must be similar, as long as culture is explicitly on the agenda and partners recognize the need to become more attuned to each other's cultural reactions to situations. A sensitive attitude to cultural differences is necessary if the alliance is to succeed.

- **Commitment and trust** To be successful an alliance should operate in a spirit of trust, cooperation, and integrity. An atmosphere of mutual distrust and domination by one partner may jeopardize the stability of the alliance.

- **Termination** A formula for termination should be built into the initial agreement as reassurance for both parties. If the alliance is to be successful, in addition to clearly defined goals, the limits of the alliance should also be recognized (Lorange and Ross, 1995).

Modes of Entry into Asia Pacific, Post-crisis

The economic liberalization and opening up of Asia Pacific to Western investors, which began in the 1980s and accelerated after the Asian crisis, has led several foreign firms to end their licensing agreements and joint ventures and to adopt other modes of entry such as: exporting, FDI, franchising, BOT, and management contracts in order to service the Asian market.

Exporting to Asia Pacific

Exporting to Asia Pacific prior to the crisis was a difficult task, especially in the consumer goods import market. The entry of a competing product was difficult, not so much because of high tariffs, but because of discriminatory measures against imported goods. Local governments often exerted strong pressures upon importers and foreign firms to promote local manufacturing of 'strategic goods'. The situation is now gradually changing with the recent liberalization process that is taking place in the region (for further details, see individual country profiles in Ch. 5).

Exporting is when a firm decides to maintain its production facilities at home and export its products to foreign countries. There are two types of exporting: direct and indirect. In *direct exporting*, export tasks are carried out directly by the company itself. Direct exporting functions include market research, study of potential international markets, international insurance, shipping and preparing export documentation, financing, pricing, and accounting. Local employees initially handle all these tasks as the orders come through. However, if the export business expands, the company may then decide to set up a separate international division to handle the increased volume of export business. Direct exporting requires relatively little capital, personnel, and resources. It also provides the company with the opportunity to test foreign markets for its product without committing much of its resources in doing so. It allows the company to sell its product overseas without transferring some of its capital into foreign markets, or exposing its personnel to the technical aspects of export trading, in preparing export documents, in dealing with customers, and in safety and security codes, as well as in local import restrictions.

Indirect exporting is when the firm is not engaged in international business operations in the full sense, but delegates this function to outsiders. These can be either agents or export firms. Export agents can either be independent intermediaries or export merchants, who may buy the product outright with the intention of reselling in foreign markets, or sell the company's products on a commission basis. The use of agents in exporting goes back at least a few hundred years, when both buyers and sellers would appoint representatives residing in each other's countries to carry out business on their behalf (Dudley, 1990: 171–2). Agents are useful in dealing with government contracts. They can also be useful for their knowledge of the local market, culture, and business ethics. Agents may also have established relationships with major customers in the foreign market or the host government, otherwise unavailable to a new exporter. Using an agent, however, carries some risks. Most agents are concerned with earning commission, and may adopt selling methods that do not reflect the company's image. Additionally, few agents act solely for one firm. They usually have other products to sell, and cannot devote all their time to a particular company's products. Therefore, and in most cases, they favour acquiring established and profitable brands, and are often reluctant to spend their time on new and untried products.

In China, for example, Pepsi Cola hired and trained people to be used by their direct distributors to promote their brand, encouraged sales, and checked product display at the point of sale. However, this sales force has been hard to manage and control because most distributors have used it to sell other products as well. Furthermore, Pepsi Cola found this method to be expensive given that the soda business was very seasonal and the sales force had to be employed all year round (Garde, 1999). Other companies, such as Mars, supplied the salespeople with vans painted with advertisements. In Vietnam, Unilever's ice-cream company, Wall's, employed similar strategies to that of Pepsi Cola by rapidly establishing several outlets and giving out special freezers, designed to keep products cool for up to six hours in the event of a power cut, to all its distributors. After launching a campaign depicting ice cream being distributed by pedicabs to the tune of a marketing jingle, Wall's set up a fleet of 120 men on bicycles to sell ice-cream from street to street around the city. Wall's provided continuous training of its army of retailers in terms of ongoing training. All distributors were backed up by a fast-response fleet of supply trucks, filling freezers within minutes when they ran out.

Using exporting firms is another alternative to using foreign agents. Exporting firms can be foreign freight forwarders, export management companies, or international trading companies. A foreign freight forwarder company specializes in the export and import of goods across national borders. Once a foreign sale has been made, the freight forwarder acts on behalf of the exporter in recommending the best routing and means of transportation based on space availability, speed, and cost. The forwarder also secures such space and storage, reviews the main Letter of Credit, obtains export licences and prepares the necessary shipping documents. The main advantage of using foreign forwarders is that they can provide advice on packaging and labelling, purchasing of transport insurance, and repackaging shipments damaged en route, and are usually up to date with the latest shipping regulations (Daniels and Radebaugh, 1992: 529). Export management companies act to some extent as the export departments of many manufacturers. They provide advice on overseas markets and help in marketing the company's product more efficiently, effectively, and at lower cost. Export management companies operate on a contractual basis, usually for two to five years, and provide exclusive representation overseas. They are particularly suitable for small companies contemplating exporting their products, because they can provide instant knowledge of the foreign market. They are also cheaper to use because their costs are spread over the sales of several manufacturers' lines, which provides for economies of scale in shipping and marketing to foreign markets (Brash, 1978). International trading companies have purchasing offices in many countries. These firms are usually the major suppliers of foreign goods in their home markets. The largest of these are the Japanese Sogo Shosha, such as Mitsubishi, Mitsui, and Sony. Together the range of products varies from advanced technology, electronics, computer software, and telecommunications to complex financial services, fashion, retailing, food processing, and consumer products. Mitsubishi Trading Corporation and Sumitomo Corporation are also deeply involved in biotechnology, and Mitsui in international telecommunications and satellite communication technology. Mitsubishi is the world's largest trading company, with a worldwide chain of subsidiaries. Its activities today include oil refineries, energy, mining, metals, chemicals banking, insurance, electronics, computers, aircraft, automobiles, shipbuilding, and electrical appliances.

Foreign Direct Investment

Despite the considerable risk associated with FDI in Asia Pacific, following the Asian crisis there is at the moment a growing trend towards a new and possibly much more effective way of doing business in Asia Pacific as wholly foreign-owned enterprises. Foreign owned enterprises, because of the flexibility and managerial control they deliver, make an excellent fit with Asia Pacific's competitive environment, particularly in China. This may well be the win–win China strategy that business people around the world have been waiting for (Vanhonacker, 1997).

Foreign direct investment simply means 100 per cent ownership by the firm of its overseas operations. There are various ways in which a company may establish its production facilities in another country while retaining total ownership. This can be achieved by acquiring foreign production facilities or by establishing a complete manufacturing system or assembly plant through direct investment by the firm in a host country. Foreign direct investment is differentiated from other forms of investment by the former's ability to have direct control over the invested capital. Usually in the form of multinational corporations, foreign investors are driven to invest overseas due to their possession of superior technology or some type of comparative advantage, to maintain international competitiveness in the midst of rising production costs at home, and/or to counter certain moves of their rivals (Tongzon, 1998: 144–5).

The advantage of wholly owned subsidiaries to the parent company is that the parent company will have total control of operations, decision-making, and control of profits, management and production decisions. Wholly owned subsidiaries also help the firm to maintain greater security over its technological assets and know-how. The major constraints of having wholly owned foreign subsidiaries are the capital requirements and the shortage of management personnel with the necessary international experience. The host government and its nationals may have some degree of anti-foreign sentiment, or may be resentful about foreign domination of its economy. The company might therefore risk expropriation, although many states in the modern world, especially less developed countries, are anxious themselves to attract foreign direct investment, and compete openly for it. Consequently, the risk of nationalization or outright expropriation has noticeably diminished.

In Asia Pacific, FDI can be achieved either through horizontal or vertical FDI, or through export-processing zones. Horizontal FDI is FDI in the same industry abroad as a firm operates in at home, for example, when large corporations open new subsidiaries worldwide. Horizontal FDI may be domestic market-oriented or export-oriented investments. For example, Toyota setting up an assembly plant in ASEAN is a domestic market-oriented investment, whereas Sumitomo's chemical complex in Singapore is an export-oriented one (Tongzon, 1998: 144–5). Vertical FDI, on the other hand, takes two forms. Backward vertical FDI is FDI into an industry abroad that provides inputs for a firm's domestic production process. Forward vertical FDI is FDI into an industry abroad that sells the outputs of a firm's domestic production processes (Hill, 1999: 197). Under vertical FDI, the corporation keeps control of the various stages of a production process. For example, Unilever in the Philippines set up a coconut oil production plant for soap production in its US factories (Tongzon, 1998: 145).

Export-processing zones are mainly located in Singapore, South Korea, Malaysia, Indonesia, the Philippines, and Taiwan. In these industrial estates, foreign companies can benefit from a labour market in which wages are far below Western standards. The productivity and discipline of labour is variable, but these zones have generally succeeded in attracting labour-intensive industries such as electronic assembly, textiles, and manufacturing. Their purpose is simple: to create a free trade environment conducive to the production of export goods in order to earn hard currency. China's Special Economic Zones (SEZs), though similar to other free trade zones in their purpose of attracting foreign capital and technology, are different from their counterparts in the following respects:

- Foreign participation is not limited to import–export business, but extends to industrial, agricultural, service, and infrastructure development. Some investment has been in the tourism, recreation, real estate, and retail sectors, such that physical and economic features are not necessarily congruent to an export orientation.

- Linkage of the SEZs with their immediate Chinese communities has not only been economic, but has also had political implications. The four SEZs were each established with a particular Chinese community Beijing wanted to make it attractive to, namely the overseas Chinese in South East Asia, Hong Kong, Macao, and Taiwan.

China's SEZs thus have three roles: 'the role of a window for China to look out into the world and for the world to look into China in the flow of capital and technology and business management skills; the role of a pioneer to blaze trails for Chinese linkage with the economies of the outside world and gain expertise in the running of a modern economy, so as to help promote the country's modernization; and the role of a catalyst to assist in the reunification of Chinese communities in East Asia by means of economic integration' (Chen, 1995: 138).

Advantages for FDI in Asia Pacific

In China, a wholly foreign-owned enterprise nowadays has substantially the same status in terms of taxation and corporate liability as joint ventures. They also operate under similar foreign-exchange rules and comparable import and export regulations for licensing, quotas, and duties. In fact, the only real technical differences are that wholly foreign-owned enterprises take less time to establish than joint ventures. Chinese authorities demand an export quota of at least 50 per cent from wholly foreign-owned enterprises (WFOEs) as a kind of fee for not working with a Chinese partner (Vanhonacker, 1997). It is expected that half of all foreign investment in China will be wholly foreign-owned enterprises by the end of 2000. For example, at the Suzhou-Singapore Industrial Park, an industrial development area that the Chinese government calls a showcase of the future, 94 per cent of the 120 business projects approved so far are WFOEs with an average investment of $40 million per project (Vanhonacker, 1997: 130–5).

Several incentives are currently available in China to attract FDI. These include priority treatment in obtaining basic infrastructure services and significant reductions in national and local income taxes, land fees, and import and export duties. Special preferences have also been established for projects involving high-technology and export-oriented investments. Foreign investors may also receive benefits by reinvesting profits. They may obtain a refund of 40 per cent of the tax paid on their share of income if the profit is reinvested in China for at least five years, and a full refund if the reinvestment is in high-technology or export-oriented enterprises. Many foreign companies have adopted a strategic plan for China that requires reinvestment of profits for growth and expansion. Johnson & Johnson is a classical example of a corporation which has been famous in China for its successful pharmaceuticals joint venture. However, in 1992, the company decided to launch its new oral-care, baby, and feminine hygiene products venture as a wholly foreign-owned enterprise. Since production began in 1994, the new venture's revenues have increased by 40 to 50 per cent per year. The project has been so successful that the company decided to make its latest investment—a business that will manufacture heart devices (Vanhonacker, 1997).

In Malaysia, tax incentives are offered by the government for those wishing to invest in the manufacturing, agricultural, and tourism sectors. These include Pioneer Status, that is, a tax holiday, ranging from five to ten years, as well as an investment tax allowance, export incentives, and grants for R & D and training (Cragg, 1992). Similar tax holidays are also offered by the Indonesian government for certain upstream industrial sectors (Goodfellow, 1997: 126).

In Singapore, there are no restrictions on the amount of capital investment, nor on the repatriation of capital or remittance of profits. There are also no percentage restrictions placed on the foreign ownership of enterprises operating in Singapore, with the exception of the manufacture of arms and ammunition, the supply of public utilities such as electricity, gas, and water and the supply of telecommunications service. The South Korean government is also slowly changing its long-time discouragement of foreign participation in the economy. Under the High-Tech Industry Cooperation Act of 1995, taxation benefits include waivers of up to 100 per cent for the first five years, and a 50 per cent exemption of corporate, income, and local taxes for the following three years. Commercial loans for the importation of equipment are allowed up to 100 per cent of the amount invested. Priority is given to investors who build production facilities in industrial zones where land can be leased at an annual interest rate of 1 per cent for twenty years. Furthermore, following the Asian crisis, on 25 May 1998 the ceiling on foreign equity ownership of domestic companies was completely eliminated, including the full liberalization of mergers and acquisitions by foreign companies.

In Thailand, the Board of Investment (BOI) offers generous incentives packages for FDI to encourage investment in 57 provinces outside Bangkok and its neighbourhood. The whole country is divided into three zones: zone 1 is Bangkok and neighbouring provinces, zone 2 is the central provinces, and zone 3 is all outlying provinces. Projects located in zone 3 receive the maximum incentive. Incentives include permanent exemption from import duties on machinery, and three-year exemption on raw material imports, an eight-year exemption from corporate income tax deductibility of water, electricity, and transport, and 25 per cent of installation costs for ten years. In the Philippines, 100 per cent foreign ownership in enterprises serving the domestic market is allowed.

Managing Successful FDI in Asia Pacific

For FDI to be successful in Asia Pacific, foreign firms ought to realize that FDI raises important questions about cultural and economic sovereignty. Asian governments don't want foreign companies taking advantage of their country. One way to avoid this is to localize production—that is, to buy as many parts and components as possible from local suppliers. Hiring local managers is another approach adopted by Western firms. Motoral's enterprise, for instance, employs only Chinese managers, very few of whom hold US passports. In Malaysia, the government, despite its willingness to allow expatriates to fill key positions in foreign firms in Malaysia, still tends to favour firms that hire *bumiputras*, individuals of Malay origin (Lemaire, 1996). Foreign companies can also be active in socially responsible projects. Several foreign companies have recently shown their commitment to public safety by buying new cars for local police departments. WFOEs can also nurture local brands. Coca-Cola, for example, recently transferred the trade-mark of its new Tian Yu Di fruit drink to Tianjin Jinmei beverage company, a local producer of concentrates. This move was warmly received as an example of the company's sensitivity, in a country where being a piece of the puzzle is more valued than being a hammer on a nail. 'Indeed, if you behave like a hammer as a foreign investor in China, the nail will probably go into your own coffin!' (Vanhonacker, 1997). Finally, foreign companies contemplating investing in the region, should put a reasonable contingency for devaluation in currency into their feasibility studies, and strive for high local content and high exports from their plants in Asia Pacific.

Franchising in Asia Pacific

International franchising operations in Asia are expected to grow rapidly in the coming few years. Examples of successful international franchises in Asia Pacific vary from service industries and restaurants, fast food, soft drinks, home and auto maintenance companies, automotive services, motels and hotels, to car rentals. Franchising is becoming a very popular and explosive business in Asia Pacific despite the crisis. The recent success witnessed by Ray Wilson California Fitness centres across Asia Pacific is quite illustrative.

In an international franchising agreement, the franchiser provides the franchisee with its trade mark and the necessary material to run the business. This may include equipment, products, product ingredients, managerial advice, and often a standardized operating procedure. Franchised operations usually have a specific set of procedures and methods and a set of quality guidelines set up by the franchiser, as well as the layout of physical facilities that the franchisee must use to produce and market the product. The franchisee is also expected to provide the capital needed to run the franchise.

The advantages of international franchising are similar to those of international licensing. In addition, international franchising provides for the expansion of brand-name recognition and requires low capital investment. The major disadvantages of franchising are the restrictions in marketing, and at the start, slight adjustments of adaptation to the standardized product or service.

Build–Operate–Transfer (BOT)

To overcome budget and financing problems, many countries in Asia Pacific including China, Indochina, Malaysia, the Philippines, and Thailand are actively promoting build–operate–transfer operations (BOT). This is a contractual agreement between a foreign investor and a state organization. Under such an agreement, the foreign investor undertakes to construct an infrastructure project and control the exploitation of the infrastructure for a given period of time, with a view to generating a usage fee to recover construction costs plus a margin of profit. Upon expiry of the agreed period and the recovery of its investment, the foreign investor transfers the operation of the infrastructure to the state organization without compensation. The essential feature of these arrangements is that project risks are clearly separated from country risk; lenders advance money against the cash flow of the project rather than the government's sovereign guarantee (Strizzi and Kindra, 1998).

Since 1996, the Philippines government, lacking sufficient financial resources to implement fundamental infrastructure needs, has encouraged BOT as a measure to attract private investment to carry out neglected infrastructure projects. As of 30 May 1998 there were 92 active BOT projects of which 27 are completed, 35 are either awarded or under construction, 10 are for public building, and 20 in the pipeline. There are also

Keeping Fit in Asia Pacific, After the Crisis

With the economic crisis still sucking the life out of businesses all over Asia Pacific, Ray Wilson California Fitness centres are taking the Asian audience by storm. With its ultra-modern look and aggressive selling techniques, California Fitness hit the Asian keep-fit scene three years ago. The US company signed up 3,000 members before its pilot centre opened in Hong Kong and started turning a profit after the first six months. The company is currently expanding, opening a fourth location in Hong Kong and a second in Singapore. The four established outlets have attracted get-fit enthusiasts in droves and carved out a definite niche for California Fitness in Asia.

'When you walk in the door, it's a totally different world. You can feel the amazing energy and excitement, which is way over the top compared to other clubs. We have a very friendly staff, with an amazingly young management team', says Eric Levine, managing director. 'It is a very cool place to be, but not intimidating. It's not snobbish or uptight; that's the last thing you'll find in California. It's a lot of fun'. The company has invested more than US$1 million in the latest computerized fitness equipment, including a cardio theatre with a wall of televisions — tune your walkman to any frequency and watch TV while you work out. The music is loud, fast, and constant. The place hardly ever shuts, heaving day and night with young professionals working their fats and pounding the treadmill in their quest for the body beautiful. 'Our facilities are far greater than other fitness centers. We have 80 aerobic classes a week and our equipment is always the best; it's state of the art. If there's anything new, we get it. We have virtual reality bikes, and we'll be converting bikes so you can surf the net while you keep fit', says Levine.

In Singapore, until California Fitness arrived, health clubs tended to be small and private affairs, tucked away in five-star hotels. Since its opening in 1998 on Orchard Road, the club started a new craze. With three floors, 25,000 sq. ft. of floor space and thirty certified personal trainers, the club brought to South East Asia a new fitness format: the American-style exercise emporium, where bigger is better, and the man or woman in the street can afford to join. In April 1999 the club will more than double its presence in Singapore with a new facility in the heart of the financial district in Raffles Place. It is expected to become the chain's global flagship store, with US$5 million worth of high-tech exercise gear and a futuristic design. The disco-style facility will feature a Philippe-Starck-style café and ten channels of television viewable from the aerobics machines.

California Fitness has plans to open more than 100 clubs throughout Asia. Having conquered Hong Kong and Singapore, it is planning to look to fresh fields, in particular Taiwan and South Korea. All this with an economic crisis still reverberating throughout the region. In fact, California Fitness has actually benefited from the crisis, as rents now make up just 30 to 50 per cent of the company's overheads, compared with about 60 per cent before the crisis began to bite. The company's response to the tidal wave of bankruptcies, redundancies, and shutdowns crashing around it has been to be more creative with its series of special offers for new members. 'Fitness makes you feel better right away; it is a guaranteed pick-me-up', says Levine.

Sources: Brian Mertens, 'Scene and Be Scene', *Asian Business*, 1 Apr. 1999. C. MacDonald, 'A California Dream', *Asian Business*, 1 Apr. 1999, Hong Kong and Singapore. http://web3.asia1.com.sg/timesnet/data

21 BOT projects for the Local Government Units. One is completed, 2 are under-way and 18 are in the planning or building process (Philippines Country Profile, http://www.state.gov/). Since the Asian crisis, the Vietnamese government has also been promoting BOT agreements. It has so far designated about a dozen projects for BOT investment. Only one or two have actually been approved with the first one, Binh An Water Treatment Plant, commencing water supply in August 1999 (http://www.tradenz.govt.nz/intelligence/profile/viet-nam.html).

International management contract

As discussed in Part I, Asia Pacific region is now on the road to recovery. Most countries in the region, particularly those worst affected by the crisis, are now gradually opening up their markets through liberalization, deregulation, and privatization. Human resource management has historically not had an important function in Asian management until the crisis. It has traditionally been regarded as a personnel function, almost totally administrative in orientation. Given the massive corporate restructuring already underway in the region, there is growing demand for a wide spectrum of Western specialized technical and managerial assistance through management contracts.

An international management contract is an agreement by which a business firm provides managerial assistance to another firm by training its personnel to assume managerial positions in return for a fee for providing such assistance. These arrangements would be beneficial for small firms which wish to expand their operations into Asia Pacific, but lack capital. No political risk is involved either, since the company simply receives a fee for providing the expertise needed. International management contracts are often operated in combination with turnkey operations. Under this type of agreement, a business firm agrees to construct an entire manufacturing plant or production facility, equip it, and prepare it for operation in a foreign country, and then turns it over to the local owners when it is ready for operation. When a turnkey operation is used in combination with a management contract, the multinational has to provide training and instruction for local personnel. Turnkey operations include the whole process of establishing an operation from design and construction through to operation. Examples of turnkey projects include road construction, factories, refineries, airports, and dams, and automobile plants. Governments, particularly in Asia Pacific, favour turnkey operations because they provide a way of acquiring Western production methods without accepting a permanent Western presence on their territory.

Counter-Trade

Finally, due to the instability of the financial system in Asia Pacific, counter-trade agreements and barter might be other alternatives for doing business in Asia. Counter-trade is a process, which links imports with exports. One of the advantages of counter-trade is that it helps to overcome foreign exchange shortages. The company can make purchases from abroad and pay for them out of future exports or in exchange for other nationally produced products. Counter-trade also helps to overcome distortions caused by inappropriate exchange rates. It also serves as a forward sales agreement, which may be valued both by exporters and importers, and provide greater access to closed markets and controlled economies. The disadvantage of counter-trade is mainly that such an operation needs particular skills and should be left to counter-trade experts. For example, many products might not measure up to world standards.

Barter is an exchange of goods and services without money, as opposed to counter-trade, which includes partial or full compensation in money. A barter agreement normally requires only one contract, while counter-trade transactions require a minimum of two contracts—one representing the initial sales agreement between the supplier and foreign customer, and the other representing details of the suppliers' commitment to purchase goods from either the foreign customer or a designated industry. Furthermore, a barter, in general, has a short time frame of one year, while counter-trade transactions may extend over several years.

Barter can take different forms:

(1) **Classical barter**, or straight barter, is when two parties directly exchange goods or service without the use of money. Barter is particularly useful when the local currency is extremely volatile. It is also very simple, can be implemented in a short time, and does not require large capital. 'Closed end' barter is when both parties exchange goods of equal value so that neither party has to acquire hard currency. It is the best method for overcoming foreign exchange controls and foreign currency shortages.

(2) **Buy-back or compensation trading** These are agreements to sell the technology, the construction of an entire project, or the licensing of patents or trade marks in return for agreeing to buy part of the output as payment.

(3) **Counter-purchase or parallel barter** is more complicated than simple barter. It involves the exchange of products that are delivered now for goods to be delivered in the future from a list mutually agreed upon between the two parties. In counter-purchase, the products received could be unrelated to the supplier's product lines, and therefore might pose some difficulties in marketing or distribution.

(4) **Switch trading** involves at least three or more countries. In a switch trade, the products exchanged might not be of any use to the importer or cannot be converted for cash unless sold in another market or country. A trading house is often used for this form of trade.

(5) **A clear arrangement** is when two parties agree to exchange their products by signing a purchase and payment agreement specifying the goods to be traded, their monetary value, and the date of settlement. This is also known as an 'evidence account transaction'. The importing country's bank of foreign trade and a bank in the exporter's country simultaneously maintain an 'evidence account' in order to ensure that transactions balance (Terpestra and Sarathy, 1991).

Obstacles to Doing Business in Asia Pacific

Western firms operating in Asia Pacific will face several obstacles other than the major challenges of adapting to different cultures and business practices, strategic planning, and the choice of appropriate international business operations. These are as outlined below.

Information Black Hole

The lack of information, especially information on the external environments of firms operating in the region, poses a serious challenge to traditional forms of strategic planning and management in Asia Pacific. Western firms entering the region cannot base their expectations of their local competitors and potential strategic partners on their prior experiences with other firms (Haley and Chin, 1996). Marketing and strategic information are also difficult to obtain, either because it is sparse or because it is unreliable. Consequently, forecasting market demand, assessing competitors, and finding local partners are clearly perceived by Western managers to be more difficult in Asia than in the USA or Europe (Schütte and Ciarlante, 1998). The lack of available knowledge has led to major differences in the manner in which strategic decisions are made and undertaken in Asia, particularly in South East Asia and China. To be effective in dealing with this 'black hole', one of the following strategies can be adopted: hands-on experience; transfer of knowledge; qualitative information and holistic information processing; and action-driven decision-making (Haley and Chin, 1996: 37–48).

Hands-on Experience

To be able to make quick decisions comfortably and without detailed analyses of hard data, a manager needs extensive knowledge and experience in the strategic environment. The manager must be a hands-on line manager who has gone through the firm's work routines and processes, and knows first-hand the product, market, business environment, and industry. This explains why many senior Chinese businessmen running huge companies are active in all aspects of their business. This level of involvement is necessary for an executive to be able to make the right decisions comfortably without data support.

Transfer of Knowledge

Western managers often have difficulties making new decisions within new environmental contexts. They tend to stick to the conventional business wisdom of staying with one's core business and pursuing only related diversification. In Asia Pacific companies often diversify successfully into new businesses, which are totally different and considered non-core. For an executive to function and to succeed in a completely new industry, in which he or she has no prior experience, the executive must have the ability to make generalizations from past experience. The executive must be able to transfer those generalizations into the new context. Successful Asian executives have the ability to see the big picture and to sense intuitively winners from losers. Whether one believes or not in the continuation of this characteristic decision-making style, it forms an accepted part of business activity in the region.

Qualitative Analysis and Holistic Information Processing ✓

Asian executives, moreover, might appear to take unnecessary risks by not undertaking sufficient research or analysis before acting. This appearance, however, may be misleading. These executives often process a multiplicity of information and consider several alternatives in depth before they take action. But this process, unlike that of their Western counterparts, is almost completely internal. Even when their decision-making may contain high degrees of articulation, they would rarely present the results in detailed, written, analytical forms. Asian executives almost always use external sources of information when making strategic decision; however, they are less likely to refer to documented evidence of data in published forms. They refer to sources of qualitative, even subjective information, such as that supplied by friends, business associates, government officials, and others in whose judgement they trust and in whom they personally trust. They may often travel to local scenes to check personally on the reliability of local information, rather than rely on secondary information.

Action-Driven Decision-Making ✓

Speed constitutes one key characteristic of decision-making in the region. Executives often make key decisions without consulting anyone. Their preference appears to revolve around action. Their decision-making model reflects an authoritative management style.

Dealing with Bureaucratic Red Tape ✓ ②

Another challenge facing Western firms in Asia Pacific is the existence of bureaucratic red tape in some countries which could tie up a project for months, if not years, in addition to legislative and regulatory barriers such as tariff and non-tariff barriers (Evans *et al.*, 1994)

Relationship Building ✓ *Soulutions.*

Establishing and maintaining sound personal relationships are absolutely essential to doing business in the Asia Pacific region. Building local contacts and relationships is the most useful form of assistance in overcoming obstacles such as the lack of local information and difficulties in dealing with the local bureaucracy. This is followed closely by market intelligence and information on local laws and customs (Evans *et al.*, 1994). Relationship building and networking are in fact not a prerequisite to any strategic development in the region. Developing and maintaining such relationships and networking, however, requires time, effort, and perseverance beyond what Western managers and corporations are used to.

Political Risk in the Region ✓ ③

Although most governments in the region welcome foreign investment, the risk of investment varies from country to country, based on four factors: country risk (i.e. stability), racial tension (especially anti-Chinese feeling), restrictions on foreign investment, and bureaucratic or regulatory conditions. The least risky countries, where it is easiest to do business, are Hong Kong and Singapore. China still presents significant political uncertainties as does Indonesia. In Malaysia, the attitude of the government towards FDI needs to be carefully monitored. Racial tension is another major source of political risk throughout Asia Pacific, especially in the South East between ethnic Chinese residents and indigenous populations. In Thailand and Indonesia particularly, having the right local people to help and lead is essential.

Corruption and Bribery

Corruption and bribery are rampant in many countries across Asia Pacific, often involving top politicians, government officials, military personnel, and business tycoons. Many leading figures in the region's business community during the crisis have been charged or jailed in numerous bribery, tax evasion, and embezzlement scandals. Currently, weak legal and regulatory regimes, chronic poverty, and widening income and wealth disparities create countless opportunities for corruption and bribery (Strizzi and Kindra, 1995).

Review Questions

1 Compare and contrast the various methods of entry into the Asia Pacific region, highlighting the advantages and disadvantages of each. Illustrate your answer with examples taken from companies known to you.

2 Why are joint ventures in Asia Pacific becoming so unpopular? What problems do they present, and how can these be overcome?

3 Western firms have conducted their operations in Asia Pacific in a variety of ways. Choose a particular company, identify the mode of entry adopted, and evaluate the advantages gained and the difficulties experienced by that company as a result of implementing such a method.

Relevant Case Studies (Part IV)

- Wal-Mart goes to Asia Pacific
- An Emerging Regional Manufacturing Network in South East Asia: The Case of Samsung.
- Nike: Ethical Dilemmas of FDI in Asia Pacific
- Coca-Cola Indochina

Further Reading

Beamish, P. W., Killing, J. P., Lecraw, D. H., and Crockell, H. (eds.), *International Management: Text and Cases*, Homewood, Il., Irwin, 1991

Lasserre, P., and Schütte, H., *Strategy and Management in Asia Pacific*, INSEAD Global Management Series, Maidenhead. McGraw-Hill, 1999.

Lorange, P., and Ross, J., *Strategic Alliances: Formation, Implementation and Evolution*, Oxford: Blackwell, 1995.

Tongzon, Jose L., *The Economies of Southeast Asia: The Growth and Development of ASEAN Economies*, Cheltenham: Edward Elgar, 1998.

Chapter 13

Marketing in Asia Pacific, Post-crisis

Although marketing principles have recently been internationalized due to the growth of multinational operations in the world, entering Asia Pacific markets can still be very complex. The region consists of several countries with different languages, cultures, histories, and customs, not to mention different tastes and preferences and levels of wealth. Different production process and marketing approaches also exist throughout the region. Furthermore, in recent years, the region as a whole has undergone dramatic transformation towards privatization, liberal trade policies, and free market forces. Western firms are finding it increasingly harder to keep up with the speed and scope of change in Asia Pacific markets, post-crisis. This chapter will explore the basic marketing issues and problems and their implications for marketing strategies in the region. It aims at providing an understanding of the distinctive nature and principles of marketing in Asia Pacific which are significantly different from those in the West, and to develop an approach most suitable to its consumers' needs.

Marketing Principles and Practices: Western Style

It is interesting to note that explicit marketing ideas were first adopted in Japan around 1650 by a member of the Mitsui family when he opened his first store in Tokyo based on the following policies, 'to be a buyer for his customers, to design the right products for them, and to develop sources for their production; the principles of your money back and no question asked; and the idea of offering a large assortment of products to his customers rather than focusing on a craft, a product category, or a process' (Drucker, 62). In the West, marketing appeared in the middle of the nineteenth century, when Cyrus H. McCormick first made the distinction between marketing as hard selling and advertising, and marketing as 'the unique and central function of the business enterprise'. He invented the basic tools of modern marketing, including market research and market analysis, pricing policies, parts and service supply to the customer, and instalment credit (Drucker, 1974: 62). Marketing as a discipline was further developed in 1905 when

W. E. Kreusi taught the first course 'The Marketing of Products', at the University of Pennsylvania, and in 1910 when R. Butler offered a course in 'Marketing Methods' at the University of Wisconsin. Marketing departments did not appear within firms until the early twentieth century, and marketing did not crystallize as a business philosophy until the mid-1950s (Kotler, 1984: 20).

Theodore Levitt made a clear distinction between selling and marketing. While selling, according to Levitt, focuses on the seller, marketing focuses on the needs of the buyer. 'Selling is preoccupied with the seller's need to convert his product into cash; marketing with the idea of satisfying the needs of the customer by means of the product and the whole cluster of things associated with creating, delivery and finally consuming it' (Levitt, 1983*b*: 45–66). Although selling starts with the firm's existing products, and calls for hard and aggressive selling and promotion to achieve profits, marketing, on the other hand, starts with the firm's target customers and their needs and wants and attempts to achieve profits through customer satisfaction. Consequently, selling is only the tip of the marketing iceberg, as Kotler put it (Kotler, 1984: 20). Marketing aims at knowing and understanding customers so well that the product fits them and sells itself. All that should be needed then is to make the product or service available (Drucker, 1974: 64–65).

E. Jerome McCarthy developed the four factor classification, which has come to be known as the famous four Ps of the marketing mix: Product, Price, Place, and Promotion (Kotler, 1984: 42).

- **Product** This includes a study of the product features, packaging, branding, and servicing policies and style.

- **Price** This refers to the money that customers have to pay for the product, such as a wholesale price or retail price, allowance and credit terms.

- **Place** This stands for various activities the firm undertakes to make the product accessible and available to consumers. These include, for example, choosing retailers, wholesalers, physical distribution firms, and intermediaries.

- **Promotion** This is simply the effort of the firm to persuade customers to buy the product and includes activities such as advertising, sales promotions, and publicity.

These marketing principles are not fundamentally different in Asia Pacific. Although the basic principles are universally applicable, entering a new market in Asia Pacific might often mean dealing with a different environment, different consumer tastes, different purchasing power, different attitudes towards new and Western products, different distribution channels and transportation logistics.

Marketing in Asia Pacific

Marketing in Asia Pacific can be defined as the process of finding out what customers want around the Asia Pacific region, and then satisfying these wants better than other competitors both domestic and international.

Product Policy for Asia Pacific Market

In recent years, the huge size and growth of consumer markets in Asia Pacific have become almost a mirage for foreign companies seeking to make a fortune. Foreign firms wishing to market their products in the region should first decide whether to adopt a standardized or a diversified strategy.

A standardized strategy is when the firm decides to produce one product and sell it in the same way everywhere in the world with the same specification and characteristics. Industrial durable products sold to manufacturing firms, businesses, and governments such as steel, hardware, machinery, and electronic components usually adopt such a strategy. This strategy is also applicable to scientific and medical instruments, laboratory equipment, and heavy machinery. The underlying assumption here is that market needs for the product are the same, and that the product would fulfil the same needs or serve the same function anywhere in the world. Consumer goods such as cameras, watches, perfumes, cosmetics, luxury goods, appliances, and automobiles often adopt a standardized strategy too.

The basic argument for adopting a standardized strategy here is the claim that national and regional differences are steadily declining due to new technology, improved communications, and transport, and that customers' needs and interests as a result are becoming increasingly homogeneous worldwide. Customers around the world, it is argued, have now one thing in common: 'an overwhelming desire for dependable, worldwide modernity in all things, at aggressively low prices which can only be achieved through product standardization' (Levitt, 1983a: 92–102). As Levitt put it: 'A powerful force drives the world towards a converging commonalty, and that force is technology . . . Ancient differences in national tastes or modes of doing business have disappeared. The commonalty of preference leads inescapably to the standardization of products, manufacturing, and the institutions of trade and commerce' (Levitt, 1983a: 92–102). Inexpensive air travel and new technologies, Levitt asserts further, have led consumers the world over increasingly to think and shop alike. Ohmae agrees with Levitt, but he takes the argument even further. He argues that the globalization of finance and information has made national geographical boundary lines on maps disappear and has given rise to what he calls a 'borderless world' (Ohmae, 1990). As the world is becoming more homogeneous, Ohmae argues, further distinctions among national markets are fading. On a political map, the boundaries between countries are as clear as ever. However, on a competitive map showing the real flows of financial and industrial activity, those boundaries have largely disappeared. What has eaten them away is the persistent ever speedier flow of information, which has made old geographic barriers become irrelevant (Ohmae, 1991). Ohmae argues further that (since) 'Information has made us all global citizens, customers needs have globalized and we must globalize to meet them' (Ohmae, 1990, 1991). Consequently, we have become global citizens, with global needs. And since global needs will lead to global products; so must the companies that want to sell us things become global. For Ohmae, then, the pressure towards globalization is driven not so much by diversification or competition as by the needs and preferences of customers. It is also claimed that standardization of production can be economically efficient, because when a product has only one production source, standardizing it will gain the economies of scale of long production runs (Terpestra and Sarathy, 1991: 253). Research and development expenses normally needed to accommodate and adapt the product to each foreign market can also be redirected towards improving the product itself and towards innovation. A standardized production policy can also maintain stronger control over design, technology, and quality, thus achieving a worldwide reputation and maintaining the global image of the product (Ohmae, 1990: 25). The idea of a 'global consumer' in Asia Pacific is of course very attractive. However, consumers in Asia Pacific are significantly different from those in the West. They may be aware of and hungry for global Western brands but their attitude towards foreign products is not the same, as shown later in this chapter.

A *diversified, or product-differentiation strategy* is when the firm realizes the need to introduce some modifications to its product in various foreign markets due to different lifestyles, tastes, religion, habits, language, or other cultural elements, legal requirements, physical differences, and different infrastructures. It thus selects only the most attractive markets and concentrates its efforts on them by adapting and diversifying its products according to local demands. There are twenty basic factors that must be considered in selecting the market or markets to target in Asia Pacific. Claudia Cragg (Cragg, 1992: 19) lists them as follows:

(1) Is there an identified need for your product or service in the country or countries of your choice and the infrastructure to sustain that need?

(2) Is there a large availability of potential customers for you and your company?

(3) What is the competition and does it enjoy significant advantages over you that might make your business unviable?

(4) Is there a wide availability of market information on your product or services for that country from specialized professional sources?

(5) What about the advertising, public relations, and general promotion of awareness of your business in that country?

(6) What is the maturity and level of the product and/or service in the market?

(7) Is there an industry using your products whose demands you could meet?

(8) What is the availability of potential outlets, agents, and distributors?

(9) What are the long-term prospects?

(10) What are the options in the market in terms of exporting, licensing, or using a local subsidiary?

(11) What is the availability of financing in the market?

(12) What are the costs of market entry?

(13) How easy is it in that market to ensure payment?

(14) How will the legal and accounting framework in that country, that is, the general operating environment, impact on your company's usual business practices?

(15) How passive or regulatory is the government's attitude to foreign businesses?

(16) What are the possibilities of incentives?

(17) How sound is the country's political stability?

(18) What are the costs of facilities and the cost and availability of necessary skilled and unskilled workers?

(19) How difficult are both cultural interaction and the spoken languages in terms of doing business?

(20) To what extent will your company's goals and interests be met by being located in this market or markets?

The main advantage of a product-differentiation policy in Asia Pacific is that it increases profits by being capable of quickly responding to changes in consumer trends, tastes, and needs. It is also claimed that with the assistance of new technology, firms are now more capable of adapting their products to specific local needs and tastes quickly and cheaply. The box (p. 253) illustrates how Pillsbury differentiated its traditional product—the dumpling—in a novel format designed to win over Chinese shoppers.

A successful differentiation strategy also requires careful attention to the particular segment of the market to be targeted.

Market Segmentation across Asia Pacific

Deep-seated differences in culture, religion, language, consumer preferences, economic development, and purchasing power exist in Asia Pacific. A pan-Asian marketing strategy would be difficult to implement. Careful attention to the various segments of the markets is essential.

By definition, a market segment is a part or section of the market. It possesses one or more unique characteristics, which set it apart and distinguish it from other segments. Market segmentation involves dividing the market into a number of distinct segments, according to some specific criteria which reflect different purchasing wants and needs. The purpose of segmentation is to make it possible for firms to produce products or services that fit more closely with people's requirements. Market segmentation involves identifying characteristics which distinguish between customers according to their buying preferences. Market segmentation is usually achieved either by geography, demography (sex, age, income, race, education level, and so on), or by social-cultural actors (social class, values, religion, lifestyle choices).

In Asia Pacific, we can distinguish four distinct segments across the region with similar interests, tastes, and attitudes, but at the same time considerably different from other segments in their respective countries: first, the young people who have unified tastes across Asia Pacific in music, sports, and cultural activities; secondly, the trend-setters and social climbers, who are the wealthier and more educated Asians. This group tends to value independence, refuse consumer stereotypes, and appreciate exclusive products. Thirdly, there is the elite group who are Asia's successful entrepreneurs and business people. They display cosmopolitan attitudes and have very similar tastes for luxury goods across the region. The fourth segment is geographic country-based segmentation.

Geographical segmentation in Asia Pacific reveals the existence of a wide diversity among consumers within the same country. Differences exist between geographically separated parts of the same country which have different mentalities, different dialects, different religions, and even different cultures. A recent survey conducted by Geng Cui

Pillsbury in China

Pillsbury, also known for its Häagen Dazs ice-cream and Green Giant vegetables, had no presence in the country before 1996. Pillsbury's famous chilled or frozen ready-to-cook buns, pastries, and breads weren't exactly good for the Chinese market. First, because of the lack of ovens available in China and secondly, because Pillsbury products needed special requirements, such as toasters, or featured unfamiliar tastes, like pizza. Pillsbury had to find a product that Chinese people eat every day, not something they think of once every three months.

In China, dumplings are very serious business. The generic English term covers everything from *shuijiao* to *tangyuan*, *dim sum* to *baozi*—varieties that range in flavour, shape, texture, and the occasions on which they are eaten. Pillsbury's research found that in Hong Kong consumers buy an average of 25 frozen dumplings at a time. In Guangzhou, the number jumps to 75, in Shanghai to 101, and in Beijing to 110. All across China people eat dumplings and in massive amounts. Before it could deliver the premium product Pillsbury felt that the market needed, the company had first to find a local partner. Hong Kong's Wanchai Ferry Peking Dumpling brand was well known in the territory but not outside. Pillsbury decided to buy Wanchai Ferry and then turn it into a new company, Pillsbury Foods Asia, owned 70 per cent by Pillsbury and 30 per cent by Chong, the local partner. That company in turn forged a partnership with Shanghai Food Group, a state-owned enterprise, that provided Pillsbury with a temporary factory, business contacts, and the land for a future plant in Shanghai. When *Wanchai Ferry Jiajuan* (home-made) dumpling arrived in store freezers to China, Pillsbury dropped 'Peking' as a concession to regional sensitivities.

Pillsbury also used all of its experience with premium brands like Häagen Dazs to differentiate its products from those of competitors, starting with the way they look. Its dumplings came in a plastic tray, whereas rival offerings tend to be loosely packed in a plastic bag. The brightly coloured packaging featured photos of the contents piping hot and ready to eat. These visual clues were a warm-up to the price tag: a package of 15 *Wanchai Ferry* dumplings sells for around 8 renminbi (a little less than $1). Market leader Longfeng Foods, a Chinese concern, sells a pack of 32 for 7.5 renminbi. Frozen dumplings surfaced in China only five years ago, and have registered double-digit growth every year since. In 1996 the market was worth $200 million, according to Pillsbury. Now, says Chong, it is worth from $300 million to $400 million. 'The key for us is really to develop a premium brand and pricing is a key lever to differentiate us', says Henry Chen, marketing director for Pillsbury China. 'We are at a stretch, but we are not beyond the consumer's reach'.

Finally, Pillsbury had to convey its brand image in terms of tradition. Pillsbury launched its first TV advertising campaign, featuring a young wife whose mother-in-law is coming to visit. Their shared meal turns out to be a steaming plate of *Wanchai Ferry* dumplings. Full of luscious shots of meats and vegetables, the advert is an attempt to hammer home the message that frozen delicacies taste as fresh as if you had made them yourself. 'Baking in the US is very traditional', says Chen. 'It is the home, it is the hearth, it is tradition. Dumplings are the exact equivalent in China. In terms of imagery and emotional feel, it is the same—just a Chinese format.'

By February 1999, Pillsbury was able to meet its projections, selling about 10 million dumplings in Shanghai and other eastern cities. In comparison, Longfeng, which distributes in every province in China, sells about 800 million a month.

Source: This case draws heavily from: Joanna Slater with Uan Zhihua, 'Retailing', *Sales Force*, 1 Apr. 1999, Shanghai. Joanna Slater 'The Case of Pillsbury: New Recipe for a New Market', *Consumer Passion*, 18 Mar. 1999, Shanghai.

and Qiming Liu (2000) examined the diversity among Chinese consumers across seven regional markets within China. Data from their national survey indicate that consumers from various regions are significantly different from one another in terms of purchasing power, attitude, lifestyles, media use, and consumption patterns. The seven regional markets identified in the study are: South, East, North, Central, South-West, North-West, and North-East. These are grouped under growth markets, emerging markets, and untapped markets.

'Growth markets' are located in the south and east. They are more advanced in economic development and have more affluent consumers than hinterland provinces. The South regional economy was the first to attract foreign investment with its four original Special Economic Zones (SEZs), and became the most outward-oriented. It also represents the *Min-Yue* culture characterized by its contacts with the outside world and great emphasis on mercantile entrepreneurship. Furthermore, each province within this region has its own main dialect, Cantonese and Fukienese. Consumers in this area, about 7 per cent of China's population, are among the most prosperous in the country. Close to Hong Kong and Taiwan, they have long been exposed to foreign products (Ariga *et al.*, 1997, quoted in Cui and Liu, 2000). East China (Hua-dong) is densely populated and highly urbanized. The region is known as the 'head of the dragon', and is the industrial and financial centre of China and the gateway to the 2000 million consumers in East China. This region has also its own culture, the *Hai-pai*, well known for having the best amenities and products for enhancing the quality of life. Consumers in this regional market are the most innovative and cosmopolitan, setting trends in fashion and lifestyles.

'Emerging markets' are located in North, Central, and South-West China. These have become increasingly attractive to global companies. This region has access to key government agencies and is making tremendous investment in industries such as telecommunications, computer technology, and pharmaceuticals (Child and Stewart, 1997. Beijing, the nation's capital, is located in this region and represents the culture of North China—the *Jin-pai* culture—attaching great value to the Confucian doctrines of hierarchy, stability, and control (Cui and Liu, 2000). Consumers here are relatively conservative and emphasize instrinsic satisfaction, yet are still open to new product ideas (Ariga *et al.*, 1997).

Finally, the North-East and North-West, are the 'untapped markets' still waiting to be explored by foreign firms. These regions emphasize heavy industries such as mining, automobile, and machinery manufacturing. With the longest winter in the country, this region has limited agricultural output, and little variety in food products. Manchurians and Koreans are the biggest ethnic minorities in the region and have a great impact on local cultures.

Product Positioning in Asia Pacific

After careful selection of the appropriate market segment, product positioning, or placing products in a part of the market where they fare well in comparison with competing products, is crucial. Product positioning involves identifying possible positions for products or services within each target segment and then producing, adapting, and marketing products and services towards the target markets.

Asian consumers are acutely sensitive to image and services. Western firms wishing to succeed in Asia Pacific will have to exert long and consistent efforts to develop the kind of reputation that these markets require. In China, for example, since the 1980s significant numbers of its consumers have become more sophisticated. They are especially hungry for luxury and personal care goods, both of which lend themselves to the efficacy of brand names (for further details see country review in Chapter 5). Because it is difficult to push a product given China's poor sales and distribution system, the ability of a brand name to pull customers to the product is therefore crucial (Wong and Maher, 1997).

Positioning of a brand in Asia Pacific can differ considerably across the region. However, there are some issues that apply to almost all product and services. First, markets in the region, with the exception of Japan, are relatively immature and in consequence are still very volatile. Not only new brands, but also the introduction of new product categories can dramatically reshape the positioning of established products. Secondly, consumer behaviour in the region is directed more towards social than individual needs. The appropriateness of an ego-centred positioning would therefore be thin in the Asian context. In many cases, companies with luxury brands have relied on the image of their country of origin instead (Schütte and Ciarlante, 1998: 129).

Finally, positioning in Asia Pacific needs to take into consideration the increasingly popular practice of *fengshui*, particularly in Hong Kong and Singapore. *Fengshui* is widely applied in Chinese culture but also in Japan and Vietnam. It means 'wind and water' and refers to the ancient art of geomancy—a calculated assessment of the most favourable conditions for any venture (Lip, 1989). It is the belief that there is a continual and ever-present relationship between the earth and the cosmos and that every spot on earth is home to either a positive or negative spirit. That spirit has the power to influence and control whatever is built or living on that location. *Fengshui*, in other words, consists of the art of proper positioning of buildings, entrances and furniture in daily business and life. Rituals and customs determine the object's precise location. Although many Westerners believe *fengshui* defies logical or scientific explanation, it is a very common practice in Asia Pacific. As Min Chen recounts:

In China, Taiwan, and Hong Kong the construction of buildings is initiated or the arrangement of furniture is attempted only after consulting a *fengshui* practioner. Decisions regarding the placement of doors and the direction in which they open are believed to determine to a large extent the future fortunes of an enterprise or of the individuals using the structure. Thus, to the Chinese, neglecting to consider the forces of *fengshui* is a very risky proposition. (Chen and Pan, 1993: 138).

There are documented cases in Hong Kong where the seriousness of complaints about buildings which were erected without first asking the advice of a *fengshui* expert has forced the owners of the building to make adjustments to satisfy superstitious concerns. The headquarters of the Bank of China in Hong Kong, for example, after it was completed in 1988, drew complaints from those in surrounding buildings because it was said that the mirrored walls on the outside of the building reflected angry spirits off on to other buildings. Trees had to be planted to appease the complainers. Even if the occupants of the building harbour no superstitious beliefs, customers can be lost and predictions of bad luck and misfortune can result by neglecting the demands of *fengshui*. Even those

Chinese who don't fully accept the veracity of the *fengshui* superstition will often follow it anyway, just to be safe (Chen and Pan, 1993). To have good *fengshui* a corporate building should face the water and be framed by mountains. At the same time, the building should not block the view of the mountain spirits. That's why a number of major office buildings in Hong Kong such as the famous headquarters of the Hong Kong and Shanghai Banking Corporation, designed by well-known architect Norman Foster, have see-through lobbies to keep the spirits happy. Sharp angles give off bad *fengshui*. That's why many people perceived the Bank of China in Hong Kong designed by I. M. Pei as having bad *fengshui*. Similarly, *fengshui* principles apply to the design and layout of hotels, restaurants, and department stores (Lip, 1989). Consequently, a company's image and reputation as well as the success of its brands can depend crucially on whether or not the company takes *fengshui* seriously—not necessarily because of the usefulness of the advice but because of consumers' perceptions. A company that consults a *fengshui* expert and publicizes it in the media tells customers and employees that it cares for their prosperity and well-being. When Marks & Spencer, the British retailer, for example, was planning and developing its new stores in Hong Kong, a master of *fengshui* was invited to evaluate the store and make recommendations regarding its layout. As a result, all Marks & Spencer's Hong Kong stores contain fish tanks with flowing water in them. Furthermore, these tanks are very carefully positioned, normally behind the cash tills, on the advice of the *fengshui* expert, in order to facilitate healthy sales.

Pricing Policy in Asia Pacific

Since the Asian crisis, consumers in Asia Pacific have become more price-conscious. Traditionally, Japanese consumers or businesses exhibited strong preferences for a high price premium. Japanese consumers' association of high prices with good product performance made them suspicious of price discounting. There is the famous instance of Chivas Regal Scotch whisky losing sales when it cut prices, thereby reducing its status as a prestigious gift (Yip, 3). Since the recession, however, and the fluctuations in the yen exchange rate in Japan, price has become an important issue to the Japanese consumer. For example, when BMW offered cheap financing for the purchase of their cars, thereby touching on a taboo topic in the marketing of luxury cars, the pay-off was increased sales in market segments entirely occupied by Japanese competitors. Offering lower prices during the crisis instead of withdrawing from the market, seemed to be the best strategy for Coca-Cola as illustrated in the box (p. 257).

Most foreign retailers in China have also adopted a similar price-cutting strategy. When, for example, Carrefour, the French retailer, opened its stores in Beijing in 1995 and in Shanghai in 1996, it emphasized low prices and warehouse-sized stores stocked with basic household goods, white goods (mostly imported), clothes, shoes, and dry goods. Carrefour promised prices as low as those in Chinese markets and state-owned stores. This approach won over the Chinese consumers in large numbers overcoming their ingrained belief that foreign-invested stores were always more expensive than domestic retail outlets (Brunet, 1999). Wal-Mart too adopted a similar approach in China by sourcing 80 per cent of its products locally and importing other parts from Asia and the USA (see case study included in Part IV). When it opened its first multi-level store in

---

Riding the Asian crisis the American way: Coca-Cola in Indonesia

We know times are tough, but Coke is an affordable pleasure.
(John Murphy, managing director at Coca-Cola in Indonesia)

Coca-Cola's Indonesian presence dates back to 1927. About 95 per cent of its raw materials are locally sourced. 'We are going to be here for a long, long time time', says John Murphy, managing director at Coca-Cola in Indonesia. The crisis presents a challenge. How do we remain close to our customer? When the Indonesian rupiah plunged in 1998, John Murphy and his team immediately tore up their carefully crafted business plan, which had focused on ways to expand sales of Coke in non-refillable packages such as cans and plastic bottles. In just three days, they wrote a new one. The gist: Coke was to be as widely available as possible, at an affordable price. Working with their bottler, they pumped up production of the single-serving refillable bottle of Coke, held the price to 700 rupiah (about 10 US cents; a can of Coke costs more than three times as much), and encouraged their distributors to get the product into small shops, street vendors' stalls, and restaurants across the country. The message for consumers: 'we know times are tough, but Coke is an affordable pleasure'.

Pricing-cutting, however, backfired on Coca-Cola in Vietnam. In 1998 a group of economists sent letters to government officials accusing Coca-Cola of price dumping when the company introduced a new 300 ml. bottle at the old 200 ml. bottle price (for further details, see case study in Part IV).

Shenzhen supercentre, Chinese local consumers bought four times the number of small appliances envisaged in Wal-Mart's original projection.

Place: Sales and Distribution Strategy in Asia Pacific

Making consumer products available in Asia Pacific is a major managerial and infra-structural problem. In China, for instance, the absence of a free market in the past resulted in scarcities. State-controlled retail outlets, manufacturers, and suppliers were often sold out before demand was satisfied. In the past, foreign firms have actually had to export many of these Chinese manufactured goods either because the government required it as a condition of the joint venture or because their particular consumer markets lay elsewhere. Although the competitive features of the open-door policy are improving matters somewhat, there is still a need for greatly improved sales and distribution networks (Wong and Maher, 1997). To overcome this problem, IBM experience in China is interesting to consider.

Since the open-door policy, IBM has raced to take advantage of the Chinese market's new openness and potential, which is growing at an annual rate of 40 per cent and was expected to reach 12 million units by the year 2000. To reach its customers through its service centres, IBM signed a joint venture with the Railway Ministry, dubbed the 'Blue Express', and was able to set up a national network of service centres, many of them in busy railway terminals. More importantly, the venture enabled 'Blue Express' to ship computer parts via the railway network around the country within 24 hours, while competitors have to book cargo space weeks in advance. The ministry's staff of more than 300 computer engineers also helped out by providing customer service on IBM products. As a result, total IBM sales have risen by 50 per cent annually between 1995 and 1997 to more than $400 million (Anon., 26 May, 1997).

Other distribution strategies in Asia Pacific are either to appoint a distributor, to go it alone, or to establish an agreement with the Sogo Shoshas. Given the important role of intermediaries in Asian life and the uncertainty of the business environment, many foreign firms favour a distributor when entering markets in the region. A major advantage of using a local distributor is that a typical local distributor will have better local contacts and possibly a better local sales force. Chinese entrepreneurs dominate the distribution sector in most countries in Asia Pacific, with the exception of Japan. Selecting one of these firms may work well in terms of efficiency, but entails certain political risks due to their unpopularity since the crisis, especially in Indonesia and Malaysia. Furthermore, Chinese distributors tend to look at distribution as a cash-management business. They might sell their products to retailers at prices below purchasing costs. This does not indicate a loss-making undertaking. Distributors may be granted payment terms of three months, stretching them to four. They will then sell to the retailer either against cash, or demand very high interest payments when granting terms of a few weeks. In adding interest earnings Chinese distributors thus achieve a positive margin, often without even having to invest in the business themselves. Also, Chinese distributors often set up the business as an activity to raise cash, which in turn can be invested in other businesses (Lasserre and Shütte, 1999: 148; see also Ch. 9).

Promotion Strategies in Asia Pacific

Despite regional variations in Asia Pacific, there are three basic factors crucial for successful promotion strategies in the region as a whole. These are: concern for aesthetics, creating a prestigious image, and enhancing quality perceptions.

Concern for Aesthetics

A general concern for aesthetics such as an attractive look, touch and feel, and attention to detail is widespread in the Asia Pacific. The region as a whole seems to share a common aesthetic style. Asians in general value complexity and decoration. Chinese, Thais, Malays and Indonesians, for example, love the display of multiple forms, shapes, and colours. Asian aesthetics, furthermore, value harmony and naturalism. In China, symbols and displays of natural objects—of mountains, rivers, and phoenixes prevail and are frequently found in packaging and advertising. From 'Dragon Air' to 'Tiger Beer' naturalism abounds in brand names and logos. In Japan, gardens, trees, and flowers are prime objects of aesthetic symbolism.

Creating a Prestigious Image

Asians are in general one of the most image-conscious consumers in the world. The 'right' image is often associated with class, market, and prestige. The marketing of alcoholic beverages, cars, and fragrances provides good examples. Johnny Walker's most recent line extension 'Honour' has been developed specifically for the East Asian markets using the classy British spelling, a proprietary bottle shape, and distinctive box design (an embossed box with seal and satin lining) to enhance the high-end positioning of the brand. Mercedes Benz, using market image advertising, is in big demand in Hong Kong, while Champagne the new fragrance by Yves Saint Laurent, is making a fortune in Asia managing corporate and brand identities in the Asia Pacific region (Schmitt and Pan, 1994).

A prestigious image is an important asset for both brands and companies. For Asian consumers, it is not only important that products be perceived as reliable and prestigious. The manufacturers should also have a positive image. It is therefore important for overseas manufacturers to promote not only their brands but also the image of the corporation. In Japan, for example, every television commercial from a consumer giant ends with a shot of the company's logo. Because brands are most successful if they are linked to companies with a respectable image, a company's image may be leveraged in the form of brand extensions. In the West a diaper by the Japanese cosmetics firm Shiseido may be judged primarily in terms of whether cosmetics and diapers go together; in Asia the image of Shiseido provides enough justification for giving the product a try. Therefore, companies operating in the region need to be very concerned about their company image because corporate identity is a major asset for marketing products (Schmitt and Pan, 1994: 32–48).

Enhancing Quality Perceptions

Quality perception in Asia Pacific is closely tied to service. Asian consumers always expect a certain level of service, even if they are price-conscious. Asians care greatly about others' perceptions of themselves and are very concerned about losing face. They are consequently less likely to complain when they receive defective products or inappropriate service; instead they change companies and products silently. Comparative advertising and quality comparisons in an Asian culture are thus seen as bad-mouthing the competition, and a company that does it loses face. A company's communal activities, on the other hand, such as sponsorships, and public relations are more important in enhancing the corporate reputation. In 1978 and 1980, chairman Kim of Daewoo, for example, donated his entire personal holdings in the corporation to the Daewoo Foundation. The Daewoo Foundation contributes to the promotion of educational services, community services, social welfare, and cultural programmes. The Daewoo Dream Village, which is a home for adolescent-run households, was also built from the copyright income of Mr Kim's autobiography published in 1989 (see Daewoo case Study in Part IV for further details).

Providing the Appropriate Level of Service

Service in Asia is often crucial for enhancing quality perceptions. Service 'Asian style', however, differs greatly from the Western style. While efficiency and time savings are crucial by Western standards, Asian customers value personal attention. Customization is more appreciated than standardization. Asian's profitable airlines are good examples of the Asian service concept. Singapore Airlines has positioned itself primarily in terms of

Service 'Asian Style': Singapore Airlines

Singapore Airlines have the highest operating profit of any airline in the world. In 1990 *Air Transport World* magazine named Singapore Airlines airline of the year; *Conde Nast Traveler* termed it the world best airline, and *Business Traveler International* called it 'best international airline'. Following the Asian Crisis, the 1998 *Review 200* pointed up a common trait among those companies that have survived and thrived through the downturn by acting quickly and decisively, being flexible and innovative in meeting demands in the new economy, embracing reforms, and focusing on core businesses. To be included in the *Review 200*, a company cannot be a niche player that is known and well regarded by the few it serves; instead it must be recognized for its achievements and leadership qualities by a broad range of people. *Review 200* comprises 110 companies based in Asia Pacific, 10 from each of 11 countries, and 90 multi-nationals that do business in Asia. As in previous surveys, Asia-based companies are ranked only in their home markets; non-Asian companies are ranked in all 11 countries of the survey.

Singapore Airlines was also ranked first in the 1999 Asia's Most Admired Companies (AMAC) survey for the fifth consecutive year. AMAC survey has little to do with numbers. Doing well in the AMAC survey comes from a combination of building a company that shareholders or owners, management and staff can be proud of; ensuring the world knows about that pride, and a good reputation. The 1999 AMAC survey also shows companies that have coped well with the regional financial crisis by improving service and products and positioning themselves for the expected economic recovery. Singapore Airlines was also the top winner in the management category, the products and services category, and was listed as a company that was seen to maintain the highest ethical standard. The fallout of the financial crisis has sharply focused attention on the abilities of companies operating in this region to cope with rapidly eroding asset values, dwindling consumer demand, rising real interest rates, and currency depreciation. In the ability to cope category, Taiwan Semiconductor came first followed by Singapore Telecom and Singapore Airlines. The other top performers are Sony and Coca-Cola. How did it all begin? How could a small island republic, measuring only 38 km. long by 22 km. wide, and with a population of 2.7 million have one of the world's largest and more profitable airlines?

When both Malaysia and Singapore became independent in the mid-1960s, the name of the carrier was changed from Malaysian Airlines to Malaysia-Singapore Airlines (MSA). However, it soon became obvious that the states had different priorities and objectives for the airlines. Malaysia wished to maintain a substantial domestic operation connecting the remote areas of the country, while Singapore, an island of less than 250 sq. m., had no interest in such an operation. Malaysia's main interest was having a flag carrier that would provide domestic and regional routes. But, being a small island, Singapore did not need domestic services; instead, its goal was to have long-distance international routes. Malaysia and Singapore agreed to divide their assets and establish two separate flag carriers.

On 1 October 1972, MSA ceased to exist and was replaced by Malaysian Airline System (MAS) and Singapore Airlines. All Boeing jets in the MSA fleet and most of the international routes were retained by Singapore Airlines. The reformation agreement of 1972 awarded Singapore Airlines most of MSAs' international routes. When Singapore Airlines first flew under its own colours in October 1972, there was a great amount of uncertainty and disbelief. How could an airline from such a small country compete in the international big league. Today Singapore International Airlines is a public company listed on the Singapore Stock Exchange, an enterprise accounting for 3 per cent of Singapore's GNP, and 54 per cent held by the Singapore government through its holding company Temasek. Although Singapore Airlines was state owned, the government role in policy-making and day-to-day management was minimal. Senior executives were told not to expect any subsidy or preferential treatment. What the government did do, however, was to offer foreign carriers the opportunity to operate out of Singapore.

Singapore Airlines Strategy: Growth and Innovation

The essence of Singapore Airlines' (SIA) corporate philosophy is dedicated teamwork and the pursuit of excellence in every sphere of the group's activities. SIA's organizational structure is rationalized on functional lines in accordance with the need to manage a wide variety of specialized functions. Members of the board of directors were drawn from the civil service and the National Trade Union Congress. There are nine function divisions, each overseen by a director. Each division is responsible for a wide range of more specific functions, which are designated as departments. This wide range of organization units is due to the complex nature of the airline business. For example, the director of engineering has over twenty managers reporting to him. In order to ensure coordination, directors meet regularly in formal committee meetings.

In 1973, instead of depending on agents to sell its services, Singapore Airlines initiated its own computer reservation and check-in system, KRISCOM. By 1991 this had been replaced by ABACUS, a computer reservation system which provided travel agents with an extended array of services including airline and hotel reservations, ground arrangements, and regional travel news. Three months before operations began, SIA signed a contract with Boeing for the delivery of two B747-200s with an option on two more. It was the first airline in South East Asia to order jumbo jets. SIA also concentrated on marketing; the airline's name and its logo—a stylized yellow bird—decorating the aircraft's dark blue tail fins soon became well known on the routes it operated. The goal was to create a distinctively different airline that would be international but retain its 'Asia' personality. Most importantly, top management insisted that it emphasize service to passengers who, they constantly reminded staff, were the unique reason for the airline's existence.

Staff Training and the Delivery of High Quality Personalized Service

Singapore Airlines has also been a success story in its branding and reputation as a well-managed airline company. The Singapore Girl—the personification of charm and friendliness—became a reality after painstaking recruiting, training, and retraining. The best-looking and most helpful young women were selected as stewardesses. They were given a maximum of three contract terms of five years each, above-average wages, and high status in the company. Better staff were given the possibility of promotion to senior jobs with SIA after the fifteen-year period. An extensive and distinctive advertising campaign promoted these stewardesses dressed in multi-coloured, ankle-length dresses made from beautiful batik fabric designed by the Paris couturier, Balmain. These women became the symbol of the airline's mission to deliver high-quality personalized service.

A service productivity index was computed each quarter in order to assess service quality standards. Multilingual in-flight surveys were used to itemize customers' impressions on key issues. This information was then compiled along with data on punctuality and baggage mishandled or recovered per 1,000 passengers. As soon as a complaint relating directly to a specific in-flight experience was received, crew members would be temporarily taken out of the system and given training. Cabin-crew members were released from their flight schedules three or four times a year to meet with training experts. Senior cabin-crew members met every Monday morning for feedback and exchange sessions with service support personnel.

Also, instead of competing on price with other airlines, Singapore Airlines preferred non-price forms of competition such as better service, more destinations, more frequent schedules, and newer fleets. The underlying company principle was that the customer came first. How customers were handled at each point of contact was considered of paramount importance. Company policy clearly stated that if a trade-off had to be made, it should be made in favour of the customer. Key people were sent on special missions to see what other airlines were doing and how customers were handled. Management firmly believed that for SIA to survive global competition it had to distinguish itself from its competitors.

Complaints were encouraged as they provided insight about problems. Complaints received from passengers were then integrated into daily simulation games, which groomed staff on ways to cope with them. Research also indicated that customers were happier when given a choice. Offering more meal variations automatically reduced the number of unhappy people. Menus, typically changed by other airlines no more than four times a year, were altered every week on SIA's high-frequency flights. Information technology enabled the chefs to fine-tune menus and immediately withdraw any dishes that were poorly received. Since this was a costly exercise, chefs were instructed to find ways to save money by, for instance, preparing meals only from ingredients in season.

A fleet modernization campaign was another tactic used to give a strong message to the market: that Singapore Airlines was a leader in aircraft technology.

Sources: Cathy Hilborn Feng, 'Asia's Leading Companies: Introduction: The Six Annual Review 2000', *Far Eastern Economic Review*, 31 Dec. 1998–7 Jan. 1999.
Asia's Most Admired Companies (AMAC), 162(1), 42–9, http://web3.asia1.com.sg/timesnet/data
Irene Chow, Holbert, Neil, Kelley, Lane, and Yu, Julie, *Business Strategy: An Asia Pacific Focus*, Singapore: Prentice Hall, Simon & Schuster Asia, 1997, 447–58; 563–89; and 755.

providing superior in-flight service, centred around the flight attendants, famously known as the Singapore Girls—the personification of charm and friendliness, and the symbol of the airline's mission to deliver high-quality personalized service. Instead of competing on price with other airlines, SIA preferred non-price forms of competition such as better service, more destinations, more frequent schedules, and newer fleets.

Marketing: The Japanese Way

Since it was the Japanese who first introduced the concept of marketing as far back as 1650, any study of marketing in Asia Pacific would be incomplete without giving some consideration to Japanese marketing principles and practices. Johnny K. Johansson and Ikujiro Nonaka's (1996) book, *Relentless: The Japanese Way of Marketing*, provides an inspiring insight into marketing, the Japanese way (this section draws heavily from the book).

Marketing, in Japan, is too important to leave to the experts. Most companies as a result

Mikoshi and Japanese Marketing

'One way to understand how the Japanese marketers view themselves and their job is through the use of a metaphor that seems to come naturally to them. They are the bearers of the company *mikoshi*, a traditional ornamented litter featured at Shinto shrine festivals. The litter supposedly carries *kamisama*, the god of the shrine, and is hoisted onto the shoulders of often up to twenty young men who are decked out in traditional half coats, sandals, and headbands. The *mikoshi* has a sturdy and heavy wooden frame, the ornamentation is in gold and brass, and the *kamisama* seat is bedecked with silk clothing, fans, paper dolls, and colourful streamers. The festival-goers are treated to a parade-like display of the *mikoshi* at the climax of the festival, when the rhythmic shouts of the carriers can be heard coming down the main streets, bound for the shrine. The Japanese marketers naturally view the customer as the *kamisama* whom they carry on their shoulders. The *mikoshi* may represent the product and service supporting the customer, and the ornamentation and streamers represent the advertising, and name, and promotion that the company does to help make the product attractive. To the onlookers, the colourful *mikoshi* and its ornamentation gives status to the *kamisama* and the shrine. Marketers help the customer look good, which helps make the product attractive to potential customers. The young men and women shout 'Wasshoi! Wasshoi!' to coordinate their movement, and rock from side to side as they parade through the crowds. The leaders are at the front, the strongest ones are in the centre crouched low, and others support the shafts extending beyond the wooden frame. One can easily see the metaphor: different kinds of people are needed to serve the customer, including channel middlemen who represent the extensions of the core company. Onlookers can also discern the obvious pride in the work done. The carriers are proud to carry the *kamisama*, and feel they are among the select few. They are eager to prove themselves better than the *mikoshi* from other shrines by parading longer, singing harder, and having more spirited carriers—but above all, by having a better constructed, more richly ornamented, and more colourful *mikoshi*. All for the glory of the *kamisama*.

This kind of traditional ceremony has long been a part of growing up in Japan and it transfers well into company life. New employees are treated to the company credo, taught the company song, and given the company lapel pin, and treated as new members of the company family. Rather than focusing on personal success, they work together towards the collective goal of carrying the customer *kamisama*.' (Johansson and Nonaka, 1996: 10).

do not have marketing managers or a marketing department. In Japan every employee in the company is a marketer.

Customer Satisfaction

The Japanese never guarantee satisfaction. For them, a guarantee of satisfaction is considered as an intrusion of privacy. 'Satisfaction guaranteed' is seen as a statement of unforgivable pride. The Japanese conception is that the buyer is God, and that the marketers are the servants of God—if God accepts them. For Western marketers 'The customer is always right'. For the Japanese, who is right or wrong is a completely irrelevant issue. The role of the seller is an advisory role, providing genuine assistance. Furthermore,

Customer's Satisfaction at Sony

Between 1987 and 1989, Sony's quality-in-manufacturing programme lowered its manufacturing defect rate for components, sub-assemblies, and finished products from 3 per cent to the targeted 1 per cent rate. But product breakdowns after purchase did not decrease. From the customer's viewpoint nothing had changed. Zero-defect manufacturing was not sufficient to improve product quality in use. Consequently in 1989, the company enlarged its zero-defects project to focus on the customer, and renamed it 'Reliability ZD'. In addition, Sony created a new slogan 'Does it satisfy the customer?' to launch a programme of cultural change within the corporation.

How could Sony make the customer satisfaction (CS) concept more real to its employee? It first expanded the notion of a customer beyond the person buying the company's products to all suppliers, agents, distributors, and retailers with whom Sony employees came into contact. Then, more importantly, a customer was redefined as any person whom an employee contacted or passed in the course of the job. Treat everyone as a customer, and you will build quality into our product and service was and remains the thinking. Today Sony regards as customer even those other Sony employees—bosses, subordinates, colleagues, and so on—with whom the employee comes into daily contact. The company also developed a sensitivity training programme for its employees. The aim was to demonstrate to the employees how traditional behaviour needed to change and to teach a new attitude. The programme, still active, takes the participants through three stages:

- **Stage 1** Products and after-sales service are treated as separate. This stage explains the pros and cons of keeping products and after-sales service separate, the traditional practice, and what Sony used to do. It also involves seminar-style interactions and lectures.

- **Stage 2** In the second stage, the notion of integrating product and service is put forward. The participants are exposed to the advantages of having service considerations adopted in the product design and manufacturing phases.

- **Stage 3** The third stage involves the bridging of the gap between company and customer by the adoption of a pro-customer attitude. This is new to Sony, and the programme involves speakers from other companies, academic experts, and workshops and role-playing sessions. The programme attempts to create a new core attitude among the participants, one that makes the employees automatically adopt a customer perspective in all activities. Even though Japanese have long been trained to listen carefully to others, company members who are not in daily contact with outside customers are not used to viewing their own jobs from others' perspectives. By redefining the customer to include also people inside the company, Sony attempts to grow the pro-consumer attitude throughout the organization.

In addition to this, Sony's other CS actions included the use of customer feedback surveys. Customer days are held four times each year, during which senior corporate managers answer customer complaints and become more sensitive to customer needs. In the typical Japanese tradition, the company also collects and rewards essays on CS improvements from its employees. Sony received more than 2,000 entries in 1989 alone. The company has published a book on its CS activities entitling it *CS 1.0.0.* where the 1 stands for best care for every one, the first 0 stands for zero defects, and the second 0 stands for zero complaints.

Source: Johansson and Nonaka (1996: 24–6).

in the West, a salesperson would take personal responsibility for satisfying the customer. The interaction between buyer and seller then becomes a contest of wills, where the salesperson attempts to convince the potential buyer about what the buyer really needs. For the Japanese, persuasion is the wrong tactic to take. A customer should not be considered as someone who needs help. Shoppers in Japan are greeted with the words 'Welcome. Thank you for coming to our store' rather than the 'May I help you?' heard in the West. Furthermore the Western conception that reliability, durability, flexibility, and similar functional attributes would be sufficient for satisfaction is unacceptable to the Japanese. To them, a customer's performance expectations of a product relate not simply to the quality of the functional aspects of a product but to a kind of emotional and aesthetic satisfaction.

The Japanese thinking about customer satisfaction relates closely to their view of quality. The quality control circles, the zero defects, and the total quality control concepts are well known, of course. In terms of quality from a customer viewpoint, the Japanese distinguish between functional quality (*atarimae hinshitsu*) and emotional quality (*miryoku teki hinshitsu*). Functional quality is largely a product of manufacturing and its zero-defects emphasis and is assumed to be taken for granted by the Japanese customer. The emotional (feel good) quality refers to more subjective criteria, including brand image, status, and style. Since all companies are generally very competitive in terms of product design, engineering, and manufacturing, the competitive edge of a company tends to be found in these softer factors.

Review Questions

1 Asian cultures, attitudes, and approaches to Western products and branded goods have often forced Western companies to re-evaluate and, in some cases, adapt their own traditional marketing strategies. Using company websites and other sources of information, describe and evaluate some of the changes adopted by Western marketers to serve their customers in Asia Pacific.

2 It is generally claimed that the advantage of accumulating learning from Asia Pacific is that lessons learned there, particularly those concerning image, quality, and customer services can be transferred back to the parent company in Europe and North America. Do you agree?

3 What are the necessary keys needed for designing and implementing a successful marketing strategy in Asia Pacific?

Relevant Case Studies (Part IV)

- Direct Selling in Asia Pacific: The Case of Dell
- Daewoo: 'The Chaebol You Never Heard Of'

End of Unit Project: Taking your Business into Asia Pacific

Aim The aim of this final project is to develop students' skills and knowledge in designing, formulating, and implementing a strategic plan for Asia Pacific, and to learn how to cooperate and coordinate their strengths and weaknesses within the group.

Assignment As an international business consultant, a local company wishing to expand

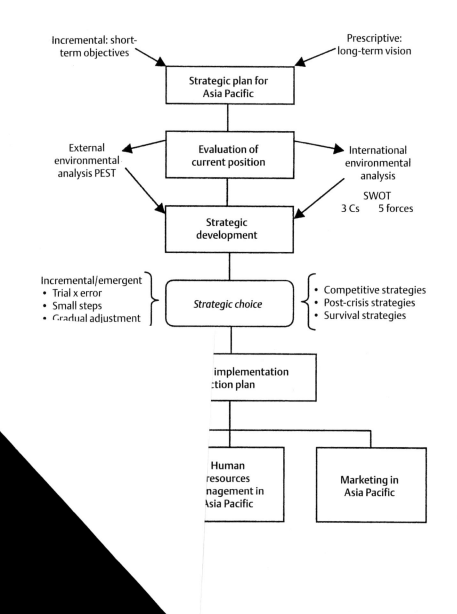

its operations in Asia Pacific has approached you for advice. The Board of Directors expects a brief presentation within three weeks, supported by a detailed strategic plan.

Format This major assignment integrates all the skills and knowledge covered in the book. Students are encouraged to work in groups, so they can identify and best utilize the strength of each member within the group and coordinate their efforts in preparing for a class presentation. To do this assignment, students may choose either a local company known to them, a local product, or a well-known brand, and formulate their own strategic plan using overheads, charts, and visual aids as they see fit.

The group presentation and supporting report should include the following:

- country selection: a country profile identifying current business opportunities, economic trends, and relevant political and socio-cultural factors that might affect the business venture;

- company profile: including an evaluation of the company's internal and external strength, competitors, and industry analysis;

- strategic formulation;

- choice of mode of entry and justification;

- human resources management;

- marketing strategy and implementation.

To assist students in formulating their own strategic plan, the model shown in Figure 13.1 can be used as a basic framework.

Further Reading

Johansson, J. K., and Nonaka, I. *Relentless: The Japanese Way of Marketing*, Oxford: Butterworth Heinemann, 1996

Lasserre, P., and Schütte, H., *Strategy and Management in Asia Pacific*, INSEAD Global Management Series, Maidenhead: McGraw-Hill, 1999.

Levitt, T., 'The Globalization of Markets', *Harvard Business Review*, May–June 1983*a*: 92–102

Ohmae, K., *The Mind of the Strategist: Business Planning for a Competitive Advantage*, London: Penguin, 1983.

Part IV

Case Studies

List of Case Studies

Daewoo: The Chaebol You Never Heard Of

Company history and the 'Daewoo spirit'

Five enterprising young men established Daewoo in 1967 as a garment and textile exporter and importer. Daewoo has focused on pioneering overseas markets from the start. Its philosophy is summarized as follows: commitment to globalization and to mutual prosperity through exercising creative innovation, pioneering new business and markets, building a worldwide network, and cultivating long-term customer relationships. The motivation behind Daewoo's expansion has been 'the Daewoo Spirit', which is the spirit of 'creativity' to seek greater insight through innovation and the recognition of infinite possibilities; the spirit of 'challenge' to boldly confront and triumph over adversity to achieve excellence; and the spirit of 'sacrifice' to set aside one's own interests and to devote oneself to a greater cause.

Daewoo's initial business activities were concerned with the manufacture and export of textiles and garments to Singapore and Indonesia. Its export sales grew from US$580,000 in 1967 to about US$40 million in 1972. It soon became the second largest Korean exporter and was awarded the 'order of Industrial Merit, Gold Tower' from the national Korean government. Its success in the US market resulted in a doubling of its exports in 1970. Predicting a US government quota on textiles based on recent exporting performance, Daewoo pushed its textiles in the USA at all costs. Exports to that country quintupled, and when the quota was imposed in 1972, Daewoo was awarded 30 per cent of Korea's share. Since then, Daewoo has diversified into construction, financial services, shipbuilding, and the manufacture of automobiles, home appliances, and telecommunication devices. In 1975 Daewoo was designated a 'general trading company' by the Korean government, which gave it preferential access to export financing and enhanced its international standing.

In 1998, Daewoo was listed eighteenth in *Fortune* magazine's list of 'Global 500—The World's Largest Corporations'. The major activities of the group are in general trading, resource development, construction, and customer service network. The group has 25 affiliates with over 190,000 employees (108,000 overseas), and a worldwide network of over 116 branch offices, trading in more than 3,000 products in more than 165 countries. In 1998, Daewoo group had emerged as South Korea's second largest conglomerate after Hyundai group with total assets of 78.18 trillion won (US$65 billion). Daewoo's primary focus today is on motor vehicle manufacturing. Daewoo Motor on its own operates five major production facilities at home and 13 localized facilities in 12 countries, shipping its products to almost 150 countries all over the world. In 1998 alone, the auto-maker manufactured a total of 1.1 million cars, 800,000 and 300,000 units respectively on its domestic and overseas production lines.

International Expansion Strategy

Daewoo expanded into related light industries by taking over ailing local manufacturing firms lacking overseas marketing competence. In 1976, the company was asked by the South Korean Development Bank to take over Hangook Machinery Ltd, one of South Korea's largest producers of diesel engines. The company had never made a profit in the 38 years of its existence and its debts were twice Daewoo's equity. Daewoo's executives renamed the company Daewoo Heavy Industries and closely monitored its turn-around. Kim, Daewoo's chief executive, quickly noticed that workers were putting in overtime to enhance their wages, but producing little. Instead of cutting back hours, Kim incorporated more business through aggressive marketing and improved quality. Production costs were lowered and break-even was achieved in the first year.

In 1978, again at the South Korean's government request, Daewoo took over another nearly bankrupt business, the Okpo shipbuilding company and created Daewoo Ship Building and Heavy Machinery. Through hard selling and aggressive pricing, Kim succeeded in turning the company into a profitable one. In 1978, Daewoo acquired a 50 per cent share, owned by the Korean Development Bank, of Saehan Motor. The automobile manufacturer later changed its name to Daewoo Motor Co. Ltd and has since become one of the most important companies within the group.

Daewoo Motor Company Joint Venture with General Motors

General Motors entered the Korean automobile industry in 1972 when it bought out Toyota's stake in Shinjin Motor and established GM Korea. Shinjin enjoyed a 50 per cent share of the domestic car market at the time. Production of Opel-designed passenger cars started in December 1972, followed by heavy trucks in March 1973, with the technical assistance of GM affiliate Isuzu Motors. However, despite the rapid rate of new production introduction, GM was unhappy with Shinjin's management. In 1976 GM asked the US embassy in Seoul to persuade the Korean government to find it another partner. Meanwhile, facing increasing financial difficulties, Shinjin transferred its 50 per cent stake in the venture to the government-owned Korea Development Bank.

In 1978, the Korean government asked Daewoo to take over the 50 per cent stake in the venture from the bank. Daewoo's ambition was to become a major international carmaker. By joining forces with such a reputable and prestigious firm, Daewoo hoped to acquire the much-needed Western technology, and enhance production expertise for the future. Under the agreement, Daewoo would be responsible for sales performance in the local market, and could take advantage of GM's capital and overseas network to promote its exports. The joint venture also presented a good fit with the diesel engine manufacturing capabilities of another division within Daewoo, Daewoo Heavy Industries. Daewoo also believed that Korean companies were not yet big enough to manage US sales networks. Consequently its products appeared in the USA under GM's name, while in the Korean market it competed with its own-branded vehicles. Daewoo also relied on GM for technology and marketing channels, including after-sales facilities.

GM, on the other hand had different expectations from the joint venture. It had no other manufacturing capabilities in Asia Pacific. Korea was seen as an attractive site for the production of inexpensive cars, with a cheap but hard-working labour force. Additionally, GM needed a local partner to gain access and operate in the highly regulated Korean market and to share market and financial risks in this highly capital-intensive venture.

Disagreements between GM and Daewoo ranged from quality, technology, capital infusion, to marketing strategy, market access, sales support, management style, and commitment. By 1983 Daewoo took over complete operational responsibility for the joint venture and changed its name to Daewoo Motor. Under the agreement, GM would continue to provide assistance in engineering technology, financing, and overseas marketing to Daewoo Motor, which in turn would assume sole responsibility for the vehicle production and domestic sales. The first model released after Daewoo took over management responsibility from GM was the Maepsy-Na, a small car based on the rear-wheel-drive Chevette. Following the success of this model, Daewoo planned to collaborate with GM for the production of a new front-wheel-drive subcompact model to be named Le Mans. The negotiation called for a transfer of GM's technology via its European subsidiary Opel to Daewoo Motor for local manufacturing and assembly in its Puyong plant. Marketing of the Le Mans in Korea, it was agreed, would be carried out by the joint-venture domestic sales force, and the GM network of US dealers would have sole responsibility for marketing the exported models in the USA. Le Mans series production started in 1985, and was introduced to the Korean market in July 1986. Exports arrived in the USA in 1987. Le Mans enjoyed tremendous success, which brought confidence to Daewoo Motor. Soon after, Daewoo started experimenting with its own designs and testing techniques for further adaptation of its products to the domestic market. It committed more resources to developing its own engineering capabilities, and sometimes even relied on outside stylists to design its passenger cars. When Daewoo insisted on investing more aggressively in Korea's domestic market, especially in the car sector, GM disagreed. GM's industrial strategy was mainly focused on increasing sales at home, even at the expense of bottom-line profits. GM's executives were not pleased with Daewoo's seemingly extravagant strategy of expansion and were not interested in making extensive additional investment in Korea. Daewoo, furthermore, had to rely on GM because of its lack of brand identity to sell its other brands, but GM refused to sell any other Daewoo vehicle than the Le Mans in the US market. GM also refused to allow Daewoo to enter the European market except through GM marketing channels. Realizing that it would be difficult to become a world-class auto-maker as long as GM influenced manufacturing decisions and controlled sales in North America, Daewoo concluded that if it wanted to compete more aggressively in the domestic market, it would have to do so alone. It then turned to Suzuki for technological assistance and launched production of its mini cars. This ended the fourteen-years partnership with GM. The separation in 1992 was acrimonious. In October 1992 Daewoo acquired GM's 50 per cent stake for $170 Million. The settlement allowed Daewoo to commence independent distribution of its cars in developing countries but it was barred from the USA and Western European markets until 1995.

Daewoo Motor Company: New Ventures in Developing and Emerging Markets

In November 1992, following the break-up with GM, Daewoo signed a licence with Honda to produce the Japanese Honda's Legend luxury car. Sales were initially restricted to South Korea and sold under the Daewoo brand name, competing against Hyundai Motors' Grandeur, and Kia Motors' Potentia. Daewoo also acquired a 51 per cent stake in Oltcit, Romania's second largest car company, for $156 million, thus giving the company a local presence in Eastern Europe which accounted for 15 per cent of Daewoo's exports in 1993.

Since Daewoo's expansion in global markets had to be outside the USA, Western Europe, and Japan until 1995, the company decided to venture into developing countries and emerging markets. The decision was primarily based on the calculation that it would prosper along with the growth of these countries once their economic development took off. In January 1994, Daewoo Motor expanded further into Eastern Europe after signing a joint-venture agreement with Automobile Craiova of Romania to form Rodae Automobile. In 1994, Daewoo also acquired F. S. Osobowych (FSO) and became the second largest car producer in Poland overnight. The Polish government was seeking a foreign acquirer for the troubled outdated company. They initially wooed GM. GM, however, insisted on dismissing two-thirds of the workers as a condition of acquiring the company. FSO officials and the Polish government could not approve such a deal. Despite five years of negotiations, both sides could not reach an agreement. However, as soon as Kim Woo-Choong was approached, a deal was struck in less than fifteen minutes. He not only pledged that he would not lay off any of the 21,000 workers for three years, but also promised a further investment of US$1.1 billion to bolster the production level to 220,000 units by the year 2001. When the deal was finalized, the ownership of the company was split between DMC (70%), FSO employees (15%), and the Polish government (15%), making DMC the second largest car producer in Poland overnight. Daewoo sold 636,000 motor vehicles worldwide in 1995 alone. By the end of 1996 Daewoo Motor had a total of 11 overseas production plants, and by 1998 it had full operations in Poland, the Czech Republic, India, China, and Romania. It also had smaller operations in the Philippines, Vietnam, Indonesia, and Iran and plans to make further investments in Libya, Pakistan, Tatarstan, Russia, Latin America, and China.

Thus, Daewoo's globalization strategies were different from other Chaebols. They were in part formulated as a reaction to Daewoo's poor international market presence in the early years, the need to build a quality brand name, and to create consumer identification with and loyalty to Daewoo products. The main problem was that Daewoo had a limited technology base, negligible brand recognition overseas, and hardly any international presence. Consequently its main drive was to venture into new unexplored markets where it expected less intense competition.

Daewoo's Operations in Europe after the GM Ban

In Europe where the car market was already saturated with global players, Daewoo, after the GM ban, concentrated on car sales rather than production. An extensive survey of the UK market involving 200,000 car buyers revealed that customers disliked dealers and were worried about hidden costs, frequent breakdowns, and repair costs. They also did not want to be stuck without a car and were not pleased with the car-buying process, which involved the intimate involvement of sales persons. In April 1995 Daewoo launched its Nexia and Espero cars in the UK. The launch was unique. Daewoo sold the cars from 32 fully owned showrooms staffed by Daewoo personnel who were not paid on commission, thus eliminating both dealers and car-sales people. Additionally, to ensure a hassle-free buying process, Daewoo introduced free-phone services to provide information on retail locations and price and employed non-commissioned customer advisers who did not haggle or pressurize customers for sale. Finally, to ensure peace of mind, Daewoo offered its customers the following package: a comprehensive three-year or 60,000 miles warranty scheme, three-year free parts and labour servicing, three-year comprehensive AA coverage, six-year anti-corrosion warranty; 30-day money-back guarantee, fully inclusive fixed price with free number plates, 12 months road licence, full tank of fuel, mobile phone, security registration, and free car pick-up and delivery for servicing with a complementary car during servicing. The result was one of the most successful new models entries in the history of British motoring. Daewoo, in its first year of operation in the UK, exceeded its initial sales target by selling over 13,000 units. It equalled or even performed better than some of the smaller Japanese competitors such as Mitsubishi and Suzuki.

Daewoo's Retail Concept and Telemarketing Strategic Success

Daewoo's advertising campaign described it as 'the biggest car company you've never heard of' and won multiple British advertising industry awards. By 1996 Daewoo became the fastest growing car brand on record in the UK.

Daewoo cars have been awarded the top sports prize in the 1998 Marketing Telemarketing Awards and Daewoo has been named 'Marketing Telemarketing Champion' for its effective low-budget launch of three new ranges in 1997 with a minimal budget. The models were launched in September with sales targets 15 per cent above 1996 and no TV advertising available until Christmas.

The strategy was devised by agency Duckworth Finn Grub Waters relying totally on telephone marketing and heavyweight advertising in the weekend supplements. The decision was taken to try to dominate the national Saturday and Sunday supplements, maximizing impact by combining at least three pages of ads each time. The theme was the Competitive Test Drive Challenge, designed to get people to experience both the new cars and the service. Telephone response was central to the operation's success, and every ad carried a free phone number. Callers were directed to their nearest Daewoo outlets. After driving one of the new cars, they were invited to complete a detailed questionnaire, which compared the test experience with their attitude to their existing car, and the service levels they had encountered elsewhere. As an incentive, 100 cars were on offer for a free one-year test. Follow-up calls were used to keep interest alive. Daewoo achieved its sales target for that year. The campaign generated 95,000 calls, resulting in 78,000 people visiting Daewoo centres and 21,000 test-drive questionnaires being completed with 70 per cent rating Daewoo much better than the competition in terms of service and quality.

Daewoo's telemarketing strategy turned conventional wisdom on its head by promoting service quality rather than technical specification or the emotional pull of its cars. It has also won the group a cluster of prizes including a gold in the Direct Marketing Association/Royal Mail Awards and a silver in the IPA Advertising Effectiveness Awards. Daewoo Motors also won the DRTV category and picked up a couple of commendations in the 1996 Marketing Telemarketing awards.

More recently, on 22 April 1999 Daewoo Motor Benelux B.V. was awarded the 'Exprix award' for the company's sales promotion 'Scratch weeks' campaign. This successful sales promotion campaign was launched at the end of 1998. Hundreds of thousands of car drivers found a 'scratch card' attached to their side window. With this card they could scratch off to win a maximum of 10,000 francs, which is greater than the official second-hand trade-in price list when trading in their car for a new Daewoo model. The 'Exprix award' is a famous and desired award for direct marketing and sales promotion in the Netherlands. The jury judges the promotional campaign on strategy, creativity, and effectiveness.

Daewoo's direct retail concept has also been granted 'Millennium Products' status by the UK Design Council in recognition of the revolutionary approach to car retailing introduced to the UK. The announcement was made in London by Stephen Byers MP, the Secretary for Trade and Industry. The recognition by the Design Council of the Daewoo strategy follows Prime Minister Tony Blair's challenge to UK businesses to show that Britain is a centre of excellence in creative and industrial terms. Patrick Farrell, Daewoo's director of sales operations, said: 'We are very proud that the Design Council has recognized our unique position in the UK car market. "Millennium Products" status give us the stamp of a forward-thinking and challenging company, and endorses Daewoo's continuously innovative approach'. To be considered for 'Millennium Products' status, a product or service must demonstrate that it fulfills one or more of the following criteria: opens up new opportunities; challenges existing conventions; is environmentally responsible; demonstrates the application of new or existing technology; solves a key problem; or shows clear user benefits. Chief Executive of the Design Council Andrew Summers said: 'I am delighted that Daewoo's retail strategy has been announced as "Millennium Product" and is going to form part of our collection of the most innovative products and services created in Britain for the new millennium'. All 'Millennium Products' qualify to be short-listed for possible inclusion in a Millennium Dome showcase of British innovation and are entitled to use the distinctive 'Millennium Product' logo in communications, brochures, point-sale materials and advertising.

Daewoo's Drive to Globalization through Technology

Believing that the future of Daewoo and of South Korea lies in high technology, Kim acknowledged in an interview with *Le Monde* in 1988 that they were 'very poor in basic technologies and too dependent on the United States and the West'. 'Our research', he stated, 'isn't developed enough. We lack scientists and we need to buy our technology and licences and create joint ventures'. In the early 1990s Daewoo executives initiated an internal campaign called 'Daewoo technology', under which, among other measures, they established Daewoo's own academic-industrial think-tank, the Institute for Advanced Engineering (IAE) in Seoul in 1992. The IAE acted as both an educational institution offering doctoral programmes and as the focal point of Daewoo's global research and development efforts.

In 1993 Daewoo launched 'Vision 2000', a campaign designed to guide member companies towards becoming global industry leaders in the next century. The theme for the campaign was 'Daewoo Globalization through Daewoo technology'. The programme included various numerical targets for the year 2000. For example, the total number of overseas trade, production, and sales subsidiaries was due to reach 150 countries. The group's total sales, which amounted to $42.5 billion in 1994 and $51.4 billion in 1995 were due to reach $72 billion in 1996 and $186 billion in the year 2000. As part of the campaign, the group's three strategic business areas consisted of telecommunications, motor vehicles, and electronics. Daewoo aimed to capture 10 per cent of the world market in each area with a top product family by the year 2000. These products included a wide range of automobiles, commercial vehicles, televisions, washing-machines, and refrigerators. Technology would focus on automobiles and six major electronics products, diesel engines, and satellites. This globalization through technology plan would ideally involve a greater ratio of goods produced overseas; non-Korean executives on the track to top management, multinational board members overseeing operations; decentralized decision-making; flexibility in research and development programmes; successful management of triple identities and loyalties; and a global rather than national image.

Daewoo's Training Programme: 'Creativity, Challenge, and Self-Sacrifice'

Daewoo's six training objectives are as follows:

(1) to implement the Daewoo business philosophy and business spirit;

(2) to develop managerial techniques and improve professional knowledge and specialized ability;

(3) to foster adaptability to meet changing business environments;

(4) to maximize organizational efficiency;

(5) to enhance the special identity of Daewoo employees;

(6) to motivate self-development.

A number of specific training programmes are offered at Daewoo to facilitate these objectives. Ungson *et al.* (1997) provide a detailed examination of these four programmes as an example of the variety and depth of these training programmes.

First, at the entry level for new employees destined for managerial positions, Daewoo offers the 'Newcomers' Training Programme'. This programme lasts eleven days and nights and covers the following topics: (1) 'Daewoo-manship' and the business philosophy, (2) an introduction to the affiliated companies of the Daewoo Group, (3) a case study of job performance, (4) freshman's life planning, (5) a tour through affiliated companies, (6) a team demonstration, and (7) a videotaped speech by the chairman.

Secondly, moving up the ladder, the Middle Manager's Training Programme consists of fifteen days and focuses on improving managerial abilities, especially those relating to human resource management. Emphasis is also placed on understanding corporate strategy.

Thirdly, once a manager reaches the director level he is sent to the Advanced Management Training Programme. This consists of four days and examines such topics as the nature of the business environment and long-range corporate strategy. In addition, this programme includes talks with the chairman.

Fourthly, in a move that is uncommon for a Korean company, Daewoo offers training programmes for managers' wives. For directors' wives, for example, the company offers a three-day programme that includes such topics as (1) Daewoo's business philosophy and spirit, (2) the relationship between office and home, (3) 'economic common sense', and (4) 'what makes a happy home life'. The basic thrust of the wives' programme is to demonstrate that the entire household—not just the husband—belongs to the Daewoo family and that the husband's success is influenced by a supportive home life.

Daewoo's Social Role

Daewoo contributes to the promotion of educational services, community services, social welfare, and cultural programmes. These programmes are initiated and executed by the Daewoo Foundation. Chairman Kim donated his entire personal holdings to the foundation in 1978 and again in 1980.

Daewoo Foundation sponsors various academic projects, including the creation and translation of higher-level textbooks entitled the Daewoo Academic Series. More than 340 textbooks have been published since the programme was launched in 1983. The Foundation also provides grants and funds to other educational institutions such as the Daewoo Educational Foundation, the Jisung Educational Foundation, and other South

Korean universities. In addition to educational services, the Foundation has been operating medical facilities in remote regions of Korea since 1978. The Foundation operates four hospitals on isolated islands and in the interior regions of Korea where adequate healthcare services and facilities are lacking. The hospitals treat an average of 70,000 patients each year. The Foundation also supports the Daewoo Dream Village, which is a home for adolescent-run households. The Daewoo Dream Village was built from the copyright income of Mr Kim's autobiography published in 1989, *It's a Big World and There's Lots to be Done*. The village provides not only scholarships and tuition expenses but also counselling and guidance to the children, as well as a wide variety of cultural programmes. Daewoo also supports Ajou University, rated first among Korean universities, through the Daewoo Educational Foundation. Furthermore, Daewoo promotes Korean journalism through the Seoul Press Foundation. The Foundation provides opportunities for selected Korean journalists to study abroad. The Daewoo Group also sponsors three professional sports teams: the Daewoo Royals football team and the Daewoo Zeus basketball team in Korea, and the Legia Daewoo football team in Poland. Daewoo Cars Ltd. in the UK was the official car supplier to the 1999 Cricket World Cup.

Daewoo's Strategic Response to the Asian Crisis

Following the Asian crisis, President Kim Dae Jung threatened to impose financial sanctions on Korea's leading Chaebols if they continued to drag their feet in downsizing. Under government and creditor pressure, Daewoo agreed to undertake massive restructuring and downsizing. Measures taken were to scale down its business structure comprising 34 affiliated companies and designate its automotive, trading, financial services, and heavy industries as its core business. Daewoo's vision post-Asia crisis was to configure a three-point organizational structure, earmarking its automotive operations at the top of the operational hierarchy with trading and financial services at the bottom.

Daewoo announced its plan to slash its debt from 59.8 trillion won (US$49.8 billion) at the end of 1998 to 30.37 trillion won (US$25.3 billion) by the end of 1999. That would reduce its debt-to-equity ratio to 199.5 per cent, just meeting the government requirement of 200 per cent or below. Additionally, the group informed its creditor banks that it would pay about 29 trillion won (about US$24 billion) of debt by the end of 1999 through the sale of assets and the introduction of foreign capital. The group also intends to offer Daewoo Heavy Industries shipbuilding unit to Mitsui and other Japanese shipbuilders for about 5 trillion won (US$ 4.1 billion) and will seek buyers for its two Hilton hotels, located in Seoul and Kyongju for around 300 billion won (US$250 million), as well as the group's ownership in domestic telecommunciations companies such as Dacom, Korea Telecom Freetel, and Hanaro Telecom valued at about 660 billion won (US$550 million). In late April 1999, Daewoo Group Chairman Kim Woo-Choong also announced that his group would sell 11 subsidiaries by the year's end to repay 29 trillion won (US$24 billion) of the company's debt. He said that Daewoo would also sell such key businesses as the bus, truck, and engine divisions of Daewoo Motors and the Hilton hotel to overseas investors, reducing the number of group affiliates from the current 34 to 8 by December 1999. Daewoo also announced that it had concluded a contract with Delphi Automotive Systems, a US Subsidiary of General Motors for the sale of Daewoo Precision's business unit that produces shock absorbers. That unit had constituted nearly 30 per cent of Daewoo Precision's total annual sales, about US$118 million. Furthermore, at the time of writing, Daewoo Group is currently negotiating with a Korean company for the sale of TV DCN, a cable TV network. The group is also selling its ownership in Kyobo Life Insurance, as well as its distribution businesses.

Daewoo has now designated its automotive sector to be its core business and will concentrate its efforts on its main business platform. Future investments will be concentrated into the automotive business in order to improve its competitiveness.

Sources

'An Introduction to the Daewoo Group'. *Daewoo Corporate Culture Series* no. 3, Nov. 1992.

Anon., 'Why GM and Daewoo Wound up on the Road to Nowhere', *Business Week*, 23 Sept. 1991.

—— 'Can this Marriage last'? *Korean Business World*, 2 Mar. 1995: 25.

—— Daewoo to Spend $11bn on Strategy Development', *Financial Times*, 8 March 1995: 38.

—— 'Non-television Advertising', *Marketing*, 18 June 1998.

—— 'The Marketing Telemarketing Champion', *Marketing*, 18 June 1998: S7–8.

—— 'Is the GM Daewoo Deal Running on Empty', *Business Week*, 12 Sept, 1998.

—— 'Chaebol Suddenly Reverses Course', *Business Korea*, 16(5), May 1999: 19–20, Seoul.

—— 'Global Status is in Reach', *Business Korea*, 16(5), May 1999: 53–5, Seoul.

Badaracco, J. L., 'The New General Motors', *Harvard Business School*, case no. 9-387-171, 1987.

—— 'General Motors' Asian Alliances', *Harvard Business School*, case no. 9-388-094, 1988.

Carr, W. I., 'The Korean Auto Industry', *Far East Ltd*, Apr. 1988, Seoul.

Education and Training Department, *Daewoo Corporation*, 1991.

Gofton, K., 'Daewoo Scoops Telemarketing Champion Prize', *Marketing*, 18 June 1998: 1, London.

http://www.daewoo.com/brief.htm

http://www.daewoo.com/gallery.htm

http://www.dm.co.kr/english/news/June99.htm

Hoo, S. J., 'Chaebols Set Massive Downsizing Plans', *Business Korea*, 16(6), June 1999: 23–4, Seoul.

Lasserre P., and Schütte, H., *Strategy and Management in Asia Pacific*, INSEAD Global Management Series, Maidenhead: McGraw–Hill, 1999: 295–329.

Lee, S. C., 'Saving the Body', *Far Eastern Economic Review*, 162(20), 20 May 1999: 42–4.

McDermott, M., 'The Development and Internationalization of the South Korean Motor Industry', *Asia Pacific Business Review*, 2, winter 1995: 23–45.

Oh, Donghoon, Choi, Chong Ju and Choi, Eugene, 'The Globalization Strategy of Daewoo Motor Company', *Asia Pacific Journal of Management*, 15, 1998: 185–203.

Ungson, G. R., Steers, R. M., and Seung-Ho, P., *The Korean Enterprise: The Quest for Globalization*, Boston: Harvard Business School Press, 1997: 197–200.

Wal-Mart Goes to Asia Pacific

This case study places students in the position of identifying and analysing the strategic post-crisis competitiveness of China and Korea for multinational corporations wishing to either maintain or expand their operations in that region.

Information Background

Wal-Mart is a US-based retailer that employs more than 850,000 people worldwide and generates in excess of $137 billion in annual revenue. Sales, according to company information, are increasing by about 17 per cent annually, translating into an increase of more than $20 billion annually.

Company Philosophy/Strategy

In the fiscal year 1998, the Wal-Mart International division increased its sales by 50 per cent to $7.5 billion and profits multiplied tenfold to $262 million. Building the Wal-Mart brand means making the customer number one. Wal-Mart's enduring progress hinges mainly on two ideas. One is that, above all else, the customer comes first. The second is that Wal-Mart must consistently try new things, to experiment. According to Sam Walton, owner of Wal Mart,

'Wal-Mart is obsessed with delivering value to the customers. Maybe in a different way, in a different package or form, but the Wal-Mart brand will be synonymous with customer service in all our markets. The customer doesn't care whether Wal-Mart has 3,000 stores or 10,000 stores. All too often management gets enamored with its own size. They think that impresses consumers. It doesn't at all. All that matters is whether what he or she wants to buy is available in a store that is satisfying price-wise, quality-wise and displays-wise. Management executives must accept this as a critical realization'.

Wal-Mart and the Asian Crisis

Unlike a number of other retailers, Wal-Mart officials devoted a great deal of time and effort to maintaining growth as opposed to putting out fires. The Asian financial crisis, the currency devaluation, companies closing down or merging provided a number of opportunities for Wal-Mart to expand inexpensively in the region.

In Indonesia, the world's fourth most populous country where business is extremely concentrated, and foreign retailers operate under tight restrictions, Wal-Mart teamed up with Lippo Group, the most powerful Indonesian conglomerate outside of the almost royal Suharto family. The licence is a very close working arrangement with Wal-Mart paid by the Lippo Group, on a fee-for-services basis. Jakarta Indonesia Wal-Mart has quickly made a strong impression in the country since its opening in 1996.

In June 1998 Wal-Mart announced plans to build at least six more stores in China over the next two years, tripling the number it already had in that country, bringing its total there to nine. China has 1.2 billion people, all viewed by company officials as potential Wal-Mart customers.' Making the mark even more attractive is its 10 per cent growth rate. Start-up costs in Asia Pacific are extremely high. It usually takes about two to three years to realize profit. 'Long term, I am a big believer in China' says Jon Menzer, Wal-Mart's executive vice-president and chief financial officer.

When Shenzhen Supercentre, Wal-Mart's first multi-level Wal-Mart store in the world, opened, it attracted crowds of shoppers. Chinese local consumers bought four times the number of small appliances envisaged in Wal-Mart's original projection. Other popular categories are telephones, electronics, convenience products from bottled water to soup mixes, and home décor items such as area rugs, decorative pillows, and framed art. Shoppers also enjoy the chain's broad selection of basic apparel and juvenile furniture, not to mention Barbie dolls.

Wal-Mart, however, had to be careful in outperforming competitors not to cause their common partner—the local Chinese government—undue consternation. The chain had to reassure business and political leaders it would play hard but fair. The issue of product sourcing inevitably arose here, leading to a legal challenge to Wal-Mart. But the retailer's approach was pragmatic: 'our worldwide sourcing is a real competitive strength'. Wal-Mart International president and chief executive officer Bob Martin told DSN (*Discount Merchandiser*): 'You want a constantly flowing introduction of new products to bring to the consumer the best value worldwide. It creates added value'.

In July 1998, the Wal-Mart chain announced that it will enter South Korea with the purchase of four stores and six additional sites. The four units, each exceeding 100,000 sq. ft., were previously operated by Korea Makro, a wholesale club hybrid, originating in Holland. Three stores are located near Seoul and one in the central city of Taejon. Annual sales for these units topped $160 million but the terms of the purchase were undisclosed. Wal-Mart's decision to enter Korea, according to Dale Ingram, a spokesman for Wal-Mart International, was taken after studying the Korean market for four years. We're already accelerating our expansion into Asia. Anyone who looks to Asia has to look at China. On the short list, you have to look at Korea. Korea is an exciting, high-potential market and an excellent next step in our Asia expansion, said Bob Martin, president and chief executive officer of Wal-Mart International.

Sources

Busillo, T., 'Wal-Mart Opening 10 Stores in Korea', *Home Textiles Today*, (19)45, 20 July 1998: 4

Johnson, J., 'Borderless Wal-Mart', *Discount Merchandiser*, 38(4), Apr. 1998: 43.

—— 'A Korean "bridgehead", *Discount Merchandiser*, 38(8), Aug. 1988: 24.

—— 'The Wal-Mart Express', *Discount Merchandiser*, 39(4), Apr. 1999: 25–32

—— and Ratliff, D., 'Wal-Mart Goes Global, *Discount Merchandiser*, 37(7), July 1997: 36–7

Saccomano, A., 'Wal-Mart Goes to Korea', *Traffic World*, 255(4), 27 July 1998: 46.

Questions

1 A foreign correspondent once pointed out: ' multinational companies can be referred to as large aircraft carriers. They are traveling around the world and call only at attractive ports. They stop in the US, which is full of capital and high tech, Italy for design, and China for cheap labour'. Based on the information provided in Chapter 5 (Country Reviews), what is the attractiveness of the port of Korea for Wal-Mart?

2 The competitive landscape is undergoing rapid changes in Asia Pacific. Carrefour is about to arrive and Dutch membership warehouse Club Makro is on the scene in five locations. What should Wal-Mart do to survive this increased competition?

Dell: Direct Selling in Asia Pacific Post-crisis

This case study reveals how Dell, the world's third biggest personal-computer maker, plans to keep expanding its operations in Asia Pacific despite the heightened risk and turmoil in the region, by subverting the model of using traditional distribution models, selling through dealers and retail outlets, with its famous direct-sales strategy.

Background Information and Company Philosophy

Dell Computer Corporation is the world's leading direct computer systems company and a premier supplier of technology for the Internet Infrastructure. Company revenue for the last four quarters totalled $25.3 billion. Dell is also the second and fastest-growing among all major computer systems companies worldwide, with more than 36,500 employees around the globe. The company ranks number one in the USA, where it is a leading supplier of PCs to government agencies, educational institutions, and consumers.

Dell was founded in 1984 by Michael Dell on a simple concept: that by selling personal-computer systems directly to customers, Dell could best understand their needs, and efficiently provide the most effective computing solutions to meet those needs. Through the direct business model, Dell offers in-person relationships with corporate and institutional customers; telephone and internet purchasing (the latter now exceeding $40 million per day); customized computer systems; phone and online technical support; and next-day, on-site product service.

Dell arranges for system installation and management, guides customers through technology transitions, and provides an extensive range of other services. The company designs and customizes products and services to the requirements of the organizations and individuals purchasing them, and sells an extensive selection of peripheral hardware and computing software. Nearly two-thirds of Dell's sales are to large corporations, government agencies, and educational institutions. Dell also serves medium and small businesses and home PC users.

Information taken from Dell.com home page at: http://www.dell.com/us/eng/gen/corporate/factpack.html

Dell's Unique Direct-to-Customers Business Model

Dell's unique direct-to-customer business model refers to the company's relationships with its customers, from consumers to the world's largest corporations. There are no retailers or other resellers adding unnecessary time and cost, or diminishing Dell's understanding of customer expectations.

Dell's unique mode offers the following benefits to its customers:

- **Price for performance** With the industry's most efficient procurement, manufacturing, and distribution process, Dell offers its customers powerful, richly configured systems at competitive prices.

- **Customization** Every Dell system is built to order. Customers get exactly what they want.

- **Reliability, service, and support** Dell uses knowledge gained from direct customer contact before and after the sale to provide award-winning reliability and tailored customer service.

- **Latest technology** Dell introduces the latest relevant technology much more quickly than companies with slow-moving indirect distribution channels. Dell turns over inventory every six days on average, keeping related costs low.

- **Superior shareholder value** Since Dell's initial public offering, its stock has appreciated more than 40,000 per cent.

Dell's corporate headquarters are in Round Rock, Texas, near Austin. Austin is the company's birthplace and home to Dell Americas, the regional business unit for the USA, Canada, and Latin America. Dell also has regional headquarters in Bracknell, England, for Europe, the Middle East, and Africa; in Hong Kong, to serve Asia Pacific, and in Kawasaki, Japan, for the Japanese market. The company manufactures its computer systems in each of six locations: Austin, Texas; Nashville, Tennessee; and Eldorado do Sul, Brazil (Americas); Limerick, Ireland (Europe, Middle East, and Africa); Penang, Malaysia (Asia Pacific and Japan); and Xiamen, China (China). Dell maintains offices in 34 countries around the world, and sells its products and services in more than 170 countries and territories.

Dell Goes to Asia Pacific

Dell first set up shop in Asia Pacific in 1996. It opened its first Asia Pacific Customer Center (APCC) in Penang, Malaysia in 1996. From there it manufactures and sells desktop and notebook computers, workstations, and network servers and ships them to customers throughout Asia except China. From APCC it also provides local-language technical and sales support throughout the region including Japan. Although the firm was a late entrant in Asia, it soon expanded its direct operations into Thailand, South Korea and Taiwan. In China, Dell opened its first 135,00 sq. ft. integrated manufacturing and sales complex in Xiamen, a city between Hong Kong and Shanghai, in August 1998.

Dell's strategy there is to sell build-to-order computers directly to customers in China and Hong Kong. The company founder believes that China will be Dell's second most valuable revenue generator after the USA within five years. In 1998 Dell's Asia Pacific sales totalled US$863 million, up 85 per cent from 1996, despite the regional slowdown. Currently, Dell's Asia-wide operations represent 7 per cent of annual turnover, and sales in the region grew by 48 per cent in 1998. Currently, Australia, China, and Japan are Dell's fastest growing markets.

The Secret of Dell's Success in Asia Pacific

How does Dell's impersonal direct business approach work in a region where so much depends on contacts and *guanxi?*

Dell's strategy in Asia Pacific has been to shift its emphasis away from the machines and towards marketing, customization, and service. Its most successful innovation lies in changing the way computers are sold. To buy a Dell, you just call a toll-free operator and detail the specific hardware and software configuration you want. An even easier way is to visit Dell's website currently generating sales of more than US$4 million a day. By not having a distribution channel, Dell does not have to worry about bad debts building up or a slow channel bleeding profits into the currency void.

The build-to-order method also limits big inventory backlogs. Inventory is a key factor for PC companies, because things go obsolete so fast, says analyst Edwin Goh of Keppel Securities in Singapore. Thanks to fanatical inventory management and improved supply of component parts, Dell has managed to shrink its inventory levels to just 7days, down from 31 in 1996.

Asian Pacific corporate customers also appreciate Dell's flexibility. It is like building your own PC without having to worry about compatibility, quality, and reliability. This also allows for tremendous cost savings, because when the price of components fall, the benefit is almost immediately passed on to the customer.

Dell's sales to individual consumers are only a small percentage of its total revenues in China, despite the rapid growth of Chinese internet use. Between 1997 and 1998, according to technical consultants at International Data Corp, the number of internet users in China jumped 71 per cent, to more than 2 million. But, so far Dell sells only 5 per cent of its PCs in China through the net, compared with 25 per cent worldwide. Part of this problem is that few Chinese consumers use credit cards, which is how most buyers pay for their purchases when ordering direct over the phone or the internet. They also prefer face-to-face sales when buying big items such as a PC. Most of Dell's sales in China are to large businesses where payment methods are different. Michael Dell admits sales through the internet which account for 35 per cent of his company's global sales but only 2 to 3 per cent of sales in China will take a while to take off. Dell says that direct selling isn't just about getting consumers to use telephones or the internet to place orders. It is also about building a direct relationship, which the company accomplishes with sales visits to individual companies. In a lot of these markets, the computer companies think that their customer is the dealer. Our customer is the end-user says the CEO.

'Relationship Marketing', Asian Style

Despite the current crisis, 'relationship marketing' does not have to be dropped, even if a company puts its expansion plans on hold. Creating and maintaining relationships will be critical to being a player in the region when it recovers. Today's opportunities in this region lie in building business ties. Relationships are not only an advantage but a requirement in Asia business culture. 'Unless you get face to face with people, unless you have a relationship, unless you give them some context about who you are, then you get nowhere in Asia' says Lou Hoffman, president of San Jose-based public relationships firm, the Hoffman Agency, and specialist in Asian marketing. 'Relationship marketing' in Asia means learning how to market in countries where personal contacts, not marketing campaigns, drive sales. Traditional promotion vehicles for tech-advertising, media coverage, trade shows are still immature in Asia. Making face-to-face contact with customers, distributors, and the press is one of the most powerful yet most neglected marketing tools in the region. In Asia, you need to develop relationships over a long period of time before you can market effectively. If you have a press release, the best thing to do with it is physically deliver it to top reporters. Getting in front of people is extremely important with the press, with partners, and with customers. Once markets are identified, assessing customers' education needs is particularly important. Without close customer contact, a marketer can easily target messages incorrectly, either by being too patronizing or by assuming too much knowledge. Real winners will be able to adapt messaging to the local market while preserving the best aspects of the international brand identity.

Dell Computer is a master of 'relationship marketing'. It has built its business on developing close ties with large corporations via thousands of field and outbound call sales representatives. The inbound calls and web sales from individuals and small businesses have recently become better known by the masses, and these are one of the company's fastest growing customer segments. 'In and around the region, doing business with people you know is how its done', says Peter Scacco, a veteran of marketing in Asia and director of corporate public relations for Dell. Despite the myth that to sell in China requires padding the egos and wallets of capricious bureaucrats—usually during long and boring banquets, Dell is winning over the chief information officers of state-owned companies the American way: with speed, convenience, and service. 'We don't have to change the formula', insists Dell salesman Peter Chan. 'It will work in the US, China, and India or even in space'. In response, IBM, Hewlett-Packard, and other PC makers are now changing tactics. Furthermore, Dell historically has said it is passing along price savings on components to its customers. In response to the Asian crisis, Dell Computer sliced prices by up to 15 per cent on selected models in its line of business PCs, attributing the modest cuts to savings on components resulting from Asian currency devaluations. Dell has thus become the first major US PC manufacturer to ascribe price reductions to the weakened economies in Japan, South Korea, and Taiwan.

The Market and Competition

China is already the fifth largest PC market, behind the USA, Japan, Germany, and the UK. But if PC shipments in China continue to grow at an average annual rate of 30 per cent as they have over the past three years, China's PC market will surpass Japan's in only five years. Not even the Asian crisis has slowed this growth. Though competition is intense, Dell is confident it has a strategy that will pay off in China. It has decided not to target retail buyers, who count for only about 10 per cent of Dell's China sales. That way, Dell avoids going head-to-head against entrenched local market leaders like Legend. Right now in China, Dell is ranked number eight in PC shipments. Competitors are beginning to copy its build-to order business model. However, Dell is not worried about this. 'We don't have to beat Legend to be successful in China', says Jon Legere who heads the company's Asia operations. With consistent 30 per cent annual growth rates, there's plenty of businesss. With such differing business models and market focus, head-to-head competition between Dell and Legend isn't on the agenda for the moment. Furthermore, because of the cost savings derived from cutting out the middleman, Dell believes it can sell computers at lower prices than its competitors, and thus steal market share. Already the gambit seems to be working: at the end of 1998, Dell's market share tripled to 1.2 per cent, while Compaq's fell from 3.5 to 2.7 per cent. Dell's shipment in Asia through direct selling jumped 15 per cent, while Hewlett-Packard, IBM, Compaq, and other PC makers that go through sellers saw shipments decline by 3 per cent. In 1999, 40 per cent of Dell's Asia PC shipment was ordered directly, up from roughly 30 per cent in 1998. Dell is also starting to rattle Chinese PC makers like Legend by nibbling into their most valuable client base: state-owned enterprises. Two-thirds of Dell's corporate customers in China are state-owned enterprises.

Getting the PC to the customer quickly also saves Dell a ton of cash. Because its just-in-time model forces Dell to keep its inventory levels low at about 6 days' worth of supply, compared with 40 for Chinese PC leader Legend, Dell saves time and money that would otherwise be wasted on warehousing. Shorter inventory cycles also give Dell a greater degree of control over price and profitability than its Chinese competitors have.

Also greasing the efficiency of Dell in China is money, or to be more precise, stock options. David Chan says the options scheme is meant to 'instill a sense of ownership', but most Chinese workers are likelier to see a direct link between their output and the stock price which is, after all, not a bad way to look at it. Around August 1999, every employee in Xiamen got roughly 200 shares of Dell, at a time when its stock was trading at $60. Three months later Dell's shares had shot up to $110, giving each employee a paper gain of about $10,000. That equals roughly one year's salary for the average Xiamen worker.

Challenges for the Future

A major problem Dell faces in China is software piracy. Microsoft estimates that over 95 per cent of the software in use in Chinese corporations is stolen. In fact, setting up a factory in China was Dell's defence against pirates. But Dell's biggest problem is that its direct-selling model can be copied easily. That is just what Legend is now doing. Legend is also copying Dell's cash management model by reducing the time it takes to get payment from its distributors by half, to 30 days. It is also rapidly moving toward Dell's just-in-time delivery model, trying to sell directly to its corporate customers and shaving excess inventory. It is even offering stock options to employees. All these copy-cat moves will make Legend a more formidable company and should therefore have Dell worrying.

Another cause of concern is China's nationalistic politics, which can quickly turn against US corporations. An example is the anti-American demonstrations that swept across China after NATO's accidental bombing of the Chinese embassy in Belgrade in mid-May 1998. Given the billions at stake in the telecom and PC markets in China, high-profile US companies, like Motorola or Dell, could be vulnerable to the ups and downs in Sino-American relations. Furthermore, US companies, especially information technology companies, cannot just go into China and grab the entire market. The Chinese government, warns Dong Tao of Crédit Suisse First Boston Securities in Hong Kong, has made no secret of the fact that it wants to promote its own national industries like IT.

Where will Dell be in China five years from now? It will probably never be the number one PC maker in China, or even number two. These slots are likely to be occupied by local manufacturers, which will always be able to sell more cheaply to China's masses. Ironically that seems to suit Dell admirably. 'Grabbing market share, in the USA, China or anywhere else, has never been its highest priority. Profits are, says Jong Legere. Of the estimated $25 billion in revenue that computer sales will generate in China by 2002, even if we get 1 per cent of $25 billion, that's a lot. You don't need to be the market leader in China to be profitable.'

Internet Leadership

It is the internet in particular which is the signpost for the future as far as Dell is concerned. Dell has the company objective of achieving 50 per cent of sales on-line by the year 2000. At the moment, it generates about 15 to 20 per cent of total revenue from internet sales. To get to the 50 per cent target, it has invested and revamped its current website to make it more user-friendly.

Dell led commercial migration to the internet, when it launched its www.dell.com in 1994 and added e-commerce capability in 1996. Today, Dell operates the highest volume internet commerce site in the world, based on Microsoft Corp's Windows NT operating system. The site supports $40 million dollars in sales every day, which currently account for almost 50 per cent of overall revenue. The company's website receives 35 million visits per quarter at nearly 80 country-specific sites. The company is increasingly applying the internet throughout its business, including procurement, customer support, and relationship management. At www.dell.com, customers may review, configure, and price systems within Dell's entire product line; order systems online; and track orders from manufacturing through shipping. At valuechain.dell.com, Dell shares information on a range of topics, including product quality and inventory, with its suppliers. Dell also uses the internet to deliver industry-leading customer services such as 'E-Support—Direct From Dell', which provides advanced online customer support capabilities; Del Talk, an online discussion forum; and Ask Dudley, Dell's natural-language technical support tool. Today, more than 40,000 corporate, governmental, and institutional customers worldwide use Dell's Web-enable Premier Pages to do business with the company.

Sources

Bickers, C., 'Sharing the Pie: Companies Take Different Paths in China's PC Market', Hong Kong, 17 June 1999, *http://www.feer.com/Restricted*

Chowdhury, N., 'Dell Cracks China', *Fortune*, 139(12), 21 June 21 1999: 120–4.

http://www.news.com/News/Item/0,4,17917,oo.html

Lydgate, C., 'Cutting Out the Middleman', *http://we.3.asia.com.sg/timesnet/data*, 1999.

Oeler, K., 'Dell cuts PC prices', *Asia*, 8 Jan. 1998.

Tristram, C., 'Crisis Marketing', *MC Technology Marketing Intelligence*, 18(11), Nov. 1998: 40–50, New York.

Weldon, L., 'Direct Dell: A Winning Strategy in Asia', Feb. 1999, Special to Worldinvestor.com

Questions

1   Multinationals already established in Asia Pacific must decide whether to stay put and risk further turmoil or cut their losses and concentrate on other markets. Evaluate Dell's strategy in Asia Pacific. What lessons can we learn from Dell's operations in the region?

2   A major challenge for the computer industry in Asia Pacific is software piracy. Dell's added problem is that its direct-selling model can be easily copied. What should Dell do to keep its competitive edge in the region?

Nike: Ethical Dilemmas of FDI in Asia Pacific

Manufacturing overseas has become common for US-based companies. Whatever the reason or reasons, lower labour costs, lower land costs, less union involvement, fewer government regulations, proximity to markets, or desire to get in early in emerging economies, companies have been doing it for a long time. Today, however, multinationals are under pressure as never before to justify their dealings with abusive regimes and their treatment of employees in developing countries. Firms used to brush off criticism, saying that they had no control over Third World suppliers, and that politics was none of their business anyway. This is no longer good enough. In the past few years, Nike among others has been rocked by the public criticism of human rights groups and labour unions. This case illustrates some of the issues faced and how, following a wave of negative publicity against its image in the world sporting goods market, from 1997 to 1998 Nike's market share actually dropped, from 42 to 41 per cent. At its $31 low in the summer of 1998, Nike stock was down by more than a half from its 1997 high. However, one year later, Nike stock crept back up to $58 and it is interesting to try and account for this positive swing.

Company History

Named after the Greek goddess of victory, Nike's headquarters is located at 1 Bowerman Drive, in the small American town of Beaverton, Oregon. The address honours one of the two co-founders of Nike, the former University of Oregon track coach Bill Bowerman. The other founder is Philip H. Knight, a former middle-distance runner on Bowerman's teams in the late 1950s. Philip Knight hit on the idea of importing running shoes from Japan to compete with the German brands such as Adidas and Puma which were then dominating the US market. The advantage was that the Japanese shoes were cheaper because labour was cheaper in Japan.

Knight started out selling the shoes from the back of his car at athletic meetings, but sales soon took off dramatically. In the 1970s, Knight and his growing company spotted early the jogging revolution and began marketing to non-professional runners as well. Soon wider markets opened as running shoes became a fashion statement and everyone from children to grannies began wearing them. By 1979 Nike had half the market in the USA and a turnover of US$149 million. By 1998 Nike had sales of over $9.5 billion controlling over 400 per cent of the athletic shoe market in the USA, and 37 per cent worldwide.

Nike Philosophy

Nike sports shoes and clothing are easily identified by the company's distinctive logo, the 'swoosh' tick, and its slogan 'Just Do It'. The essence of the Nike message embedded in 'Just Do it' seems to be free-spiritedness, self-empowerment, a will to do what one wants, and indeed can do. The company's ethos involves a strong dedication to sport and fitness. Staff at the company's headquarters, the Nike WorldCampus at Beaverton, Oregon, are expected to spend a few hours each day in the gym. They are described by a former Nike director as 'athletic, outdoor, let's-do-it-together types'.

Nike's International Operations in Asia Pacific

The international sphere is vital for Nike. Nike entered the Canadian market in 1972. It opened its first manufacturing plant in 1974, before which its shoes had been made in Japan. In 1977, attracted by the cheap labour, Nike opened factories in Taiwan and Korea. In that year its shoes were sold for the first time in Asia Pacific. Instead of owning its own plants, Nike contracted production out to local Korean and Taiwanese companies. As Nike boss Phil Knight has said: 'There is no value in making things any more. The value is added by careful research, by innovation and by marketing'. Nike is now basically a designer and marketer of shoes while manufacture is done by its Korean and Taiwanese suppliers. In the 1980s Nike tried to set up production in China, in partnership with state-owned enterprises, but that proved disastrous. However, just after the open-door policy, negotiations led to the to production of Nike in China, and production was handed over to Taiwanese investors who simply moved across the Taiwan Strait into mainland China to take advantage of the cheaper labour there. In 1981 Nike joined forces with the Japanese trading company, Nissho Iwai (which had worked with Nike on letters of credit ten years earlier), to form Nike-Japan. By 1988 nearly a third of Nike shoes were sourced in Indonesia alone. Most of the production is subcontracted to 11 main contractors and dozens of subcontractors in Indonesia. In 1996 it began manufacturing in Vietnam, North Korea, Cambodia, and India. The relationship between Nike and its contractors is quite close. There are Nike personnel in each of the plants of the contracted suppliers, checking that quality and workmanship meets Nike's stringent requirements. Most of the factories producing for Nike are located in the newly developed light industrial areas in Tangerag and Serang, to the west of Jakarta. In the Korean-owned plants (and in several of the Indonesian-owned ones as well), the top management is Korean. Middle-level managers and superiors may be either Korean or Indonesian.

Nike today has become a $9 billion powerhouse that dominates the athletic shoe market. Through its contractors Nike provides work for about 383,000 people each day at 200 factories throughout Asia mainly in China, Vietnam, Indonesia, and Thailand. Together, they employ 80 per cent of the workers making Nike sports goods worldwide, and make 90 per cent of the products themselves. The production of Nike shoes is a truly global operation. Products are designed in the USA, labour is carried out in cheap labour countries in Asia, using raw materials from several countries and Korean, Taiwanese, and Japanese capital, while marketing is done all around the world. Although Nike stipulated a code of conduct for its contractors' factories as far back as 1991, growing reports of strikes, worker abuse, and even the use of child labour at the plants aroused the fury of a Nike-saturated public in the USA. First, church groups and later students' associations, ethical-investment funds, and finally the US Congress became its critics.

The Attack against Nike

Nike has suffered much in recent years over accusations by human rights groups about the use of cheap labour in factories in South East Asia and its labour practices in general. In addition to child labour, critics accused Nike of not paying a living wage to its workers in Asia Pacific. They claimed that Nike in Asia paid workers in China and Vietnam $1.60 a day and workers in Indonesia less than $1, when these employees say they need $3 a day to maintain an adequate living standard. Nike's cachet has been clouded by a new image of Asian workers in hot, noisy factories, stitching together shoes for as little as 80 cents a day. 'Suddenly, Nike doesn't seem so cool anymore.'

According to Community Aid Abroad's report, Nike workers in Indonesian plants were forced to work overtime until production targets were met. Overtime was mandatory in nearly all factories. Working till 11 p.m. was not infrequent, and any overtime after 11 p.m. was unpaid. Often, workers were obliged to work a 12-hour shift every day, and if they refused to work overtime, they got punished. Punishment for asking not to work overtime included cleaning toilets, sweeping factory floors, and dismissal. Workers received no religious leave and were allowed only two days off per month. The normal working pattern was seven days per week for two weeks, then six days for the next two. Although workers were paid the official minimum wage, this was only reached if transport and meal allowances, which were supposed to be extras were included. Although the factories were paying what was required by law, the official minimum wage is not enough for workers to meet their basic daily needs. Workers were also provided with grossly overcrowded accommodation, with tiny rooms 3 m. by 3 m. holding a dozen people. Workers were also often abused by their supervisors, such as being smacked on the head with an outsole.

Nike's Response 'Wages may be Low, but people want these Jobs'

Dusty Kidd, Nike's public relations director, in a 1995 article in the British newspaper the *Observer*, justified Nike's conditions in factories in Indonesia as follows:

'It is true that workers in shoe factories in Indonesia enjoy conditions which are better than those in many other industries, and for some, better than those at home in the village. And the jobs are sought after. But what this means is that, while things may be bad in these factories, they are even worse elsewhere—especially for the unemployed. For despite the increase in the number of factory jobs in Indonesia, unemployment among 20 to 24 years olds is still very high. The people who work in these factories have not, as the quote above implies, been drawn away from subsistence agriculture by better incomes in manufacturing. Rather they are drawn from those who have no prospects in agriculture. Subsistence agriculture in Indonesia, especially in Java, has absorbed about as many people as it can. There is no more new land for the growing population and land holdings are already too small to be further sub-divided'.

He further stated that

'The overwhelming share of workers in our subcontract factories there have had a positive experience, as evidenced by the fact that the turnover rate in those factories is the lowest in the business . . . The workers, if you will, vote with their feet. It is clear to them that manufacturing jobs pay a steady wage, and offer the kinds of benefits that are prized in a country where half the work force is still earning a subsistence income on a farm, often with neither running water nor electricity'.

He also stated that

'in a country where the population is increasing by 2.5 million per year, with 40 percent unemployment, it is better to work in a shoe factory than not have a job. All the evidence suggests that the new factory jobs are absorbing (to some extent) the growing numbers of young people who have no access to land, and for whom the alternative is unemployment or possibly destitution. For those who have prospects in agriculture, the wages in factories are not good enough to draw them away'.

Nike's Code of Ethics

In 1996, amid a growing public outcry, Nike's founder and chief executive Phil Knight announced the company's new labour initiative. Knight promised to raise the minimum age for workers at Nike's contract plants in Asia to 18. He also agreed to open its plants in Asia Pacific to monitoring by non-governmental organizations. At the annual shareholders' meeting in that same year, Knight invited the Labor Practices Department to form an independent third party of observers to visit Nike's contractor facilities. Nike also promised to offer schemes to provide free education and business loans to workers' families, and fund research into global companies' labour practices. It also vowed to improve air quality in plants by switching to more costly water-based glues and by improving ventilation. Nike has agreed that NGOs will begin monitoring parts of its operations in Vietnam, China, and Indonesia from mid-1999, while factories have been given until 2002 to introduce education for workers. Nike's decision to use local NGOs, however, has been heavily criticized. But Brad Figel, Nike's director of governmental affairs, says, 'the company chose local NGOs because they have well developed community contacts. As long as we maintain the principle of using credible and independent NGOs, everyone should be happy'.

Nike's revised Code of Conduct was released in March, 1997. It included the following statement:

Nike Inc. was founded on a handshake. Implicit in that act was the determination that we would build our business with all of our partners upon trust, teamwork, honesty and mutual respect. We expect all of our business partners to operate on the same principles. At the core of the Nike corporate ethic is the belief that we are a company comprised of many different kinds of people, appreciating individual diversity, and dedicated to equal opportunity for each individual. Nike designs, manufactures and markets sports and fitness products. At each step in that process, we are dedicated to minimizing our impact on the environment. We seek to implement to the maximum extent possible the three R's of environmental action: reduce, reuse and recycle.

There is no finish line

Nike has also established its own Code of Conduct for itself and its business partners. A Memorandum of Understanding was issued requiring all Nike's contractors to sign as part of their contractual arrangement with the company. What Nike expects of its contractors according to the Memorandum is: compliance with all applicable local government regulations including health and safety, and workers' insurance; on the use of forced labour; environmental responsibility including non-use of CFCs; non-discrimination and equal opportunity practices; and documentation of their compliance with the Code and Memorandum.

Nike's Memorandum of Understanding

Wherever Nike operates around the globe, we are guided by our Code of Conduct and bind our business partners to those principles with a signed Memorandum of Understanding.

- **Government regulation of business** Subcontractor/supplier certifies compliance with all applicable local government regulations regarding minimum wage; overtime; child labour laws; provisions for pregnancy, menstrual leave; provisions for vacation and holidays; and mandatory retirement benefits.

- **Safety and health** Subcontractor/supplier certifies compliance with all applicable local government regulations regarding occupational health and safety.

- **Work insurance** Subcontractor/supplier certifies compliance with all applicable local laws providing health insurance, life insurance, and worker's compensation.

- **Forced labour** Subcontractor / supplier certifies that it and its suppliers and contractors do not use any form of forced labour—prison or otherwise.

- **Environment** Subcontractor/supplier certifies compliance with all applicable local environmental regulations, and adheres to Nike's own broader environmental practices, including the prohibition on the use of chloro-fluoro-carbons, the release of which could contribute to the depletion of the earth's ozone layer.

- **Equal opportunity** Subcontractor/supplier certifies that it does not discriminate in hiring, salary, benefits, advancement, termination, or retirement on the basis of gender, race, religion, age, sexual orientation, or ethnic origin.

- **Documentation and inspection** Subcontractor/supplier agrees to maintain on file such documentation as may be needed to demonstrate compliance with the certification in this Memorandum of Understanding, and further agrees to make these documents available for Nike's inspection upon request.

To monitor the implementation of its code, Nike has assigned an expatriate staff member to each factory. These employees are as responsible for the daily adherence to the Memorandum of Understanding as they are for product design, development, and quality control issues. Moreover, like production managers, they are expected to send formal update reports on the implementation of the Memorandum on a semi-annual basis. Currently there are more than 800 staff members in Asia Pacific alone to monitor adherence to the Memorandum.

Recent Developments and Improvements at Nike's Factories

In March 1998, a delegation from the Interfaith Center on Corporate Responsibility visited factories producing for Nike in China, Indonesia, and Vietnam. Their report found that health and safety standards had improved and that progress was being made in limiting excessive overtime.

On 15 October 1998, Nike announced that it would raise the pay for minimum wage workers in its Indonesia-based sport-shoe factories by 25 per cent, from 200,000 rupiah (a little over US$20) per month to 250,000 rupiah (just over US$25).

In March 1999, Nike set the standard for the industry by opening its shoe factories to inspectors. In a report 'Beginning to Just Do It' released in March 1998, Nike allowed researchers from Community Abroad to inspect their factories to assess whether the situation had improved. The report found that significant dangers to workers remain, and that considerable improvements are still needed before conditions meet the US Occupational Health and Safety Administration (OSHA) standards which Nike pledged to meet. Nonetheless the report describes important safety improvements in the factory.

In June 1999, in its latest response to the international campaign against it, Nike partnered with the World Bank, the International Youth Foundation, and Mattel in what they call a 'Global Allliance for Workers and Communities'.

Nike and the Asian crisis

Nike's strategy in dealing with the crisis thus far has been to maintain its usual business course. Nike became one of the companies most affected by the Far East turmoil, because it chose to maintain its market presence in Indonesia despite the crisis. According to Joe Vernachio, Nike's raw materials manager, Nike is not sourcing any more or less in Asia Pacific than it did before the crisis. In fact, most of Nike's contract manufacturers in the 40 Asian countries in which the company sources are also exporters and are doing better than they have ever done, he noted. Nike have also tried to come up with a price-sharing policy to take advantage of the improved exchange rates, at least in US dollars.

In Japan, however, the Asian economic meltdown has turned a $125 million operating profit in Japan for 1997 into a $40 million loss. The company has shifted from its strategy of using Japan as sourcing and allowed Japanese manufacturers to produce to their own needs.

Future Challenge

The new strategy for the firm is true globalization. Obviously Nike has been doing business internationally for a long time, but its director-general wants it to become global. He plans to have the Nike brand mean the same to consumers in each of the 80 plus countries it operates in. The ultimate goal is to get their brands to stand for the same thing in all those parts of the world and to have Nike's employees on the ground on the same wavelength as in the home office. He even asserts that, even though such a strategy may be hindered by differing levels of economic development in different countries, it is still possible to achieve.

Sources

Bolderson, C., 'Knight of the Pack', BBC Worldwide, British Broadcasting Commission, Oct. 1994.

Community Aid Abroad, http://www.caa.org.au/campaigns/nike/sweat2.htm

Gallagher, Lei, 'Rebound', *Forbes*, 163 (9), 3 May 1999: 60–1.

Gilley, Bruce, 'Sweating it out', *Far Eastern Economic Review*, 161(50) 10 Dec. 1998: 66–7.

Global Alliance for Workers and Communities, website, www.theglobalalliance.org

Goozner, M. 'Nike Manager Knows Abuses do Happen', *Chicago Tribune*, 7 Nov. 1994: 6.

Hardjono, J. 1993, 'From Farm to Factory: Transition in Rural Employment in Majalaya, West Jaa', in C. Manning and J. Hardjono (eds.), Indonesia Assessment 1993, Political and Social Change Monograph No. 20, Canberra: Australian National University.

Holbert, Neil, 'Nike Inc. Just do it', in Irene Chow, Neil Holbert, Lane Kelley, and Julie Yu, *Business Strategy: An Asia Pacific Focus*, Singapore: Prentice Hall, Simon & Schuster Asia, 1997: 327–53.

Kidd, D. 'Letter to American Friends Service Committee, Portland, Oregon from Dusty Kidd, Nike Public Relations, 19th April 1993.

Kostova, Tatiana, and Zaheer, Srilata, 'Organizational Legitimacy under Conditions of Complexity: The Case of the Multinational Enterprise', Academy of Management, *The Academy of Management Review*, 24(1) 64–81.

McCall, William, 'Nike Battles Backlash from Overseas Sweatshops', *Marketing News*, 32(23), 9 Nov. 1998: 14–15.

Murdoch, Adrian, 'Just doing it', *Accountancy*, 123(1267), Mar. 1999: 30–1.

Nike, Production Primer, Oregon, USA, 1994.

—— Nike Establishes Labor Practices Department, 2 Oct. 1996.

—— website, http: www.nike.com

Questions

1   How important is it for the future of Nike to be a player in Asia Pacific Region?

2   Based upon the information provided in the case, and using the corporation internet site, comment on the following statement 'While the creation of industrial jobs in Indonesia by Nike is certainly beneficial, the jobs created must be non-exploitative, and contribute more to the host country and particularly to its workers in the form of decent wages and safe and healthy working conditions' (Nike Watch).

3   Following the events at Tiananmen Square in 1989, few firms left but most stayed, arguing that a US presence would eventually improve the situation. Levi Strauss, however, decided to end many of its business dealings in China because of what the company called 'pervasive human rights abuses'. Levi's decision to leave China, it was claimed, was based on its shared values in social responsibility and employee rights which apply not only to the USA but to all Levi's employees around the world. Critics of Levi have charged that the decision to leave China was nothing more than a publicity stunt aimed at luring more customers. With Nike's case in mind, do you agree that Levi's decision was 'a pure business decision related to bottom-line profitability'?

An Emerging Regional Manufacturing Network in South East Asia: The Case of Samsung

Yongwook Jun

This case study describes the formation of a regional manufacturing network in South East Asia by a conglomerate in the Korean electronics business sector in response to the changing global business environment which is characterized by globalization, regionalization, and informatization. The study will specifically focus on the interrelationship among four major sister companies of the Samsung Electronics Group which are in a vertically integrated relationship for the production of consumer electronics goods. A few salient characteristics of such a network by a 'minor league' firm in global competition will be identified along with an assessment of the network in terms of benefits enjoyed by member firms and its limitations.

Introduction

We are witnessing a new form of organization in today's business world, namely network organization (Nohria and Eccles, 1992). This network organization not only appears in domestic organizations, but also shows up in international corporations (Ghoshal and Bartlett, 1991, Gilroy, 1993). Three forces seem to drive the formation of network organization in the global setting. One is the globalization force which is manifested in faster global communication and transportation infrastructures and homogenization of consumer needs (Levitt, 1983). The conclusion of the Uruguay Round and the formation of the World Trade Organization will hasten the realization of a global village. The second

Yongwook Jun is a Lecturer at Chung-Ang University, Seoul, Korea.

force is the regionalization trend in major economic zones of the world economy, namely, the formation of the North American Free Trade Agreement and the European Union. The formation of such regional blocs will aid major international firms to integrate operations which had previously been scattered in those regions. They are now in a better position to form an economically sound network and exploit the economies of scale thanks to the expanded market size and the removal of barriers on cross-border transactions. A third force which facilitates international networking is rapid innovation in information technologies (Elbert, 1990). Though the first two forces are providing the necessary ground for networking, it is innovation in information technology which makes it possible to take advantage of the new economic environment. Without the assistance of information technologies, the full-scale integration and coordination required in successful networking is not possible.

Taking the changed global business setting as a background, this case study tries to present a networking attempt by a Korean Chaebol in South East Asia. The case study will show an example of internal networking among sister firms of the Samsung electronics business sector. This case may contribute to the existing literature on networking by providing a case of a 'minor league' firm in global competition. Samsung electronics sector was chosen simply because it has achieved the most advancement in international networking among Korean firms.

After this introduction, the section following will describe the business details of member firms comprising the Samsung electronics sector. The third section explains the formation of internal networking among Samsung firms in South East Asia in detail. A few salient characteristics of such networking will be identified. The final section will make an assessment of the networking and some future issues will be raised.

The Samsung Electronics Sector

Samsung Group is a representative Korean business conglomerate, a so-called 'Chaebol' which is characterized by strong family ownership and wide diversity in business interests which are often quite unrelated. Samsung is the largest Chaebol in Korea with $87 billion in turnover and 255,000 manpower as of 1995. The business domain of Samsung Group is composed of five major businesses and the electronics business sector is the flagship business of Samsung. In 1995, the electronics business sector represented 30.7 per cent of total group sales and 40.2 per cent of employment.

In terms of membership, the electronics business sector is composed of five sister companies which are vertically integrated among themselves. At the downstream end of the vertical chain is the flagship company, Samsung Electronics Corporation (SEC) which produces system and set items such as audio and video products, telecommunication gears, and computing equipment. It is also the largest producer of memory chips in the world. SEC is the second largest maker of video-cassette recorders and microwave ovens and the sixth largest colour television producer in the world. The second member firm of the electronics group is the Samsung Display Device (SDD) whose major product lines consist of colour picture tubes (CPTs) and colour display tubes (CDTs) which are fed into the production of colour television and computer monitors of SEC. SDD is the largest colour picture tube producer in the world with a 17 per cent global market share. The third member firm is the Samsung Electro-Mechanics (SEM), the principal product lines of which are parts for consumer electronics items produced by SEC (e.g. turner, transformer) as well as parts for colour picture and display tubes manufactured by SDD (e.g. deflection yokes). The company is second to none in the world in the production of deflection yokes and fly-back transformers. The fourth member firm is the Samsung Corning Corporation (SCC) which is a fifty-fifty joint venture between Samsung Group and Corning Glass Work of the USA. The main product of SCC is picture tube glass of colour picture tubes made by SDD. SCC is one of the three largest producers of tube glass in the world along with Ashai Glass and Nippon Electric Glass (NEG) of Japan. The last member of the electronics group is the Samsung Data System (SDS) whose business domain lies in system integration and software development.

Internal Networking in South East Asia

The Formation Process

SEC has spearheaded the international expansion of the Samsung electronics sector into South East Asia. The first direct involvement in foreign production began with the establishment of a joint venture with Saga Group of Thailand in 1989 for the production of colour television. Samsung provided production facilities and brand name and Saga supplied land, factory accommodation, and labour force. In return, Samsung got a 51 per cent share in the equity and Saga, the remaining 49 per cent. After this investment, SEC made five more investments in South East Asia; one in Indonesia in 1990 for the production of refrigerators for domestic sales; another one in the same country in 1992 for the production of audio equipment and VCR for exports; a third one in Malaysia in 1991 for the production of microwave ovens; and a fourth and fifth one in 1995 in Malaysia and Vietnam for production of colour monitors and colour TV, respectively.

Following the lead of SEC, Samsung Display Devices, the major producer of colour picture tubes, invested in Malaysia in 1990 with a 100 per cent wholly owned subsidiary. The basic motivation for such capital-intensive investment was to restore the competitiveness of 14-inch CPTs which had been lost in Korea due to wage hikes and to provide a stable supply of CPTs to its in-house customer's (SEC) operations in the region. However, it has to be noted that only 22 per cent of SDD's Malaysian production found its way to SEC's factories in South East Asia as of 1996. This is because of the difference in economies of scale between the capital-intensive CPT production and labour-intensive colour television assembly processes. The remainder of the production volume was to supply mostly foreign customers in the region such as Sanyo, Funai of Japan, and Thomson of France as well as other clients outside South East Asia. Another point to notice is the location decision by SDD in 1990. SDD chose Malaysia over Indonesia which was favoured by SEC which had a vision to develop an integrated production complex in Indonesia at that time. Malaysia was selected due to its conformity to the capital-intensive nature of the investment given its better social infrastructure and stable supply of electricity and water. The production capacity of SDD in Malaysia increased from 1.2 million sets in 1990 to 3.5 million sets in 1994 to 4.2 million sets in 1995.

Samsung Corning was the next player in the networking game in the region. SCC followed SDD in Malaysia in 1992 with 100 per cent ownership. The dominant motivation was to supply its largest client at the location where it operates. Besides this reason, SCC also considered the strategic position of its rival Japanese glassmakers in the region: Asahi had already had production facilities in the region; one in Singapore and the other one in Thailand. NEG was considering an investment in Malaysia. In order to maintain a global competitive alliance with its rival firms in the globally oligopolistic industry, SCC had to capture a strategic position in this region. The location decision was rather straightforward because of the need for geographical proximity to its major client (in this case, SDD). By being near to its major client, significant cost savings in terms of logistics and utilities cost were expected. In fact, SDD procured a plant site next to SCC, expecting follow-the-customer investment by SCC. SDD also installed a common utilities infrastructure which it could share with SCC. The production capacity of SCC has increased from 2.4 million sets in 1992 to 3.6 million sets in 1994 to 4.8 million sets in 1995. Most of the production of SCC found its way to its next-door sister company.

The last entrant in the regional networking was Samsung Electro-Mechanics (SEM). SEM started its first foreign manufacturing in Thailand for the production of tuners, deflection yokes, and fly-back transformers in 1993. The reason for this late entry was the lack of secure market demand in the region. However, as it witnessed the increasing investment of its in-house customers such as SEC and SDD in South East Asia as well as the increasing entry of Japanese customers which came to the region due to 'endanka', SEM finally decided that the time had come to invest. SEM chose Thailand for its local site due to the more favourable labour conditions in Thailand and given the labour intensive nature of its production process. As for the initial production capacity, it chose to go for an optimal scale which could achieve full use of economies of scale. SEM production capacity were set to produce 1.9 million sets of tuners a year, 2.4 million sets of fly-back transformers, which far exceeded the in-house demand by the Thai colour television operation of SEC and the Malaysian CPT operation of SDD at that time. As of 1996, around 20 per cent of the production volume was consumed by its sister companies in South East Asia. The rest of production was for sale mostly to Japanese firms in the region and other clients outside South East Asia

The Relations in the Network

As we observed in the formation process, the network of the Samsung electronics sector in South East Asia is a vertical network among related companies, which copied their relationship at home. There are two main streams of parts flow in the vertical chain. One flow starts from Samsung Corning's Malaysian operation, which supplies tube glass to the Samsung Display Malaysian factory, as a major input for the latter's colour picture tube production. A proportion of these picture tubes are, in turn, sold to Samsung Electronics's operations in Thailand, Indonesia, Vietnam for colour televisions, and in Malaysia for computer monitors. The other flow begins from the Samsung Electro-Mechanics Thailand operation. It supplies tuners, deflection yokes, and fly-back transformers to Samsung Electronics's Thailand, Vietnam, and Malaysian operations for colour televisions and computer monitors, tuners to the Indonesian operation for VCRs, and oil capacitors to the Malaysian operation for microwave ovens. The same operation also provides deflection yokes to Samsung Display Devices Malaysian operation for colour picture tubes.

If we look at the relations in greater detail, the following four pairs of relations are identified: SCC v. SDD; SDD v. SEC; SEM v. SEC; SEM v. SDD. Let's review the relations one by one. The relation of the first pair, SCC v. SDD, is a captive one, SCC being a captive supplier of SDD. SCC depends on SDD for 100 per cent of its production volume. Thus, SCC enjoys a secured market for its product and SDD likewise a stable supply source next door. Being in the same location in the same country, their relationship is a very cooperative one. SCC benefits especially from the local operating experiences (e.g. labour management and public relations) of SDD which invested there earlier than SCC. Both parties also benefit from each other because they can share utility infrastructures in the same location. The relation between the second pair of SDD and SEC is rather tenuous. Only 22 per cent of SDD production is sold to SEC due to the limited business volume of the latter's operation in South East Asia. SDD has to sell the remaining 78 per cent to outside firms both in the region and outside of region. SEC benefits more than SDD from the relationship by having a secure in-house supply line in the region. However, SEC also assists SDD in improving the quality of picture tubes by providing customer feedback on picture tube quality and by sharing an after-service database.

The relationship between the third pair of SEM and SEC is rather diverse in the sense that SEM supplies different sets of items to six different factories of SEC scattered in Thailand, Indonesia, Vietnam, and Malaysia. Though there are multiple links between the two firms, the actual business volume is not significant. SEC consumes less than 20 per cent of the production volume of SEM. SEM sells most of its product to Japanese customers in the region and other clients outside the region.

The relation between the last pair of SEM and SDD is the most tenuous one of the four. It involves only item (i.e. deflection yoke) between the Thai operation of SEM and the Malaysian operation of SDD and the demand of SDD for deflection yokes represents only a minimal portion of the production volume of SEM. However, from SDD's point of view, it depends on SEM for 80 per cent of its requirements.

Salient Characteristics of the Samsung Network

From the formation process of the network and the specific relations among member firms in the network, we can identify a few interesting aspects of the Korean firm's networking.

First, there seems to be a sequence informing the network. The set maker takes the lead and it is followed by parts makers, first by firms of major parts and then by firms of minor parts. SEC made a series of investments for the production of set items such as colour televisions, CR, and microwave ovens. If we follow the investment track related to the production of colour television, SEC started with the investment for colour television in Thailand in 1989. This investment was followed by SDD's investment for the production of colour picture tubes in Malaysia in 1990, which is the single largest cost item for the production of colour television. The SDD's investment was, in turn, followed by both SCC's investment for tube glass in 1992 in Malaysia and SEM's investment for deflection yokes in 1993 in Thailand. These items are rather minor parts *vis-à-vis* colour picture tubes in terms of both cost and their value-added contribution to the production of colour television

Secondly, the Korean firm's networking seems to be the outcome of a revolutionary process rather than that of a master-minded grand plan. The Samsung network was not planned far in advance of their actual investments. This aspect of behaviour was well demonstrated in the very independent location decisions of each member firm. Instead, Samsung's Asian network has been formed over time in response to changing market and competitive environments. Although the sister companies followed each other in part to provide a secure local supply source for in-house demand, they also reacted to the changing structure of the international division of labour in the regional electronics industry. In particular, the surge of Japanese set makers' investment in South East Asia in the 1980s and 1990s as a way to overcome the yen appreciation and high labour costs at home had motivated some of the Samsung firms to invest in the same region to serve their erstwhile export clients. This kind of motivation was very evident in the cases of SEM's investment in Thailand and SDD's investment in Malaysia. As we have seen in the previous section, the lion's share of their production volume found its way to these Japanese firms.

Thirdly, even in the same network, there exist both strong and weak links together (Gillroy, 1993). The relationships between SEC and SDD for the supply of colour picture tubes and between SDD and SEM for deflection yokes are rather tenuous because the latter party's economies of scale far exceeded the demand of the former members. SDD and SEM paid more attention to Japanese customers' demand than to the in-house demand simply because of the large size difference in the order quantity. In contrast, the link between SDD and SCC in the colour picture business was quite strong. It was not only because of their geographical proximity, but also because of heavy dependence on each other for business transitions.

Finally, there exists a strong 'Single Samsung Spirit' prevailing in the network. Being member firms of Samsung Group with one corporate culture, the firms made explicit endeavours to help each other and thus, create a synergy effect from the network (Jun and Han, 1994). Know-how in labour management, public relations, local employee education, and government affairs were extensively shared among member firms through regular get-together meetings as well as occasional task-force team activities. The newcomer to this region did not need to start from scratch thanks to the local management information provided by other sister firms which had invested there earlier. Furthermore, there was close synchronization between the home offices of each member firm in Seoul on the issue of transfer pricing on internal flow of parts as well as production volume, so that they could achieve synergistic competitive advantage as a group *vis-à-vis* local or Japanese competitors in the region. The most transparent aspect of the Single Samsung Spirit is reflected in the supply guarantee or supply priority given to sister firms by the member firms in this region.

An Assessment of the Samsung Networking in South East Asia

The Samsung electronics sector seems to enjoy a few benefits from the networking. One major benefit is the possession of secure local supplies of key parts by transferring the same vertically integrated production system at home to the local market-place. This may contribute to improving competitiveness in terms of cost, service, and delivery time. Another expected advantage is the improved bargaining power *vis-à-vis* local customers or governments, which could be marshalled from the fact that Samsung has an integrated production system in the region. Lastly, the firm has built up a system to share information and know-how among member firms if needed, even though the current utilization has yet to be much improved.

On the other hand, the Samsung network has a long way to go in order to create a significant advantage deriving from the economies of scope expected from such networking. First of all, there is no significant traffic volume between the multiple nodes of the network. As we have seen in the previous section, most of the links are of a tenuous nature in terms of quality of relations. Many of the member firms depend on outside Japanese firms for most of their business rather than on in-house demand. Furthermore, there is no sign of significant use of information technologies in integrating the network. Most communication and synchronization of business activities among member firms are performed in traditional ways such as meetings and business travel. There is not even much interaction among local operation units because most critical decisions such as transfer pricing and volume are made at the headquarters in Seoul. Finally, a more fundamental issue with respect of the network is the potential problem of Single Samsung Spirits. Though Single Samsung Spirits may contribute to improving the competitiveness of the Samsung electronics sector in regional or global competition, it may backfire because of the tendency of overdependence on family members. The future core competence may lie in creating more diverse networking even including competitors. Besides internal networking, a company has to learn how to make external networking or strategic alliances with outside firms. The in-house breeding may block another avenue of building competitiveness in global competition, and one which is becoming more significant these days.

Sources

Elbert, Bruce R., International Telecommunication Management Norwood Artech House, 1990.

Ghoshal, S., and Bartlett, C. A., 'The MNC as an Inter-organizational Network', *Academy of Management Review*, 15(4) 603–25, 1990.

Gillroy, B. M., *Networking in Multinational Enterprise*, Columbia, SC: University of South Carolina Press, 1993.

Jun, Y. W., and Hams, J. H., *The Road to an Excellent Company: Samsung Group's Growth and Transformation* (in Korea). Seoul: Kimyoungsa, 1994.

Levitt, T., 'The Globalization of Markets', *Harvard Business Review*, 92–102, 1983.

Nohria, N., and Eccles, R. G., *Networks and Organizations*, Boston: Harvard Business School Press, 1992.

Questions

1   What were the major forces driving member firms of Samsung Electronics Sector to go abroad to South East Asia?

2   Can the regional networking concept in South East Asia be applied to three regions of Samsung operations?

3   How might the network evolve over time? What might be the principal factors shaping the future network?

4   In the current Asian crisis, will the transfer of the Korean Chaebol structure to South East Asia be a workable idea?

Matsushita: Putting the Employee First

In the mid-1980s Matsushita Electric Industrial Co. was often cited as one of the premier examples of the management practices and style that had made Japan into a global power. What makes the Matsushita group different from most large companies in Japan, stated President Toshihiko Yamashita, was the unique management philosophy of its founder.

Company History and Philosophy

Matsushita was founded in 1918 by Konosuke Matsushita, one of Japan's legendary entrepreneurs. Matsushita had joined the Osaka Electric Light Co. at the age of 15, convinced that electricity had a great future in Japan. Seven years later, he resigned to form his own company. Starting with capital of 100 yen (about $50 at that time), the Matsushita Electric group of companies grew to become one of Japan's largest consumer electronics groups, employing 1,516,000 employees worldwide.

Matsushita operates 46 production facilities in 27 countries and 34 sales companies in 28 countries. In addition, it has a series of licensing arrangements with foreign companies, notably RCA and Phillips, with the latter owning a minority position in Matsushita Electric Co. Matsushita has had a variety of ownership arrangements in various host countries from full ownership to joint ventures, but has never had less than a 50 per cent board position.

Company Philosophy

Despite its enviable record of profitability, the company insists on putting service to society before profits. According to the company creed, a business can exist only by using resources—people, real estate, municipal services, and so on. Therefore the primary goal should be to contribute to society in return for the use of its resources. This belief formed the basis of a unique 250-year mission established in 1932: 'Throughout our industrial facilities, we strive to foster progress, to promote the general welfare of society and to devote ourselves to furthering the development of world culture'.

Matsushita has developed its own unique and extraordinarily powerful philosophy. Matsushita's stated mission is to continue to contribute to the well-being of mankind by providing reasonably priced products and services in sufficient quantities to achieve peace, happiness, and prosperity for all. This is supported by five principles:

- growth through mutual benefit between the company and the consumer;
- profit as a result of contributions to society;
- fair competition in the market-place;
- mutual benefit between the company, its suppliers, dealers, and shareholders;
- participation by all employees.

Matsushita strongly believes that progress and development can be realized only through the combined efforts and cooperation of each member of the company.

The company's seven spiritual values are:

(1) national service through industry;

(2) fairness;

(3) harmony and cooperation;

(4) struggle for betterment;

(5) courtesy and humility;

(6) adjustment and assimilation;

(7) gratitude.

Every morning at Matsushita's plants in Japan (and in most areas throughout the world) every employee attends a morning meeting, at which the Matsushita creed, principles, and/or spiritual values are recited aloud. Only a skeleton force of telephone operators, guards, and process controllers are not present. In Japan the meeting begins with pre-arranged exercises learned in early grade school. Then in 'relaxation exercises' each person massages and pounds the back of another person, and then both turn around to give or receive similar benefits. Following the company song and the recitations, a discussion leader—a task rotated daily—poses a question for the group to discuss and try to resolve. This can be an operating problem, a new opportunity, or an important philosophical issue designed to provoke interest. After 15 minutes or so, everyone goes off to work. At work stations the exercise routine is repeated for 5 minutes at the end of each hour and for 1 to 15 minutes mid-morning and afternoon.

Matsushita also provides 8 months training for all its university graduates. This involves 3 weeks of headquarters training classes, 3 months in retail stores, 1 month in the factory, 1 month in cost accounting, and 2 months in marketing including lectures and activities. Less time, but equal attention, goes into training rank and file workers. Job rotation is common throughout all ranks. Five per cent of all employees comprising one-third managers, one-third supervisors, and one-third workers are usually rotated from one division to another each year, and some 80 per cent of all employees participate in quality circle activities.

Matsushita views employee recommendations as instrumental to making improvements on the shop floor and in the market-place. It believes that 'a great many little people, paying attention each day to how to improve their jobs, can accomplish more than a whole headquarters full of production engineers and planners'. Thus, praise and positive reinforcement are an important part of the Matsushita suggestion scheme. Employees whose suggestions are implemented by their supervisors may win coveted awards; sponsors of patentable suggestions receive patents and monetary awards in their own names. Workers are not only encouraged to suggest improvements, they can stop the production line if they are not satisfied with quality.

Production plants are usually spotlessly clean. Cleanliness standards are firmly dictated from headquarters and subject to interpretation anywhere in the world. Work stations are typically separated by 8 to 10 ft. with aisles extremely wide at 15 to 30 ft. Noise levels around work stations are kept relatively low, and the production lines move more slowly than is typical in Western plants. A substantial amount of small-scale automation was generally visible at individual work stations. Individual workers are directly responsible for quality results at their own stations, but heavily automated quality control and test facilities are in evidence all along the electronics and consumer product lines. Employee turnover in Japan is extremely low. But even overseas plants tend to have a quarter of the turnover of comparable plants in their host countries.

More recently, realizing that the old lifetime system was enshrined in the pay system and put iron links that chained employees to their employer, Matsushita introduced short-term contracts to attract young graduates. Under the old system, workers could not leave because rises were limited during their employment until they reached their mid fifties when they received a huge lump sum. Under the new system of short contracts, wages can be drawn from this fund each month. It is up to the workers to decide whether they invest it in a private pension scheme, use it to improve their skills, or spend it. According to Atsushi Murayama, personnel director at Matsushita Electric, this new system was introduced because they realized that under the old system, people were loyal to the company even after they lost interest in their actual work. Matsushita did not want a half-hearted workforce. They want their workers to stay with them because they share a common interest with the company. This, they believe, will create a more active and conscious loyalty among their staff. Of the 800 graduates recruited each year since the introduction of the new system, 40 per cent of the graduates have already taken this option.

International Operations in Malaysia

Matsushita Electric Co. (Malaysia) was established in September 1965. It was the first company to begin manufacturing electronic products in Malaysia. As such, it was granted pioneer status for all the products it planned to manufacture. Towards the late 1960s the government of Malaysia changed its industrialization strategy, moving away from import substitution. In an effort to sustain economic growth and provide greater job opportunities in a rather small domestic market, exports of manufactured goods began to be emphasized for the first time. In 1968, the Pioneer Industries Ordinance (1958) was repealed and a more comprehensive Investment Incentives Act (1968) was passed. This Act maintained the notion of pioneer industries status, but added provisions for granting investment tax credits and export incentives.

Matsushita made a great effort to transfer management practices developed in Japan to Malaysia. Its success could be attributed to the step-by-step fashion it used to introduce its culture, to the nation's own avowed intention to learn from Japan as part of the 'Look East' policy, and to the supporting policies that accompanied the transfer of organization-specific practices. The latter included the policy of minimizing line–staff and blue–white collar differences, and a personnel evaluation system that stressed not just job performance but also such aspects as positive attitude, eagerness to improve, and attendance at quality control circle meetings. However, despite the enormous resources put into educating employees in appropriate skills as well as their attitude to work, the company was conscious that some culturally rooted differences between Japanese and Malaysians would remain. The task of moulding the two cultures was a difficult one, made even more so by the presence of three distinct ethnic groups in Malaysia—Malays (54% of the population), Chinese (35%), and Indians (10%) and by a somewhat large employee turnover.

Based on its philosophy of harnessing 'collective wisdom' a suggestion committee was set up in 1976 with eleven subcommittees in various departments and factories, each consisting of three to four members. In 1982, some 20,975 suggestions were received, of which 986 were graded as being valuable, In 1977, of 7,329 suggestions, only 182 were graded. The number of suggestions per employee increased from 3.5 to 17.2 between 1978 and 1982. Another successful transfer of Japanese management practices was in the introduction of quality control circles at MELCOM starting in March 1982. Since its inception, 129 QCs were formed with a total of 950 participating members out of a workforce of 1,200.

Sources

BBC 2, *Video Bubble Trouble*, Jan. 2000.

Chow, I., Holbert, N., Kelley, L., and Yu, J., 'Matsushita Electric Industrial Company', *Business Strategy: An Asia Pacific Focus*, Singapore: Prentice Hall, Simon & Schuster Asia, 1997: 207–24.

Cruikshank, J., 'Matsushita', *Harvard Business School Bulletin*, Feb. 1983.

Kono, T., *Strategy and Structure of Japanese Enterprises*, Armonk, NY: M. E. Sharpe, 1985.

Turpin, D., and Shen, X. (eds.), 'Matsushita in Malaysia', in *Casebook on General Management in Asia Pacific*, Macmillan, Business, IMD, 1999: 282–99.

Questions

1 Identify and evaluate Matsushita's management philosophy.

2 To what extent are Matsushita's management practices applicable to other companies? Which practices could be adopted outside Japan?

Quality Circles at Land Rover: The UK Experience

Geraldine Hammersley and
Ashly Pinnington

Company Background

Land Rover commenced manufacturing four-wheel-drive vehicles at its West Midlands site in 1948. As a strategic business unit of the Rover Group, Land Rovers' ownership has mirrored that of the UK nationalized motor industry. Initially part of the Rover Motor Co., it was subsequently part of BLMC, British Leyland, Jaguar Rover Triumph, and then in 1988 following privatization was merged back with Rover Cars to form Rover Group. The Rover Group was owned by British Aerospace until 1994. Subsequently it was sold to BMW Group, who remained in charge until April 2000, when the entire group was broken up and the Land Rover marque purchased by Ford.

Land Rover manufactures four vehicles: Defender, Discovery, Freelander, and Range Rover, spanning the utility, leisure, and luxury segments of the four-wheel-drive automobile market, with 800 model variations. Employing 9,000 people, its corporate strategy is defined as 'Introducing world class products, increasing investment in facilities and people, expanding its export market base and improving the competitiveness of its cost base' (Rover Group, 1992).

The company has developed its customer and market profile over the last two decades, moving away from the situation in 1980 when 83 per cent of its products were sold in developing countries. A major business review indicated an over-reliance on sales in declining Third World markets along with falling demand in the heavy duty sector which accounted for most of Defender sales. It thus became imperative for the company to exploit opportunities in developed markets in the leisure and luxury sectors. As a low-volume niche market manufacturer, the company saw an overall contraction in Third World markets accompanied by intensified Japanese competition. Its response was three-fold: to move its model range upmarket to meet the demand for more sophisticated vehicles in developed countries, to rationalize from fourteen production sites to the

Geraldine Hammersley is Senior Lecturer at Coventry University, UK. Ashly Pinnington is Senior Lecturer at the University of Queensland, Australia.

single Solihull plant, and to address the quality in its finished vehicles. By 1992 Land Rover's market profile had changed so that only 11 per cent of its products were sold in Third World markets with developed countries accounting for 89 per cent of sales.

Land Rover management also determined that increased productivity was necessary for the organization to maintain its competitiveness. It was taking on average twice as many man hours to produce a car in a European owned plant in Europe than in a Japanese-owned plant in Japan (Womack *et al.*, 1991). Lean production techniques were introduced and necessitated a change from the traditional hierarchical structure to a team-based organization structure. As a consequence three layers of supervision were removed and in their place Land Rover introduced cell-based manufacturing, with team leaders who lead teams of between ten and twenty-four employees but have none of the supervisory role of the traditional foreman position.

Production is organized into cells; few robots are used other than on the body in white framing lines. The majority of trim and final assembly operations are carried out by hands-on production assembly lines.

Land Rover's objectives of moving its models upmarket and reducing its reliance on Third World markets necessitated a review of the vehicles' quality. At the same time, introduction of lean production techniques to facilitate improvements in quality also brought about a change in working methods. Alongside this was the development of a company culture possessing many of the elements of a 'strong' corporate culture (Deal and Kennedy, 1992). According to the managing director (MD), 'A strong commitment to innovation, vision and leadership ensure the company is market driven with a strong customer focus and global perspective underpinned by an open management style with flat hierarchies' (Morgan, 1993). Nevertheless, elements of collective industrial relations persist alongside the more direct communications with management and new methods of team-based working. Five main trade unions are recognized and have negotiation rights on pay and conditions and health and safety via collective bargaining. In general, industrial relations are said to be good—an indication being that no working days have been lost due to disputes in ten years. Over the 1990s substantial increases in productivity have been achieved as shown by vehicle sales that increased by 300 per cent over seven years.

Total Quality Improvement

Land Rover's pattern of changing ownership is similar to other British car companies, but its quality management is somewhat atypical for having had a thriving quality circle programme that lasted for over nine years. Quality Circles were established at Land Rover in 1988 after a strike at the plant lasting for six weeks over failure to agree the annual pay deal. The MD explained, 'as senior managers we knew people were proud of working for Land Rover and so we had to ask ourselves why they felt it necessary to strike for six weeks in order to communicate a message to us' (Wheatley and New, 1994: 4).

Following the strike, communications became a management priority. Techniques were adopted that would promote two-way communication; cascade briefing groups were introduced along with attitude surveys and the launch of a total quality improvement (TQI) programme, so named because, 'in the immediate post-strike workplace environment, the less an initiative smacked of management, the better' (Wheatley and New, 1994: 5). An external consultant was appointed to work on the programme with a designated manager. The implementation plan identified eight necessary cultural changes required: the need for total quality leadership, empowerment of fact holders, ownership of problems, shared values, business orientation, common objectives, effective communication, and creation of a learning environment. All employees received four days off-the-job training in total quality and were issued with a handbook which set out the basic principles of total quality improvement:

- prevention not detection;
- management-led;
- everyone responsible;
- cost of poor quality;
- right first time;
- company-wide;
- continuous improvement (IRS 1992: 2)

The TQI handbook emphasized that total quality is achieved via prevention of problems rather than reliance on problem-solving after the event, and formed part of a series of initiatives that aimed to create a new quality culture with the company.

Quality Circles

Following the introduction of the TQI programme the company introduced quality circles starting with a pilot of nine groups. Initial reaction from the workforce was hostile; the trade union representatives vetoed them and the employees involved were subjected to boos and catcalling as they left the assembly line to attend circle meetings. The MD changed their name to discussion groups and made his commitment to them visible by asking discussion groups permission to attend their meetings. Subsequent growth of the groups is illustrated in Figure C1.

Membership of a group was voluntary, with groups being made up of between four and twelve employees from a common work area. Members were free to leave groups whenever they wished. Groups met either weekly or fortnightly and meetings were scheduled to fit in with their work area pattern and agreed between the group and local management teams to facilitate production requirements. Meetings were usually of between one and two hours duration. They met to discuss work-related problems and remained in more or less permanent form.

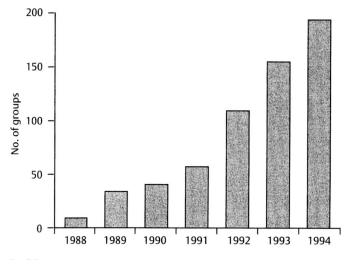

Fig. C1 Growth of discussion groups

The Communications and Involvement Manager along with three Involvement Co-ordinators oversaw and promoted all discussion group initiatives. They provided training and assistance to new groups. A steering committee chaired by the MD and comprising senior management and directors monitored the overall discussion group programme, set objectives and allocated resources.

The objectives of discussion groups were to:

• improve quality;
• create an outlook of solving problems and completing projects;
• involve people in their work;
• improve communications and teamwork;
• help personal development;
• increase motivation;
• improve job satisfaction.

The company perceived the benefits of discussion groups as:

• cost saving;
• quality improvement;
• creation of a better skilled workforce;
• improved teamwork;
• fostering a greater commitment to the organization.

Recognition of the effectiveness of discussion groups has come through national awards won by Land Rover among which was the 1992 NSQT Perkins Award for the company demonstrating the most significant progress in its quality improvement programme;

1993 winners of the Michelin Award; and 1993 winners of Management Today Most Improved Factory Award.

The trade union response to TQI initiatives was initially sceptical, fearing an erosion of the shop stewards role and the possibility that the unions would become marginalized. However, once it became clear that traditional union negotiating issues would not be affected, many shop stewards began to take an active role in discussion groups. An interview with a shop steward who is a member of a discussion group elicited this response: 'Because as a T.U. rep I was brought into contact with managers outside my normal working area it's broken down the traditional shop steward image. It's opened up doors and other departments and how they operate—you get a better vision of what is happening around you. It gives you a good feeling for the company' (Hammersley, 1995).

The period of the quality circle programme coincided with a change in the culture of the organization. Land Rover instituted a programme of culture change supported by the New Deal in employment that was agreed with the company's trade unions and launched by Rover Group in 1992. The New Deal included harmonization of terms and conditions to a single-status company; employees were called 'associates' and provided with work-wear, clocking in was abolished, revised holiday and sick pay arrangements were implemented alongside a no redundancy agreement guaranteeing job security. The process of recruitment and selection was revised to incorporate psychometric testing for all potential shop-floor associates and selection extended from a single interview to a two-day, team-based process of assessment.

During the first half of the 1990s, Land Rover was operating two other employee involvement initiatives alongside discussion groups—the suggestion scheme and quality action teams. In order to reinforce these activities the company introduced the Recognition of Involvement Scheme for Employees (RISE) in 1992. RISE awarded points to individual employees which could be accumulated and exchanged for awards. Each acceptable suggestion submitted to the suggestion scheme earned five points, joining a discussion group and attending at least ten meetings earned ten points, making a presentation about a concluded discussion group project earned fifty points and so on. Three hundred points could be exchanged for the use of a Range Rover for the weekend plus £50; 1,000 points entitled the employee to dinner for two up to the value of £60, the use of a Range Rover for a week, and £100; 2,500 points could be exchanged for a Rover 100 1.4SL car, while the top award of 5,000 points won a Rover 214 car, two weeks' holiday in the USA, four weeks' base pay, and two extra weeks' holiday. Within three years of the commencement of the RISE scheme, seven Rover 100 cars had been awarded to employees.

By 1996, quality circles had grown to 200 groups covering 14 per cent of the workforce, which is comparatively high membership for companies in the automotive and also other industries (Brennan, 1991). At the end of 1996, senior management reviewed the contribution that discussion groups were making and agreed to phase them out. Their review coincided with an increase in volume production from 68,104 vehicles in 1993 to 126,334 in 1996. One consequence of such volume increases was that it became increasingly problematic for employees to be released from their jobs to attend meetings; concomitant were the necessary changes in shift patterns brought about by volume uplifts. Arguably, it was not the case that discussion groups had failed; rather they were superseded by other forms of quality management.

Continuous Improvement Groups

Some members of discussion groups were selected by Land Rover management to participate in the pilot of continuous improvement groups. They had worked on quality improvement through the quality circle programme and most had been employed with the company long enough to have experienced the culture change brought about since the New Deal. Continuous improvement groups were established with the deliberate intention of increasing management's influence on processes and outcomes by selecting team members and determining tasks and priorities.

Ten pilot groups were established in the second quarter of 1997. The expertise in these groups varied according to the quality tasks and individuals were selected from a variety of occupations, job positions, and parts of the plant. Each group was based in a manufacturing zone and contained approximately six or seven people drawn from a manufacturing cell, including the team leader. Their task was to concentrate on the immediate work area and restricted to activities leading to process and quality improvement.

The benefit for Land Rover employees of continuous improvement groups is very similar to quality circles (Pinnington and Hammersley, 1997). These quality groups are work systems enabling employees to get to know other areas of the business. Improving quality in the immediate work area often means consulting employees working on other tasks in other similar areas, and sometimes will lead to communicating and migrating 'quality solutions' to people in other parts of the company. Both continuous improvement groups and quality circles provided employees with opportunities to contribute their ideas and become more involved in their own work and in the broader operations of the business, with the consequence that their self-confidence was improved. In addition to intrinsic and developmental benefits, continuous improvement groups were extrinsically motivating by providing additional means whereby employees perceived they would increase their individual chances of promotion and enhance their own and others' job security.

The main difference between the two types of group was that quality circles were perceived more negatively and as being inferior to continuous improvement groups because they failed to concentrate on critical issues of quality improvement. As one former discussion group member said: 'Basically we could have talked about anything from the fridge in the rest room to a process issue' (Hammersley and Pinnington, 1999). Discussion groups played an important role by introducing the philosophy of involvement and quality improvement to the workforce. While the level of discussion group membership enabled management to maintain and reinforce a high profile for quality issues, their weakness from a quality management perspective, was the latitude of topics they were allowed to investigate. A second related difference was that employees said that they preferred continuous improvement groups because they involved more guidance and control from management, meaning that they felt the group was more likely to achieve significant improvements in quality.

When discussion groups were subject to review in 1996, senior management concluded that their contribution was difficult to measure and they had outlived their usefulness. It was recognized that they had performed an important role in involving and educating the workforce. Land Rover management wanted to introduce more rigour through improvement groups and hence the brief was prescriptive, with activity limited to process and quality improvements within the immediate work area. The inclusion of team leaders in the pilot groups was improved to increase the likelihood of them remaining focused on relevant issues of quality improvement. Management envisaged that improvement groups would become a mainstream part of the business whereas discussion groups initially attempted little more than gaining better workforce involvement. The success of continuous improvement groups, according to the managers we interviewed, will be measured through process improvements, process adherence, and quality improvements:

The idea of getting people involved, with support from ourselves, was set up to facilitate discussion groups and it was an easy transition to improvement teams. We took with us all the expertise, one of the things that saved us having to preach the philosophy from new, because it was already ingrained to some extent in the philosophy of the business, it made it easier, we were pushing at an open door. What we had to do in 1988 when we launched discussion groups was go out and almost preach the gospel to people. (Communications and Involvement Manager).

In the eyes of the employees, the benefits for employee development have been expressed in both programmes, suggesting that the reduction in the number of people participating may mean less development for the overall workforce. However, continuous improvement groups operate differently from discussion groups and the employees interviewed spoke positively about the requirement to concentrate on quality and process issues at local level. This suggests that employees perceived their time was better utilized through a more controlled focus of attention, and additionally the emphasis on local zone-based issues may make it easier for them to identify workplace benefits due to quality improvement activities.

Sources

Brennan, M., 'Mismanagement and Quality Circles: How Middle Managers Influence Direct Participation', *Employee Relations* 13(5): 22, 1991.

Deal, T., and Kennedy, A., *Corporate Cultures*, London: Addison-Wesley, 1995: 3–20.

Hammersley, G., 'Evaluation of Discussion Groups in Land Rover: Impact on the bottom line', unpublished MA thesis, Leicester University, 1995: 11.

—— and Pinnington, A., 'Employee Response to Continuous Improvement Groups', *The TQM Magazine*, 11(1), 1999: 29–34.

IRS, 'Lean Production and Rover's New Deal', *IRS Employment Trends*, 514, 1992: 12–15.

Morgan, T., 'Rover Group Associates Roadshow', Transcript, 1993: 17.

Pinnington, A., and Hammersley, G., 'Quality Circles under the New Deal at Land Rover', *Employee Relations*, 19(5), 1997: 415–29.

Rover Group, *Annual Report*, 1992: 8.

Wheatley, M., and New, C., 'Britain's Best Factories Land Rover, Solihull', *DTI/Management Today/ Cranfield School of Management Case Study*, 1994: 4–5.

Womack, J., Jones, D., and Roos, D., *The Machine that Changed the World*, New York: HarperCollins, 1990: 13.

Bad Luck or Bad Management? Peregrine and the Asian Financial Crisis

Leong H. Liew

A Victim of the Asian Financial Crisis: Peregrine

> There is only a thin line between daring and irresponsibility.
> (David Chiu, Hong Kong legislator and developer)[1]

> We got caught in a completely unprecedented meltdown. The wealth loss in Asia . . .
> must be unprecedented in world history—even 1929.
> (Philip Tose, Peregrine's co-founder)[2]

Until its liquidation on 12 January 1998, Peregrine Investment Holdings was Asia's largest home-grown investment bank outside Japan. At its peak, it had assets of over US$5 billion and offices in 16 countries (Sender and Granitsas, 1998). The immediate cause of its insolvency was its exposure of over US$400 million in Indonesian corporate debt (Table CT1). Peregrine's largest exposure was an underwriting loan of US$235.8 million to the Indonesian company Steady Safe, which amounted to about one-third of Peregrine's equity. Peregrine granted this loan to Steady Safe as part of a deal where Peregrine was the underwriter for the bonds that Safety Safe was issuing to refinance its short-term debt and a US$118 million loan from Hong Kong Bank. Peregrine was to square its position once the bonds were sold. Unfortunately for Peregrine, investors' interest in the bonds disappeared when the financial crisis broke and it was unable to square its position. A debt–equity swap was not feasible because the collapse of the Indonesian economy following

Leong H. Liew is Associate Professor in the Faculty of International Business and Politics, Griffith University, Australia.

[1] Quoted in Hirsh (1998: 52).
[2] *Newsweek* interview (1998).

Table CT1 Peregrine's biggest exposures as at 31 October 1997

Corporation	$US million
Steady Safe (Indonesia)	235.76
Borneo Pulp & Paper (Malaysia)[1]	150.00
APP International Finance (Singapore)	
APP Global Financial (USA)	113.15
Medco Energi Corporation (Indonesia)	57.70
Pelabuhan Indonesia (Indonesia)	43.73
Rekasaran (USA)	34.00
Perkebunan Nusantara (Indonesia)	31.00
Robinson Dept. Store Co. (Thailand)	27.00
Polysindo Eka Perkasa (Indonesia)	25.30
Panasia Indosyntoc (Indonesia)	21.00
Total	738.64
Indonesian exposure	414.49

Note: [1] Denominated in ringgit.
Source: Pritchard (1998*b*).

the massive depreciation of the rupiah had drastically reduced the market value of Steady Safe to only US$4.7 million (Pritchard, 1998*a*).

Foundation of Peregrine

Peregrine's co-founders were Philip Tose and Francis Leung. In November 1988 Tose and Leung, with the backing of several influential business persons in Hong Kong, registered Peregrine International Holdings (PIH) in the Cayman Islands with an initial capital of US$38.4 million (HK$300 million). Their most influential backers included property magnate, Li Ka-shing, building and construction magnate, Gordon Wu, and chairperson of the Chinese government-owned China International Trust and Investment Corporation Pacific (Citic Pacific), Larry Yung. Tose and Leung provided 35 per cent of the initial capital, Li Ka-shing's Hutchison Whampoa and Gordon Wu's Hopwell Holdings, each provided 8 per cent; Citic Hong Kong, which owned 49 per cent of Citic Pacific, provided 5 per cent; and 15 other shareholders provided the remainder. After a series of corporate takeovers and restructuring, PIH became the controlling shareholder of Peregrine Investment Holdings, a listed company on the Hong Kong stock exchange.

Li, Wu, and Yung are very successful businessmen in Hong Kong and have impeccable political connections in China. Li's flagship companies Cheung Kong (Yangtze River) Holdings and Hutchison Whampoa were rated by the *Far Eastern Economic Review* (1998–99: 48) as two of Hong Kong's top ten companies in 1996, 1997, and 1998. Li was a business partner with Deng Zhifang, the second son of China's deceased supreme leader,

Deng Xiao Ping in property development and other ventures. He was invited on as a board member of Citic at its foundation in 1979 as an investment arm of the Chinese government and served on various Beijing-appointed bodies overseeing the transition of Hong Kong to Chinese rule. Although perhaps not as influential as Li in Beijing, Wu's and Yung's connections in Beijing are not to be underestimated. Wu is a major player in highway and other infrastructure developments in China and Yung's father was head of the entire Citic Group before he was promoted to be China's State Vice-President in 1993.

Peregrine's Philosophy

Peregrine's business philosophy reflected very much the philosophy of Tose. It was seen as akin to the British Special Air Service (SAS) motto of 'Who dares, wins'. Peregrine relied on its carefully cultivated connections to make the sort of quick business decisions that other investment banks were unwilling to make. It had a can-do attitude. There was less justification of business decisions based on careful analysis in Peregrine compared to other investment banks. Its organization was not structured in a manner that was amenable to checks and balances on important decisions. Power and decision-making were heavily concentrated at the top. For a long time, risk assessment and management was not taken seriously and was introduced only rather belatedly (Hirsh, 1998: 49).

Peregrine's can-do attitude typifies many of its business decisions. In 1996, Cheung Kong Holdings invited several investment banks to underwrite its placement of a huge share offering. The investment banks Merrill Lynch and Morgan Stanley were invited together with Peregrine to peruse its proposal. Merrill Lynch and Morgan Stanley decided they needed more time to evaluate the proposal. Tose without hesitation accepted the deal on offer and agreed to lead-manage the US$679 million share offering. It took Peregrine just one hour and a half in one afternoon to place all the stock (Hirsh, 1998: 51; Sender, 1996: 70). The fact that Cheung's major shareholder is Li Ka-shing helped to cement the deal, but the speed at which the deal was completed was no doubt due to Tose's can-do attitude to business.

Peregrine's Strategy

Tose was the driving force behind Peregrine's business strategy. Right from the start, Tose's strategy for Peregrine was to focus on marketing its banking services to Chinese businesses in Hong Kong and Mainland China by making use of his wide range of connections in the Chinese business and political community. Tose had foreseen the emergence of Greater China[3] and the rise of Chinese businesses and the competition they

---

[3] Mainland China, Hong Kong, and Taiwan.

would offer to established British businesses in Asia well before the British investment banks, which had dominated Hong Kong finance. He realized before many others that the end of colonial rule in Hong Kong would mean that the traditional influence enjoyed by British businesses would shift to Chinese-managed businesses. When he was a broker in the Hong Kong office of the British brokerage firm Vickers da Costa and Francis Leung was his subordinate, he cultivated the long-neglected Chinese business community for business. His astute cultivation of future Chinese business leaders in Hong Kong enabled him to form close relationships with Li and others in the Chinese business community that proved so critical to him when he started Peregrine and his subsequently built up client base.

Tose wrote a report on Li Ka-shing's Cheung Kong. The report is the first analysis ever undertaken for a Western investment house on a Chinese-managed firm. To do business with the Chinese entrepreneurs, Tose relied on 'guanxi' or connections. The term 'guanxi' used in the Chinese world has two meanings. The first refers to the use of official connections to circumvent official regulations. It is the method of the backdoor or 'houmen' and is illegal. The second meaning refers to the development of long-term social relationships to acquire information and build trust in the face of imperfect information in the marketplace in order to facilitate business transactions. This latter meaning is not dissimilar to the meaning of the Western term networking. Although Peregrine was reprimanded by Hong Kong's Securities and Futures Commission (SFC) for misleading the markets as to the real demand for the shares in the companies that it was underwriting (Sender, 1993), it had never been accused of engaging in any illegal activity. Hence, Tose's 'guanxi' is best described as networking with Chinese characteristics.

Peregrine became a pioneer in the listing of Chinese mainland companies in Hong Kong. Among the 'H-share' and 'red-chip' companies[4] that Peregrine had acted as adviser, arranger, or lead underwriter for were China Overseas Land & Investment, China Travel International, Guangzhou Shipyard, Hai Hong (a subsidiary of China Merchant Holdings), Shanghai Industrial, Shanghai Petrochemical, Stone Electronic Technology, and Denway Investments. The share issue of Denway Investments in 1993 became the most oversubscribed issue in the history of the Hong Kong Stock Exchange (Hirsh, 1998; Sender, 1993).

Besides acting as adviser, arranger, or underwriter for Chinese Mainland companies, Peregrine was also a direct investor in some of these companies. By 1993, it had invested to the tune of HK$1 billion in Chinese industrial assets. It was a business partner with the Beijing's municipal and Guangzhou's and Jiangsu's provincial governments, and became a broker for Chinese firms wanting to place shares on the Shanghai and Shenzhen stock exchanges. Its relationship with the Chinese authorities was so good that it was the only overseas firm that had a seat on the Shanghai Stock Exchange in 1994 (Anon., 1994: 99).

Peregrine's willingness to take a stake in the new issue of shares of companies that it was underwriting strengthened its relationship with its clients and was one of its strong marketing points. However, this was sometimes interpreted as attempts to influence the public's perception as to the true demand for those shares.

---

[4] H-share companies are companies registered in Mainland China that have a listing in Hong Kong. Red-chip companies are companies registered in Hong Kong where Chinese mainland companies exercise control over more than 35 per cent of the stock.

While Peregrine's strategy focused its attention on Chinese-managed businesses, it did not neglect business opportunities elsewhere in Asia. In 1992, Hong Kong provided 91 per cent of its operating profit and its investments outside Hong Kong were designed as much to reduce its dependence on Hong Kong as they were to exploit business opportunities in new and emerging markets. Within four years of its foundation, it had opened offices in Indonesia, Malaysia, the Philippines, Singapore, and Thailand. It later opened an office in Myanmar (Burma) and another in South Korea. As well as its offices in Asia, it had offices in London and New York. Peregrine's business was expanding rapidly and it sought to increase its capitalization. By 1995, Peregrine's initial capital of $US38.4 million in 1988 had grown to US$690 million and it announced further plans to boost its capital to US$1 billion (Hirsch, 1998: 51).

Peregrine's belief that it could rely on good political connections to hedge against political risk was an important factor behind its decision to invest in Myanmar. Myanmar is a country with a poor human rights record and the likelihood of political instability. However, the country is rich in natural resources and has liberal foreign investment laws. Peregrine entered into partnership with the Union of Myanmar Economic Holdings to set up an investment company named Myanmar International Trust and Investment Company (MITIC) to attract foreign investments into Myanmar. As with Steady Safe, the company that subsequently caused the collapse of Peregrine, MITIC appeared to have strong political connections. It is a company with strong links to the Burmese army (Anon., 1995: 70).

In 1994, buoyed by the success of Peregrine in the equities business, Tose headhunted a team of bond traders led by Andre Lee, a Korean-American, from Lehman Brothers, with the aim of dominating the emerging Asian fixed-income market. Lee became somewhat of a pioneer in the Asian junk bond market and developed a reputation for his ability to raise cash for fast-growing companies. Between January 1996 and August 1997, he managed to raise $US2.6 billion capital for such companies in Indonesia and Thailand (Anon., 1998: 87). Peregrine's can-do attitude in its equity business was repeated in its fixed-income business but, as it later turned out, with devastating consequences.

Peregrine's Pre-crisis Performance

Peregrine's company philosophy and strategy served it well until the Asian financial crisis. Within five years of it commencing business, it became the most successful brokerage firm in Hong Kong. In 1993, it accounted for 60 per cent of the new listings on the Hong Kong Stock Exchange and it led 33 per cent of all rights issues in Hong Kong (Anon. 1994: 99). Peregrine was involved in raising HK$19 billion (US$2.4 billion) in 1992. Its profits of HK$608 million (US$78 million) in the year ended November 1992 were double what they had been a year before (Sender, 1993). In 1993, its profits rose by over 40 per cent to US$110 million (Anon., 1994: 99) and by 1995, profits had reached the HK$1 billion (US$128 million) mark (Sender, 1996: 71).

Just Bad Luck?

Peregrine's management style was an important factor in its collapse. But the Asian financial crisis surprised many in business, government, and academia. Even the International Monetary Fund and World Bank did not anticipate the crisis. In the immediate years before the crisis, GDP growth in the Asian countries was strong and their government budgets were healthy. The average annual GDP growth of Indonesia in the decade before the crisis was about 8 per cent and the government budget was in surplus. Its savings ratio was close to 30 per cent of GDP and, although it had a current account deficit of 3.3 per cent GDP, this was lower than the current deficits of the 1980s.

In his interview by *Newsweek*, Tose defended his stewardship of Peregrine by arguing that it was the Asian crisis and not bad management that caused the collapse of Peregrine. In his words, 'in the first seven days of January the rupiah went from 5,000 to 11,000 [per US dollar]. No one in their wildest dreams would have anticipated . . . that the rupiah could go anywhere near that level'.

Tose finds some support from the well-known Harvard economist Jeffrey Sachs, who sees the Asian financial crisis as a classic case of financial panic. In Indonesia, when available foreign exchange reserves were insufficient to cover short-term foreign liabilities, a sudden loss in investor confidence led to 'a rush for the exits' by foreign investors leading to a dramatic collapse of the rupiah. Many corporations, which would otherwise have been profitable, were made insolvent because over-depreciation of the rupiah increased the domestic value of their foreign debts to unsustainable levels.

It was likely that Peregrine believed that the good political connections that it enjoyed in Indonesia were sufficient compensation for the relatively weak financial position of Steady Safe. The main earnings of Steady Safe came from a Jakarta taxi franchise. Steady Safe had no dollar revenues and its annual income was equivalent to only US$9 million. Its high price–earnings ratio before the crisis was due to its yet-to-be realized promises of railway and ferry businesses that were contingent on its close relationship with President Suharto's daughter. However, the political fortunes of the Suharto family fell in tandem with the collapse of the Indonesian economy and any business relationship with members of the family was no longer seen as an advantage.

Peregrine's management's mistake of being overconfident in the power of good connections was compounded by its decision in 1995 to organize the company along product rather than country lines without making sure that information flowed horizontally as well as vertically. Consequently, Peregrine's total exposure in each country was not transparent. Although the management of Peregrine was highly centralized, Lee was given a lot of independence to run Peregrine's fixed-income business, perhaps because Tose was a stockbroker and was not as familiar with the bond business. As it turned out, only a small number of senior managers were aware of the excessive exposure to Indonesian debt. Even Tose and the head of Peregrine's office in Jakarta were apparently unaware of the total amount of Indonesian bonds held by the company. Senior management was alerted to the company's large exposure to Indonesian paper only after the rupiah was devalued (Pritchard, 1998*b*).

Several lessons from the perspective of country risk can be learnt from the experience of Peregrine. The first is that political connections, no matter how strong, are no guarantee of the safety of a corporation's investments. The political fortunes of individuals in countries where politics matter much in business are highly uncertain and unpredictable. They wax and wane and it is unwise to put all eggs into one basket. The willingness of Peregrine to risk about one-third of its capital on one firm, even if it was to be for a short period, violated a fundamental principle of risk management. Political connections cannot substitute for solid business fundamentals. Steady Safe would not have been able to honour its debt to Peregrine even had the Indonesian economy not collapsed from the IMF-imposed tight fiscal and monetary polices. With no dollar revenues, the upward valuation of Peregrine's dollar debt in rupiah from the massive depreciation of the rupiah would have written off its entire capital base.

Sources

Anon., 'Banker to the Bureaucrats', *The Economist*, 10 Sept. 1994: 99.

—— 'Peregrine's Blind Spot', *The Economist*, 11 Feb. 1995: 70.

—— 'Talons Pulled', *The Economist*, 10 Jan. 1998: 87.

Bank for International Settlements, *The Maturity, Sectoral and Nationality Distribution of International Bank Lending: First Half 1997*, Basle: BIS, Jan. 1998.

Far Eastern Economic Review, 31 Dec.–7 Jan. 1998–99.

Hirsh, Michael, 'Cronyism Crashes', *Newsweek*, 26 Jan. 1998: 49–52.

IMF, *World Economic Outlook: Interim Assessment*, Dec. 1997.

Liew, Leong, 'A Political-Economy Analysis of the Asian Financial Crisis', *Journal of the Asia Pacific Economy*, 3, 1998: 301–30.

Newsweek, 'They Killed a Peregrine, Too', interview with Philip Tose, 26 Jan. 1998: 52–3.

Pritchard, Simon, 'Indonesia Debt leaves Peregrine in the Cold', *South China Morning Post*, internet edn., 9 Jan. 1998*a*.

—— 'Peregrine Exposure Stuns Chiefs', *South China Morning Post*, internet edn., 14 Jan. 1998*b*.

Sender, Henny, 'Hong Kong Regulators Reprimand Peregrine', *Far Eastern Economic Review*, 30 Sept. 1993.

—— 'Peregrine's Great Leap', *Far Eastern Economic Review*, 9 May 1996: 70–2.

—— and Granitsas, Alkman, 'Broken Wings: Peregrine's Collapse Raises Troubling Questions', *Far Eastern Economic Review*, 22 Jan. 1998: 52–3.

Taylor, Michael, 'Swooping to Conquer', *Far Eastern Economic Review*, 10 Oct. 1991, 63–5.

The Economist, 'East Asian Economies Survey', 7 Mar. 1998.

World Bank, *Global Economic Prospects and the Developing Countries: Beyond Financial Crisis*, Washington: World Bank, 1999.

Questions

1 What were the factors responsible for the early rapid growth of Peregrine?

2 While Peregrine's use of connections or '*guanxi*' was an advantage in its dealings with Chinese-managed businesses, why did the reliance on '*guanxi*' fail so badly in the case of Steady Safe?

3 Suggest possible reasons why Peregrine's management made a US$236 million loan to Steady Safe, despite it having no dollar revenues and earning an annual income of only US$9 million. Was it due to Peregrine's failure to undertake a country-risk analysis for Indonesia or was it an example of its aggressive venture into the Asian junk bond market?

4 Was the collapse of Peregrine due more to bad luck or bad management?

P.T. BIT: An Indonesian Textile Case Study

Malika Richards

Description of the Business

P.T. BIT, located just outside Jakarta, Indonesia, spins synthetic yarns to supply the needs of weaving mills and knitting factories. The company was first started in 1990 with an initial investment of 22 billion rupiah. Seventy per cent of this capitalization was in the form of a syndicated bank loan. At that time, the exchange rate was 1,400–1,500 rupiah to the US dollar. BIT is an outgrowth of an Indonesian family-owned knitting business. When BIT was first established, there were few spinning mills in Indonesia and these tended to be part of vertically integrated conglomerates. The family decided to integrate backwards when they found it increasingly difficult to find a reliable, on-time source of quality yarn for their knitting mills. At first, BIT was able to manufacture only two products: rayon, and TR (a polyester/viscose blend). Its products now include viscose, modal, polynosic, acrylic, polyester/viscose blends, and viscose/polyester blends. BIT's mission is 'to be the finest yarn manufacturer in terms of quality, on-time delivery, and reasonable prices'.

One of BIT's strengths is that it benefits from being a family-supervised company, and at the same time is managed and run by professionals. So, the decision-making process is quite fast compared to the larger spinning companies. The company utilizes a just-in-time inventory and production management system. They also use computers intensively to control inventory, accounting and expenses. From time to time the firm also comes up with new products developed by technical advisers. Even though most spinning companies produce similar items, BIT considers its competitive advantage to be that of providing consistently high-quality products and on-time delivery.

BIT is currently the only yarn manufacturer in Indonesia that spins 100 per cent modal and 100 per cent polynosic. These two products are very expensive items and used mainly for high-value garments and for advanced industrial applications. BIT was the first to develop a relationship with LZ AG, the modal fibre supplier, and FJB Junlon, the polynosic fibre supplier. In addition, BIT is the first in Indonesia to spin and market these yarns.

Malika Richards is Assistant Professor of Management at Drexel University, Philadelphia.

Based on engineering specifications, the most efficient minimum production level of a spinning mill is 30,000 spindles. A 10,000-spindle machine costs between US$8 to US$15 million. BIT has 22,000 spindles. The key to flexible spinning production is at the pre-spinning stages. The four pre-spinning stages are: blow room, carding, drawing, and roving. These four stages involve 20 to 40 per cent of the plant's total investment (see Fig. C2). It is very costly to switch from one type of fibre to another. The problem is directly related to efficiency. Usually, a spinning mill will lose 20 per cent (for the period of one to two weeks) of its output when it switches fibre type. In the 'off season' BIT can run a different fibre in each of its four blow rooms. Alternatively, if one of the fibres is in particularly high demand, it could be processed in all the blow rooms.

BIT can produce four items at once, while other Indonesian spinning companies of the same size are capable of running only two items at a time. In such a cyclical industry, it is a risky strategy for a 20,000–22,000 spindle company to have only two lines. The company would be entirely dependent on the market demand for these two products. In addition to producing viscose—a commodity and a price-sensitive product, BIT can also produce modal and polynosic—products others do not spin and which sell at a much higher price. This enables BIT to enter markets that have not yet been developed (see Table CT2). Having a production layout like GT or DX would lead to stockbuilding during the 'off season'. Viscose yarn is a seasonal and price-sensitive item. Therefore, BIT's production layout enables the firm to diversify risk.

By manufacturing a variety of products, BIT can spread its risk and at the same time become a player in several markets. As the world demands more innovative products, BIT also develops new items. For example, they were the first company to spin R/T (a viscose/polyester blend), which has since become a desirable item. BIT also tries to introduce to the market interesting new synthetic fibre blends. Another way they differentiate their products is by adjusting the percentage ratio of the blends. For example, the T/R yarn ratio is usually 63:35, but BIT also develops a T/R ratio of 50:50 and 80:20. These days customers have become very price sensitive and quality conscious. In order to both please customers and maintain profitability, BIT applies a flexible pricing strategy. For example, they give quantity discounts as an incentive.

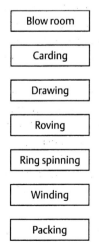

Fig. C2 Spinning process

Table CT2 P.T. BIT product list

Item[1]	Seasonal product	Pricing	Count (Ne)[2]	Weaving[3]	Knitting[4]
100% viscose bright	No	Low	20/1	Yes	Yes
			30/1	Yes	Yes
			40/1	Yes	Yes
			30/2	Yes	Yes
			40/2	Yes	Yes
			60/2	Yes	Yes
100% viscose semi dull	Yes	Moderate	15/1	Yes	No
			30/1	Yes	No
			40/1	Yes	No
100% polynosic junlon	Yes	High	30/1	Yes	Yes
			40/1	Yes	No
			40/2	Yes	No
			60/2	Yes	No
100% modal	Yes	High	30/1	No	Yes
			40/1	No	Yes
			60/2	No	Yes
Polyester/viscose (65/35)	No	Low	30/1	Yes	Yes
			40/1	Yes	Yes
			30/2	Yes	No
Viscose/polyester (70/30)	Yes	Moderate	30/1	Yes	Yes
			40/1	Yes	No

Notes:
[1] These are BIT's primary products. Of the six items, four can be manufactured at the same time.
[2] Count (Ne) refers to the English system yarn count number.
[3] Commonly used for weaving.
[4] Commonly used for knitting.

BIT visits new customers once every three months, so they become familiar with the company. The company also promotes its logo and brand on the outside of the carton box, so customers will become increasingly familiar with the firm. In addition, BIT differentiates itself by making a firm commitment to deliver the goods on schedule.

BIT's products are promoted worldwide by the large trading companies Marubeni, Itochu, Nichimen, Toyomenka, Yagi Co. and Samsung. Currently, BIT is the price and quality leader in the Korean market for 100 per cent viscose, viscose/polyester, and poly-ester/viscose yarn. These trading companies have a good performance record, selling textile products in the Korean market.

Considering the current economic crisis, it is necessary for BIT to keep more cash to avoid any difficulties. Thus, to persuade their customers to pay in advance or by T.T. (telegraphic transfer, BIT gives cash discounts. Production is based on orders and letters of credit (LCs) in hand. BIT's financial policies are conservative. They allow only spending related to the core business. Compared to other Indonesian companies, BIT has a low level of debt. This offers a safety cushion in the face of rising interest rates (see Tables CT3 and CT4).

The spinning industry is cyclical. When the number of orders drops, spinning companies either switch fibres and/or reduce output. Lay-offs during downturns are common

Table CT3 P.T. BIT statement of income, year ended 31 December (thousand rupiah)

	1991	1992	1993	1994	1995	1996	1997
Net sales	24,561,137	20,397,661	18,213,802	21,714,550	27,088,843	21,924,991	25,453,621
Cost of goods sold	18,362,453	15,366,607	13,542,290	16,807,532	22,143,095	18,193,587	20,435,903
Gross profit	6,198,684	5,031,053	4,671,512	4,907,018	4,945,748	3,731,405	5,017,719
Operating expenses							
General and administrative expenses	837,935	925,703	913,485	1,044,953	1,077,417	764,095	786,393
Selling	140,174	148,256	413,591	456,448	1,008,172	1,118,270	1,137,973
Total operating expenses	978,109	1,073,959	1,327,075	1,501,401	2,085,590	1,882,366	1,924,366
Income from operations	5,220,575	3,957,094	3,344,437	3,405,617	2,860,158	1,849,039	3,093,353
Other income (charges)							
Interest income/expense	(6,838,495)	(5,465,306)	(3,139,287)	(1,765,847)	(1,748,745)	(1,320,324)	(999,258)
Gain on sale of properties			10,932	11,505	34,282		
Loss of foreign exchange				(63,637)	(40,239)	(37,864)	
Miscellaneous	166,283	26,979	72,005	214,178	562,498	693,052	875,737
Other charges—net	(6,672,213)	(5,438,326)	(3,056,350)	(1,603,801)	(1,192,203)	(665,136)	(123,521)
Net profit (loss)	(1,451,638)	(1,481,232)	288,086	1,801,816	1,667,955	1,183,903	2,969,832
Beginning of year profit (loss)	(1,207,318)	(2,658,955)	(4,140,187)	(3,852,101)	(2,050,285)	(382,330)	801,573
End of year profit (loss)	(2,658,955)	(4,140,187)	(3,852,101)	(2,050,285)	(382,330)	801,573	3,771,406

Table CT4 P.T. BIT balance sheet, year ended 31 December (million rupiah)

	1991	1992	1993	1994	1995	1996	1997
Assets							
Current assets							
Cash	789	0.8	51	65	94	1,003	161
Bank							13
Accounts receivable							
Trade	7,892	6,212	3,362	3,342	1,788	578	2,929
Others	56	31,751	87	43	7	10	2
Inventories	1,461	2,282	4,479	4,464	5,473	5,535	5,792
Prepaid taxes and expenses	45	108	204	259	1,252	667	544
Total current assets	10,243	8,635.8	8,183	8,172	8,614	7,793	9,442
Property, plant and equipment net of accumulated depreciation	21,968	20,480	19,874	20,701	19,237	17,423	14,555
Equipment under capital lease — net of accumulated depreciation				161			
Pre-operating expenses — net	666	480	294	108			
Total assets	32,876	29,595.8	28,351	29,143	27,851	25,215	23,997
Liabilities							
Current liabilities							
Accounts payable							
Trade	4,568	1,943	3,538	4,029	6,990	7,365	6,916
Others	619	450	20	600	64	595	310
Accrued expenses	475	1,644	1,339	1,282	488	424	629
Taxes payable	306	131	6	4	5	2	2
Current maturities of long-term loans							
Bank loans	7,522	11,922	13,822	16,222	11,755	7,072	3,500
Obligations under capital lease				73	75	10	
Total current liabilities	13,490	16,090	18,725	22,211	19,378	15,559	11,357
Long-term loans net of current maturities							
Bank loans	13,200	8,800	4,633	83	10		23
Obligations under capital lease				55			
Total long-term loans	13,200	8,800	4,633	138	10		23
Due to stockholders	4,845	4,845	4,845	4,845	4,845	4,845	4,845
Capital							
Capital stock — 1 million rupiah par value							
Authorized — 5,000 shares							
Subscribed and fully paid — 4,000 shares	4,000	4,000	4,000	4,000	4,000	4,000	4,000
Profit/deficit	(2,659)	(4,140)	(3,852)	(2,050)	(382)	802	3,771
Total capital	1,341	140	148	1,950	3,618	4,802	7,771
Total liabilities	32,876	29,595	28,351	29,143	27,851	25,215	23,997

among all spinning companies. Maintaining the current workforce size but reducing the number of working hours across the board is not typically done.

BIT's worker turnover rate is 25 per cent annually. Most workers stay no longer than ten years. This high turnover rate is mainly due to the composition of BIT's workforce. Ninety-five per cent of the workers are female. Because of superior dexterity, female workers have proved to be more suitable for this type of industry. However, due to child-rearing responsibilities and marriage, they also leave their jobs more often than do men.

Indonesian workers are not yet familiar with computers and electronics. BIT employs more people than a European or Japanese plant of the same size. This way, quality and output quantity can still be achieved using manual techniques. Still, as a result of intensive training, BIT has been able to reduce the number of plant workers by 30 per cent over the past two years. To ensure good and stable quality, BIT has a working standard for each spinning stage. In addition, within each section, BIT appoints one supervisor to ensure that the workers follow the quality standards.

A spinning mill is both a capital-intensive and a labour-intensive business. To this end, BIT strives to take care of its employees. The company built a canteen in 1990 and dormitories for female workers within the factory premises. Most companies do not have dormitories for their workers. Having workers stay within the factory premises provides BIT with a competitive advantage in terms of production efficiency. It means that workers are able to get to work on time.

In addition, BIT gives health and life insurance to all workers. In Indonesia, it is not common for a company to give health and life insurance directly to the workers. Each company in Indonesia is obliged to pay a negotiated sum of money to a government support foundation called 'Jamsostek'. In return, Jamsostek pays compensation to workers' families for accidents and death during employment. A pension plan is also part of the Jamsostek programme.

BIT has built strong ties with the local community and has a good relationship with its workers' union. The company also has an established relationship with nearby police and the army, as a precaution in the event of riots. Given Indonesia's unstable political situation and recent history of social unrest, this is a possible threat to any company. On many occasions BIT has helped the surrounding community by building roads and by participating in social activities, such as charity bazaars and sports events with neighbouring factories.

However, there are also some issues facing BIT. The minimum efficient number of spindles for a plant of its size should be 30,000. Also, the company's marketing department has not been aggressive. BIT simply gets its publicity through its good relationship with the trading giants Marubeni, Itochu, Nichimen, Toyomenka, Yagi Co., and Samsung.

Competition

Thirty years ago in Indonesia, there were only a few government-owned spinning companies and the BL group. Today, textiles rank behind oil and gas as Indonesia's second largest industry. Because of its potential to earn foreign exchange, the Indonesian government supports textile industry growth. Some of the government-owned spinning companies are still running, but they focus on the domestic market only. Also, their quality is not stable and delivery is often not on-time—both necessary to compete in the global market.

The largest synthetic yarn manufacturer is the BL group (see Table CT5). BL's factories have a total of 200,000 spindles in Indonesia. The BL group concentrates on the domestic market (roughly 80%). Their domestic market share is approximately 50 per cent. Recently, they have been trying to export their products in order to take advantage of the weak Indonesian rupiah. As noted above, most spinning companies do not produce many items. The BL group, however, can produce many items at one time. The BL group is BIT's toughest competitor. BIT usually manages to get a higher price for its products than does BL in Indonesia. However, BL's manufacturing costs are lower. As Indonesia's economic situation worsens, it is possible that BL will build up more and more unsold inventory and will have to dump it on the market.

There are over twenty synthetic-yarn spinning companies the same size as, or smaller than, BIT. One of these, Kanindotex (or AIC), is now a public company, although Suharto's son is a major shareholder. In order to overcome the negative public relations associated with the Suharto family, the company has changed its home to 'Apac'.

Table CT5 Main competitors in the Indonesian synthetic-fibre spinning industry

Name	No. of spindles	Ownership	Investment[1]
BL group	200,000	Foreign	Japan, Germany
IRA	125,000	Domestic	India
KTX	125,000	Domestic	Taiwan
LA	77,000	Domestic	Germany
BIT	22,000	Domestic	Japan, Germany
GT	22,000	Domestic	Japan
DX	22,000	Domestic	Italy
MU	16,000	Domestic	Japan

Notes:
[1] The investment column indicates that machines from a particular country are used for production. The buyer can determine the approximate quality level of each company's yarns by looking at the origin of its spinning machines (see below):

Most expensive investment	Japan and Germany
Expensive	Japan and Italy (although Italian manufacturers are known for poor after-sales service)
Moderate	Taiwan
Less expensive	China
Cheap	India, Soviet Union

Other recent developments: most of the local Indonesian competitors are planning to expand capacity. They have ordered new machinery to replace the old. These new machines should be delivered soon. On the other hand, many Japanese and Korean firms have closed down their spinning plants in Japan and Korea, and have scrapped the old machinery.

The Japanese and Korean markets remain in recession. China, Pakistan, and India present even stronger global competition in cotton, though Indonesia still has an advantage in synthetic fibres.

Major Customers

BIT has two basic customer groups: weavers and knitters. These two make all the textile fabrics in the world. They are capital-intensive globalized businesses. It is very costly for these customers to have their knitting and weaving machines break down due to inconsistent yarn quality. Therefore, the most important things customers look for are stable yarn quality and on-time delivery. Furthermore, similar yarn quality and specifications—uniformity, tenacity, and evenness—are demanded no matter where in the world the weaver or knitter is located. BIT's four product groups are regularly demanded staples throughout the world. Since this is a cyclical industry, customers are in a stronger bargaining position during the 'off season'. Having flexibility in the types and quantities of fibres, as BIT has, provides a cushion against such customer bargaining strength.

BIT sells very little to the domestic market (see Fig. C3). The company relies primarily on the Korean market. It takes 12 to 15 days for BIT to make and deliver the spun yarn to Jakarta's Tanjung Priok Port. It takes another 12 days to ship goods directly from Tanjung Priok to Busan Port in South Korea. So, Korean customers can begin to use BIT's yarn in 30 days. Other market destinations include the USA, Australia, Japan, Taiwan, Italy, Greece, and occasionally, Germany and Sri Lanka.

Most of BIT's customers are medium- and small-sized companies. A small customer would order one to two shipping containers a month. Medium customers order three to five containers a month, while large customers order five to ten containers a month.

Major Suppliers

Fibre is the only raw material for a spinning mill. There are many types of synthetic and natural fibres, such as polynosic, polyester, modal, acrylic, cotton, and so on. However, to spin many varieties, a spinning mill would have to invest in a substantial amount of machinery. Since viscose, viscose/polyester, polyester/viscose yarns are so affordable, there are no significant substitutes that can pose a threat. Even if fibre manufacturers came up with a new fibre, it would probably be rather expensive to spin and to market.

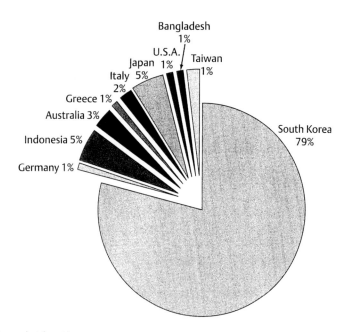

Fig. C3 BIT's market locations

Table CT6 BIT's main suppliers

Name	Product	Location
FJB	Polynosic	Japan
IBR Rayon (of the BL group)	Viscose	Java, Indonesia
IIU Rayon (a local firm)	Viscose	Sumatra, Indonesia
LZ	Modal	Austria
SPV (of the LZ group)	Viscose	Java, Indonesia
TFC (a Japanese MNC)	Polyester	Java, Indonesia
TRY (a Japanese MNC)	Polyester	Java, Indonesia

Suppliers to the spinning industry are very large. It costs a minimum of $US200 million to build a new fibre plant. Their sales are approximately $US250 million a year. Major synthetic suppliers, ranked by quality and price, are: (1) P.T. IBR Rayon (a member of the BL group), (2) P.T. SPV (a member of the LZ group), and (3) P.T. IIU Rayon (a new company owned by a local group). However, P.T. IIU has recently been shut down due to many problems, including those concerning the environment, surrounding community, and the government (see Table CT6).

These three suppliers are viscose fibre manufacturers. Monthly, each can produce up to 12,000 metric tons. P.T. BIT's monthly consumption is roughly 400 metric tons. To maintain stable quality, BIT chooses only the best quality (and highest priced) fibre. So, the company purchases all its viscose fibre from IBR Rayon.

It is not easy to spin 100 per cent modal or 100 per cent polynosic. Even if they are able to, spinning companies need to get certification from the supplier that their products have met strict quality standards. After five years of experimentation, BIT was finally successful in meeting LZ's strict quality-control requirements. LZ wants to develop its modal market, but needs the help of both spinners and weavers/knitters.

Industry Background

Key success factors in the spinning industry are: (1) good and stable quality yarn, (2) on-time delivery, (3) yarn consistency, (4) reasonable prices, and (5) innovation. Since they are among the basic necessities, the world will never stop buying textile products. It is now a matter of who can produce at the cheapest cost, produce the best quality, at a reasonable price, and also ship the goods on schedule.

There has been a steady decrease in the number of spindles in Japan, Korea, and Europe. The world's weavers and knitters are now turning to the more affordable yarns manufactured in the developing Asian countries—including China, India, Pakistan, and Indonesia, all countries with low labour costs. Ten years ago Japan had almost 20 million spindles in production. Today, due to high labour costs, that number is below 2 million. On the other hand, Indonesia, with over 200 million people, only operates 6 million spindles. Five years ago, Indonesia had only 4 million spindles. Capacity is still insufficient to meet the current domestic demand. In light of the opening of promising new markets, such as China and the former Soviet Union, the Indonesian spinning industry is expected to further expand production over the next five years.

China, including Hong Kong, is the world's largest producer of textile items. Indonesia ranks fourth after India and South Korea. Hong Kong is gradually replacing its weaving and knitting products with garment manufacturing—a higher value-added process. Likewise, firms in the USA, European Community, and Turkey are moving away from spinning and investing more in the weaving and knitting industries. Most of the spinning companies now in the USA are open-end mills. Although the output of an open-end mill exceeds that of a spinning mill of the same size, open-end yarn is of inferior quality.

China, India, and Pakistan spin most of the world's cotton yarn today. The Chinese are still using poor quality local spinning machines. In another ten years, however, these three countries are likely to move into the mid-quality synthetic yarn market. A few years ago large Japanese trading companies started to invest in new machines in China. However, due to unsatisfactory returns, many have now shifted their investment focus into other industries, such as banking and automobiles.

Spinning technology has changed only incrementally. The basic principles of spinning have remained the same over the past fifty years. So, when a company buys a new machine they simply buy one that is more productive and will yield a better quality output with less maintenance. Some companies change their machines every ten years, others change them every twenty-five years. The decision to update spinning machines is at the discretion of each company's top management policy. For example, even in

Japan some firms still operate 60-year old plants without any modernization—only minor modifications.

The most recent process innovation is an integrated online production system that connects the whole plant, now used by a few spinning companies in Europe and Japan. Although it is not easy to maintain these new plants, there are considerable labour-cost savings. For example, a 30,000 spindle factory with this new production system in Japan might need fewer than fifty workers. In existing Indonesian factories, at least 300 people would be required. However, another factor to consider is that European and Japanese workers are more familiar with electronics and have better computer skills. These are critical to the successful implementation of online production process.

Over the past five years, textile exports have increased from Indonesia because of both increasing demand from global markets and the expansion of the Indonesian textile production capacity. In addition, trade barriers are falling in the textile industry world-wide. Countries with high labour costs realize that it is simply not cost-effective to manu-facture textiles locally. Also, the prices of new spinning machines have fallen, so local businesses in developing countries, like Indonesia, are now more able to afford this investment.

Relative to other more developed nations, Indonesia's labour-intensive industries have a competitive advantage because of the country's low wage levels and plentiful labour supply. Nevertheless, in the next six to seven years, Indonesian spinners will probably start to invest in more technology in order to reduce the amount of labour required, increase efficiency, and increase quality.

Indonesian synthetic spinning mills have several competitive advantages: (1) they are close to the raw material sources (wood and petroleum), (2) they enjoy low labour costs—for now, the lowest in South East Asia due to the currency devaluation, (3) the govern-ment provides tax holidays as an export incentive, (4) the textile market (weavers and knitters) is the largest in South East Asia—in fact much larger than the combined textile markets of the other nine ASEAN countries (Malaysia, Singapore, Thailand, the Philip-pines, Brunei, Vietnam, Laos, Cambodia, and Myanmar), and (5) the end-customer base, the Indonesian population, is the largest in South East Asia (over 200 million people) and the fourth largest in the world.

Future Challenges

As Asia entered a severe recession in 1998, survival strategies are becoming very import-ant. For example, due to the financial crisis, the Indonesian government increased lend-ing interest rates to 70 per cent per annum for the Indonesian rupiah and 15 per cent per annum for US dollars. As a result, 80 per cent of the local industries have collapsed and need to be restructured. In addition, the world demand for textiles has decreased, which has led the weavers and knitters to become very price-sensitive. Thirdly, as the spinning industry continues to mature, quality has become a crucial factor. Customers are not only price-sensitive, but have become quality-sensitive as well. Also, globlization has created increasingly specialized synthetic yarn markets. While this means that companies like BIT must struggle to forecast demand, it also offers new niche opportunities. Furthermore, there is the threat of future competition from spinners in other emerging markets, such as China.

Sources

P.T. BIT kindly provided access to its financial data and allowed extensive interviews with company representatives.

Questions

1 Perform an analysis of the Indonesian spinning industry. You may find it useful to apply Michael Porter's 'five forces' framework. What seem to be the key success factors in this industry?

2 Discuss the environmental trends (economic, political, regulatory, societal, and technological) that affect the Indonesian spinning industry. You may find the following websites useful in tracking trends:

coombs.anu.edu.au/wwwvlpages/indonpages/wwwvl-Indonesia.html
www.asiannet.com/indonesia/
www.asiabiz.com/indonesia/index.html

3 Discuss P.T. BIT's strengths, weaknesses, opportunities, and threats.

4 What business strategy is P.T. BIT following? Is it suitable given the industry environment and company resources?

5 Propose strategic alternatives for P.T. BIT. What actions should they take now? What might they consider five to ten years in the future?

Coca-Cola Indochina Pte. Ltd.

Jeff Barden and Marjorie Lyles

On 18 May 1998, *Vietnam Investment Review* reported that a group of economists had sent a scathing letter to government officials denouncing recent business practices of Coca-Cola Indochina Pte. Ltd. The letter declared, '[Coca-Cola] is taking advantage of its management rights to hand down decisions by itself on dumping and promotion, and this has brought huge losses to the Vietnamese side . . . They are selling their products under cost price and spending excessive amounts on advertising.' Vietnamese editorialists accused Coke of financing the scheme by charging unfairly high transfer prices for the soft drink syrup base, which was imported from the USA. Domestic soft drink producers, who had watched their market shares cut in half since the arrival of Coke and Pepsi, were already complaining about Coke's tactics. However, this letter marked a dangerous escalation in the accusations levelled against Coca-Cola's Vietnamese joint ventures (see Fig. C4).

Now Coke's own business partners and distributors were beginning to feel seriously threatened. Managers from Coke's Ho Chi Minh City partner, Chuong Duong, sent their own letter agreeing that Coke was attempting to post huge losses in an effort to force Chuong Duong to either inject millions of dollars it didn't have or sell out its share of the partnership. Meanwhile, Coke's managers strongly felt that an additional $42.2 million investment in the Ho Chi Minh City joint venture would be critical to its long-term success. On the other hand, they had to be mindful because the public backlash against Coke was reaching a crescendo. Only four years after the lifting of the US trade embargo, the inner workings of the Vietnamese communist government were still a mystery. If government officials felt compelled to react, Coke's $100 million dollar investment in Vietnam could be seriously damaged.

Jeff Barden is a Ph.D. candidate, Fuqua School of Business, Duke University and Marjorie Lyles is Professor of International Strategic Management and Kimball Faculty Fellow, Kelley School of Business, Indiana University.

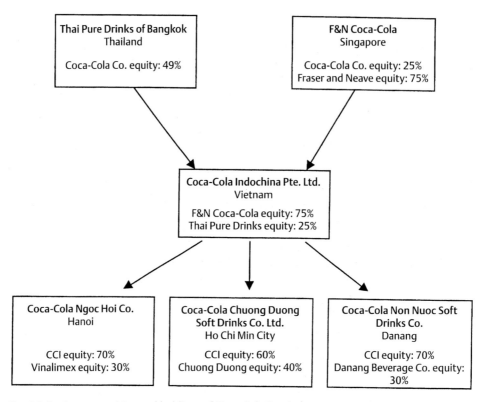

Fig. C4 Equity composition and holdings of Coca-Cola Pte. Ltd.

The Hundred Years Cola War

Today, the Coca-Cola Company and Pepsico, Inc. are the two largest soft drink producers in the world. With bottlers and distributors in nearly every region of the world, the two jointly control over 70 per cent of the world soft drink market.[1] 1997 revenues and operating income for Coke stood at $18.9 billion and $5.0 billion, while Pepsi earned $10.5 billion and $1.2 billion respectively.[2] The majority of profits made by Coke and Pepsi come from the manufacture and sale of soft drink concentrate or syrup base. Syrup is generally sold to either independent or company-owned bottlers to be mixed with carbonated water and sweeteners, packaged, and distributed to retailers, such as grocery stores, convenience stores, or mass merchandisers. Sweetened syrup is also sent directly to restaurants and fast-food chains where it is sold to the public as a fountain drink.

---

[1] *Beverage Digest*, 19 Sept. 1997.
[2] Excludes revenues and income from Pepsi's Frito-Lay food business.

The rivalry between Coke and Pepsi began as early as the late 1800s when both were exclusively sold as fountain drinks. No soft drink brand held a significant market share in the USA or the world until the Second World War. At that time, General Dwight D. Eisenhower fortuitously endorsed Coke as a morale builder for the troops and a symbol of the American way of life, helping the Coca-Cola Company to secure a rare exemption from sugar rationing during the war. By the end of the war, the US government had effectly subsidized dozens of Coca-Cola bottling plants throughout Europe and Asia. After the war, Coke continued its focus on global expansion until nearly two-thirds of its volume was overseas in the 1970s.

Meanwhile, Pepsi chose to focus on the domestic market by aggressively advertising to a younger, hipper 'Pepsi Generation' and targeting the rapidly growing grocery store distribution channel. Rivalry between Pepsi and Coke, which had been steadily increasing with Pepsi's domestic market share, reached a crescendo in 1974 with the confrontational comparative ad campaign, 'the Pepsi Challenge'. Early success of the ads set off one of the most famous price and advertising wars in history, a war that ended in an expensive stalemate. By 1984, Coke and Pepsi were spending over $300 million on worldwide advertising.

As domestic market growth slowed during the late 1980s to about 2 per cent,[3] Coke and Pepsi realized that head-to-head competition could seriously damage them both to the benefit of third-party manufacturers. To the dismay of many second-tier drink producers, the two began clogging distribution channels by signing exclusivity agreements with bottlers and sharing prime display space in major retailers. Coke and Pepsi also eased direct competition between the flagship products by introducing new brands, such as Slice, Cherry Coke, Snapple, PowerAde, and Nordic Mist. However, while the two seemed to be coming to a tacit understanding of the rules of the game in the domestic market, rivalry in foreign markets began heating up where growth rates were expected to reach 7 to 10 per cent.[4]

The transitional and developing regional economies of the world presented the most exciting opportunities for growth (see Table CT7). For example, Coke could double its size by matching per capita consumption of soft drinks in China to that of the USA. 'It might seem a little strange for a 112-year-old company to say, but we believe our business is in its infancy', elaborated Coke CEO, Doug Ivester. The expansion strategies for Coke and Pepsi were relatively simple: get into the emerging markets quickly on a country-by-country basis and make the long-term investments necessary to stay. 'We never leave. We go to these places on a permanent basis', Ivester added.[5]

Recognizing the regulatory and cultural challenges of entering emerging markets, Coke and Pepsi usually chose to create joint-venture bottling agreements with local partners in order to expedite market entry. For example, in South East Asia, Coke used Singapore-based Fraser and Neave, Ltd. to negotiate the establishment of sixteen different bottling facilities in eight different countries. In countries where the establishment of joint ventures proved difficult, the soft drink giants often imported from the closest bottler in

---

[3] S. Foley and D. B. Yoffie, 'Cola Wars Continue: Coke vs. Pepsi in the 1990s', *Harvard Publishing*, 1994.
[4] Value Line, *Soft Drink Industry*, 20 Aug. 1993.
[5] Z. Coleman, 'Asia won't Slow Coke Expansion, CEO Says', *Atlanta Business Chronicle*, 24 Apr. 1998.

Table CT7 World soft drink industry market share

Country	Population (1000's)	8 oz per capita	Coca-Cola (%)	Pepsico (%)	Cadbury-Schweppes
Brazil	162,661	252	52.0	10.0	0.7
Cambodia	10,861	2	40.0	49.1	—
China	1,210,005	19	26.0	13.0	—
Germany	83,536	356	56.0	5.0	0.9
India	952,108	4	57.0	40.1	1.2
Indonesia	206,612	13	85.0	7.0	3.6
Japan	125,450	214	52.0	8.0	1.9
Laos	4,976	4	7.0	90.4	—
Malaysia	19,963	87	62.0	35.9	2.1
Philippines	74,481	156	75.0	14.2	—
Russia	148,178	51	24.7	15.0	3.5
Saudi Arabia	19,409	256	18.0	81.3	0.7
Singapore	3,397	264	61.0	36.0	3.0
Thailand	58,851	118	57.3	41.0	0.2
UK	58,490	337	33.6	12.0	8.1
US	265,563	838	43.1	31.0	14.8
Vietnam	73,977	14	33.0	55.0	3.0
Total Worldwide	5,772,000	119	48.0	22.3	8.5

Source: From *Beverage Digest,* 19 Sept. 1997.

order to build brand image for the future. However, such expansion was not always so easy. For example, Coke was forced to leave India for nineteen years because it refused to divulge its secret syrup-base formula to the government. In addition, the tacitly understood 'rules of the game' in the US market were neither as apparent nor as applicable in the vast emerging markets. In Venezuela, Coke responded to Pepsi's market dominance by buying up Pepsi's largest franchisee in secret negotiations. In India, Pepsi accused Coke's re-established subsidiary of unfairly luring away personnel with aggressive incentives. Such vast opportunity and hardball tactics also seemed present in Vietnam.

Vietnam: The Latest Frontline

Initiated in 1986, 'Doi Moi', Vietnam's economic liberalization plan, had demonstrated significant progress. During the mid-1990s, inflation fell to around 10 per cent while real economic growth grew to almost 10 per cent.[6] As Vietnam's middle class grew in urban

[6] D. A. Rondinelli and Le Ngoc Hung, 'Administrative Restructuring for Economic Transformation in Vietnam', *International Review of Administrative Sciences*, 63, 1997.

areas, foreign direct investment by Western multinational companies increased to over US$8 billion.[7]

By the time the US trade embargo on Vietnam was lifted in 1994, Coke already had a head start in developing the Vietnamese market. In fact, Coca-Cola had been operating in the country for over ten years and was selling over 20 million cases of soda per year when the last Americans were airlifted out of Vietnam in 1975.[8] Coke's operation in Vietnam during the war included bottling plants in Saigon, Danang, and Qui Nhon (see Fig. C5). When Coke could not meet demand, local production was supplemented with imports. Pepsi, on the other hand, was unable to develop local brand recognition at that time, having opened its first bottling plant just months before evacuation. Even after the American evacuation, Coke maintained its popularity as independent profiteers from other parts of South East Asia illegally smuggled the soft drink into the country and sold it for approximately 70 cents a can. In fact, Coke's brand awareness was so strong in 1994 that its initial marketing slogan was best translated as 'Good to see you again!' Although no reliable data existed, analysts estimated that Coke maintained a significant market share in Hanoi while 7up was the most popular soft drink in Vietnam in 1993. Other popular local brands Tribeco Cola, Festi, and Saigon Cola also held significant market shares along with soft drink alternatives such as fruit drinks, iced tea, and soya milk.

As the likelihood of the US lifting its trade embargo on Vietnam increased in the early 1990s, both Coke and Pepsi began establishing relationships and ramping up marketing preparations for entry into the Vietnamese market. As required by Vietnamese law, the soft drink giants would have to enter into joint ventures in order to bottle soft drinks locally. Initially, both companies began courting the same local bottler, Ho Chi Minh City (Saigon)-based International Beverage Company (IBC). Formed in 1991, IBC was a fifty-fifty joint venture between a consortium of Vietnamese state-owned enterprises, including Tribeco, and Singapore-based Machondray & Company. IBC had already signed an agreement to produce Cadbury-Schweppes products in 1992. Ultimately, Pepsi won out in negotiations with IBC. IBC's managers attributed their decision to Coke's injection of several unfavourable conditions into negotiations, such as equity and distribution requirements. However, Pepsi's success was most likely due to the fact that Machondray & Company was already working with Pepsi in the Philippines.

Pepsi came off the starting line quickly, starting domestic production in Vietnam within hours of President Clinton's announcement of the end of trade restrictions. Pepsi chose to immediately access Vietnam's market through its established, ad hoc distribution network of around 1,000 small, privately owned distribution agents who supplied smaller retail outlets. The remaining 20 per cent of production would be sold directly to larger retail outlets such as schools and fast-food restaurants. On the day after production began, Pepsi marketers set up a huge inflatable can under the red flags marking the sixty-fourth anniversary of the country's Communist Party and handed out 40,000 bottles of Pepsi from the first day's production as free samples to a frenzied crowd of thirsty Vietnamese. On the following Friday, Pepsi had launched a TV advertising campaign featuring the popular Miss Vietnam, Ha Kieu Anh, and proclaiming Pepsi as the 'Choice of the

[7] 'Foreign Investment in Vietnam Continues to Fall', *Japan Economic Newswire*, 4 July 1998.
[8] Prendergast, M., *For God, Country, and Coca-Cola*, Touchstone Books, 1997.

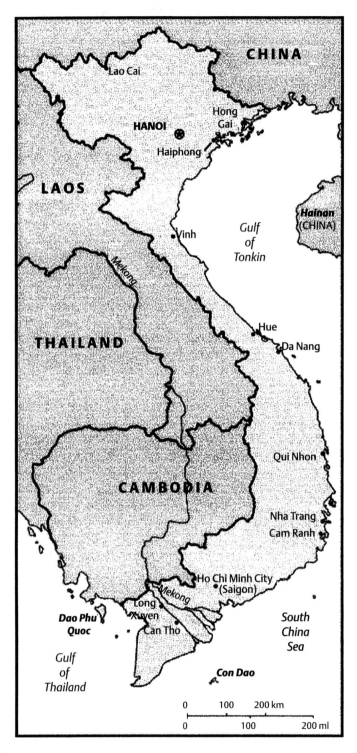

Fig. C5 Vietnam map

New Generation'. In spite of a minor problem with the carbon dioxide, which made the first batches of Pepsi taste funny, Pepsi's launch was a success.

Coke's response was delayed, but aggressive. Coca-Cola initiated its own television advertising campaign just a week after Pepsi's started. Yet, despite shipping over 6 tons of promotional signs to Vietnam, Coke's overall campaign was quiet compared to Pepsi's. By late 1994, Pepsi had risen from relative obscurity to claim a 55 per cent market share while Coke's share was only 39 per cent.[9]

While Coke failed to strike a deal with IBC, it did succeed in partnering three other regional bottlers during the next few years. Until production arrangements could be made, Coke supplied the market with imports. Without the competition for partners from Pepsi in Hanoi, Coca-Cola Indochina (CCI) quickly signed a government-approved Memorandum of Understanding with state-owned enterprise Vinalimex (Vietnam Food Export-Import Corporation) to jointly build and operate the 'greenfield' Ngoc Hoi plant 16 kilometres west of the city. Coca-Cola initially invested $20.4 million dollars in exchange for a 70 per cent stake in the joint venture. Production was set to begin in 1995 and initial capacity was planned to be about 36 million litres. In mid-1996, Coca-Cola Indochina invested an additional $15 million in the Ngoc Hoi joint venture, doubling capacity and adding several delivery trucks. Cans were eventually to be supplied locally by another joint venture between Vinalimex, US-based Crown Cork & Seal Co., and Swire Pacific Co. Ltd. of Great Britain. Coke officials boasted that once the can plant was built and running, 90 per cent of Coca-Cola Ngoc Hoi's raw materials, including sugar and packaging, would be supplied locally. Unfortunately, construction of the can plant was delayed until complicated land-usage procedures could be settled and geological surveys conducted.

CCI's negotiations in Ho Chi Minh City did not go as smoothly as negotiations in Hanoi. In 1993, Coke came to a preliminary agreement with state-owned enterprise Chuong Duong; however, it was nullified when the State Committee for Cooperation and Investment rejected the plan. The two primary reasons given for the rejection were that Chuong Duong was only given a 35 per cent share of the joint venture and production was to be done in a refitted plant in the centre of the city. The objections were eventually overcome in 1995 when CCI agreed to give Chuong Duong a 40 per cent share and plans to build the plant in an authorized 'industrial zone'. Whereas Coca-Cola contributed $48.75 million in cash and assets for its 60 per cent share, Chuong Duong contributed the 30-year land-use rights of a 6 hectare lot in the industrial zone for its share. Chuong Duong, run by the Ministry of Light Industry, was in fact Coca-Cola's partner prior to 1975; however, at that time it was known as Brasserie Glacières Indochine and was owned by French investors.

---

[9] 'Pepsi Claims Lead in Cola Wars', *Vietnam Investment Review*, 18 Dec. 1994.

Aggressive Advertising or Cultural Pollution?

In late 1995, Coke and Pepsi's battle for brand recognition in the new market intensified as both spent millions of US dollars on marketing. Vietnamese cities were covered with banners, large electric signs and brightly coloured street sellers. Coke became the second largest advertiser on Vietnamese television. Both companies sought to associate their drink with leisurely lifestyles by sponsoring sports, cultural events, and concerts. Local soft drink producers were overwhelmed, prompting one manager to observe, 'It's amazing. These signs are really expensive. They can spend US$350 for the entrance of a tiny [shop]. I do not think they can expect any return from their investment before two years, but they have a very long term strategy.' Two years after Coke and Pepsi entered the market, local soft drink producers had lost an estimated 60 to 70 per cent of their market share, forcing them to redirect efforts into niche strategies like developing rural markets away from the deluge of Coke and Pepsi signs.[10]

In early 1996, the Vietnamese government also became concerned with the growing number of aggressive American advertising campaigns. In an effort to crackdown on 'cultural pollution' from the West, officials ordered police to paint over many of the billboards. After some pressure from investors, the government softened its position by requiring advertisers to reduce the amount of writing on signs in English while increasing the size of the Vietnamese words. In another backlash against Western marketing practices, the local government of Ho Chi Minh City banned a Coca-Cola contest in which matching sets of bottle caps could be collected to win a mountain bike. In response to reports of Vietnamese children spending large amounts of money on sodas to find the rare bottle cap that completed the winning set, a director at the Trade Department described the contest as a lottery-related promotion considered 'deceiving and cheating, fomenting an unhealthy, over-consuming trend'. All advertising had to be submitted to and approved by local advertising boards. Anything deemed to be too sexy, provocative, or disrespectful would be denied. Local industry sources claimed that roughly one-third of all ads were rejected.

The Foreign Exchange Cash Crunch

Procurement from international sources and repatriation of capital from Vietnamese sales were particularly difficult problems for Coca-Cola Indochina because foreign currencies were not readily available in exchange for the Vietnamese dong. Some inputs, like sugar and packaging materials, could be obtained locally, but other raw materials and equipment had to be imported by Coke's joint ventures, particularly before supporting can and bottle factories were built near the new bottling plants. The problem was so bad

---

[10] 'Local Firms seek Protection from Overseas Brands', *Vietnam Investment Review*, 3 June 1996.

that some other multinationals in Vietnam even had to default on fixed loan payments denominated in foreign currencies. Coke could apply for a conversion licence, which would allow the company to purchase dollars directly from the Vietnamese government. Unfortunately, the hurdles for obtaining the licence, including annual tax payments over 100 billion dong (US$8 million) and high minimum employment numbers, were insurmountably high. Coke could also apply for a revolving line of credit with a foreign bank in order to cover accounts payable; however, that required Coke to assume some risk by providing a letter of guarantee to cover the Vietnamese partner. In addition, Coke had to consider the cost of holding more debt denominated in foreign currency, particularly if inflation began to rise again. Devaluation of the dong was already costing Coca-Cola Indochina's partners a great deal in foreign exchange losses.

Coke Goes on the Offensive

At the end of 1996, Coke raised the stakes in the battle for local market share by introducing a new 300 ml. bottle at the old 200 ml. bottle price. Local producers, already bruised by the entrance of foreign competition, immediately cried foul, accusing Coke of 'price dumping'. Pham Hong Chuong, managing director of Tribeco Saigon, elaborated, 'Coca-Cola intentionally sells their product lower than cost to try to dominate the market and finish off domestic producers'. Phan Nhu Tam, Director of Festi Hanoi, went a step further by suggesting that 'the government needs to force foreign companies to obey the masterplan'. Coke managers adamantly denied selling below cost and claimed Coke only had a 35 per cent market share.[11] However, even IBC's general director Pham Phu Ngoc Trai, who has been described as the most experienced man in the Vietnamese soft drink industry, declared that Coca-Cola Indochina must be selling the 300 ml. product at a loss. Among the chorus of protests, Vu Ngoc Khanh, vice-director of Tribeco Hanoi, called for government price controls to prevent the practice. Under the legislation of the time, price dumping of any kind was technically legal.

Reactions by government officials to the price-dumping accusations were mixed. While it was not immediately clear whether Coke was making a loss on the new product, Coke did raise prices on the new product by 10 per cent six months after introducing it. In addition, an independent study by Nielsen SRG Vietnam placed Coke's market share at 52 per cent.[12] Coke's move into the top spot was also confirmed by IBC's studies (see Table CT8). Some officials recognized that price promotions were an accepted practice in the international business environment while others promised that 'The government will enact documents to deal with controlling monopolies and fighting against unfair pricing-oriented competition'. In spite of the publicized row, no officials made direct accusations against Coke, but all agreed that the government would deal firmly with any business practices deemed unfair. In February of 1997, Vietnamese Prime Minister Vo Van

[11] 'Bottlers Call for "price dumping" law', *Vietnam Investment Review*, 16 Dec. 1996.
[12] 'Coca-Cola pips Pepsi in Battle of the Soft Drink Giants', *Vietnam Investment Review*, 24 Mar. 1997.

Table CT8 Vietnam statistics, 1997

	Ho Chi Minh City	Hanoi	Danang	Cantho (Mekong Delta)	Vietnam Total
Population (MM)	11	34	7	12	78
Urban GDP per capita in US$ (Rural)	920 (348)	700 (180)	475 (166)	230	296
Pepsi market share	41%	11%	27%	32%	30%
Coca-Cola market share	35%	65%	43%	20%	36%

Source: IBC.

Kiet announced that, with the exception of special projects, no more licences for joint ventures would be granted in the soft drink industry.

According to some, market share may not have been the only motivation for Coke's price cuts. A Vietnamese newspaper reported in early 1997 that a coalition of Coke wholesalers had accused Coca-Cola Ngoc Hoi of trying to bankrupt them. About 20 of Coke's 46 wholesalers contended that the joint venture dumped inventories of the 200 ml. bottles on them at the original price just days before announcing the new, lower-priced 300 ml. bottle. Wholesalers then said that Ngoc Hoi added insult to injury when it began requiring them to cover the cost of getting soft drinks from the joint-venture's warehouse to their own inventories, contrary to previous practice. Joint venture trucks were then allegedly used to sell the larger-sized products elsewhere at lower prices. Eventually, after the bitter public skirmish, Ngoc Hoi began compensating wholesalers for thousands of dollars for losses incurred as a result of the price promotion.

Within the year, Coca-Cola would find itself embroiled in another public exchange with its own partner, Chuong Duong. In a November 1997 report, Chuong Duong stated that the Ho Chi Minh City joint venture had lost $2 million in the past year. The report also claimed that Coke's marketing expenditures made up more than 10 per cent of total expenditures. This was more than twice the maximum of 5 per cent permitted by Vietnamese law. Coke managers responded by pointing out that losses were expected during the second full year of operation and that sales had increased dramatically, putting the joint venture in a prime position to earn future profits.

Despite the losses and disputes surrounding Coca-Cola's two joint ventures, the Vietnamese government approved Coca-Cola's third joint venture with the Danang Beverage Company in January of 1998. Plans included a new $25 million bottling plant which was to be built on a 4 hectare plot adjacent to Danang Beverage Company's existing facility. Sources within the government say the plan was approved on the basis of a feasibility study projecting an internal rate of return of 17.78 per cent, after-tax profits of $7.85 million per year and a payback period on the investment of 5.5 years. The report also estimated that the new plant would create 300 new jobs for locals.

As 1998 wore on, accumulating losses in the joint ventures began to take their toll on the patience of Vietnamese managers despite assurances by Coke managers that profitability would be reached by 2001. Under Vietnam's traditional economic culture, managers could literally be jailed for showing significant losses. While Coca-Cola Indochina managers refused to divulge exact figures, analysts estimated that combined losses for all of Coke's joint ventures had reached around $13 million. The cash-poor Vietnamese state-owned enterprises were not capable of injecting any more capital, yet re-capitalization of the order of several million dollars was vital to short-term liquidity and long-term success.

When the economists' letter charging Coca-Cola Indochina with intentionally trying to force out Vietnamese partners was published in May, Coke managers knew they were going to have some tough decisions to make. On the one hand, they could simply pro-vide the needed capital and then hope to renegotiate the best deal they could for a greater share of the joint venture. On the other hand, Coke could simply sell out its share and look for better places to invest in the world. Finally, Coke could take its chances by insisting that Chuog Duong provide the needed cash or sell out. In any event, Coke would need the blessing of the Vietnamese government.

Questions

1 What are the roles and contributions of Coca-Cola and the local partners in these joint ventures? How sustainable is this arrangement?

2 What are the primary factors in the Vietnamese business environment that should influence Coca-Cola's decision?

3 How should Coca-Cola approach the Vietnamese government?

4 How do other constituents in the Vietnamese soft drink industry (i.e. Pepsi, local competitors, Coke's distributors) view Coca-Cola Indochina? How should they respond to CCI's recent manoeuvres?

5 What is Coca-Cola's best course of action?

Telecommunications in Thailand: The Mobile Phone Sector

Shaukat Ali

Introduction

South East Asia is the fastest-growing region for telecommunications and Thailand has been identified as a key market. According to Teleglobe, the US-based international carrier, Thailand is the third largest communication market in South East Asia. By the year 2000,[1] Asian mobile phone users are estimated to number 560 million. Total demand for mobile phones worldwide will be about 1,040 million users[2]. Prior to the Asian financial crises, the Thai economy expanded significantly, with annual growth rates of approximately 6 to 8 per cent.[3] As Thailand's economy grew during the 1980s and the first half of the 1990s, it became clear that developments in infrastructure were creating a bottleneck and hindering industrial growth. Various governments, buoyed by a favourable economy, initiated reforms in an attempt to meet these demands by giving priority to developing the telecommunications sector. As a result, by 1994 Thailand's telecommunications industry more than doubled in size.

The Telephone Organization of Thailand (TOT) aimed to increase the number of telephone lines to no fewer than ten lines per 100 inhabitants as well as upgrading the quality of telecommunications services to international standards. Because of the importance of these changes and the realization on the part of the government that huge financial resources are required in such an undertaking, it invited the private sector to participate.

The private sector, realizing the potential profits, responded with enthusiasm and over

Shaukat Ali is Senior Lecturer at the Wolverhampton Business School, University of Wolverhampton.

[1] The authorities set a nominal date of 2000 for the completion of certain tasks. Due to the continuing political uncertainty and slower than expected recovery of the Thai economy, none of the deadlines has been met.

[2] *Bangkok Post Economic Review*, 1996.

[3] *Bangkok Bank Quarterly Report*, 1st quarter, 1997.

a period of some ten years, Thailand has established a telecommunication infrastructure that, while still lagging behind developed countries, is thought to be helping, rather than hindering, economic growth. As a result, the telecommunications infrastructure includes the fixed line network (using optical fibre, land-lines, submarine cables, and satellites); Data communication (Datanet offers point-to-point connection and broadcasting services. Main users of this services are government departments, state-owned enterprises, and international companies, including providers of news services); television and radio broadcasting;[4] information technology (advanced applications such as teleshopping, telebanking, LAN/WAN networks, email systems, as well as smart cards) and the mobile network.[5]

This case study explores the mobile phone sector in Thailand and examines the strategies of the main players in the industry. It also focuses on the impact on and response of, these firms to the Asian financial crisis that began in Thailand in 1997 and engulfed most of South East Asia.

Thailand Telecom Market

The main established players in the Thai Telecom market are Shinawatra, Telecom Asia, Ucom, Jasmine, TT&T, while relative newcomers include players such as Loxley, Samart, Comlink, Sahaviriya, Future Hi-Tech, and Lenso (paging services), who will compete with each other to get the various government-conceded contracts.

Thailand's telecommunication policy and its regulation is managed by a myriad of governmental bodies consisting of the Ministry of Transport and Communication (MOTC), the Post and Telegraph Department (PTD), the Telephone Organization of Thailand (TOT), and the Communications Authority of Thailand (CAT).[6]

Mobile Phone Industry

In Thailand, the mobile phone was first introduced in 1986 by TOT (the NMT 470 Nordic Mobile Telephone), followed by the AMPS-800A (Advance Mobile Phone System-Band *A*) introduced by CAT. Both of these were analogue systems.

The Telephone Organization of Thailand and the Communications Authority of Thailand recognized that the key factors in the development of the telecommunications

---

[4] In addition to the five state-owned national stations, the subscription-based stations (IBC, Thai Sky TV, UTV), and a number of free to-air stations (TV3, 5, 7, 9, 11, ITV), new licences have been granted to various cable operators. There are also 76 radio broadcasting stations in Bangkok with 401 channels throughout the country.

[5] Analogue mobile phone systems are provided by the Telephone Organization of Thailand (TOT), the Communications Authority of Thailand (CAT), while both analogue and digital mobile phone systems are provided by Advanced Information Services (AIS) and Total Access Communications (TAC).

[6] The PTD, TOT, and CAT are under the supervision of the MOTC.

infrastructure were ample sources of funds and advanced technology. In line with government policy that encouraged the private sector to join with the public sector, both in expanding the main services and especially in value-added services, they allocated the mobile phone services concessions to Advanced Info Service (AIS) of the Shinawatra group in 1990 and to Total Access Communications (TAC) of the UCOM group in 1991.

Current Market Situation

For numerous reasons (business needs, shortage of fixed lines, feeling of eliteness, a way of being reachable in Bangkok's notorious traffic jams, and a generally convenient way to keep in touch), the mobile phone has become very popular in Thailand. There were also other factors such as overall economic prosperity, the growing unequal wealth distribution, the growth of suburbs around Bangkok, such as Nontaburi, Samutprakarn, and Patumthani. There were also opportunities and potential in the provinces because of the shortage of fixed lines and the relatively low air charges for long-distance calls on mobile phones. All these factors contributed and will contribute, for some time, to the growth of the mobile phone industry.

At present, mobile phone services have developed and adjusted to suit each group of user. Improvements in efficiency and reduced costs of services, as well as the adaptation of analogue systems to digital systems that can deliver messages, visual, and voice have further increased their popularity and use. Moreover, improvements in service and other value-added components better serve the needs of each group of users.

Most subscribers in Thailand are still using analogue handsets which account for 70 per cent of the total subscriber base. This is due to the limited geographic coverage offered by digital systems as a consequence of limited coverage of digital networks as well as handset prices. During 1996, the growth in new cellular subscribers had not shown any noticeable slowdown even though economic indicators such as credit growth and vehicle sales had undergone a marked slowdown. It was thought that growth in the subscriber base would continue through continued discounting of air-time charges and handset prices. The temporary promotions, which the market was already used to, will, it is thought, increasingly become a permanent future of the operating landscape. As a pointer to the feature direction of the industry, TAC, with its significantly lower handset prices and aggressive promotion campaign (e.g. capping air-time charge at 600 baht per month), had been eating into AIS's market share in both analogue and digital systems.

TAC's analogue system added more monthly new subscribers than AIS since it started to expand its analogue coverage upcountry in late 1995. Moreover, prices of handsets under the TAC analogue were falling faster than those of AIS (around 15,000 baht) and proved to be best sellers in the provinces. On the digital side, the price of PCN handsets (under TAC and service providers) fell 33 per cent from close to 40,000 baht at the beginning of 1995 to only 26,900 baht at the end of 1997, while the price of GSM handsets (under the Advance system) fell only 13 per cent from the same level to 35,000.

The mobile phone industry in Thailand consists of four main operators (two public and two private) who currently provide mobile phone services in Thailand. There are two mobile phone systems, analogue and digital. The analogue system has already been in operation for almost a decade. A chronic problem of the system is that the capacity of the system continuously lags behind demand and needs. This results in poor performance of the mobile telephone systems, because of a narrow radio frequency band. Capacity problems are concentrated in Bangkok. Sometimes it is difficult to gain access to a frequency and some calls are cut off. Most problems are solved through the expansion of the number of base stations.

There are four analogue systems, namely:

- NMT 470 operated by TOT. The system only has 50,000 subscribers, mainly due to the limitation of phone numbers and because the handsets are rather large. TOT plans to reduce prices and will target customers in provincial areas.

- NMT 900 operated by AIS. The system enjoys high sales due to its large number of base stations—approximately 500—with wider transmission zones than TAC. This has led AIS to capture the highest market share. In 1997 sales of NMT 900 and GSM mobile phones were around 550,000 but dropped below 450,000 in 1998.

- AMPS 800-B operated by TAC. This system has a better quality in the cities than the NMT 900 system. Since 1994, incoming calls with TAC are no longer charged.

- AMPS 800-A operated by CAT. This system is only used by government employees and government institutions.

There are two digital mobile operating systems in Thailand. Digital GSM 900 operated by AIS allows easy frequency management and maintenance, more capacity, and more importantly, a lower investment than analogue systems. But for customers it also has some major advantages, such as better voice quality and use for various value-added services such as fax integration, data communications, short messages, international use, vehicle remote tracking, calling waiting, calling holding, call transfer, and voice mailbox. AIS has tried to differentiate its analogue and digital systems through the introduction of new value-added services, such as roaming possibilities with Hong Kong.[7]

PCN 1800 is operated by TAC. Each handset costs between 19,900 and 41,500 baht. Digital phone concessionaires are quarrelling about whose system is better. TAC's PCN 1800 system has 25,000 subscribers, whereas AIS's GSM 900 system has fewer than 20,000 subscribers (which is much lower than expected). PCN covers a wider area than GSM and its costs are 10 to 15 per cent cheaper than GSM handsets. PCN subscribers do not have to travel to Bangkok to register their handset. All these factors suggest that PCN is going to be the leading system. Another factor which will be of influence is the availability of value-added services on the systems. TAC also has made roaming deals to set up a roaming network for its PCN 1800 to cover thirty countries worldwide.

The advantage of an analogue mobile phone system like NMT 900 over GSM is that

---

[7] Roaming means that a subscriber can use the same phone, with the same phone number, anywhere in the world.

they offer better coverage areas at a lower price. NMT 900 is good for local service while GSM is better for international use.

Table CT9 shows the current market position of the main cellular phone providers.

Table CT9 Cellular phone market share, January, 2000

Operator	System	No. of subscribers
TAC	AMP 800	625,883
AIS	NMT 900	720,000
AIS	GSM 900	440,000
TAC	PCN 1800	434,137
TOT	NMT 470	33,612
CAT	CDMA 800	5,000

Source: Bangkok Post.

The Main Private Operators

The main private players in the mobile industry are the Shinawatra group (owners of AIS), and the UCOM Group (operators of TAC).

Shinawatra, a Thai company, originally a service provider, is developing itself more and more as a systems integrator. Its main activities include broadcasting (IBC), satellite provision (Thaicom), cellular mobile phones (GSM and NMT 900), and data communications. The Shinawatra group includes Shinawatra Satellite Co., owner of the 30-year-old Thaicom Satellite BTO[8] concession (Thaicom), as well as operating the NMT 900 cellular mobile phone system, and owning the concession for publication of Bangkok telephone directories. The Shinawatra group recently signed a contract to develop the telecommunications infrastructure in Laos. The agreement calls for the installation of 20,000 domestic and 500 international circuits, a cellular mobile network, and paging and television broadcasting services. Shinawatra also operates the most used paging system Phonelink 152 under a concession from the TOT. Phonelink has 310,000 subscribers.

The UCOM group, owned by the Bencharongkakul family, was originally a Thai engineering company with very close links with the military, more recently it has increasingly become a service provider. Their main business is cellular mobile phones. TAC is responsible for more than half of UCOM's revenues. UCOM is also close to Motorola, which holds an equity stake in UCOM. Ucom is also one of the participants in Motorola's iridium project (the satellite mobile phone) and negotiated exclusive selling rights for Motorola equipment in Thailand. Because of the high investments needed in PCN and iridium projects, UCOM's philosophy has been to concentrate on the Thai market.

---

[8] Under the BTO contract, the concessionaire must build its own cellular network and then transfer the ownership of the complete network to either TOT or CAT. After the transfer, the company starts to operate within the concession period under the conditions of revenue sharing with the concessionaires (both TOT and CAT).

Thai Mobile Phone Industry Structure

Thailand's mobile phone industry is structured around a duopoly industry, consisting of only two private operators, AIS and TAC. The reasons for this duopoly are mostly governmental. First, any private company wishing to invest in the mobile phone business must purchase a concession from one of the Thai government institutions, such as TOT and CAT under the BOT (build–transfer–operate) system. This automatically becomes a barrier to entry for other newcomers in the market. Another major disadvantage of a BOT contract is that it is limited only to Thai investors so there is no opportunity offered to foreign telecommunication companies who have very advanced technology and more financial strength compared with Thai telecom companies.

The duopoly of the Thai mobile phone industry is becoming an obstacle to the development of a basic telecommunications infrastructure in Thailand and restricting opportunity for other private sector operators to fully provide telecommunication services. The lack of a competitive environment will not motivate the two operators to improve the efficiency of their services while it is allowing them to gain monopoly power to set high prices.

In line with global privatization trends to improve the efficiency of public utilities, particularly in developing countries, the Thai government, too, has recognized the need for a more flexible. business climate and thus, for deregulation. The Thai government lacks the financial resources to deal with the new demands and, instead of the muddling-through strategy of issuing BOT contracts to private partners, has decided to liberalize the telecommunications market according to a master plan. Under the plan, operators would be put in three categories—service or network providers, and those handling both businesses. The national telecommunications committee would determine the conditions for each group. Services currently run on concession from the state agencies would be turned into ventures with joint shareholdings.

The master plan also envisages the privatization of the two state-run telecom agencies—TOT and CAT—and the establishment of a regulatory body called the National Telecommunications Board (NTB). The plan is seen as honouring Thailand's commitment to the World Trade Organization to deregulate the telecom market. But delays mean Thailand will be ready to liberalize in 1999, a year later than intended, and to allow foreign participation in 2006.

Operations and Marketing Strategies

AIS, the subsidiary of the Shinawatra group, was established in 1986 and registered on the SET (Stock Exchange of Thailand) in 1991. The major shareholder is Shinawatra group which holds 57.7 per cent. In 1990, AIS received a 20-year concession, under the BOT scheme, to operate mobile phone NMT 900 from the Telephone Organization of

Thailand. Under the concession, AIS must share its revenue with TOT. For the first five years, it would give TOT 15 per cent of its earning before tax and this amount would increase 5 per cent every five years. In 1994, AIS launched the Digital GSM onto the market. The strength of AIS is that it has strong political connections through the founder of the Shinawatra group, Dr Taksin Shinawatra, a former cabinet minister, and friend of prime ministers of various parties. In terms of technology, AIS has no specific suppliers, neither does it cooperate with any specific foreign company. Rather, it uses bidding processes to select the most appropriate suppliers who can meet the specifications that AIS requires. After selecting a supplier, AIS hands over turnkey project responsibilities to the supplier, who will install the network for AIS. On completion of the project, the supplier provides training and know-how to AIS employees, who then operate the network. Maintenance requirements and repairs, should the system fail, are carried out by the supplier.

From AIS's viewpoint, it's not necessary to develop its own technology and it doesn't have to invest in research and development (R & D). Buying technology from suppliers saves money, because the suppliers have experience and know-how, both of which are important since the concession period is very limited. Thus, if AIS had spent time in developing its own technology, it would, most likely, not have been as successful in exploiting business opportunities so quickly and so profitably.

As an example, for its analogue system NMT 900, AIS hired Nokia from Finland and Ericsson from Switzerland to install the mobile phone network. Nokia installed the mobile telephone exchange (MTX), radio-based station (RBS), and other communication equipment. Ericsson was responsible for the system expansion. Similarly, for the digital system, AIS hired Nokia, Ericsson, and Motorola to install the network.

The other main player is TAC, a wholly owned subsidiary of the UCOM Group. Established in 1989, TAC accounts for more than half of UCOM's revenues. Initially TAC was granted a 15-year concession from CAT for its AMPS 800-B mobile phone. Later, TAC, planning for a listing on the SET, asked CAT to extend the concession period from 15 to 22 years in order to meet SET rules. Under the terms of the concession, in the first four years of TAC's operation, it had to give CAT 12 per cent of its revenue before tax, for the next ten years it has to give 25 per cent, and 30 per cent for the remaining years. UCOM has a close relationship with Motorola (USA) which holds an equity stake in UCOM. Thus, Motorola and UCOM are strategic allies, with Motorola providing technical support to UCOM.

AIS entered the mobile phone market a few years ahead of TAC, gaining first-mover advantages, especially in gaining market share over TAC. Furthermore, in the beginning, as with fixed-line phones, TAC used seven-digit numbers for its phones, which meant it soon ran out of numbers for its subscribers. Another major weakness of TAC is that subscribers have to pay for both incoming and outgoing calls while AIS subscribers pay only for outgoing calls. To remedy these problems, TAC asked for changes to its concession specification, requesting to change its line numbers to be similar to AIS (01-xxx-xxxx) and to allow it to charge only for outgoing calls. Currently, both AIS and TAC are defending their respective market shares and position, with neither gaining real competitive advantage over the other. We shall discuss their competitive strategies later on.

Both AIS and TAC operate under the same regulatory agencies and rely on similar suppliers. They also have the same target customer market. In the global telecommunications industry, there are only a few main suppliers in the world (such as Nokia, Ericsson, Motorola, Siemens, and so on), thus both AIS and TAC have to deal with similar suppliers.

The key issue in the external environment that both companies have had to be aware of is the Information Technology Agreement (ITA) that Thailand and members of World Trade Organization (WTO) ratified at the beginning of 1997. Under the ITA, Thailand and every country member would have to open the country for foreign investment in information technology sectors. This will end the monopoly power of the Thai telecommunications industry and is likely to become the main threat to AIS and TAC in the very near future.

Product Strategy

The mobile phone is a product that has unique characteristics and/or brand identification for which significant groups of buyer are habitually willing to make a special purchasing effort. This entails purchasing only at WorldPhone store[9], Telewiz stores (of AIS), or from other distributors and individual mobile phone stores in department stores or shopping centres.

Initially, mobile phones were bulky and cumbersome, and viewed as specialty items; as technology developed, phones have become small in size and lighter, some weighing only 200 g. adding to their popularity, and have become more or less commodities. To differentiate their products, companies have used various added features such as use of numerous colours to attract the different segments.

At present, there is a serious problem of misuse of phones with some subscribers tuning the receivers illegally to make phone calls on other people's numbers. Consequently, some customers have been asked to pay more than 200,000 baht per month without using their phone. Both AIS and TAC are aware of these security problems and how these reduce consumer confidence. In response, they have attempted to try and adjust their systems as well as developing protection methods in cooperation with the police and the Communication Authority of Thailand. Specific remedies taken include international call barring without permission of the owner, the use of credit limits whereby consumers can set a monthly budget in order to limit the number of calls and to be secure from illegal usage, the use of pin numbers for identification purposes, and so on.

---

[9] A TAC-owned outlet. AI is a distributor of many mobile brands such as Nokia, Ericsson, Panasonic, Dancall, Hitachi, Philips, Sahaviriya, Benefon, and NEC. UCOM is the main distributor under the Motorola name and other brands such as TELLABS, HARIS, VMX, CELWAVE, etc.

Price Strategy

Due to the very short life cycle, with some models having a lifespan of less than six months, price and promotion competition has been fierce, with various segments targeted differently. For the high-end market, amounting to 20 per cent of the total market, the target consumers includes businessmen and image-conscious individuals, who place great emphasis on reliability, size, price, and so on. The price range is approximately 30,000 baht upwards. For the mid-end market, amounting to 40 per cent of the total market, the target consumers include mid-ranking executives and white-collar staff, both of whom look for quality of product as well as reasonable price. The price range is approximately[10] 20,000 to 30,000 baht. The lower end of the market, amounting to 40 per cent of the total market, consists of price-conscious consumers, such as workers and students. For this segment, the emphasis is on durability and utility, so the products are priced in the range 12,000 to 20,000 baht.

Place Strategy

Due to fierce competition in the mobile phone industry, and the lack of alternative, existing distribution infrastructure, each company has had to create and expand its own distribution channels, both in retailing and wholesaling. Main channel distribution outlets include Telecom World, Telewiz, Smart shops, IEC, department stores, and computer branches.

More recently, largely due to the sharp rise in cellular mobile telephone subscribers and paging users, a number of new telecommunication retailer branches have opened. The main players in the paging and cellular market have set up their own retail channel for strategic reasons. The retail market can therefore be characterized as a fast-growing market with an increasing number of players and still relatively high prices, although these can, and will, come under pressure in the future. The increasing competition and the domestic production of equipment will, in due course, lead to lower prices. Some retailers, such as IEC, are trying to stay ahead of the increasing competition in the retail market of telecommunication products by selling all mobile phone systems (NMT 470, AMPS 800, NMT 900, GSM 900, and PCN 1800). IEC is trying to set up a leasing firm, called Q-zone, so that people on middle incomes can afford a mobile telephone. IEC will set up a joint venture with TAC to set up a Q-zone.

Telecom World is a retail outlet of UCOM. It distributes mainly Motorola equipment largely because it has exclusive rights to sell Motorola equipment. Since June 1995, Worldphone shops also provide fax and air-courier services. TAC, a subsidiary of UCOM,

---

[10] These prices are prior to the devaluation. Due to constant exchange rate fluctuations and promotional activity, it is not possible to give accurate figures for recent years.

works together with Federal Express. Worldphone had 100 outlets in 1994, of which 27 were owned by TAC and 63 by its franchisees.

Shinawatra's Telewiz sells only 300 models. Shinawatra's GSM mobile phones are sold by Technical Telecom Co., New Technology, and Shinawatra Telewiz Co. Jasmine's Smart Shops provide various telecommunication products and services, including consultation to retail customers. In 1994, ten shops were opened, with a further thirty predicted for 1997. Central department stores such as Robinsons and Central Department, wholesalers such as Siam Makro, and specific telecommunication and computer retail channels such as Sahaviriya also sell a lot of telephone equipment.

Promotion Strategy

In the mobile industry, companies have to implement various types of advertising and promotion strategies. For advertising, the companies utilize all media types such as television, newspapers, magazines, cinema, and outdoor. Newspapers rank number one in terms of total spending, followed by television and outdoor, magazines and cinema respectively. From the total advertising industry perspective, the mobile industry is considered to be ranked fourth, with spending amounting to some 1.4 billion baht annually.

Short-term sales promotions to encourage purchase or sales of a product or service form an increasingly important component of the promotion strategy. Incentives include free IBC Cable TV subscription, free calls for 120 minutes per month, free IBC instalment, free calls of double the amount of the previous month, free calls in the same area, and so on. For the mobile industry, personal selling is not popular and rarely used.

The Asian Economic Crisis

The Asian financial crisis, about which much has been written, began in Thailand in 1997 and spread to Indonesia, Malaysia, and other South East Asian countries.

In the case of Thailand, the reasons for the crisis were many and deep-rooted.[11] First, huge deficits in the current account (the deficit was 8% of GDP in 1995 and 7.9% in 1996; in addition, the export growth rate decreased from 23.6% in 1995 to zero in 1996) caused the country to rely heavily on external borrowing. In 1997, the IMF estimated that the country's external debt was about $99 billion, or about 55.5 per cent of GDP. The majority of this debt, privately incurred, was estimated at $71.7 billion. On the other hand, the external debt of the public sector was $27.3 billion, making Thailand one of the least publicly indebted countries.

Phatra Research Institute reported that the average debt–equity ratio of listed non-

---

[11] Thammavit Terdudomthan, *Bangkok Post*, 1997.

finance sector companies increased from 1.58 in 1994 to 1.98 in 1996, and the ratio of earnings before tax and interest payments to liabilities decreased from 14.2 per cent in 1994 to 10.7 per cent in 1996, making many firms vulnerable.

The second major cause was the collapse of the property sector. This sector began to boom in the late 1980s. With the liberalization of international capital flows after the introduction of the Bangkok International Banking Facilities in March 1993, the sector grew rapidly. By 1995, an oversupply of housing emerged, which became into a major problem. With loans increasingly expensive and hard to get under the central bank's squeeze on lending, the sector began to collapse in 1996. The sector's debts totalled around 800 billion baht in 1996. Debts of the 26 share-market-listed developers had been put at 200 billion baht the year before. The slump in the property sales market and the lending squeeze worsened developers' cash-flow troubles and increased defaults on interest payments. For example, in February 1997, Somprasong Land Plc defaulted on interest payments on euro-convertible debentures worth $80 million. Many finance companies and some small banks faced liquidity problems, with 16 finance companies suspended in June 1997, and another 42 in August. In December, 56 of them were closed permanently.

The third cause of the crisis was exchange rate mismanagement. With a fixed exchange rate and the liberalization of international capital flows, foreign money poured in between 1993 and 1996, attracted by high interest rates. The baht became overvalued against other currencies, partly slowing down growth in exports for 1996. However, the central bank persisted in pegging the baht to a basket of currencies in which the dollar had 80 per cent influence. Speculators attacked the baht in February and May 1997. To defend the currency, official foreign reserves were used, and these fell from $39.2 billion in January to $32.4 billion in June. In addition, the central bank sold $23.4 billion of the reserves on the forward market—a sale hidden from the public until August. On 2 July, the central bank had to replace the fixed exchange rate regime with a 'managed float', as it could no longer tap the reserves. The baht fell steadily from 25.8 to the dollar on 1 July to a trading range of 45–9 to the dollar in late 1997, recovering over the past two years to the current level of around 38 baht (Mar. 2000).

The Impact and Response of the Telecom Companies

In the Chinese language two characters represent the word 'crisis', one for 'danger', the other for 'opportunity'. Thailand's telecommunication firms, along with most other businesses, being ethnic Chinese-owned, took the old saying to heart and responded with determination and, some would say, enthusiasm.

Following the devaluation of the baht, some telecom companies increased their product charges while others secured favourable fixed exchange rates from their suppliers, which somewhat reduced their profitability but allowed them to carry on with their plans, albeit drastically curtailed or delayed. Some saw their profits wiped out by the decline in the value of the baht, while others had to revise their projections severely. In some cases, help was forthcoming from some major suppliers—notably both Epson Corp and the Acer Group came to the rescue of their distributor in Thailand, the Sahaviriya OA Group. Inevitably, many companies had to lay off staff, initiate austerity plans, cut salaries (as did Samart, Sahaviriya, and Datamat).

As the crisis deepened, some government projects were scaled back or cancelled. For example, TOT halted, cancelled, or scaled back projects worth 1.6 billion baht as part of a programme to shave government spending. The biggest announced cut was to slow down work on switching the Bangkok analogue phone network to digital, a saving of 145 million baht; the TOT also put off part of the installation of 800,000 new land-lines, to save 81 million baht.

Private companies have had their own problems. Total Access Communication were put on a credit watch by Standard & Poor (S & P), who stated that even TAC's BBB-/A-3 corporate rating was at risk. S & P said TAC had an above-average business position and cash-generating ability, but was under heavy pressure because of the crash of the baht. S & P had previously warned that TAC faced major refinancing difficulties in 1998 unless it could get an infusion of foreign capital.

The initial impact of the Asian financial crisis was severe.[12] All telecom companies listed on the SET faced a combined loss of 30 billion baht in the third quarter of 1997. Although AIS recorded a profit of 2.4 billion in the first nine months of 1997, its parent company, Shinawatra Computer and Communication, suffered a consolidated loss of 2.8 billion for the same period. UCOM (owners of TAC) recorded a loss of 11 billion baht, mostly from the impact of foreign exchange changes following the crash of the baht. All these telecom giants began restructuring to survive by cuts in pay, staff, and other spending and investment, while looking for foreign partners to ensure smooth cash flows.

By the middle of 1999, the Thai telecom industry showed signs of slight recovery with improved operating revenues, despite the burden of hefty foreign exchange losses, and some progress towards debt restructuring. The ten major telecommunication companies listed on the SET reported third-quarter combined losses of 17.48 billion baht against earnings of 5.47 billion baht a year earlier.[13]

Advanced Info Services (AIS) reported net gains of 884 million baht, mostly improving mobile phone sales in the second half. In the third quarter alone, AIS had 80,000 new subscribers, making it the leading phone operator with an almost 50 per cent share of the 2.3 million subscribers market. At the end of 1999, AIS had about 1.2 million subscribers, with 360,000 new subscribers, up from 200,000 in 1998. The parent company Shinawatra corporation registered net profits of 82 million baht in the third quarter, an increase of 32 per cent compared with 668.11 million baht in the same period the previous year.

UCOM (United Communication Industry), on the other hand, reported losses of 6.7 billion in the third quarter against 1.76 billion net profit in the same period the previous year. UCOM's subsidiary TAC posted third-quarter losses of 3.54 billion against a 3.94 billion baht net profit for the same period in 1998. However, TAC recorded a 19.3 per cent increase in operating income year-on-year. The surge in operating income was a result of

---

[12] Vivat Prateepchaikul, *Bangkok Post*, Jan. 2000.
[13] *Bangkok Post*, Jan. 2000

rising revenues in its core mobile phone business, to 4.69 billion baht at the end of the third quarter, up from 3.752 billion baht. However, TAC was hard hit by unrealized foreign exchange losses of 4.06 billion baht for the third quarter.

Metropolitan fixed-line carrier, TelecomAsia Corporation Plc, posted the highest net losses of 6.79 billion baht in the third quarter, against 1.76 billion baht net profit in the same period the previous year. This was caused mainly by losses from the baht's depreciation. But the company's earnings from the fixed-line operation rose to 795 million baht from 713 million baht because it successfully reduced operating costs.

Meanwhile, the debt-ridden provincial fixed-line-carrier, Thai Telephone and Telecommunication Plc, recorded third-quarter net losses of 2.43 billion baht, against a 410.07 million baht net profit in the corresponding period the year before. Of that total loss, 1.86 billion baht was a result of foreign exchange losses. However, TT&T's overall operating performance improved, with total revenues increasing from 1.42 billion baht in the third quarter of 1998 to 1.52 billion baht in the third quarter of 1999, following improvements in its fixed-line service earnings. The company attributed its better operating results to a decline in operational costs, from 2.3 billion baht to 2.08 billion baht.

In contrast, state telecom firms have reported losses from operations in the past nine months up until mid-1998. The Telephone Organization of Thailand (TOT) reported a huge drop in revenue in 1998, due mainly to foreign exchange losses and a decline in demand for telephone services. The TOT said its net profit plunged by more than 80 per cent, to 2.08 billion baht from 16.5 billion baht the previous year. The decline was also attributed to a decrease in telephone service demand, due mainly to the popularity of mobile phones and the commercial launch of the personal communication telephone (PCT) by TelecomAsia.

While TOT has been trying to slash operating costs, foreign exchange losses still weigh heavily on the company's balance sheet. Analysts say TOT has reason to be discouraged by its dismal financial results since it needs to go ahead with privatization to prepare itself for the intense competition expected when the telecom market is fully liberalized in 2006.

The shortfall prompted TOT to start collecting fees for its eight special phone services (SPCs), beginning the following year, to bolster its falling revenues. TOT has indicated that the move was necessary as it needed more funds to finance the operation and development of the SPC project, which required a great deal of investment.

From January 2000, the monthly fee for a single service will be 30 baht per line, three services will be 80 baht per line, and a further 25 baht will be imposed for every additional service per line. By charging customers for the services, TOT expects to gain an additional 12 million baht per month.

Currently, fixed-line companies earn an average of 650 baht to 750 baht from each line per month. However, provincial fixed-line operator Thai Telephone and Telecommunication Plc (TT&T) indicated that its subscribers who use the special services will not be charged until April 2000.

Meanwhile, the long-delayed 8 billion baht synchronous digital hierarchy (SDH) project made progress when TOT's board of directors approved a proposal to reopen bidding. The project is a crucial part of TOT's plan to increase its domestic telephone network capacity to 6 million lines and to introduce new services using high-speed technology. However, since the SDH was proposed three years ago, the technology has advanced and it is now called the Transmission and Network Expansion project (TNEP). TNEP is a vital element in the success of TOT, which wants to introduce high-speed technology to its local telephone network.

SDH bidding was first opened in 1996 but was postponed after rumours circulated of widespread collusion among the bidders. Under the new bidding arrangements, with revised criteria, international companies are allowed to join in the bidding process, regardless of whether or not they have subcontractors or joint-venture companies in Thailand.

There are several companies bidding for the consultancy tenders including the German consultancy Detecon Deutsche Telepost, Norconsult Telemetics Ltd., Telia Swedtel, and Tele Denmark Consultant A/S. The winning bid will formulate the specification details for the project, review terms of reference, supervise project progress, design technical specifications, and select potential investors.

To ensure transparency, the qualifications of the consultant will also be vetted by the World Bank and the National Electronics and Computer Technology Centre. The consultant would spend at least two months designing the specification before inviting bids from suppliers. The while process would take eight months.

Under the new bidding terms of reference, the winning foreign bid will have to purchase locally manufactured products worth at least 50 per cent of the successful bidding price, as part of a counter-trade agreement. The conditions were included to support the local industry and promote the export sector.

TOT is confident that it will achieve its objective of receiving a bid of around 8 billion baht, a projection lower than the 10 billion baht proposed in the first bid, in order to prevent criticism of overspending.

The board also endorsed a recommendation that the TOT separate the bidding procedure into two parts: the fibre-optic supply process and the transmission network supply process. Each process is searching for just one winning bid to prevent renewed accusations of collusion among the bidders.

The original round of bidding saw TOT divide the project into six zones, which it was forced to change after the rumours of collusion began. But the second half of 1999 also saw some major telecom firms make progress in their debt-restructuring talks.

Debt-ridden TelecomAsia Corporation Plc (TA), the metropolitan fixed-line operator, signed a memorandum with 45 local and foreign creditors over its 63.11 billion baht debt-restructuring plan, scheduled for completion by the end of 1999. The debt-restructuring frameworks approved by the creditors include payment rescheduling and the issue of convertible preference shares.

However, the creditors were only willing to write off less than 2 per cent of the group's debt. The group's outstanding debt of 49.56 billion, which was in the form of secured loans, will be rescheduled by 2000. The secured loans will be repaid in instalments from the second quarter of 2002. The last payment will be made before the end of 2008. Interest will be limited to the London Interbank Offered Rate. The remaining 13.46 billion baht of unsecured loans will be settled through a combination of debt forgiveness, an immediate cash repayment of about 5.61 billion baht, and the issue of promissory notes worth 6.71 billion baht. As part of the package, German export bank Kreditanstalt für Wiederaufbau, which is the group's largest creditor, will inject fresh funds of US$150 million by taking up 702 million convertible preference shares. The injection will lift the German bank's stake in TelecomAsia to 24 per cent of its paid-up capital. The capital injection will dilute the stakes of the Charoen Pokphand group and its affiliates, which currently hold 37 per cent and Bell Atlantic, which holds 18 per cent through Nynex Network System (Thailand) Co. TelecomAsia will use the extra funds to repay debt to its unsecured creditors. The restructuring plan will enable TA to attain cash-flow and meet debt service obligations in the foreseeable future as well as maintain the company's position in the telecom industry.

However, provincial fixed-line operator Thai Telephone and Telecommunication Plc (TT&T) was slow in its debt-restructuring talks and still could not meet the year-end deadline for debt rescheduling set by the central bank's debt advisory committee—the Corporate Debt Restructuring Advisory Committee (CDARC). It is the only listed telecom company that has not been able to secure a debt-restructuring agreement with its creditors under the supervision of the committee.

TA, TT&T, and Jasmine International Plc sought supervision from the advisory committee to hasten their debt-restructuring procedures. The central bank set up the debt advisory committee as a state-run mediator to help corporations handle the debt problems that emerged during the economic crisis. Most indebted businesses prefer the advisory committee to the bankruptcy court and lawsuits from lenders.

Negotiations between TT&T and its lenders have been delayed since neither could agree to the other's demands. While TT&T wanted its lenders to give in to a compromise deal and allow the company to covert debt to equity, its lenders said that TT&T must accept the pain itself by diluting the ownership of its shareholders.

One factor discouraging the lenders from granting the company a new debt term is high revenue-sharing of 43.1 per cent with the TOT, which made the firm's income projections fall below the original target. A local bank recently said that other deterrents for TT&T included the drop in earnings as a result of the unfair tariff structure between the fixed-line and mobile phone business.

Meanwhile TT&T's holding firm, Jasmine International, expected to secure terms on its $60 million debt-restructuring plan by the end of 1998. Its subsidiary, Jasmine International Overseas, concluded a separate $80 million agreement with its lenders. Two major creditors of Jasmine are Bangkok Bank and Chase Manhattan Bank. The second half of 1998 also saw Shin Corporations Plc approach TT&T with terms of a takeover, following a suggestion by TT&T's lenders who floated the idea as one option. But TT&T declined the overture.

Samart Corporation Plc, a debt-ridden telecom firm, reached agreement in October 1998 with most of its creditors to roll over the 7.2-billion-baht debt burden as a major part of a debt-restructuring plan. Most creditors passed a resolution to grant an extension of debt payments to the company for seven years for the roll-over. Samart Corp. is one of the cash-strapped telecom firms now making a breakthrough in a long, drawn-out debt-restructuring plan.

Total Access Communication Plc (TAC) was also granted a six-year extension on the maturity of loans, worth $537.7 million, by its creditors. TAC's creditors also agreed to extend the repayment of short-term loans until November 2004. The rolled-over loans account for 54 per cent of the company's outstanding loans of $1.18 billion.

TAC's parent firm, United Communication Industry Plc (UCOM), also passed the most critical stage of its struggle for survival by clearing $573 million of debt. UCOM's total debt consists of the equivalent of $208 million in bank facilities, $264 million in euro-convertible bonds, and 3.6 billion baht in baht debentures. The euro bonds and baht debentures will be converted into equity of $120 million, according to the debt-restructuring agreement.

The government is actively seeking foreign partners to take a stake in the privatization of TOT and CAT, by offering equity stakes of up to 25 per cent. One possible investor in CAT is the US-based international carrier Teleglobe. Teleglobe offers voice and data services, broadcast, calling cards, and private leases to carriers. Teleglobe recently opened a representative office Bangkok to explore potential opportunities.

Future Trends

Although the existing private operators, Advanced Info Service (AIS) and Total Access Communications (TAC), are protected by the terms of their licences, pressure has been steadily building up to break up the duopoly and allow greater competition. The pressure has been coming mainly from private interests which either missed out or did not bid for the original licences. The current government, as well as regulators, have been trying to find a way out of their contractual obligations. The first 'window of opportunity' was a reclassification of PHS[14] systems as value-added mobile services, and thus in theory outside the scope of the original cellular licences. However, having opened one 'loophole' it was difficult to stop ongoing discussion of other technologies.

As a result, both TOT and CAT are negotiating with their respective concessionaires (AIS and TAC) to cancel (or more appropriately, renegotiate) their exclusive rights. Meanwhile, the Ministry of Transport and Communications (MOTC) asked the Judicial Council to give an opinion on the exclusivity rights of AIS and TAC. AIS has proposed eight conditions while TAC has proposed five conditions to amend their concessions in return for cancellation of exclusive rights. The main conditions proposed by AIS include an extension of its concession life by another five years, a waiver of revenue-sharing on promotions, and permission for AIS to install, use, and earn revenue from transmission networks. Other conditions aim to make AIS more flexible in running its service in the future.

In addition to pure cellular systems, TOT has also announced that the personal hand-phone system (PHS) will be allowed as a value-added service to all fixed-line operators. Since the service is considered to be a value added to land-lines, PHS handsets will use the same seven-digit number as the land-lines and a PHS subscriber needs to have a fixed line. TelecomAsia (TA) has signed a contract with TOT to provide PHS service for the Greater

---

[14] Personal hand-phone system.

Bangkok area while TT&T is currently negotiating to sign a contract to provide the service in provincial areas. TA also received approval from TOT to provide PHS for TOT's fixed-line subscribers under the TOT network. This means that TA has effectively increased potential PHS subscribers under the TOT network by another 1.5 million under TOT's network in addition to the 2.6 million under TA's own network.

TOT itself might introduce another PHS system by joining with a Japanese company-KDD. The holding structure will be 49 per cent held by TOT, 49 per cent by KDD and 2 per cent by the Crown Property Bureau. The TOT system will be different from TA's in terms of the numbering plan. TOT's PHS subscribers will use a nine-digit number which means that the number of subscribers will not be limited by the fixed-line subscribers. The PHS will make its debut in the Thai market in the near future. PHS is expected to grow slowly, tapping low-end cellular users. Due to its limited capability in comparison with cellular service, PHS will probably not attract core cellular subscribers. It will create a new market segment, which accepts its limitations.[15] The target audiences are housewives, college students and paging subscribers. Moreover, the cost gap between using and owning the cheapest cellular and PHS is not high enough to justify buying the lower-feature PHS.

The growth of the digital system will most likely be fuelled by the introduction of the new operators, with all of them expected to be offering digital services in 1999. At the end of the decade, it is expected that analogue subscribers will stop growing and digital subscribers will account for more than 40 per cent of the total subscribers. The recently introduced PHS is likely to face competition from the new generation of pagers that incorporate personal digital assistance (PDA), which builds a phonebook, computer games, a dictionary, a calculator, and karaoke services into one unit.

When the Thai telecom market is fully liberalized in 2006, the mobile phone concept itself will have undergone tremendous changes. As the recent telecom fair in Switzerland showed, in the next few years, international companies plan to introduce new mobile phones that are more like personal computers than phones. These will incorporate full fax, internet, and visual technology that will make current devices (and systems) obsolete. For Thai telecom companies, whether the future represents a crisis or an opportunity is as yet uncertain.

QUESTIONS

1. What are the dominant characteristics of the telecommunications industry?

2. What is competition like in this industry? Which competitive forces are strongest, which weakest?

3. How would you characterize the strategies of TAC and AIS? What are the key elements?

4. How attractive is the telecommunications industry? What competitive threats should the main players be concerned with?

---

[15] Small-cell site coverage of a radius of 200–300 metres makes seamless coverage almost impossible. Therefore, connectivity through the PHS network is unreliable. Calls will be disconnected if travelling more than 30 km. per hour.

5 What are the strengths and weaknesses of the main players, their external opportunities and threats?

6 Why is collaboration with other companies such an important facet of the telecommunications industry?

7 What are the key success factors in the industry? What do companies have to do and achieve in order to be successful?

8 What role can the government play in ensuring a viable telecom sector?

9 What impact will the Asian financial crisis have on industry as a whole and on mobile phone service providers in particular?

Select Bibliography

Abonyi, George, *Thailand: From Financial Crisis to Economic Renewal*, ISEAS Working Papers, Institute of Southeast Asian studies, 1999.

Adams, D., 'The Monkey and the Fish: Cultural Pitfalls of an Educational Advisor', *International Development Review*, 2(2), 1969: 22–4.

Adlan, D. N., 'APEC and the Asia Crisis: Can APEC make a difference?' Address of Ambassador Dato Noor Adlan at the Sir Hermann Black Lecture on Tuesday 5 May 1998, Sydney, Australia.

Aggarwal, Raj., 'Lessons for America', *Multinational Business Review*, 7(2), Fall 1999*a*.

—— 'Restoring Growth in Asia after the late 1990s Economic Crisis: Need for Domestic and International Economic Reforms', *Multinational Business Review*, 7(2), Fall, 1999*b*.

Akira, Kojima, 'APEC and the Lessons of the Asian Economic Crisis', *Journal of Japanese Trade and Industry World Reporter (TM)*, 11 Jan. 1999.

Alburo, Florian, 'The Asian Financial Crisis and Philippine Responses: Long Run Considerations', *The Developing Economies*, 37(4), Dec. 1999: 439–59, Japan.

Altfest, Lewis, J., 'Why Asia's Still a Great Place for your Money', *Medical Economics*, 75(4), 23 Feb. 1998: 40–4.

Annual Report on the Asian Economies, 1999, http://www.epa.go.jp/99/f/19990622f_asia_e.html

Anon., 'How can you win in China', *Business Week*, European edn., 26 May 1997: 40–5.

—— 'Asia Currency Crisis Enters Second Phase', *FX Manager*, 10 Oct. 1997: 1, London.

—— 'Causes of the Crisis—Mr Severino's Speech', *Sydney Morning Herald*, 17 June 1998.

—— 'The Chicken or the Egg?' *Asian Business*, 1 Aug. 1999. http://www.web3.asia1.com.sg/timesnet/data

APEC, Asia Pacific Economic Cooperation, http://www.apecsec.org.sg/

Apmforum.com, Capsule Review update, 1999.

Ariff, Mohamed, and Abubakar, Syarisa Yanti, 'The Malaysian Financial Crisis: Economic Impact and Recovery Prospects', *The Developing Economies*, 37(4), Dec. 1999: 417–39.

Ariga, M., Yasue, M., and Wen, G. X, 'China's Generation III: Variable Target Market Segment and Implications for Marketing Communication', *Marketing and Research Today*, Feb. 1997: 17–24.

Asian Development Bank, *Emerging Asia: Changes and Challenges*, An Asian Development Bank Publication, 1997.

—— *Asian Development Outlook, 1998: Population and Human Resources*, New York: Oxford University Press, 1999.

Bartlett, C. A. and S. Ghoshal, *Managing across Borders*, Boston: Harvard Business School Press, 1989.

Beamish, P. W., Killing, J. P., Lecraw, D. H., Crockell, H. (eds.) *International Management: Text and Cases*, Homewood, Ill: Irwin, 1991.

Bhaskaran, Manu, 'Is Asia Recovering Too Quickly'? *Far Eastern Economic Review*, 162(23), 10 June 1999: 90–1.

Biersteker, T. J., 'Reducing the Role of the State in the Economy: A Conceptual Exploration of IMF and World Bank Prescriptions', *International Studies Quarterly*, 34, Sept. 1990: 477–92.

Bisson, T. A., *Zaibatsu Dissolution in Japan*, Berkeley: University of California Press, 1954.

Bond, M. H., *Beyond the Chinese Face*, Oxford: Oxford University Press, 1991.

Boulas, C., Fryling, J., and Buchanan, I., *Asian Business*, 1 Jan. 1999, http://web3.asia1.com.sg/timesnet/data/ab/docs

Brahm, L., and Daoran, Li, *The Business Guide to China*, Singapore: Butterworth-Heinemann Asia 1996.

Brash, J., 'Export Management Companies', *Journal of International Business Studies*, 9(1), spring–summer 1978: 59–72.

Brook, Timothy, and Luong, Hy V. (eds.), *Culture and Economy: The Shaping of Capitalism in Eastern Asia*, Ann Arbor: The University of Michigan Press.

Brown, David, H., and Porter, Robin (ed.), *Management Issues in China*, London: Routledge, 1996.

Brunet, P. M., 'Beijin Wang Fuging Dept Store Group Ltd', INSEAD, CEIBC, Fontainebleu, France, Case Study No. 399-1-2-1, 1999.

Butterfield, Fox., *China: Alive in Bitter Sea*, New York: Coronet Books, 1983.

Byung-Nak, Song, *The Rise of the Korean Economy*, New York: Oxford University Press, 1990.

Camdessus, M., Statement by the Managing Director on the IMF Program with Indonesia, News Brief No. 98/2, 15 Jan. 1998*a*.

—— 'Is the Asian Crisis Over?' Address at the National Press Club, Washington, 2 Apr. 1998.

—— Managing Director of the International Monetary Fund, 'Australia and Asia in the Global Economy', paper presented at the Australia Unlimited Round Table, Melbourne, Australia, 5 May 1998.

—— 'The IMF's Role in Today's Globalized World', Address to the IMF Bundesbank Symposium, Frankfurt, Germany, 2 July 1998.

Camp, R. C., 'Learning from the Best Leaders to Superior Performance', *Journal of Business Strategy*, May–June 1992: 3–6.

Capsule Review Update: Asia, 30 Mar. 1999.

Cateora, P. R., *International Marketing*, 7th edn., Homewood, Ill.: Irwin, 1990.

Chaiyasoot, Naris, 'Industrialization, Financial Reform and Monetary Policy', in Medhi, Krongkraw (ed.), *Thailand's Industrialization and its Consequences*, London: Macmillan, 1995.

Chang, Y. S., Labovitz, G., and Rosansky, V., *Making Quality Work*, Essex Junction: Oliver Wright publications, 1992.

Chaponniere, J. R., and Lautier, M., 'Breaking into the Korean Market—Invest or License', *Long Range Planning*, 28(1), 1995: 104–11.

Chen, M., *Asian Management Systems*, London: Thomson Business Press, 1995.

—— and Pan, W., *Understanding the Process of Doing Business in China, Taiwan and Hong Kong: A Guide for International Executives*, Lewiston, NY: The Edwin Mellen Press, 1993.

Cheng T. C. E. and Podolsky, S., *Just in Time Manufacturing: An Introduction*, 2nd edn., London: Chapman and Hall, 1996.

Chi, Aelim, and Miyake, M., 'Japan and Asia: Development Ties', *The OECD Observer*, 217–18, Summer 1999: 70–1, Paris: Organization for Economic Cooperation and Development.

Child, J., *Management in China during the age of reform*, Cambridge: Cambridge University Press, 1994.

—— and Stewart, S., 'Regional Differences in China and their Implications for Sino-Foreign Joint Ventures', *Journal of General Management*, 23(2), 1997: 65–86

Ching, Ng R. M., 'Culture as a Factor in Management: The Case of the People's Republic of China', *International Journal of Management*, 15(1), Mar. 1998: 86–93.

Chong-Tae, Kin, 'Korea Swings Door Wide Open', *Business Korea*, 16(6), June 1999: 26–8.

Chow, Irene, Holbert, Neil, Kelley, Lane, and Yu, Julie, *Business Strategy: An Asia Pacific Focus*, Singapore: Prentice Hall, Simon & Schuster Asia, 1997.

Chua, C. C., 'Kiasuism is Not All Bad', *The Straits Times*, 23 June 1989, Singapore.

Clad, James, *Behind the Myth: Business Money and Powers in Southeast Asia*, London: Unwin, 1989: 52–3.

Clyde-Smith, D., 'The Acer Group: Building an Asian Multinational', Fontainebleau, France: INSEAD–EAC, 1997 Case 397-1-5-1.

Collins, Susan, and Bosworth, Barry, 'Economic Growth in East Asia: Accumulation versus Assimilation', *Brookings Paper on Economic Activity*, 1996.

Congressional Report, 'Asian Financial Crisis', Congressional Research Service Report for Congress, No. 97–1021, 25 Nov. 1997.

Connelly, Thomas, J., 'The Great Asian Fire Drill', *Journal of Financial Planning*, 11(2), 1998: 32–7, Denver.

Cragg, Claudial, *Hunting with the Tigers: How to Achieve Commercial Success in the Asian Pacific Rim*, London: Mercury Books, Gold Arrow Publications Ltd., 1992.

Crosby, S. G., 'The Myths and Realities of Asia Growth', *Asia Money*, Sept. 1997, London.

Cui, Geng, and Liu, Qiming, 'Regional Market Segments of China: Opportunities and Barriers in a Big Emerging Market', *Journal of Consumer Marketing*, 17(1), 2000.

Daniels, J. D. and Radebaugh, L. H., *International Business: Environments and Operations*, 6th edn., Reading, Mass.: Addison-Wesley, 1992.

David, P., 'Opportunity from Chaos', *World Trade*, 12(3), Mar. 1999.

De Gruyter, Charles J. Walter, *The Japanese Industrial System*, New York: Macmillan, 1989.

De Keijzer, A. J., *China Business Strategies for the 90s*, Berkeley: PacificViews Press, 1992.

Department of Trade and Industry at http://www.dti.gov.uk/worldtrade/regional.html

Diddiqi, Moin, 'Asia Double-Edge Sword', *African Business*, London Issue 234, July–Aug. 1998: 18.

Diederman, David, 'Spring Time in Maine and Asia', *Traffic World*, 258(7), 17 May 1999: 20–2.

Dohyung, Kim, 'IMF Bailout and Financial and Corporate Restructuring in the Republic of Korea', *The Developing Economies*, 37(4), Dec. 1999: 460–513.

Drucker, P., *Management*, New York: Harper and Row, 1974.

Dudley, J., *1992: Strategies for the Single Market*, London: Kogan Page, 1990.

Dumaine, B., 'Asia Wealth Creators Confront a New Reality', *Fortune*, 8, Dec. 1997: 42–52.

El Kahal, S., *Introduction to International Business*, Maidenhead: McGraw-Hill, 1994

Embassy of Japan, 'Japan's role in Asian Financial Crisis', 16 Nov. 1998a at http://www.embjapan.org/features

—— 'Japanese Economic Measures, Japan's Role in Asian Financial Crisis', 16 Nov. 1998 at http://www.embjapan.org/features/JCONASIA.html

Engardio, Pete, 'The Chinese Deal Makers of Southeast Asia', *Business Week*, 11 Nov. 1991: 60–2.

Engholm, Christopher, *When Business East Meets Business West: The Guide to Practice and Protocol in the Pacific Rim*, New York: John Wiley & Sons, 1991.

EPU White Paper, 'The Status of the Malaysian Economy', paper tabled at the Malaysian Parliament on 6 Apr. 1999, Prime Minister's Department, Economic Planning Unit, in Mohamed Arief and Syarisa Yanti Abubakar, 'The Malaysian Financial Crisis: Economic Impact and Recovery Prospects', *The Developing Economies*, 36: 417–38.

Erland, H., 'Pacific Basin: Restoring US Economic Leadership', *Business Economics*, 29(2), Apr. 1994: 7.

Evans, T., Grant, M., and Nevison, D., 'Profiting in the Asia Pacific Region', *Canadian Business Review*, 31(3), autumn 1994: 27–9.

Far Eastern Economic Review, 'If Korea was Doing the "Right Things", So How do we Account for the Financial Calamity?' 1996: 151–5.

Feldstein, M., 'Refocusing the IMF', *Foreign Affairs*, 77(2), 1998: 20–33.

Fisher, Stanley, 'The Asian Crisis: A view from the IMF', Address by Stanley Fisher, First Deputy Managing Director of the International Monetary Fund at the Midwinter Conference of the Bankers' Association for Foreign Trade, Washington, 22 Jan. 1998a.

—— 'The Asia Crisis and Implications for Other Economies', presentation by Stanley Fisher, First Deputy Managing Director of the International Monetary Fund for delivery at the seminar on the Brazilian and the World Economic Outlook, organized by Inter News, São Paulo, 19 June 1998b.

—— 'The Asian Crisis and the Changing Role of the IMF', *Finance and Development*, June 1998c.

Flight, H., 'The ASEAN Financial Crisis: A Harbinger of Things to Come?' 120/1251, *Accountancy*, Nov. 1997: 58–9, London.

Franklin, B. H., 'The Asia Crisis: The US Outlook in the Global Economy', *Vital Speeches of the Day*, 64(14), 1 May 1998: 428–31, New York.

Freeman, Nick, 'Realism Reigns', *The Banker*, June 1996: 65–6.

Fries, A., 'The Battler for the Pacific': Gordon Redding Interviews Alexis Fries', *Long Range Planning*, 28(1), 1995: 92–4, 1005.

Fukuda, K. John., *Japanese Style Management Transferred: The Experience of East Asia*, New York: Routledge, 1988.

Garde, P., 'China: Shanghai famous Pops', Case 599-0251-1, France: INSEAD/CEIBS, 1999.

Genzberger, Christine A., *Hong Kong Business: The Portable Encyclopedia for Doing Business with Hong Kong*, California: World Trade Press, 1994.

Gibney, Frank B., 'Creating a Pacific Community: A Time to Bolster Economic Institutions', *Foreign Affairs*, 72(5), Nov.–Dec. 1993, New York.

Gleick, J., *Chaos*, London: Penguin Books, 1988.

Global Intelligence Update, 'The IMF and the World Bank bow toward Malaysia', 10 Sept. 1999 at www.stratfor.com

Goodfellow, Rob, *Indonesian Business Culture: Insider Guide*, Reed Academic Publishing, Butterworth-Heinemann, Asia, 1997.

Goodman, David, P., 'Opportunity from Chaos', *World Trade*, 12(3), Mar. 1999.

Gore, C., Murray, K., and Richardson, B., *Strategic Decision-Making*, London: Cassell, 1992.

Gough, Leo, *Asia Meltdown: The End of the Miracle*, Oxford: Capstone Publishing, 1998.

Greenspan, A., US House of Representatives—Testimony of Chairman Alan Greenspan before the Committee on Banking and Financial Services, 30 Jan. 1998.

Gross, R., and Kujawa, D., *International Business: Theory and Managerial Applications*, 2nd edn., Boston: Irwin, 1992.

Gwynne, S. C., 'What a drag!', *Time New York*, 152(11), 14 Sept. 1998: 26–33.

Habbib, G. M., and Burnett, J. J., 'An Assessment of Channel Behaviour in an Alternative Structural Arrangement: the International Joint Venture', *International Marketing Review*, 6(3), 1989: 7–29

Haley, G. T., and Chin, T. T., 'The Black Hole of South-East Asia: Strategic Decision in an Information Void', *Management Decisions*, 34(9), 1996: 37–48.

Hall, E. T., *Beyond Culture*, Garden City, NY: Doubleday, 1977.

Hamel, G., and Prahalad, H. K., *Competing for the Future*, Boston: Harvard Business School Press, 1994.

Hannan, M. T., and Freeman, J., *Organizational Ecology*, Boston: Harvard Business University Press, 1988.

Hatakeyama, Noburo, Chairman of Japan External Trade Organization, 'Japan's Economy and the Asian Crisis: Domestic Demand-Led Growth and Other Challenges', speech presentation made at the South Africa Institute of International Affairs, 15 Feb. 1999, and at the Cape Chamber of Commerce, 16 Feb. 1999, http://www.Jetro.Co.Za/

Hattori, Tamio, 'Ownership and Management in Modern Korean Enterprise', *Asian Economy*, May–June 1984.

Henderson, Callum, *Asia Falling: Making Sense of the Asian Crisis and its Aftermath*, Business Week Books, New York: McGraw-Hill, 1998.

Hill, C., *International Business*, New York: McGraw-Hill, 1999.

Hinkelman, Edward, G. (ed.), *Hong Kong Business. The Portable Encyclopedia for Doing Business with Hong Kong*, Country Business Guide, California: World Trade Press, 1993.

—— (ed.), *Japan Business: The Portable Encyclopedia for Doing Business with Japan*, Country Business Guide series, California: World Trade Press, 1994.

—— (ed.), *Korea Business: The Portable Encyclopedia for Doing Business with Korea*, Business Guide Series, California: World Trade Press, 1995*a*.

—— (ed.), *Taiwan Business: The Portable Encyclopedia for Doing Business with Taiwan*, Business Guide Series, California: World Trade Press, 1995*b*.

Hiroshi, Okumura, *Six Largest Business Groups in Japan*, Tokyo: Diamond Publishing, 1976.

Ho, D. Y. F., 'On the Concept of Face', *American Journal of Sociology*, 81, 1976: 867–84.

Ho, J. T. S., Ang, C. E., Loh, J., and Ng, I., 'A Preliminary Study of Kiasu Behaviour—Is it Unique to Singapore?' *Journal of Managerial Psychology*, 13(5–6), 1998.

Hookeun, Shin, *Characteristics and Problems in Korean Enterprise*, Seoul: Seoul National University Press, 1985.

Howard, Flight, 'The ASEAN Financial Crisis: A Harbinger of Things to Come?' *Accountancy*, 120(1251), Nov. 1997: 58–9, London.

Hsu, F. L. K., 'Psycho-social Homeostasis and Jen: Conceptual Tools for Advancing Psychological Anthropology', *American Anthropologist*, 73, 1971: 23–44.

http://www.apecsec.org.sg/97brochure/97brochure.html

http://www.apecsec.org.sg/member/indoec-report.html

http://www.apmforum.com/research/asia.html

http://www.dti.gov.uk/worldtrade/regional.html

http://www.epa.go.jp/99, 'Ideal Socioeconomy and Policies for Economic Rebirth', Economic Council, 5 July 1999.

http://www.usfca.edu/pac-rim/pages/publications/report8.html.

Hu H. C., 'The Chinese Concept of Face', *American Anthropologist*, 46, 1994: 45–64.

'IMF approves SDR 15.5 billion standby credit for Korea', Press Release No. 97/55, 4 Dec. 1997.

'IMF conclude Article IV. Consultation with Malaysia', 7 July 1999, Executive Board, IMF, Public Information Notice PIN No. 99/88, 8 Sept. 1999, Washington.

IMF home page. 'The IMF's Response to the Asian Crisis', Apr. 1998.

'IMF Press Release, IMF approves SDR 15.5 billion standby credit for Korea', Press Release No. 97/55, 4 Dec. 1997.

'IMF Approves Stand-by Credit for Indonesia, 1997', Press Release No. 97/50, 5 Nov. 1997.

Jacobs, J. B., 'A Preliminary Model of Particularistic Ties in Chinese Political Alliances', *China Quarterly*, 78, 1979: 237–73.

James, David, 'Adversity and Opportunity', *Upside*, 10(6), June 1998: 60–2.

Japanese Human Relations Association, *The Idea*

Book: Improvement through Total Employee Involvement, Tokyo: JHRA, 1998.

Johansson, J. K., and Ikujiro, Nonaka, *Relentless: The Japanese Way of Marketing*, Oxford: Butterworth Heinemann, 1996.

Jomo, K. S. (ed.), *Tigers in Trouble: Financial Governance, Liberalisation and Crises in East Asia*, London: Zed Books Ltd., 1998.

Jordan, T., 'Straight Talk—Direct Assault', *Asian Business*, 1 Jan. 2000.

Ju Choi, Chong, and Wright, Nigel, *How to Achieve Business Success in Korea: Where Confucius Wears a Three-Piece Suit*, London: Macmillan, 1994.

Kagda, S., 'Totally Opposing Traits', *The Business Times, Executive Lifestyle*, p. 2, 1993.

Kang, T. W., *Is Korea the next Japan?*, New York: The Free Press, 1989.

Kaukuchi, S., 'Problems and Pills—The Soft Touch', *Asian Business*, 1 Dec. 1999 at http://web3.asia.com.sg/timesnet/data

Kay, J., *Foundation of Corporate Success*, Oxford: Oxford University Press, 1993.

Keys, B. J., Wells, R. A., and Trey Denton, L., 'Job rotation, Japanese Managerial and Organizational Learning', *Thunderbird International Business Review*, 40(2), Mar.–Apr. 1998: 119–39.

Kienzle, Rene, and Shadur, Mark, 'Developments in Business Networks in East Asia', *Management Decision*, 35(1), 1997: 23–32.

Killing, P. J., 'How to Make Global Joint Ventures Work', *Harvard Business Review*, May–June 1982: 72–89.

Kindel, T. I., 'A Partial Theory of Chinese Consumer Behavior: Marketing Strategy Implications', *Hong Kong Journal of Business Management*, 1, 1983.

Koberstein, Jan Wayne, 'How Hot is Asia? Economic Chaos Clouds Industry Expansion', *Pharmaceutical Executive*, 18(1), Jan. 1998*a*: 42–53.

—— 'Regional Structures: A Company Survey', *Pharmaceutical Executive*, 18(1), Jan. 1998*b*: 64–8.

Kojima, K. A., 'APEC and the Lessons of the Asian Economic Crisis', *Journal of Japanese Trade and Industry—World Reporter*, 11 Jan. 1999.

Kotler, P., *Marketing Management: Analysis, Planning and Control*, 5th edn., Englewood Cliffs, NJ: Prentice Hall, 1984.

Kraar, Louis, 'Korea's Tigers Keep Roaring', *Fortune*, 12 Apr. 1995: 62.

Krongkaew, M., 'Capital Flows and Economic Crisis in Thailand', *The Developing Economies*, 32(4), Dec. 1999.

Krugman, M., 'The Myth of the Asian Miracle', *Foreign Affairs*, 73(6), 1998.

Kunimune, Kozo, 'Crisis in Japan and the Way Out: A Counter Argument to Pessimistic Views', *The Developing Economies*, 37(4), Dec. 1999: 514–39.

Lall, Rajiv, 'Market Surge Signals Recovery', *Far Eastern Economic Review*, 162(24), 17 June 1999: 53–4.

Lasserre, P., 'Information Black Hole', *Long Range Planning*, 31(1), Feb. 1998: 30–50.

—— and Schütte, H., *Strategies for Asia Pacific*, London: Macmillan, 1995.

—— —— *Strategy and Management in Asia Pacific*, INSEAD Global Management Series, Maidenhead: McGraw-Hill, 1999.

Lauridsen, Laurids S., 'Thailand: Causes, Conduct and Consequences', in K. S. Jomo (ed.), *Tigers in Trouble: Financial Governance, Liberalisation and Crises in East Asia*, London: Zed Books, 1998: 136–61

Lebra T. S., *Japanese Patterns of Behavior*, Honolulu: University of Hawaii Press, 1976.

Lee, C., 'Modifying an American Consumer Behavior Model for Consumers in Confucian Culture', *Journal of International Consumer Marketing*, 3(1), 1990: 27–50.

Lee, S. M., and Yoo, S. J., 'The K-type Management: A Driving Force of Korean Prosperity', *Management International Review*, 27(4), 1987: 68–77.

—— —— 'Management Style and Practice of Korean Chaebols', *California Management Review*, 27, 1987: 68–78.

Legewie, J., 'Maturing Strategies for South East Asia after the Crisis: Europe, US and Japanese Firms', *Business Strategy Review*, 10(4), 1999: 55–64.

Leggett, Chris, J., and Bambeer, Greg, J., 'Vogel in Pacific Tiers of Change', *Human Resource Management Journal*, 6(2), 1996: 7–19.

Lei, D., and Slocum, J. W., Jr., 'Global Strategic Alliances: Payoffs and Pitfalls', *Organization Dynamics*, winter, 1991: 44–62.

Leipziger, Danny M., and Vinod, Thomas, 'Roots of East Asia's Success', *Finance and Development*, 31(1), Mar. 1994: 6.

Lemaire, Dan, 'Malaysia: Vision 2020'. *Canadian Business Review*, 23(2), summer 1996: 44–7.

Levitt, T., 'The Globalization of Markets', *Harvard Business Review*, May–June 1983*a*: 92–102

—— *The Marketing Imagination*, New York: The Free Press, 1983*b*.

Li, J., Khatri, N., and Lam, K., 'Changing Strategic Postures of Overseas Chinese Firms in Emerging Asian Markets', *Management Decision*, 37(5), 1999: 445–56.

Lim, C., 'Kiasu Tag Merely Adds to Global Treasury of Humour', *The Straights Times*, 1 Mar. 1995, Singapore.

Lim, Linda, Y. C., 'Social Welfare', in Kernial S. Sandhu and Paul Wheatley (eds.), *Management of Success: The Moulding of Modern Singapore*, Singapore: Singapore Institute of Southeast Asian Studies, 1989: 186–7.

Limlingan, Victor Simpao, 'The Overseas Chinese in ASEAN: Business Strategies and Management Practices', *Manila Vita Development Corp*, 1986: 88–9.

Lip, E., *Feng Shui for Business*, Singapore: Times Books, Int., 1989.

Lorange, P., and Ross, J., *Strategic Alliances: Formation, Implementation and Evolution*, Oxford: Blackwell, 1995.

Lorriman, J., and Kenjo, Takashi, *Japan's Success*, Oxford: Oxford University Press, 1994*a*.

—— —— *Japan's Winning Margins: Management, Training and Education*, New York: Oxford University Press, 1994*b*.

Low, L., and Toh, M. H., 'Regional Outlook: South Asia 1994–1995', ASEAN Institute of Southeast Asian Studies, 1994: 35–54.

Lynch, R., *Corporate Strategy*, London: Pitman Publishing, UK, 1997.

Maddison, Angus, 'Dynamic Forces in Capitalist Development', in Jon, Rohwer, *Asia Rising*, Oxford: Simon & Schuster, 1991: 51–60.

Mair, A., *Honda's Global Local Corporation*, New York: St Martin's Press, 1994.

Manu, Bhaskaran, 'Reviving for Recovery', *Far Eastern Economic Review*, 162(15), 15 Apr. 1999: 79–80.

Martin, Josh, 'If not Asia, where?' *Management Review*, 87(8), Sept. 1998: 16–20.

Marubini Corporation, *The Unique World of the Sogo Sosha*, Tokyo: Maruei Corporation, 1979.

Masaaki, Imai, *Kaizen: The Key to Japan's Competitive Success*, New York: McGraw-Hill, 1986.

Mason, Edward S., *The Economic and Social Modernization of the Republic of Korea*, Cambridge, Mass.: Harvard University Press, 1980.

Medhi, Krongkaew, 'Capital Flows and Economic Crisis in Thailand', *The Developing Economies*, 37(4), Dec. 1999: 395–416.

Mee Kam, M. G., and Wing-Shing, Tang, 'Land-use Planning in One Country, Two Systems: Hong Kong, Guangzhou and Shenzhen', *International Planning Studies*, 4(7), Feb. 1999: 7–27.

Mei Ching Ng, Rita, 'Culture as a Factor in Management: The Case of the People's Republic of China', *International Journal of Management*, 15(1), Mar. 1998: 86–93.

Mitsui & Co. Website http://www.mitsui.co.jp)

Mitsui in Action, 36(4), July– Aug. 1999.

Mitsuru, Taniuchi, 'The "East Asian Miracle" Deserves More Credit', *Tokyo Business Today*, Apr. 1995: 42–6.

Miyashita, Kenichi, and Russell, David, *Keiretsu: Inside the Hidden Japanese Conglomerates*, New York: McGraw-Hill, 1994.

Mi-Young, A., 'Sharing the Wealth', *Asia Business*, 1 Mar. 1999, South Korea at http://web3.asia.1.com.sg/timesnet/data

Montes, Manuel F., *The Currency Crisis in Southeast Asia*, Singapore: Singapore Institute of Southeast Asian Studies, 1998.

Mroczkowski, T., Hanaoka, Masao, 'The End of Japanese Management: How Soon?' *Human Resource Planning*, 21(3), 1998: 21–30.

Murray, Geoffrey, and Perera, Audrey, *Singapore: The Global City-State*, New York: St Martin's Press, 1996: 17–28.

Naisbitt, John, *Megatrends Asia*, London: Nicholas Brealey Publishing Ltd., 1996.

Naito, W., 'State-Owned Enterprises: No Longer State Run', *Beijing Review*, 16–22 Nov. 1991: 17–21.

Nikkei Business, 'Japanese Market Barriers', 6 June 1994: 126–9.

Nishumuro, Taizo, President, Toshiba, 'Bubble Trouble: Changing the Japanese Way'. BBC2, recorded 16 Jan. 2000.

Noboru, H., Chairman of Japan External Trade Organization, Japan's Economy and the Asian Crisis: Domestic Demand–Led Growth and Other Challenges', speech presentation made at the South Africa Institute of International

Affairs, 15 Feb. 1999 and the Cape Chamber of Commerce, 16 Feb. 1999 at http://www.jetro.co.za/

Nunnenkamp, Peter, 'Dealing with the Asian Crisis: IMF Conditionality and Implications in Asia and Beyond', 33(1), Mar.–Apr. 1998: 64.

Ohmae, K., *The Mind of the Strategist: Business Planning for a Competitive Advantage*, London: Penguin, 1983.

—— *The Borderless World: Power and Strategy in the Interlinked Economy*, London: Collins, 1990.

—— 'Managing in a Borderless World', in *Going Global: Succeeding in World Markets*, Cambridge, Mass.: Harvard Business Books, 1991.

Okumura, H., *The Six Largest Business Groups in Japan*, Tokyo: Tokyo Diamond Publishing, 1976.

'OTN Explores South Korea: Yes, But What Exactly Are the Chaebols?' 28 Sept. 1998 at http://www.megastories.com/

Page, John, 'Asian Miracle: Building a Basis for Growth', *Finance and Development*, 31(2), Mar. 1994, Washington.

Parsons, T., *The Social System*, Chicago: Free Press, 1951.

Porter, M., *Competitive Strategy: Techniques for Analyzing Industries and Competitors*, New York: Free Press, 1980.

—— *The Competitive Advantage of Nations*, Basingstoke: Macmillan, 1990.

Punnett, B. J., and Yu, P., 'Attitudes towards Doing Business with the PRC', *International Studies of Management and Organization*, 20(1), 1990: 149–60.

Pye, Lucian, *Chinese Commercial Negotiating Style*, New York: Quorum Books, 1992.

Quah, Stella R., and Quah, Jon S., *Friends in Blue: The Police and the Public in Singapore*, Singapore: Oxford University Press, 1987.

Quanyu, Huang, Leonard, Joseph W., and Tong, Chen, *Business Decision-Making in China*, New York: International Business Press, 1997.

Quinn, James B., *Strategies for Change—Logical Incrementalism*, Homewood Ill: Irwin, 1980.

Rahul, J., 'Believers in a Miracle: American Companies in Asia Shrug Off the Market Turmoil, Partly Because they were Prepared for It', *Hong Kong Times Business*, 150, 17 Nov. 1977: 20.

Redding, S. G., and Ng, M., 'The Role of "Face" in the Organizational Perceptions of Chinese Managers', *Organization Studies*, 3, 1982: 201–19.

Reuters, 'Malaysia Economy Recovering: Problems Still', 2 Feb. 2000, IMF Global News, Reuters, Washington.

Rick, Steve, 'Think Globally: Act Locally', *Credit Union Magazine*, 64(1), Jan. 1998: 69–70, Madison.

Rohwer, J., *Asia Rising*, London: Simon & Schuster, 1995.

Rong, I. W., 'Taiwan's Role in Asia Financial Crisis', delivered at Conference on The Asian Economic Crisis: Remedies and Implications of Asia Pacific Economies, co-sponsored by Center for Taiwanese Chamber of Commerce, Washington, and Institute of International Development Studies, Washington, Apr. 1998.

Ross, J. E., and Ross, W. C., *Japanese Quality Circles and Productivity*, New York: Restow Publishing Company Inc., 1982.

Roubini, Nouriel, 'An Introduction to Open Economy Macroeconomics: Currency Crises and the Asian Crisis', 1998, http//www.stern.nyu.edu/~nroubini/NOTES/macro5.htm#9.

Rowen, Henry, S. (ed.), *Behind East Asian Growth: The Political and Social Foundations of Prosperity*, London: Routledge, 1989.

Ruthstrom, C. R., and Matejka, K., 'The Four Meanings for the Word Yes in Asia', *Industrial Marketing Management*, 19 Aug. 1990: 191–2.

Sachs, Jeffrey, 'The Wrong Medicine for Asia', *New York Times*, 3 Nov. 1997.

—— 'Global Capitalism Making it Work', *The Economist* at http://www.stern.nyu.edu/~nroubini/Asia/sachsEco.html

Sangiin, Yoo, and Sang, Lee, 'Management Style and Practice in Korean Chaebols', *California Management Review*, summer 1987: 95–110.

Sarel, M., 'Growth and Productivity in ASEAN Economies', paper presented at an IMF Conference in Jakarta, Nov. 1996.

Saunders, Heather A., Renaghan, Leo M., 'Southeast Asia: A New Model for Hotel Development', *Cornell Hotel and Restaurant Administration Quarterly*, 33(5), Oct. 1992.

Savage, Victor R., Kong, Lily, and Warwick, Neville, *The Naga Awakens: Growth and Change in Southeast Asia*, Singapore: Times Academic Press, 1998.

Saving, Thomas R., Cheung, Steven N. S., Hall, Jane V., Kawai, Masahiro, 'Thailand's Exchange-Rate Crisis Relationships to East Asia and the

Global Economy', *Contemporary Economic Policy*, 16(2), Apr. 1998: 136–56.

Schmitt, B. H., and Pan, Y., 'Managing Corporate and Brand Identities in the Asia Pacific Region', *California Management Review*, 36, summer 1994: 32–48.

Schültz, Clifford, J. II, and Pecotich, Anthony, 'Marketing and Development in the Transition Economies of Southeast Asia: Policy Explication, Assessment and Implications', *Journal of Public Policy and Marketing*, 16(1), spring, 1997: 55–68.

Schütte, H., *Marketing in Indonesia*, Jakarta: Intermasa Publishing, 1974.

—— and Ciarlante, D., *The Black Hole of South East Asia: Strategic Decision-making in an information void*, *Consumer Behavior in Asia* , MacMillan Business, London, 1998.

Seah, J., 'Whah, Recognition at Last . . . and it is Free Too', *The Straits Times*, 12 Feb. 1995, Singapore.

'Setting the Stage for the 21st Century', *Mitsui in Action*, Nov.–Dec. 1998, 35(6), Dec. 1998.

Sharma, S. D., 'The IMF and Asia's Financial Crisis: Bitter Medicine for Sick Tigers', http://www.usfca.edu/pac-rim/pages/publications/report8.html, 1998.

Shin, Ji-Young, 'Consumption is Recovering, but is Not the Same', *Business Korea*, 16(5), May 1999. 16–18.

Shirazi, Javad, K., Regional Manager East Asia and the Pacific, World Bank, 'The East Asia Crisis: Origins, Policy Challenges, and Prospects', paper presented at the National Bureau of Asia Research and the Strategic Studies Institute's Conference, East Asia in Crisis, Seattle, 10 June, 1998.

Siew, V.C., 'Taiwan Weathers the Asia Crisis', by Premier Vincent C. Siew, The Republic of China, at the 68th Conference of the International Law Association, 29 May, 1998, at http://www.ey.gov.tw/

Simon, Fred (ed.), *Corporate Strategies in the Pacific Rim*, London: Routledge 1995.

Siow-Yue, Chia, 'The Economic Development of Singapore: A Selective Review of the Literature', in Basant K. Kapur (ed.), *Singapore Studies: Critical Surveys of the Humanities and Social Sciences*, Singapore: Singapore University Press, 1986.

Slater, Jim, and Strange, Roger (eds.), *Business Relationships with East Asia: The European Experience*, Boston: Routledge Advances in Asia Pacific Businesses, 1997.

Smith, Esmond D., and Cuong, Pham, 'Doing Business in Vietnam: A Cultural Guide', *Business Horizons*, May–June 1996: 47–51.

Smith, Jeffrey, 'State of the Industry: The Asia-Pacific Cosmetics and Toiletries Sector, 1995', *Drug and Cosmetic Industry*, 59(3), Sept. 1996: 24–5.

Song, Byung-Nak, *The Rise of the Korean Economy*, New York: Oxford University Press, 1990.

Sowinski, Lara, 'Asia: Prospects for Japan, South Korea and Taiwan', *World Trade*, 12(6) June 1999: 28–32, Irvine.

Stalk, G. Jr., and Hout, T. M., *Competing against Time: How Time-Based Competition is Reshaping Global Markets*. New York: The Free Press, a division of Macmillan, Inc. and London: Collier Macmillan Publishers, 1990.

Stiglitz, Joseph, 'Bad Private Sector Decisions', *The Wall Street Journal*, 4 Feb. 1998.

Stitt, H. J., and Baker, S., *The Licensing and Joint Venture Guide*, 3rd edn., Toronto: Ministry of Industry, Trade and Technology, 1985.

Strizzi, Nicolino, and Kindra, G. S., 'Emerging Issues Related to Marketing and Business Activity in Asia Pacific', *International Marketing Review*, 15(1), 1998.

Suzaki, K., *The New Manufacturing Challenge*, New York: The Free Press, 1987.

Tae-Kyu, 'Confucian Values and Contemporary Economic Development in Korea', 125–36.

'Taming the Tigers: The IMF and the Asian Crisis'. Nicola Bullard.

Tarlton, Dudley, 'Asia Economies to Produce Miracle Recovery by 2000', *Oil and Gas Investor*, 19(1), 8.

Terpestra,V., and David, K., *The Cultural Environment of International Business*, 3rd edn., Cincinatti: South Western, 1985.

——and Sarathy, R., *International Marketing*, 5th edn., New York: Dryden, 1991.

Testimony of Chairman Alan Greenspan before the Committee on Banking and Financial Services, US House of Representatives, 30 Jan. 1998.

The Banker, 'China: One State, Two Currencies', Nov. 1996.

The Economist, 'Wobbly Tigers', 340(7980), 24 Aug. 1996: 13, London.

The Economist, 'Asia's Precarious Miracle', 342(8006), 1 Mar. 1997*a*.

——— 'Asia's Population Advantage', 13 Sept. 1997*b*.

——— 'Asian Values Revisited: What Would Confucius Say Now', Anon., 3328(8078), 25 July 1998: 23–8.

——— 'Business: Asia Online', 351(8115), 17 Apr. 1999: 69–70, London.

Theravaada, R. C. L., *Buddhism in South East Asia*, Ann Arbor: University of Michigan Press, 1972.

Tobin, James, and Ranis, Gustab, 'Flawed Fund', *The New Republic*, 218(10), 9 Mar. 1998: 16–17.

Tongzon, J. L., *The Economies of Southeast Asia: The Growth and Development of ASEAN Economies*, Cheltenham: Edward Elgar, 1998.

Tsang, Eric W. K., 'Can Guanxi be a Source of Sustained Competitive Advantage for Doing Business in China?' *Academy of Management Executive*, 12(2), 1998: 64–73.

Tsang, Shu-ki, 'The Political Economy of China', *Asia Pacific Business Review*, 2(3), spring 1996.

Ungson, Gerardo R., Steers, Richard, M., and Park, Seung-Ho, *The Korean Enterprise: The Quest for Globalization*, Boston: Harvard Business School Press, 1997.

Usha, C.V. Haley, Linda Low, and Toh. Mun-Heng, 'Singapore Incorporated: Reinterpreting Singapore's Business Environments through a Corporate Metaphor', *Management Decision*, 34(9), 1996: 17–28.

——— ——— 'Crafted Culture: Governmental Sculpting of Modern Singapore and Effects on Business Environments', *Journal of Organizational Change Management*, 11(6), 1998: 530–3.

Vanhonacker, W., 'Entering China: An Unconventional Approach', *Harvard Business Review*, Mar.–Apr. 1997: 130–5.

Vernard, Bertrand, 'Vietnam in Mutation: Will it be the Next Tiger or a Future Jaguar?' *Asia Pacific Journal*, 15(1), Apr. 1998: 77–99.

Waters, Dan, *21st Century Management: Keeping ahead of the Japanese and Chinese*, New York: Prentice Hall, 1991.

Weihrich, H., 'The TOWS Matrix: A Tool for Situational Analysis', *Long Range Planning*, 15(2), Apr. 1982: 54–66.

Weldon, L., 'Only Gateway, A Smaller Competitor is a Direct Supplier in Some Parts of Asia—Direct Dell: A Winning Strategy in Asia', Feb. 1999 Special to Worldinvestor.com

Welsh, James, 'World Economies Weather the Asian Flu', *World Trade*, 11(1), Jan. 1998: 68–71, Irvine.

Werther W. B. Davis, K., Schwind, H. F., and Das, H., *Canadian Human Resource Management*, 3rd Canadian edn., Toronto: McGraw-Hill, Ryerson Ltd., 1990.

Whitehill, Arthur, *Japanese Management. Tradition and Transition*, London: Routledge, 1991.

Wilhelm, Kathy, 'China out of Business, Beijing and Handan, Hebei province', http://www.feer.com/Restricted, 18 Feb. 1999.

Wong, H. Y., and Maher, T. E, 'New Key Success Factors for China's Growing Market', *Business Horizons*, May–June 1997: 43–52.

Wood, Andrew, 'Investment Pace Slows: More Firms Go it Alone', *Chemical Week*, 160(32), 26 Aug.–2 Sept. 1998: 39–44.

Woodall, Pam, 'Survey: East Asian Economies: How Many Paths to Salvation?' *The Economist*, 346(8058), 7 Mar. 1998, S14–S17, London.

World Bank, *The East Asian Miracle, Economic Growth and Public Policy*, World Bank Report, New York: Oxford University Press, 1993.

——— *Asian Development Outlook, 1998: Population and Human Resources*, Asian Development Bank, New York: Oxford University Press, 1999.

World Trade Organization, 'WTO Annual Report: 1997', Lausanne and Geneva: WTO Secretariat Information and Media Relations Department.

Wu, I. R., President of Taiwan Institute of Economic Research, 'Taiwan's Role in Asian Financial Crisis', paper delivered at Conference on The Asian Economic Crisis: Remedies and Implications for Asia Pacific Economies, co-sponsored by Center for Taiwanese Chamber of Commerce, Washington and Institute of International Development Studies Inc., Washington, Apr. 1998.

Yadong, Luo, 'Guanxi Principles, Philosophies and Implications', *Human Systems Management*, 16, 1997: 43–51.

Yamazawa, Ippei, 'Introduction', *The Developing Economies*, 37(4), Dec. 1999: 385–94.

Yang, S. L., 'The Concept of Pao as Basis for Social Relations in China', in J. K. Fairbank (ed.), *Chinese Thought and Institutions*, Chicago: University of Chicago Press, 1957: 291–309.

Yau, O. H. M., 'Chinese Cultural Values: Their Dimensions and Marketing Applications', *European Journal of Marketing*, 22(5), 1988: 44–57.

—— *Consumer Behaviour in China*, London: Routledge, 1994.

Yellen, Janet, Chair Council of Economic Advisers, 'Lessons from the Asian Crisis', *Council on Foreign Relations*, New York, 15 Apr. 1998.

Yeon-Ho, Lee, *The State, Society and Big Business in South Korea*, New York: Routledge, 1997.

Yi-Chi, C., 'Asia Crisis Project', Country Report on Taiwan, University of Washington, 1998.

Yip, George S., *Asian Advantage: Key Strategies for Winning in the Asia-Pacific Region*, London: Addison-Wesley, 1988.

Yoshino, M. Y., and Lifson, Thomas B., *The Invisible Link: Japan's Sogo Shosha and the Organization of Trade*, Cambridge Mass.: The MIT Press, 1986.

Young, I., 'Hope amid the Crisis', *Chemical Week*, 4 Mar. 1998, 160(8), 25–7.

Young, S. M., 'A Framework for Successful Adopting and Performance of Japanese Manufacturing Practices in the United States', *Academy of Management Review*, 17(4), 1992: 677–700.

Yunhua, Liu, 'Post-Crisis Development in Trade Investment in Asean countries', at http://www.pes.org.ph/April2000.

Zimmerman, M., *Dealing with the Japanese*, London: George Allen and Unwin, 1985.

Index